Getting started

Machen Sie sich fit für Ihren neuen Englischkurs. Bearbeiten Sie diese neun Seiten, um die einfachen Grundlagen aufzufrischen. Die Querverweise helfen Ihnen dabei, Ihr Kursbuch besser kennenzulernen.

1 CLASSROOM LANGUAGE

→ Language for speaking: *hintere Umschlagklappe*

Work with a partner. Match the situations (1–8) to the phrases you can use (a–h) in these situations. Then take turns to practise the situations.

You …

1 are late for class.
2 can't hear what someone says.
3 don't know how to say a word.
4 don't understand a word in the text.
5 don't understand the teacher.
6 know the German word but you don't know the English word.
7 need to go to the toilet.
8 want the speaker to stop talking so fast.

a Can I go to the toilet, please?
b Could you repeat that, please?
c Could you speak up, please?
d How do you pronounce that?
e How do you say … in English?
f Could you please slow down a bit?
g Sorry I'm late.
h What does … mean?

2 PARTS OF SPEECH*

*parts of speech = *Wortarten*

A **Think:** Make a list of five English words you know. Try to find one word for each of the parts of speech. The table below will help you start off. Copy it and add your five words.

parts of speech				
noun	**verb**	**adjective**	**preposition**	**pronoun**
school	live	happy	near	you

Pair: Show your list to the person sitting next to you. Together add five new words, one word for each column.

Share: Work with another pair. Add the words of the other pair to your table. If any of the columns are short on words, try to fill them.

B **Use words from your *parts of speech* table above to write six short statements (*Aussagen*). You don't have to use every part of speech in every statement.**

EXAMPLE: *I live near the school.*

REMEMBER ! *a/an*

Change **a** to **an** before a vowel sound (a, e, i, o, u).

a film **an** English film

3 THE SIMPLE PRESENT OF THE VERB "TO BE"

A **Look at the photos. Use the information to complete what the people say.**

I'm ...

I'm from ...

I'm a ...

I use English in / at / to ...

Name	Pat Kruger
From	Cape Town, South Africa
Age	32
Job	waiter

He uses English in the restaurant.

Name	Anika Chopra
From	Delhi, India
Age	23
Job	call centre agent

She uses English to help people from around the world.

Name	Chris Brady
From	Wellington, New Zealand
Age	34
Job	flight attendant

He uses English to explain the safety regulations.

Name	Maria Baumann
From	Stuttgart, Germany
Age	25
Job	hotel receptionist

She uses English to speak to guests.

B **Work with a partner. Take turns to ask and answer questions about the people. Ask about their name, where they are from, how old they are, what their job is, and where or when they use English.**

REMEMBER !

Where is he/she from?	~~Where is he/she coming from?~~
He's/She's a/an (+ job). She's **an** engineer.	~~He/She is (+ job).~~ ~~She's engineer~~

C **Now take turns to ask and answer personal questions. Use one of the jobs above, or choose another job, to answer the last questions. (You can use a fantasy person if you like.)**

1 What's your name?
2 Where are you from?
3 How old are you?
4 What's your job?
5 Where do you use English?
6 When do you use English?

D **Introduce your partner to another pair.**

Start like this:
This is ... He's/She's from ...

4 PREPOSITIONS OF PLACE

Work with a partner. Look at the picture. Use the prepositions in the box to say where people and things are.

at ▪ behind ▪ between ▪ in ▪ in front of ▪ next to ▪ on ▪ under

EXAMPLES: *The teacher is* ***in front of*** *the board.*
The dictionaries are ***on*** *the trolley.*

REMEMBER !

next to ~~next~~

5 SOME/ANY

→ Quantifiers, S. 264

A **What things do you take to school? Work in groups and brainstorm a list. Here are two things to start you off.**

pencils
mobile

B **Take turns to ask and answer questions about what is in your schoolbag.**

EXAMPLES: *Have you got* ***any*** *water with you today?*
No, I haven't got ***any*** *water with me today. I've got* ***some*** *iced tea.*

REMEMBER ! ***some, any***

Use **some** in positive statements.
Use **any** in questions and negative statements.

C **Report back to the class.**

EXAMPLE: *Mario has got* ***some*** *iced tea, but he hasn't got* ***any*** *water.*

6 THERE IS/ISN'T ... THERE ARE/AREN'T

REMEMBER ! *Es gibt*

Es gibt ... = There is/are ...
~~It gives~~

A **You are going to describe your dream school. Work with a partner. Decide together what rooms and facilities there are. Make a list or a mind map.**

What about a billiard room?

OK. That's a good idea. What about a café?

B **Work with another pair. Take turns to ask and answer questions about your dream schools. Use *there is/are* and *some/any* when you need to.**

EXAMPLES: *Is there a cinema in your dream school?*
Yes, there is. / No, there isn't.
Are there any places where we can sleep?
Yes, there are. / No, there aren't.

C **Work in groups of four. Two new students have arrived at your school. Two of you play the new students, while two of you are the old students. Take turns to ask and answer questions about the rooms and facilities.**

7 PLURALS

→ Plurals, S. 263

A **Copy the table below into your notebook. Complete the "rules for plural" column and add more examples. Two of the rules have been added for you.**

	nouns	rules for plural	examples
1	Most nouns	*add s*	book → books school → schools
2	Most nouns that end in *-ch*, *-sh*, *-s*, *-x* or *-z*	▬	box → boxes church → churches
3	Most nouns that end in a vowel (a, e, i, o, u) followed by *y*	▬	boy → boys day → days
4	Most nouns that end in a consonant followed by *y*	▬	family → families country → countries
5	Most nouns that end in *-f* or *-fe*	▬	shelf → shelves knife → knives
6	Nouns that end in *-o*	*add s or es*	piano → pianos hero → heroes

B Not all nouns follow the rules above. Match these exceptions* (1–4) to the rules (a–d).

*exception = *Ausnahme*

1	child → children	**a**	Certain English nouns change a vowel sound when they become plural.
2	fish → fish sheep → sheep	**b**	Some nouns are always plural.
3	foot → feet man → men tooth → teeth	**c**	Some nouns don't change when they become plural.
4	jeans scissors	**d**	Some nouns have their own special plural form.

8 'S AND S'

A Read the sentences and decide if 's is the genitive or the short form of *is*.

EXAMPLE: The student always comes to school by car. The student's car's in the English teacher's parking space.

student's = genitive; car's = car is (short form of is); teacher's = genitive

1 Ian's from Edinburgh. Edinburgh's the capital of Scotland.
2 That's my friend's phone.
3 These are the boy's books.
4 That book's not yours, it's Jane's.
5 The dog's bowl's empty. Its food's in the cupboard.

REMEMBER ! it's and its

it's = it is	its = pronoun

This is my cat. **Its** name is Sparky. **It's** a big cat.

final s + genitive

James' book	James's book

Both forms can be used.

B Add the correct genitive singular or plural ending.

EXAMPLE: (Peter)[a] (parents)[b] car is dirty.
Peter's parents' car is dirty.

1 (Frank) scooter is cool.
2 Where are (Lenny)[a] (sisters)[b] books?
3 I can't see (James)[a] name on the (teacher)[b] list.
4 The (teachers) room at school is large.
5 The (girls)[a] dictionaries are at home. They are using (Patrick)[b].
6 The (football players) boots are dirty.

REMEMBER !

genitive singular and plural

the boy**'s** father =
the father of the boy

the boy**s'** father =
the father of the boys

9 PERSONAL PRONOUNS AND POSSESSIVE ADJECTIVES

→ Personal pronouns and possessive adjectives, S. 267

A Copy and complete the speech bubbles with the correct forms of the pronouns. The first one has been done for you.

B Work with a partner. Decide together if the German "Sie/sie" in sentences 1–4 is *she*, *you* or *they*, then translate the sentences. Say what helped you decide.

1 Sie mag Techno.
2 Sind Sie aus England?
3 Sie ist 18 Jahre alt.
4 Sie sind alle Fußballfans.

C Now decide with your partner if "Ihr/ihr" in sentences 1–4 is *her*, *your* or *their*, then translate the sentences. Say what helped you decide.

1 Shazia ist 16. Ihr Bruder heißt Sadiq.
2 Peter und Laura wohnen in England. Ihre Eltern kommen aus Deutschland.
3 Das ist Joanna. Ihr Freund Luke wohnt zusammen mit ihrem Bruder.
4 Ist das Ihr Handy?

10 OBJECT PRONOUNS

→ Personal pronouns and possessive adjectives, S. 267

Complete these sentences with the correct pronoun.

EXAMPLE: Emily doesn't like dogs. She's afraid of ▬.
Emily doesn't like dogs. She's afraid of *them*.

1 We're going out tonight. Would you like to come with ▬?
2 Who is that boy? Why's he looking at ▬?
3 Harry left his wallet at home. Can you lend ▬ some money?
4 Your friends are late again. Please call ▬ [a] and tell ▬ [b] to hurry up.
5 Did you get your birthday present? I asked your grandad to send ▬ [a] to ▬ [b] last week.
6 We're tourists and we're lost. Can you help ▬, please?

11 MUCH / MANY / A LOT OF

→ Quantifiers, S. 264

REMEMBER ! much, many, a lot of

a lot of is used in positive sentences, especially in spoken language.

much is used for things that cannot be counted (e.g. time). "Time" is an uncountable noun.
many is used for things that can be counted (e.g. book). "Book" is a countable noun.
much and **many** are usually used in negative sentences and questions.

She likes a lot of milk in her coffee.
I don't drink much milk.

There are a lot of eggs in the fridge.
How many eggs do we need?

Choose *much*, *many* or *a lot of*. Explain your choice. Sometimes you can use two.

EXAMPLE: How ⬬ time do you spend on homework?
How *much* time do you spend on homework?
Reason: time is an uncountable noun

1 There aren't ⬬ good clubs in this city.
2 How ⬬ pocket money do your parents give you every week?
3 I see that you've got ⬬ [a] shelves but not ⬬ [b] books.
4 ⬬ [a] people are coming to my party. I'm a bit worried as I don't have ⬬ [b] beer.
5 How ⬬ people are coming to the party?
6 Paula couldn't come on holiday with us, as she doesn't have ⬬ money.
7 I want to get bigger muscles so I eat ⬬ chicken.
8 I know ⬬ people in my street but I don't spend ⬬ time with them.

12 TELLING THE TIME

REMEMBER ! the time

Use **o'clock** with the full hour only:
It's ten o'clock. ~~It's half past ten o'clock.~~

The twenty-four hour clock (e.g. **sixteen thirty**) is only used for timetables.
Say **in the morning/afternoon/evening** or **a.m./p.m.** when the time is not clear.

Be careful with the half hour. 9:30 (*halb zehn*) is **half past nine.** ~~half ten~~

A Write out the times on the right in full.

EXAMPLE: *It's ten o'clock in the morning.*
It's ten a.m.

B Work in groups. Ask and answer the following questions.

What time …
1 do you go to bed? (on a weekday / at the weekend)
2 do you get up? (on a weekday / at the weekend)
3 does school start?
4 do you get home from school?
5 does your favourite TV show start?
6 is it now?

13 COUNTRIES AND NATIONALITIES

A Make sentences by combining things from this chart. Don't use each item more than once.

EXAMPLE: *Saint Basil's Cathedral is a Russian church.*

Antalya	is a/an	American	church.
California		Australian	city.
Saint Basil's Cathedral		Austrian	holiday resort.
Tasmania		German	island.
The Matterhorn		Indian	mountain.
The Rhine		Russian	monument.
The Taj Mahal		Swiss	river.
Vienna		Turkish	state.

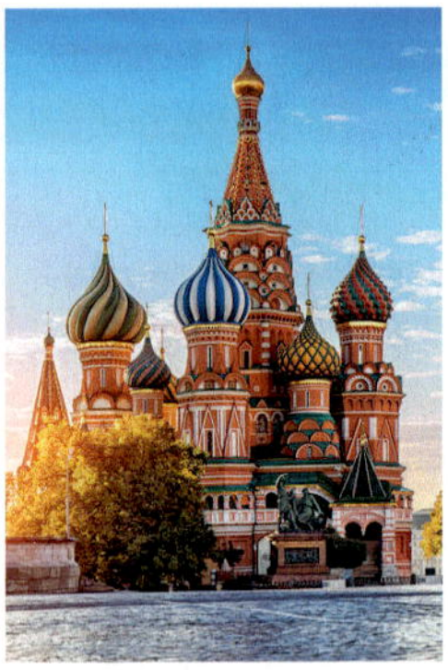

B With a partner, say where you would like to go, and why.

14 FIND SOMEONE WHO …

Your teacher will give you a photocopy. Walk around the class, ask and answer questions and fill in the names of the students.

Find someone who …	name
drinks tea.	
has got a mountain bike.	

15 COURSEBOOK RALLY

You are going to find out about your coursebook. Work in groups of four. Your teacher will give you a photocopy. Search through your coursebook to find the answers. Which group can find all the answers first?

Where can we find …	answer / page number
a photo of Prince Harry?	
the grammar pages	

The food we eat

1

A WARM-UP: TALKING ABOUT FOOD

Think: What are your three favourite meals?

Pair: Together identify the food in the photos and then talk about your favourite meals. Say why you like them.

> I like ... because it tastes good.

> It's easy to order ... by phone and get it delivered.

Share: List your favourite foods on the board. What meals are at the top of the list? Give reasons why these are your class favourites.

B FEEDING THE WORLD

SITUATION: Your school is taking part in an Erasmus+ project with a school in Scotland to make people think about global issues. You are working on a blog called "What foods can we use to feed the world?". You find a text called "Feeding the world" (p. 17) on a website and want to inform the Scottish school about it (task 5, p. 19).

1 PREPARING TO READ

→ Ein Wörterbuch benutzen, S. 228

A The following words are taken from the text. Use your dictionary to find the German translations. Write down some of the translations your dictionary gives for each word. Keep your list for later. You'll need it again in task 2A below.

1 agriculture	3 create	5 melt	7 fibre
2 protein	4 famine	6 gain	8 flour

B Follow the suggestions in the skills box below and make notes. Then answer this question: What is the text going to tell us about feeding the world?

TRAIN YOUR SKILLS: Vorbereitung auf das Lesen

vgl. auch S. 230

Versuchen Sie, das Thema eines Textes zu erraten, bevor Sie gründlich lesen. Verwenden Sie dazu alles auf der Seite, das helfen könnte:

- Die Überschrift und Zwischenüberschriften geben Ihnen eine erste Vorstellung vom Inhalt des Textes.
- Schauen Sie sich die Fotos und Illustrationen zum Text an: Was zeigen sie? Welche Information steckt in den Bildunterschriften?
- Lesen Sie die Fragen zum Text: Was genau ist Ihre Aufgabe?

2 READING AND UNDERSTANDING THE TEXT

A Read the text opposite and then look at your list of German translations from task 1A. Which of the words fits the context of the text?

B Use your dictionary to answer the following questions:

1 Was ist das entsprechende Substantiv vom Adjektiv „ill"?
2 Zu welcher Wortart gehört „average"?
3 Welche der beiden Schreibweisen „organisation" und „organization" wird in Großbritannien, aber nicht in den USA, verwendet?
4 Nennen Sie alle Wortarten, zu denen das Wort „well" gehört.
5 Welche der folgenden Wörter können als Substantiv und Verb auftreten?

feed ▪ result ▪ gain ▪ future

02

FEEDING THE WORLD

A The growing planet

The number of people on the planet is growing quickly. By 2050, there will be 9.7 billion people. According to the Food and Agriculture Organization of the United Nations (FAO), one in nine people in the world suffers from hunger. This number includes a lot of babies and young children. We need to produce more protein but the way we get meat, eggs and milk is destroying the environment and creating greenhouse gases. How can we feed the world? Nutritionists say plants and insects are the answer.

B Feeding children

In countries where there is famine, health organizations give children powdered milk. When there is no clean water to mix the powder with, the children get ill. A French doctor, André Briend, has created a food which does not need to be mixed with water.

One morning, as he reached for the chocolate spread on his table, he thought: 'Why don't we use something like this to feed the children?'. He melted chocolate bars and mixed them with the vitamins and minerals that hungry children need to eat.

The result is Plumpy'Nut®. It's a mixture of peanut butter, sugar and nutrients. One package a day helps a child gain around 900 grams a week. You don't need to mix Plumpy'Nut® with water.

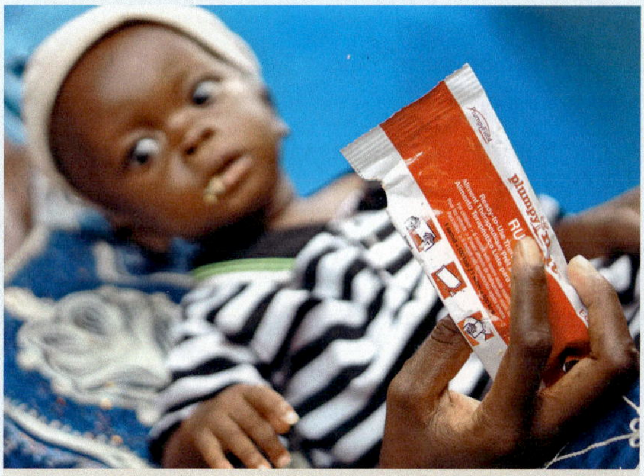

Plumpy'Nut®

C Eating insects today and in the future

In sub-Saharan Africa and south-east Asia people eat insects. They taste good and they are healthy. Nutritionists say that insects are the superfood of the future.

The average insect contains around 50% protein and a few of them contain about 75% protein, so insects compare well to other animal protein sources. Insects are also a good source of fibre. Moreover, they are not full of antibiotics and hormones. You can eat them whole or make them into flour for bread.

(301 words)

Insects on sale in a market

C **Match the sub-headings (1–4) to the three paragraphs in the text (A, B, C). There is one sub-heading more than you need.**

1 Experts focus on insects for protein
2 The French doctor and the breakfast spread
3 Using technology to make food for children
4 Why we need more sources of food

D **Work with a partner. Use information from the text to answer the following questions. The first answer has been given.**

→ Gezielt Informationen im Text finden, S. 231

1 How many people will there be on earth by 2050?
There will be nine point seven billion people on earth by 2050.
2 What is the problem with the way we produce food at the moment?
3 When can powdered milk be dangerous?
4 Who is Plumpy'Nut® made for?
5 Why is it safer than powdered milk?
6 Where do people eat insects? Why?
7 Why will insects be the superfood of the future?

Go to File 1 on page 182.

E **Now compare your answers with your notes from task 1B (p. 16).**

3 LANGUAGE IN USE: QUESTIONS

→ Simple present, S. 247

A **Form questions using the words in brackets, and then answer them. The first question has been given.**

1 ▬ a big meal in the evening? (your parents – eat)
Do your parents eat a big meal in the evening?
2 ▬ insects? (your teacher – eat)
3 When ▬ breakfast? (you – eat)
4 How much ▬? (a hamburger – cost)
5 ▬ cook a good meal? (you – can)

REMEMBER ! questions in the simple present

To ask a question in the simple present, you need to add "do" or "does" (for he/she/it).

Do you **like** Thai food? ~~You like Thai food?~~
What **does** he **eat** for breakfast? ~~What eats he for breakfast?~~

Questions using a modal auxiliary (e.g. can, should, may) and "be" do not need "do".

Can you give me a slice of pizza? ~~Do you can give me a slice of pizza?~~
Are you in the kitchen? ~~Do you be in the kitchen?~~

B **Work with a partner. Brainstorm three questions based on information in the text (one question for each paragraph). Write down your questions and give them to another pair. Ask them to answer your questions without looking at the text.**

EXAMPLES: *How can we feed the world? Why don't we use ... to feed children?*

4 WORKING WITH WORDS

→ Ein Wörterbuch benutzen, S. 228

A Work with a partner. The words below appear in the text. Use an English-German dictionary (print or online) to find words that belong to their families. Write down the German translations of all the words. One word has been added to start you off.

1	nutritionist (noun) (l. 7)			*Ernährungswissenschaftler/in*
Find	a	a noun	*nutrient*	*Nährstoff*
	b	another noun		
	c	an adjective		
2	agriculture (noun) (l. 3)			
Find	a	an adjective		
	b	another noun		
3	healthy (adjective) (l. 27)			
Find	a	a noun		
	b	an adverb		

B Make six sentences using words you and your partner found while doing task 4A.

5 WRITING AN EMAIL

→ Einen Text zusammenfassen, S. 235

Now write to the students at the Scottish school, telling them about one of the foods described in the text. Include the following points:

- the name (or type) of food
- who eats it at the moment
- what is in it
- the benefits of the food

Start like this:

Hi, I found an article about feeding the world that I think contains some interesting information. The article … .

C EATING HABITS

1 PREPARING TO LISTEN

TRAIN YOUR SKILLS: Vorbereitung auf das Hören vgl. auch S. 234

- Lesen Sie die Hintergrundinformationen – zum Beispiel eine Situationsbeschreibung und Angaben, wie viele Personen Sie hören werden.
- Denken Sie daran, dass die Fragen zum Hörtext meist in derselben Reihenfolge gestellt werden, in der die entsprechenden Informationen im Hörtext gegeben werden.

You are going to listen to an interview with Mark and Jane. Before you listen, do the tasks below.

A Read the speech bubbles and answer these questions.

1 What do the speakers eat?
2 Why do they eat their particular diet*?

*diet = *(hier) Ernährung*

Jane

I eat almost everything, including meat. I believe that you need a variety of food and that includes meat.

I'm a vegan. Vegans believe that you should never use animals for food.

Mark

B Match the words and expressions that the speakers use (1–4) to the definitions (a–d). The expressions are in the same order as they appear in the interview.

1 to survive	**a** to make something happen
2 to cause something	**b** to not have enough red blood cells
3 to suffer from anaemia	**c** to give somebody good reasons to do something
4 to persuade somebody	**d** to continue to live

03 2 LISTENING: WHAT I EAT AND WHY

Read the questions below, then listen to the interview. Which of the questions do you hear?

1 Are you a vegetarian or a vegan?
2 Do you eat meat?
3 Do you suffer from anaemia?
4 Is your diet healthy?
5 Do you have any allergies?
6 Do you have problems with any food?

3 UNDERSTANDING THE AUDIO TEXT

True or false: Listen again and say whether these statements are true or false.

1 Jane has a problem with her blood.
2 Vegans can get all the nutrients they need from their diet.
3 Mark has allergies so he can't eat some foods.
4 Jane loves all types of meat.
5 Mark would like his friends to become vegans.
6 Jane respects the food choices other people make.

4 LANGUAGE IN USE: ADVERBS OF FREQUENCY

→ Simple present, S. 247

never usually always often rarely sometimes

EXAMPLES: *I **never** have any problems with food.*
*I **often** eat meat.*

A **Draw a line in your notebook. Complete the line using the words above in the correct order. Two words have been given for you.**

– never ———————————————— always +

B **Work in groups. Ask and answer questions about your eating habits. It may help you to write down your questions before asking them. Here are some questions to start you off.**

- When do you eat your main meal?
- How often do you eat meat?
- Do you eat Chinese food?
- How often do you cook?

01

5 VIEWING

→ Videos, S. 194

Watch the video called "First vegetarian school in the US" and complete the tasks on page 194.

6 DISCUSSION

→ An Diskussionen teilnehmen, S. 245

Think: Are your eating habits like Mark's or like Jane's?
Pair: Talk about what you eat, what you don't eat, and why. What do you think of diets such as veganism, low-carb diet, vegetarianism, etc.?
Share: Report back to the class.

You work in a restaurant in London.

1 READING A MENU

Study the menu below and say which foods are

a suitable for vegans.
b suitable for vegetarians.
c not suitable for people with soya and nut allergies.

THE EAT WELL RESTAURANT
Open 6 a.m. till 8 p.m.

All-day breakfast
Breakfast cereal * with milk
Variety of yogurts – plain, soya, fruit
Fresh fruit salad
Toast and butter with jam

Starters
Lentil soup
Mixed salad

Main courses
Beefburger with green salad
Vegetarian pizza with or without cheese
Stir-fried vegetables with rice
Tofu burgers

Desserts
Ice cream (various flavours)
Cheesecake

* contains nuts

2 LISTENING: SERVING A GUEST

04

Your colleague, Brian, helps a guest choose a meal.

A Work with a partner. Read the gapped dialogue and use Brian's sentences (a–f on page 23) to complete it. There is one sentence more than you need.

Brian: Good evening. What would you like to eat today?
Sarah: I'm not sure. I'm a vegetarian. What can you recommend?
Brian: ___ 1
Sarah: Thank you. I like pizza. I'll have a vegetarian pizza with cheese and a mixed salad.
Brian: ___ 2
Sarah: I'd like a bottle of mineral water, please.
(A little later, Brian brings Sarah her meal.)
Brian: ___ 3
Sarah: Thank you. That looks good.
(Sarah has finished her meal.)
Brian: ___ 4

Sarah: Yes, I did. It was very nice, thank you. Can I have the bill, please?
(Sarah pays and starts to leave.)

Brian: ____ [5]

Sarah: Thank you. Have a nice evening. Bye.

Brian's part of the conversation

- **a** Did you enjoy your meal?
- **b** Goodbye. I hope to see you again soon.
- **c** Here you are. Enjoy your meal!
- **d** The vegetarian pizza's very tasty.
- **e** What about the stir-fried vegetables with rice?
- **f** What would you like to drink?

B **Now listen and check.**

C **Read the dialogue together. Take turns to play the roles.**

3 ROLE-PLAY: SERVING A GUEST

Work with a partner and help him/her choose from the menu on page 22. When you have finished, change roles and act out the dialogue again.

TIPS !

- I like … *Ich mag …*
- I would like … *Ich hätte gern …*
- Here you are! … *Bitte schön!*
- Enjoy your meal! … *Guten Appetit!*

Partner A: You are working in the restaurant	Partner B: You are a guest in the restaurant
→ Begrüßen Sie den Gast und fragen Sie, was er/sie gerne essen würde.	→ Erklären Sie, dass Sie Vegetarier/Veganer/ Allergiker sind. Fragen Sie den Kellner / die Kellnerin, was er/sie empfehlen kann.
→ Machen Sie einen entsprechenden Vorschlag.	→ Stimmen Sie zu.
→ Fragen Sie, was der Gast trinken möchte.	→ Bestellen Sie Ihr Getränk.
→ Sie servieren und wünschen „Guten Appetit".	→ Bedanken Sie sich.
→ Fragen Sie den Gast, wie ihm/ihr das Essen geschmeckt hat.	→ Sagen Sie, dass es gut war. Bitten Sie um die Rechnung.
→ Verabschieden Sie sich und sagen Sie, Sie hoffen, den Gast wiederzusehen.	→ Bedanken Sie sich und wünschen Sie dem Kellner / der Kellnerin einen schönen Abend.

Go to File 2 on page 182.

Your school wants to improve its canteen. You are going to work in a team and plan and present a menu.

1 NOTICE OF A COMPETITION

Work in groups. Read the notice and answer the questions.

1 Why does the school need to know what you would like to eat?
2 What do you have to do?
3 What do you have to include?
4 What should you remember when you plan your menu?

COMPETITION –
MENUS FOR OUR NEW SCHOOL CANTEEN

We need your help to make our new canteen the place where you want to eat. That's why we need you to tell us what you would like to eat.
We would like you to plan a menu.
- *Include a starter, a main course and a dessert.*
- *Remember – we want healthy, balanced meals that everyone can enjoy.*
- *Please keep the prices low.*

It's your canteen. We want you to eat there.
Go and plan the meals!

2 TALKING ABOUT THE TARGET GROUP

Discuss the following questions. Make notes.

a Who eats in your canteen?
b What age groups eat in the canteen?
c Does anyone have a special diet? If so, what do they eat/not eat?

3 PLANNING YOUR MENU

Brainstorm ideas of foods you would like to see in the canteen. Make a list. From your list, choose a starter, a main course and a dessert that will give you a healthy, balanced menu.

4 WRITING AND PRESENTING YOUR MENU FOR THE COMPETITION

A **Take a large piece of paper and write up your menu. Illustrate it with drawings or take pictures from the internet if you like. Say why your menu is healthy and well balanced.**

EXAMPLE: *Our menu includes all the food types that we need for a well-balanced diet.*

Say why students will want to eat it.

EXAMPLE: *It includes tasty and nourishing food that young people enjoy.*

B **Pin your menu on the wall and do a gallery walk. (Walk past all the menus and study them.) Then rank the posters using the categories below. Give points from 1 to 5 for each category.**

design ▪ well-balanced diet ▪ prices ▪ attractiveness ▪ overall effect

Sport

2

A WARM-UP: TALKING ABOUT SPORT

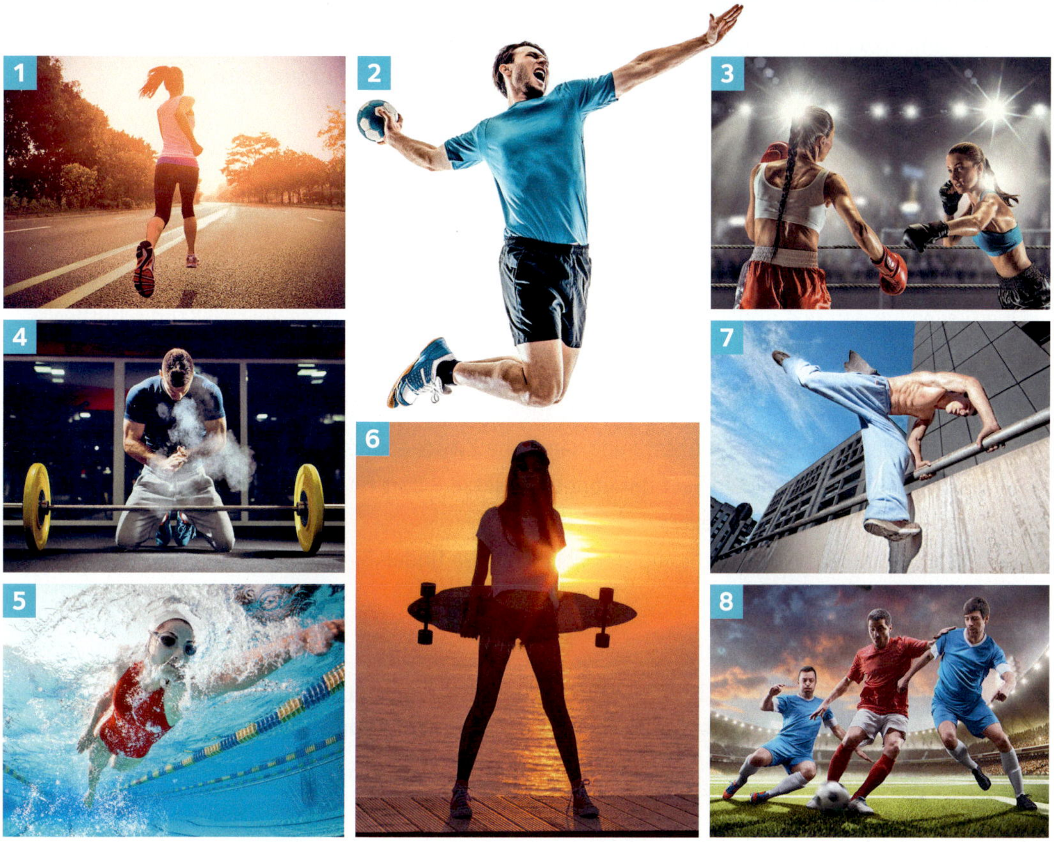

A **Identify the sports in the photos. Then copy and complete the mind map below with as many sports as you can. What do you notice about the sports that are used with "go"?**

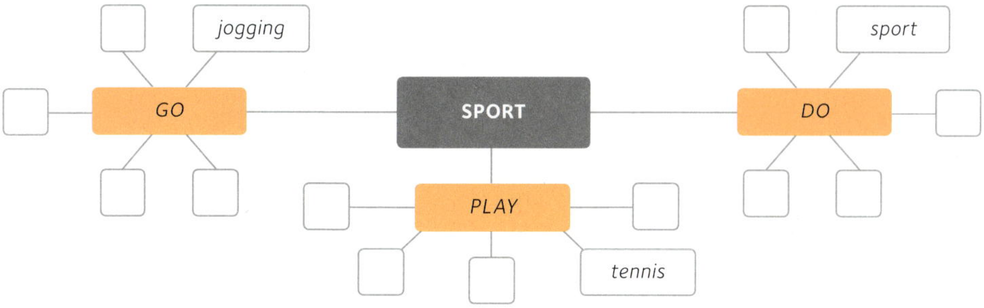

B **What sports do you enjoy playing or watching? Why? What sports do not interest you? Say why not.**

I like going to the fitness studio. I meet my friends there.

I don't like running. It's boring.

REMEMBER !

I **do** sport. I ~~make~~ sport.
It **is** fun. It ~~makes~~ fun.

B THE DIARY OF A WINNER

SITUATION: Your class is taking part in an Erasmus+ project about the importance of sport for young people in Europe. Part of the project is a competition to provide one photo with a text which shows why sport is important. The photo will be used on a website photo gallery about sport in Europe (task 6, p. 29). The material in this section will help you get some ideas.

1 PREPARING TO READ

TRAIN YOUR SKILLS: Den Sinn eines Textes erfassen vgl. auch S. 231

Überfliegen Sie den Text und schätzen Sie ein, worum es geht. Gehen Sie anschließend schrittweise vor.

- Lesen Sie die Überschrift sorgfältig – sie ist meistens eine Inhaltsangabe des Textes.
- Danach lesen Sie den ersten Absatz und sämtliche Zwischenüberschriften.
- Lesen Sie den jeweils ersten Satz der übrigen Absätze – dort finden Sie in der Regel die wichtigsten Gedanken des Textes.
- Lesen Sie den letzten Absatz komplett. Üblicherweise finden Sie hier eine Zusammenfassung des Textes.

Multiple choice: Look at the text opposite and complete each sentence below with the best ending (a–c). Use the information from the box above to help you.

1 The text is about Tony …
- **a** running in a park.
- **b** planning a sports trip.
- **c** sharing his sports activities online.

2 He is trying to …
- **a** find a girlfriend.
- **b** get his life in order.
- **c** become an athlete.

3 A Park Run is …
- **a** for everybody, no matter how fit they are.
- **b** only for fast runners.
- **c** the best place to train for a marathon.

4 Tony is happy because …
- **a** he gets a lot of likes on Instagram.
- **b** life is good.
- **c** he is making new friends.

2 READING AND UNDERSTANDING THE TEXT

05

THE DIARY OF A WINNER

By BELLA FRY

This month I'm talking to Tony. Tony spends too much time alone at home on the sofa playing video games. His mum wants him to get out, meet new friends and get fit – and she thinks sport is the answer. Tony's keeping an online diary to record his progress.

Tony's social media diary

Tony uses social media. He scrolls down to his first entry. The photo shows Tony on the sofa. His mum took the photo. 'My mum is right,' he tells me. 'She says that I'm not really doing much with my life. I'm very lazy – I just like staying at home listening to music and playing video games. It's time to get a life!'

Tony_fitnessdiary

♥ **14 likes**
Time to get a life!
#getalife #fitness #newme #nomoreexcuses #workingonmyself

He's getting his life in order

Like many teenagers, he is finding it difficult to know what he wants from life. But he is getting his life in order with the help of a personal sports trainer, Paula. 'We train in the gym and we run together twice a week,' he says. 'Paula's also teaching me mental exercises to improve my confidence.'

'It's taking time but I'm losing weight and developing muscles. I'm feeling a lot more energetic now. There are some days when I want to give up, because it is a lot of hard work, but Paula always helps me to keep me motivated.'

The Saturday Park Run is for everyone

Tony shows me another photo on his account. The tag line reads: *'We're getting ready for the next Park Run.'*

Tony_fitnessdiary

'I go to the local Park Run every Saturday morning,' he explains. 'All kinds of people turn up. In this photo you can see Sam and Oliver. We meet there every Saturday. They are faster than me, but it's fun to train with them. Most of the runners are faster than me, but I am getting better at running. We only run 5 kilometres so there's no pressure. You just do what you can and everybody accepts you. After the run, we go to a café and chat. There's a really good atmosphere.'

♥ **50 likes**
We're getting ready for the next Park Run.
#parkrun #runningmates #getalife #fitness
#newme #nomoreexcuses #workingonmyself

Today's post

Tony shows me his latest photos from a Park Run. In most of them, he's sitting in the café with a lot of other runners. He looks healthy and happy. He posts the photos on his account, then types in a tag line: *'We're relaxing after the Park Run.'* The photos which he posts online show his progress from lonely kid to a guy who is making new friends. And he's got a life.

(416 words)

Short-answer questions: In real life we often just give short answers to questions. Use information from the text to give short answers to the following questions. The first answer has been given.

1 Why is Tony doing sport? (three aspects)
to get out of the house, to meet new friends and to get fit
2 Where does he keep a record of what he does?
3 How does he describe himself?
4 What is Paula doing to make Tony more sure of himself? (three aspects)
5 How are Tony's activities changing him? (three aspects)
6 What does he do every Saturday morning?

3 WORKING WITH WORDS

Gapped summary: Complete the summary with words from the text. Use only one word for each gap. Give the number of the line in which you found the word.

The first entry in Tony's social media diary shows a ___ [1] teenager on the sofa. However, he is now sorting out his ___ [2]. Paula, his personal trainer, has helped him increase his ___ [3] and makes sure that he stays ___ [4]. Tony now has friends. They meet every Saturday and do a 5-kilometre run. This is not too long, and Tony doesn't feel under ___ [5]. His photos show his ___ [6] from unhappy boy to popular teen.

4 LANGUAGE IN USE: PRESENT PROGRESSIVE

→ Present progressive, S. 247

EXAMPLES: *Tony **is keeping** an online diary to record his progress.*
*We **are relaxing** after the Park Run.*

Study the drawings. Describe what the people are doing. Use the present progressive form of the verb.

5 DESCRIBING A PICTURE

TRAIN YOUR SKILLS: Ein Bild beschreiben und deuten vgl. auch S. 240

Sehen Sie sich das Bild genau an und machen Sie sich Notizen zur Vorbereitung:

- Wer oder was spielt die wichtigste Rolle?
- Steht ein Element im Mittelpunkt? Warum?
- Hat das Bild eine „Botschaft"?
- Wir benutzen oft die Zeitform „present progressive", wenn wir Bilder beschreiben, weil Bilder (angehaltene) Vorgänge darstellen.

Look at the photo on the right and follow the suggestions in the skills box to describe the picture.

Go to File 3 on page 183.

6 PREPARING A PHOTO

Find a photo for the website that you think shows why sport is important. Write a description of the photo and explain how it shows that sport is important.

C MY SPORT AND WHY I DO IT

1 PREPARING TO LISTEN

You are going to listen to interviews with two people. They are talking about their favourite sport and why they do it.

Before you listen, use these words from the interviews to talk about a sport you like.

league ▪ match ▪ season ▪ team ▪ equipment ▪ challenge ▪ strength ▪ skills

TRAIN YOUR SKILLS: Zuhören und Notizen machen vgl. auch S. 234

Machen Sie sich beim Hören Notizen auf Englisch. Das ist nicht immer leicht, weil die Sprecher keine Pause machen, während Sie schreiben.

- Konzentrieren Sie sich auf die Aufgabe, schreiben Sie Schlüsselwörter und wichtige Ausdrücke auf.
- Strukturieren Sie Ihre Notizen.

2 LISTENING: MY SPORT AND WHY I DO IT

06

A **Copy the grids, then listen for the questions and make notes on the answers. Two of the notes have been made for you.**

Mia	1	What sport do you do?	*football*
	2	How often do you train?	
	3	When do you play your matches?	
	4	What league are you in?	
	5	What do you like best about the game?	
	6	What's your message for women who are interested in playing?	

Fred	1	What is parkour?	*a fast running sport*
	2	Where do you do it?	
	3	What do you do?	
	4	What equipment do you use?	
	5	What do you like best about doing parkour?	
	6	Why should other people do it?	

3 LANGUAGE IN USE: SIMPLE PRESENT VS PRESENT PROGRESSIVE

→ Simple present; present progressive, S. 247

A Sort these signal words and expressions into two lists: those that are usually used with the simple present and those that are usually used with the present progressive.

always ▪ at the moment ▪ every day ▪ mostly ▪ never ▪ normally ▪ now ▪ often ▪ rarely ▪ right now ▪ sometimes ▪ this week ▪ today ▪ usually

B It's Sunday morning and Mia is at the gym with her friend Pat. Use the correct form of the verbs in brackets to complete Mia's thoughts. Tip: pay attention to the signal words.

TIP !

The following verbs are used mostly in the simple present:

agree – have – hear – know – like – need – remember – see – think – understand – want

I like ~~I am liking~~
I agree ~~I am agreeing~~

Pat and I usually ___ [1] (do) a few stretches together then we ___ [2] (split up). Mostly, I ___ [3] (run) on the treadmill first but the TV ___ [4] (not work) today, which is why I ___ [5] (train) on the exercise bike instead.

Who's that nice-looking guy at the weights? I ___ [6] (think) that he ___ [7] (smile) at me. Oh! Now I ___ [8] (remember) who he is. I ___ [9] (see) him every morning on the bus to work.

Pat ___ [10] (sit) at the juice bar right now. Normally she ___ [11] (not sit) at the bar, but she ___ [12] (wait) for her boyfriend Liam today. I ___ [13] (like) Liam – he's a great guy!

4 PRESENTATION

You have three minutes to present your favourite sport or leisure activity (*Freizeitbeschäftigung*) to the class. Use the following points in your presentation:

- What sport/leisure activity it is
- How you play it
- Why you like it
- Why others should do it

2 THE WORLD OF WORK — Volunteering at the Berlin Marathon

You are interested in a career in sport, so you decide to volunteer to help out at this year's Berlin Marathon.

1 AN INTERESTING SUGGESTION

Read the advertisement and make notes about the job under the headings on the left.

- how volunteering can lead to a career in sports
- characteristics/skills volunteers need
- negative sides of volunteering
- positive sides of volunteering

Want a career in sport? First become a volunteer

Are you interested in a career in sport? We are looking for volunteers for this year's Berlin Marathon. We need volunteers to help the athletes, organize the event and manage our website. You work long hours but you meet interesting people, see behind the scenes and learn a lot from the people organizing the event. If you enjoy hard work, like to work in a team and speak good English, join up as a volunteer at this year's Berlin Marathon. All our team leaders work in the sports business. They were volunteers once, too.

2 WRITING THE SCHEDULE

07

You are helping organize the website of the Berlin Marathon. Your team leader wants you to put a table with all the events of the Berlin Marathon weekend on the website. You have made the table below and filled in most of the information, but there are some bits missing. You ask him to go through the schedule for you again. Listen carefully and complete the table with the missing information.

day and time	name	type of competition	distance	participants
Saturday 11 a.m.	Bambini Run	running	between 400m and 1000m	___
Saturday 1 p.m.	___	inline skating	500m and 3km	children aged 6 to 13
___	Mini-Marathon	running	___	teenagers aged 13 to 19
___	Inline Skating Marathon	inline skating	marathon	adults
Sunday 8:50 a.m.	___	wheelchairs	marathon	adults
Sunday 8:58 a.m.	Handbiking Marathon	handbiking	marathon	___
Sunday 9:15 a.m.	Running Marathon	___ and ___	marathon	adults

3 FAQS ABOUT THE MARATHON

A The team leader asks you to update the FAQs on the website. Match the answers to the FAQs.

1 When does the start area open?
2 Where can I change into my running gear?
3 Where can I have a shower after the race?
4 Where can I leave my clothes?
5 Where can I get something to eat and drink during the race?
6 What if I get ill during the race?
7 What about toilets?

a There are showers in the changing tent.
b There are six first-aid stations along the route.
c There are seven refreshment points along the route and one at the finish line.
d There are WCs at the start/finish area and at all of the refreshment points.
e There is a changing tent at the start/finish area.
f The clothes drop-off is next to the changing tent.
h You can go in from 6:30 a.m. on the day of the race.

B The team leader gives you some more information about registering. You have to write the questions and answers in German for the German part of the website. One example is given.

EXAMPLE:
Frage: *Wann kann ich mich für den Marathon anmelden?*
Antwort: *Sie können sich zwischen dem 19. Februar um 12 Uhr mittags und dem 30. März für den Marathon anmelden.*

Registration begins at noon on 19 February. The final date for registration is 30 March. The race takes place on 26 September. The entry fee is 98 euros. You can pay for your registration with a credit card. A registration confirmation will be sent to you immediately via email after you have completed your registration.

4 AT A JOB INTERVIEW: DESCRIBING VOLUNTEERING

Volunteering shows employers that you want to learn as much as you can about your profession. Always remember to add relevant information about volunteering on your CV.

A Imagine you have a job interview. Make notes on your time as a volunteer at the Berlin Marathon. Use the ideas below.

I volunteered at ___ because ___.
I helped ___.
I completed and updated ___.
The benefits of volunteering are ___.

B Work with a partner. One of you is the interviewer. The interviewer asks about your experience at the Berlin Marathon. Tell her/him about why you volunteered, the benefits and what you did. Use the prompts above.

Your school is expecting a group of exchange students. Some of them would like to do sport while they are in your area. You research opportunities for doing sport and produce a flyer in English giving precise information about times and places.

1 SPORTS AND EVENTS

Brainstorm ideas about sports and events in your area. Make a list.

2 INTERNET RESEARCH

Do internet research to find out more about the top three activities in your area. Make notes. Here are some questions to think about. Add your own ideas.

- Where/When does the activity take place?
- Do the exchange students need any special equipment or clothes? (If so, where can they find equipment/clothes?)

3 MAKING A TIMETABLE

Make a list of the activities. Make a timetable showing when they can do the activities. Add information about where the activities take place.

4 MAKING A FLYER

A Use the notes and the timetable you made above to produce a flyer in English for the exchange students. Make the flyer as attractive as possible (e.g. add photos or a map of a running route from the internet).

B Put all the flyers on a table. Choose another group's flyer and comment on the activities. Vote for the best flyer.

Relationships: families and friends

3

A WARM-UP: TODAY'S FAMILIES

A **Work with a partner. You have three minutes to brainstorm English words that describe family members. Make lists. Which pair has the most words?**

father	wife	parents

1

2

3

4

5

B **Complete the definitions of the types of families (1–5) with the sentence endings (a–e). Then match the definitions to the photos above.**

1 A blended family is
2 An extended family is made up of
3 In an intercultural family,
4 In a single-parent family,
5 The nuclear family is made up of

a the parents are from different cultural backgrounds.
b three or more generations in one home.
c a parent brings up his or her children without a partner.
d a mum and dad and their children.
e a family consisting of a couple, the children they have together and their children from earlier relationships.

C **Which of the types of families above do you know? What other types of families are you familiar with?**

B FAMILIES

SITUATION: Your school is doing a project on relationships around the world. The focus is on families and friends. The school has set up a blog on which to collect interesting material. You read the story below and write a letter to the two girls mentioned in the text with questions about them and their families (task 5, p. 39).

1 PREPARING TO READ

A Work in small groups. Study the words and expressions below and say which of them you …

- **a** know and why you know them. (For example, it is like a German word.)
- **b** can guess the meaning of. (How did you guess?)
- **c** need to look up in your dictionary. (Look them up now!)

to share | to be an only child | to be sad | to adopt | double | lactose intolerant | identical | to release

B Choose one word from categories a and b and two words from category c and make four sentences.

2 READING AND UNDERSTANDING THE TEXT

A True or false: Read the text opposite and decide whether the following statements are true or false. Explain your answer.

1. Samantha sent Anaïs a link to her video.
2. Anaïs did research into the woman in the video.
3. The girls are not like each other at all.
4. A DNA test confirmed that they are twins.
5. The girls' parents were happy when the story came out.
6. The girls went on a journey to get to know each other.
7. They met their birth mother.
8. Anaïs's friend shared their story with the world.

08

DON'T FREAK OUT!

Anaïs Bordier grew up in France. Her parents adopted her from an adoption agency in South Korea when she was a baby.

Anaïs studied fashion in London. While she was there, a friend showed her a video on YouTube. In the video there was a young American actress who looked and sounded exactly like Anaïs. She was Anaïs's double!

Anaïs decided to do some research about her double. She found out that the woman in the video was born on the same day in the same place as she was – Busan, a port city in South Korea. She contacted the actress via Facebook and introduced herself and her background and she told Samantha: 'Don't freak out!'

Anais and Samantha

As Anaïs and Samantha shared photos and details of their lives, they discovered that they had a lot more in common than just a shared birthday. They both loved the Harry Potter books, they both watched the same TV programmes and they adored cheese – even though they were both lactose intolerant. They began to talk on Skype and a real friendship developed.

While Anaïs grew up as an only child in Paris, Samantha lived with her two older brothers as the only adopted child in a New Jersey family. Like Anaïs, Samantha felt that something or someone was missing in her life. When she received the message from Anaïs, she was surprised but also excited. This strange girl looked just like her.

*

After a while the two girls decided to take a DNA test together, which confirmed what they suspected – they are identical twin sisters. Their mother gave them up for adoption when they were babies. The adoption agency gave them separately to two different sets of parents. Their adoptive families did not know either.

When the story came out, the sisters' adoptive parents found the situation difficult. Anaïs's parents did not believe that Samantha was their daughter's twin and Samantha's parents were sad that their daughter had grown up without her sister.

For over a year, the twins travelled together and learned everything about each other's lives. They made thousands of videos of their journey, which included two weeks at Samantha's home in the USA, and 10 days in the place where they were born in Korea. They even visited the adoption agency together. However, when they contacted their birth mother, she didn't want to meet them. As they grew closer, Anaïs and Samantha decided to share their story with the rest of the world. They raised funds for a documentary tracking their discovery called *Twinsters*. The documentary ends with the release of their DNA results, which proves that they are indeed identical twins. Anaïs and Samantha's story is one more example of how the internet can bring the world closer together. (458 words)

B Multiple matching: Match five of the statements (1–7) with people mentioned in the text. There are two statements that do not match.

	person	statement
1	⬬	Every baby needs two parents.
2	⬬	I don't want to meet them. The past is past.
3	⬬	I watched the video and I thought: She looks just like me.
4	⬬	I'm happy she contacted me.
5	⬬	My daughter and I are the only women in a house full of men.
6	⬬	We love our daughter so much. She is our only child.
7	⬬	Skype is a great way to keep in touch.

3 LANGUAGE IN USE: SIMPLE PAST

→ Simple past, S. 249

EXAMPLES: *Anaïs **studied** fashion in London. They **began** to talk on Skype.*

A Complete the text with the simple past form of the verb in brackets.

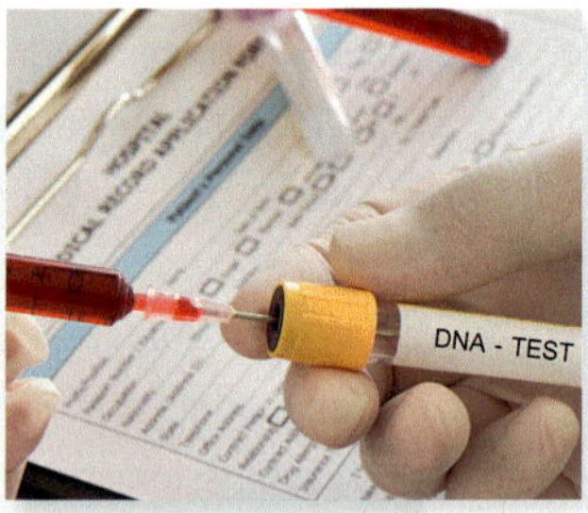

How the internet can bring the world closer

Anaïs Bordier and Samantha Futerman are twins who ⬬ [1] (meet) for the first time at the age of 27. The twins ⬬ [2] (not know) each other until the internet ⬬ [3] (bring) them together. One day, Anais ⬬ [4] (see) an American actress called Samantha in a video on YouTube. Samantha ⬬ [5] (look) just like her. Anaïs ⬬ [6] (search) the internet and ⬬ [7] (find out) that she and Samantha ⬬ [8] (share) the same birthday. Anaïs ⬬ [9] (contact) Samantha on Facebook. They ⬬ [10] (get to know) each other on Skype and in person and they ⬬ [11] (take) a DNA test that ⬬ [12] (prove) they are twins. The girls ⬬ [13] (raise) $44,000 dollars on a crowdfunding site and ⬬ [14] (make) a documentary film about their story.

B A journalist asked another mother who gave up her child for adoption why she did so. Here are the answers she gave. Write down the journalist's questions.

1 I gave up my child for adoption because I was very young.
2 I was 18 years old.
3 No, I didn't have anyone to help me.
4 No, I didn't have a job.
5 Someone in my church told me about the adoption agency.
6 I refused to meet my child because I have another family now.

REMEMBER ! how to form questions in the simple past

Yes/No questions:
Did you **meet** your friends yesterday?
Were your friends at the café?

Wh-questions:
When **did** you **tell** your friends about your new job?
Where **were** you **born**?

Go to File 4 on page 184.

4 WORKING WITH WORDS

A collocation is when words usually go together, for example "do sport" (*Sport treiben*) or "immediate family" (*engste Familie*). Add words from column A to words from column B to form collocations. All the collocations are in the text.

column A		
adoption	DNA	lactose
adoptive	identical	only

column B		
agency	intolerant	test
child	parents	twins

5 WRITING A LETTER

It is time for you to write to the twins for this part of your school project.

TRAIN YOUR SKILLS: Writing a letter vgl. auch S. 237

Die Anrede: Ein Brief fängt immer mit einer Anrede an: *Dear …*
Der Betreff: Erklären Sie, wer Sie sind und warum Sie schreiben.
Der Inhalt: Der Großteil des Briefs beschreibt Ihre Angelegenheit.
Der Schlusssatz: Hier nennen Sie Ihr erhofftes weiteres Vorgehen: *I look forward to hearing from you.*
Die Grußformel: Der Brief endet mit einer Grußformel: *Yours sincerely / Best wishes*

A Work in groups. Brainstorm ideas about what you would like to know from the twins. Make notes. Here are some ideas to start you off.

- how each of them grew up
- when they first knew they were adopted
- what type of clothes they liked as children / what they wear now

B Complete the body of the letter with your questions to the twins.

Dear Anaïs and Samantha,

I am a student at school in Germany. I read your story in a book I use at school. The school is doing a project on relationships around the world and this week we are looking at family relationships.
Do you mind if I ask you some questions about your childhood and how you grew up?

Thank you for taking the time to answer my questions.
I look forward to hearing from you soon.

Best wishes
(*your signature*)

C MY BEST FRIEND

1 PREPARING TO LISTEN

The words below are all from the text. What do you think the text is going to be about?

truth hurt friendship lies problem cheating jealous

2 LISTENING: I THOUGHT YOU WERE MY FRIEND

09

Mark and Isolde are usually good friends but today they're having an argument.

Complete the sentences with information from the text.

1 Mark heard that Isolde is ___.
2 He tells her that Tristan is ___ on her.
3 Mark knows this because he saw Tristan with ___.
4 Isolde thinks Mark is ___.
5 Mark doesn't want Isolde ___.
6 Isolde thinks Mark is ___.
7 Mark says that in a week or two Isolde will be ___.

3 DISCUSSION

Discuss these questions in groups.

1 Was Mark right to talk to Isolde about Tristan?
2 Why doesn't Isolde believe Mark?
3 Do you think Mark is right about Tristan?
4 Do you think Mark and Isolde will be good friends in the future?

4 LANGUAGE IN USE: COMPARISON OF ADJECTIVES

→ Comparison of adjectives, S. 266

EXAMPLES: John is a *good* programmer. He's *better* than David.
She's not that *old* – she's just one year *older* than I am.
He's so *funny*! In fact, he is *the funniest* person I know.

A Complete the word table. The words in the table are all in the text. The first row has been completed for you.

	adjective	comparative	superlative
1	good	*better*	*best*
2	nice	___	___
3	bad	___	___

	adjective	comparative	superlative
4	serious	___	___
5	___	funnier	___
6	stupid	___	___

B **Write six sentences using words from the table.**

C **Choose the correct form of the adjective in brackets to complete the text. The first one has been done for you.**

WILLIAM AND HARRY: Brothers and friends

Prince William and Prince Harry on TV's "DIY SOS", Manchester, 2015

Everybody knows William and Harry. They are two of the world's *most famous* [1] (famous) brothers and come from one of the world's … [2] (rich) families. William was born in 1982. He is two years … [3] (old) than Harry. Because they have a lot to do, they are not always together but they are very … [4] (close) friends.
Their mother, Diana, was called "The Princess of Hearts" because she was one of the … [5] (warm) members of the British royal family. William and Harry are both as … [6] (kind) as she was.
When William and Harry were teenagers, their mother died in a car crash. There is nothing … [7] (bad) than the death of a parent but, even though he suffered, William supported his … [8] (young) brother and helped him through this … [9] (terrible) time.
For the press, Harry is … [10] (interesting) than his brother. As a teenager, he was just as … [11] (wild) as any other boy but, because he was a member of the royal family, the media reported everything. Today, Harry is … [12] (stable) than he was then.

5 WRITING A BLOG

TRAIN YOUR SKILLS: Bevor Sie schreiben vgl. auch S. 235

Schreiben Sie nie los, ohne vorher Ideen zu sammeln und eine Struktur zu erabeiten.

- Ideen sammeln Sie am besten in Form einer Mindmap.
- Listen Sie die Ideen in einer Reihenfolge auf, die als Struktur dienen sollte.
- Finden Sie Beispiele, die Ihre Ideen untermauern.

You and a group of six students from different countries have set up a group blog to share your experiences of school, family and life. One of the group members has started a new thread and wants you all to contribute.

> "Friends are the family we choose for ourselves."

Write a comment of 120 words saying what you think of the statement. Remember that blogs are intended to be read by lots of people.

You are working as an intern at the South Manchester Youth Centre.

1 ABOUT THE YOUTH CENTRE

Read the "About" page and use the headings to make notes to describe the centre:

- who goes there
- opening days / times
- why kids go to the centre

http://www.south_manchester_youth_centre.uk/about

THE SOUTH MANCHESTER YOUTH CENTRE

Kids know that it's a great place to be!

The South Manchester Youth Centre is a centre for young people aged 12 to 18. The centre is open Monday to Friday from 4 p.m. till 9 p.m. The Centre is the place where youngsters have fun, make friends and learn new things. We have activities for everyone.

2 QUALITIES YOU NEED FOR A JOB

What qualities do you need to work at the centre?
These are essential qualities that all youth workers need: energy, patience and creativity. You also need to have an optimistic and enthusiastic attitude, because you are a role model for the youngsters. It's important to have a positive view of young people and to respect them. If you know how to communicate well and enjoy working in a team, this may be a good job for you. (A good sense of humour also helps a lot.)

What does a day look like for a youth worker?
A normal working day is a mixture of different things: We answer and write emails. We make a budget and a timetable for each project. And most of all, of course, we work with young people.

What work does a youth worker do with youngsters?
A youth worker provides fun activities, he/she plans new activities, plays the role of mentor and helps young people to think about their lives and their futures.

A Write down the qualities that a youth worker needs. Start like this:

A youth worker needs to:
- *have energy, patience and creativity.*
- *have …*
- *know …*

B You are applying for a job with a company you really want to work for. Write a personal statement describing the qualities you will bring to the job. Use the expressions in task 2A to write a description of yourself.

3 A DISCUSSION ABOUT NEW ACTIVITIES

10

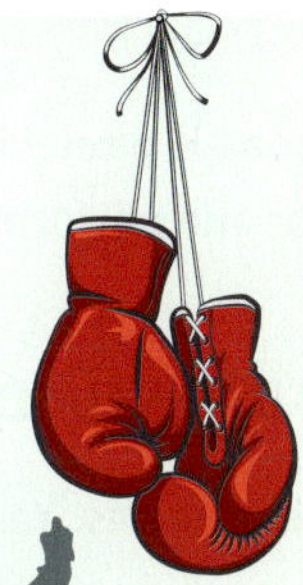

Karin, who is the manager of the Youth Centre, is talking to Andy about two new projects.

A As you listen, make notes in English of the advantages of each activity. Then make a table like the one below, listing the information in German.

Skateboarding	Boxing
Skaten ist cool.	Die Benutzung des Box-Clubs ist kostenlos.

B Below you can see the expressions Karin and Andy use in their discussion. Put them in a table under the following headings:

agreeing	disagreeing	asking for an opinion	introducing an idea

Let's have your thoughts on the matter.
That's a good idea.
I think that … is the best option.
Have you thought about … ?
The problem with that is …
That sounds good.
Let's discuss …
The main advantage is that …
I agree with you that …
I don't think that …
I disagree with you.
Another point I would like to make is …
I think you are right that …
Can I suggest that … ?
That's a good idea.

Go to File 5 on page 184.

4 GROUP DISCUSSION

The Youth Centre wants to add one new activity to its programme. You and the other interns have to choose an activity and present it to the group. Discuss the activities and make a ranking list to show which ones you should do at the Youth Centre. The activities can be found in File 1 on page 192.

Presentation phase

Each of you presents one of the activities in a one-minute speech. Explain why you think it is the best for the Youth Centre.

Interaction phase

Exchange arguments, try to convince the others that your activity is the best or at least should be the second on the list. Be willing to compromise. Use expressions from task 3B.

A docusoap is a television series that shows the real lives of people. You are going to write a script for and perform a short scene in a docusoap.

1 RELATIONSHIP DOCUSOAPS

A **Work in teams. You have three minutes to brainstorm a list of docusoaps that portray relationships.**

B **As a class, collect your titles on the board. Which is the most popular docusoap? Say why it is so popular.**

2 BACKGROUND WORK

Before writing your scene, discuss the points below. Collect your answers in a mind map on the board.

1 What topics are covered in docusoaps that focus on relationships?
2 What types of characters appear in them?
3 Where do things happen?

3 PLANNING AND PREPARING YOUR SCENE

Work in teams. Together:

- Choose a topic for your scene.
- Decide where the scene will take place.
- Decide on an interesting name for your docusoap.
- Choose two or three characters for the scene. Make notes about them (names, ages, what they look like, their characters, relationships to each other).

4 WRITING YOUR SCRIPT

A **Use the notes you made above to write the script for your scene.**

B **Give your scene a title.**

5 PERFORMING YOUR SCENE

A **When you are ready, introduce your scene as follows:**

- Tell the others the title.
- Say something about the action.
- Say where the scene takes place.
- Introduce your characters (names, ages, characters, relationships).

B **Play your scene in front of the class.**

Each member of the audience completes a viewer card, which your teacher will hand out. After all the scenes have been played, your teacher will collect the cards and announce the best docusoaps.

Role models

4

A WARM-UP: TALKING ABOUT ROLE MODELS

Malala Yousafzai: She is a courageous woman who fights for the rights of women to have education. She has been awarded the Nobel Peace Prize and has been appointed UN Messenger of Peace.

Manuel Neuer: Besides being a member of the German national football team, he donates money to charity and has his own foundation for underprivileged children.

Martin Luther King: He fought so that black people in the USA could be treated equally.

Firefighter: She does a dangerous job and saves lives every day.

Mum: She always told me I could achieve anything.

Grandad: He never stops working, even though he is an old man.

Think: Who are your role models? Could any of the people above be a role model for you?
Pair: Talk together about your role models and say why you like them.
Share: List your role models on the board. What makes them role models? How do they behave?

He is a role model because he ...

I look up to her because she ...

B GETTING BACK ON TRACK

SITUATION: A friend of yours is going through a difficult time at home and is thinking of running away. You read an interview with a young woman who overcame her problems and turned her life around. You write an email to your friend telling him or her about the young woman's experience.

1 PREPARING TO READ

The following phrases (1–8) are used in the interview. Match them with the German expressions (a–h). The phrases are in the order in which they appear in the text.

1	to live rough	**a**	auf der Straße leben
2	to turn your life around	**b**	das Beste daraus machen
3	to go off with somebody	**c**	ein offenes Beratungszentum
4	to fall behind at school	**d**	in der Schule zurückbleiben
5	to make the most of something	**e**	mit jemandem ein Verhältnis anfangen
6	a drop-in centre	**f**	Prüfungen wiederholen
7	to get back on track	**g**	sein Leben umkrempeln
8	to do resits	**h**	wieder in die Spur kommen

2 READING AND UNDERSTANDING A TEXT

A **Multiple matching: Read the text opposite. Choose the most appropriate sentence (1–6) to fill the gaps in the text (A–E). There is one sentence more than you need. The first one has been done for you.**

1	Everything I did was wrong.	**4**	I hope to become a counsellor one day.
2	I had a lot of responsibilities.	**5**	Nobody told me to behave myself.
3	I hated being told what to do.	**6**	When he left, my life changed completely.

B **Is Laura a good role model? Explain why/why not.**

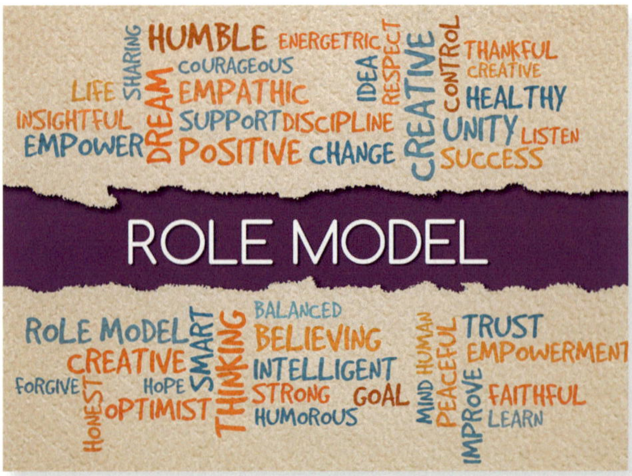

GETTING BACK ON TRACK

11

Laura was 14 when life at home became difficult. A year ago, at the age of 16, she dropped out of school and left home. She went to London where she lived on the streets. It didn't take long for her to realize that living rough wasn't good for her. Today, Laura has turned her life around. I asked her to tell us her story.

Why did you decide to leave home, Laura?

I grew up in a small town north of London. I lived with my mum and dad and my two brothers. They're twins. Everything was fine but, when I was 14, my dad went off with another woman. She had a house in the next town. She had two kids of her own and my dad didn't want to know us. **A** *When he left, my life changed completely.*

How did your life change?

My mum worked in a supermarket, so I did most of the housework and looked after my brothers when they got home from school. I didn't have any time for myself so I fell behind at school. Then, when I was 15, Mum met Andy and she went out almost every night. My brothers were 9 years old and I did the babysitting. I was supposed to do homework but instead, I watched TV all night. **B** It was just too much for me.

How did things go on?

The trouble started when Andy moved in at the beginning of last year. He made a lot of rules for me to follow. **C** I had to stay at home on weekday evenings and I was only allowed to go out at weekends, so I made the most of it. I stayed out late with my friends, drinking and doing stupid things. There was always trouble when I got home and, in the end, Mum threw me out. My dad couldn't take me in, and I didn't have any friends I could stay with so I went to London.

What did you do there?

I met some people who camped under a bridge near Charing Cross Station so I lived with them. At the beginning I liked it: I was free to do what I wanted. **D** We slept all morning, then we went out begging for money. But, one day, after six months, I woke up and thought: What have I done? I used to have goals. I can't live like this for ever. And it's dangerous: other youngsters have been harmed or have died on the streets. Why have I thrown my life away? I went to a drop-in centre, where I spoke to a social worker. She helped me to get back on track. I have never been so grateful to anyone.

What has happened since then?

I've been back with my family for the last six months and I'm now hanging out with friends who have goals in life. I've started school again and I've just done my resits. **E** I haven't applied for a place at college yet, but I've already visited schools and given talks about my experience and the way things have turned out for me. Last month I met the social worker from the drop-in centre – she was so happy and impressed! I really have turned my life around. (559 words)

3 LANGUAGE IN USE: SIMPLE PAST VS PRESENT PERFECT

→ Simple past, S. 249; present perfect, S. 251

EXAMPLE: *I've just done my resits.*

A Sort these signal words and expressions into two lists: those that are usually used with the simple past and those that are usually used with the present perfect.

ago ▪ already ▪ just ▪ last month ▪ never ▪ since ▪ when ▪ yet

B Look at lines 8–52 and find examples of the simple past. Say why they are in that tense.

C Look at lines 53–65 and find examples of the present perfect.

D When do we use the simple past? When do we use the present perfect? Complete each of the sentences below with one of the endings, a–d below.

1 Wir verwenden *simple past* für ___
2 Wir verwenden *present perfect* für ___

a Ereignisse, die in der Vergangenheit begonnen haben und noch andauern.
b vollständig abgeschlossene Ereignisse.

E How would you say the sentences below in English?

TIP ! *seit* in English

since 2016 seit 2016 *(bezogen auf einen Zeitpunkt)*
I have lived on the streets since 2016.

for six months *seit sechs Monaten* *(bezogen auf einen Zeitraum)*
I have lived on the streets for six months.

Note: Last year I lived on the streets for six months.
Letztes Jahr lebte ich sechs Monate auf der Straße.

EXAMPLE: Ich wurde 2001 geboren. *I was born in 2001.*

1 Vor sechs Monaten habe ich meine Prüfungen bestanden.
2 Ich wohne seit meiner Kindheit in London.
3 Letzten Winter habe ich eine Sozialarbeiterin getroffen.
4 Haben Sie je auf der Straße gelebt?

F Ask your neighbour questions beginning with: When did …? – How long …? – Have you ever …? – Did you … last year/month? – Where/What … five years ago?

4 WORKING WITH WORDS

A phrasal verb is when a verb and a preposition are put together and have a meaning that is different from the original verb. They are very common in English.

EXAMPLE: drop *She dropped her book.* drop out of *She dropped out of school.*

A Go through the text and find all the phrasal verbs. The first few are shown in the table.

phrasal verb	German	line in text
drop out of school	*die Schule abbrechen*	*2–3*
turn your life around	…	…
…	…	…

B Decide which prepositions from the box on the right can be used with the verbs in brackets in the text below.

back to ▪ through ▪ up ▪ up ▪ up to

It often helps to have a good role model when we …[1] (go) a difficult period in our lives. A good role model is someone who you …[2] (look) and who is positive and …[3] (lift – you). A good role model is ambitious and does not …[4] (give) easily. But it is not just about them – the best role models also …[5] (give) society.

5 MEDIATION

TRAIN YOUR SKILLS: Mediation vgl. auch S. 243

Mediation ist das Übertragen wesentlicher Informationen aus einem Text von einer Sprache in eine andere.

- Lesen Sie die Anweisungen sorgfältig. Stellen Sie fest:
  - warum Sie schreiben,
  - für wen Sie schreiben,
  - welche Art von Text Sie schreiben (z. B. Brief, Onlineartikel).
- Suchen Sie die Textpassagen, die die relevanten Informationen enthalten.
- Schreiben Sie die wichtigsten Punkte des Textes in klarem, einfachem Deutsch auf.
- Überprüfen Sie, dass Sie nur die relevanten Informationen übernommen haben und dass der Text adressatengerecht ist.

Sie haben den Text über Laura gelesen und denken, dass das für Ihren Freund / Ihre Freundin hilfreich wäre, da er/sie darüber nachdenkt, wegen Familienproblemen auszuziehen. Schreiben Sie Ihrem Freund / Ihrer Freundin eine E-Mail auf Deutsch, in der Sie über Lauras Erfahrungen erzählen und wie ihm/ihr diese Informationen helfen könnten. Erwähnen Sie Folgendes:

- warum Laura weglief
- was ihr geschah, als sie nach London zog
- wo sie sich jetzt aufhält

C HOW ROLE MODELS INFLUENCE US

1 PREPARING TO LISTEN

You are going to listen to a podcast on the influence of role models.

A Before you listen to the podcast, read the introduction and study the highlighted words and expressions below. Match them to the expressions (1–4).

Why do we look up to certain people? Why do we choose a certain person as a role model? Sometimes it's because they are famous or successful or talented. Role models usually set an example that we wish to follow. They can serve as ambassadors for certain causes. Today, I'm talking to Marion and Robin about their role models and how they influence their lives.

1 encourage and inspire people to behave in a similar way
2 being naturally able to do well at something
3 the effect role models can have on people
4 person who represents an organization by educating the public

B Make sentences using the highlighted expressions from the text.

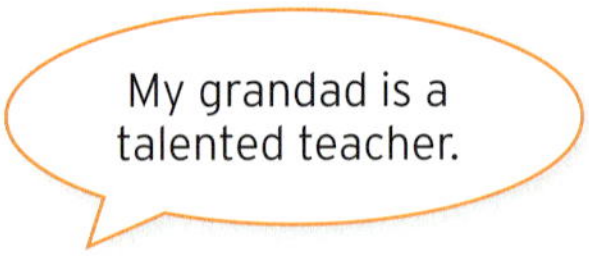

2 LISTENING: WHO'S YOUR ROLE MODEL?

12

True or false: Decide if the following statements are true or false. Explain your answers.

1 Sara Nuru won first place in the last series of Germany's Next Top Model.
2 Sara is an ambassador for "Menschen für Menschen".
3 "Generation ABC – 2015" supports people with health problems.
4 Marion speaks to young women in Africa about their problems.
5 Leonardo DiCaprio goes to disaster areas to help people.
6 He once criticized the US President for his poor judgement on climate issues.
7 Robin has never been actively involved in environmental issues.

Sara Nuru, at a children's home in Ethiopia supported by "Menschen für Menschen", 10 May 2012

3 LANGUAGE IN USE: RELATIVE CLAUSES

→ Relative clauses, S. 267

EXAMPLES: *We choose **a person who** is popular among other teenagers.*
*It's one of these **shows which** are shown all over the world.*

Complete the text using *who* or *which*.

Role models always set an example. That's fine when the role models are people ⬬ [1] do good things. Sometimes, however, a role model might encourage us to do things ⬬ [2] are bad. Some of the celebrities ⬬ [3] we admire do things ⬬ [4] are stupid. Some of them take drugs or get drunk. Doing things like that, ⬬ [5] are against the law, might get you into trouble. The thing is people don't just want role models ⬬ [6] are perfect. They want to see role models make mistakes but get up again. Weaknesses are the things ⬬ [7] allow us to identify with role models. Of course, if your role model is someone evil like Ramsay Bolton, ⬬ [8] was one of the most sadistic characters in *Game of Thrones*, the chances are that you won't turn out to be a good person. Choose a role model ⬬ [9] will make you a better person.

REMEMBER ! *used to*

We use **used to** to talk about how you did something or how you thought about something in the past. With negatives and questions we use **did not use to / Did … use to …?**.

I **used to admire** Justin Bieber but I don't like him now.
Früher habe ich Justin Bieber bewundert, aber jetzt mag ich ihn nicht mehr.
I **didn't use to like** Lady Gaga but I really like her now.
Lady Gaga mochte ich früher nicht, aber jetzt stehe ich auf sie.
Did you use to watch KiKa?
Hast du früher KiKa geschaut?

02

4 VIEWING

→ Videos, S. 195

Watch the video called "Matt Damon calls for action on clean water access" and complete the tasks on page 195.

5 DISCUSSION

→ Interaktion, S. 245

What do you think about role models and the way they influence us? Think about what you know about role models and reflect on what you have learned from the pages in this unit. Discuss in groups, make notes and report to the class.

You are interested in meeting people from other cultures. Your teacher points out the following announcement online. You apply for a place to meet and greet visitors from China.

http://lokalstadt.de/Veranstaltungen

Visitors from our twin town in China

Would you like to be an ambassador for your school? Next month, we are going to welcome a group of people from our twin town in China. They are interested in finding out about our vocational training programmes. We have an exciting programme for our guests, including visits to local factories, workshops and places of further education.

We would like to invite students, who will represent local schools, to take part in a "Meet and Greet" event. If you are between 17 and 20 and interested in meeting people from other cultures, apply here.

You should have a friendly and open personality. Good spoken English is a must. If your application is accepted, you will be invited to a training session.

13

1 HOW TO BEHAVE WITH CHINESE VISITORS

Your application has been accepted and you go to the training session. The first session is about how to behave when you meet the visitors.

Listen to the trainer and complete the grid below, making notes on how the Chinese behave and how you should behave.

Behaviour	Chinese people	You
1 Greetings	*shake hands when they meet people*	▬
2 Clothes	▬	▬
3 Body language	▬	▬
4 Being prepared	▬	▬
5 Language	▬	▬

Go to File 6 on page 185.

2 MAKING SMALL TALK WITH GUESTS

A What is small talk? Choose the best definition.

1 a child's first words
2 using simple language to communicate
3 polite conversation about ordinary or unimportant things

B **Work with a partner. Decide together which of the topics in the box you should not talk about with people you do not know well.**

about the journey to the meeting place ▪ food ▪ hobbies ▪ money ▪ problems at school ▪ religion ▪ sex ▪ sport ▪ the weather ▪ your training

14

C **Your trainer practises small talk with a member of the class who takes the role of one of the Chinese visitors. Read the gapped dialogue and add the questions and statements (a–g) to complete it. The first question has been added for you. When you have finished, listen and check.**

Trainer: [1] *How was your flight to Germany?*
Visitor: Very good, thank you. There weren't any delays. [2]
Trainer: That's nice. I'm sorry about the weather here. It's not usually so cold at this time of year.
Visitor: [3] The hotel is warm and the food here is very good. I like German food.
Trainer: [4]
Visitor: Yes, I have. I visited the Black Forest two years ago. It's a very beautiful region. Now, I'm happy to be here and to meet everyone. [5]
Trainer: There are 24 students. [6]
Visitor: Oh, our classes are very big. Sometimes we have as many as 40 students in one class. They are all training for the same profession. What about you? [7].

a Have you been to Germany before?
b How big are the classes in your country?
c How many students are in your class?
d ~~How was your flight to Germany?~~
e I don't mind the cold.
f It was good weather for flying.
g What do you want to do when you have left school?

3 ROLE-PLAY: MEETING AND GREETING A VISITOR

It is time for the Meet and Greet event. With a partner take turns playing the role of the visitor.

Partner A: You are one of the students	Partner B: You are one of the visitors
→ Sie grüßen den Gast und stellen sich vor. Heißen Sie den Gast willkommen.	→ Erwidern Sie den Gruß und sagen Sie, wie angenehm es ist, hier zu sein.
→ Machen Sie etwas Smalltalk, z. B. zu seiner/ihrer Reise.	→ Reagieren Sie. Fragen Sie etwas zurück, z. B. zum Thema Unterrichtsstoff.
→ Reagieren Sie auf die Frage des Besuchers / der Besucherin.	→ Sagen Sie, dass es schön war, sich mit dem Schüler / der Schülerin zu unterhalten.
→ Sie reagieren entsprechend und schließen das Gespräch freundlich ab.	→ Wünschen Sie dem Schüler / der Schülerin viel Erfolg mit seinen/ihren Berufsplänen.

You are going to research and give a presentation on a good role model.

1 CHOOSING A ROLE MODEL

Work in small teams. Decide together if you are going to present a celebrity or a local person you all know. Write down the name of the person.

2 WHAT MAKES THE PERSON YOU HAVE CHOSEN A GOOD ROLE MODEL?

Talk about what the person does that makes him/her a good role model. Make notes.

3 RESEARCHING YOUR ROLE MODEL

Research the background of your role model. Make notes on any details that may have helped the person become a good role model.

Here are some ideas to start you off:

- where they were born
- what their profession is
- what their family background is
- what they have achieved
- what makes them special

4 PREPARING YOUR PRESENTATION

A Structure the notes you made above for a presentation. Conclude by saying why the person you have chosen is a good role model.

B Make copies of photos, newspaper articles and anything else that is relevant.

C Make handouts.

5 GIVING YOUR PRESENTATION

→ Präsentation, S. 244

A Take turns to present your role model. Answer any questions from the audience. (Remember that your audience will be making notes. See task B below.)

B While you are listening to a presentation, make notes on the categories below. Give points from 1 to 5 for each category.

structure of presentation ▪ use of language ▪ body language ▪ answering of questions ▪ handouts

Health today

5

A WARM-UP: ALTERNATIVE TREATMENTS

A Look at the different ways in which people deal with illnesses. What do you think about the treatments shown?

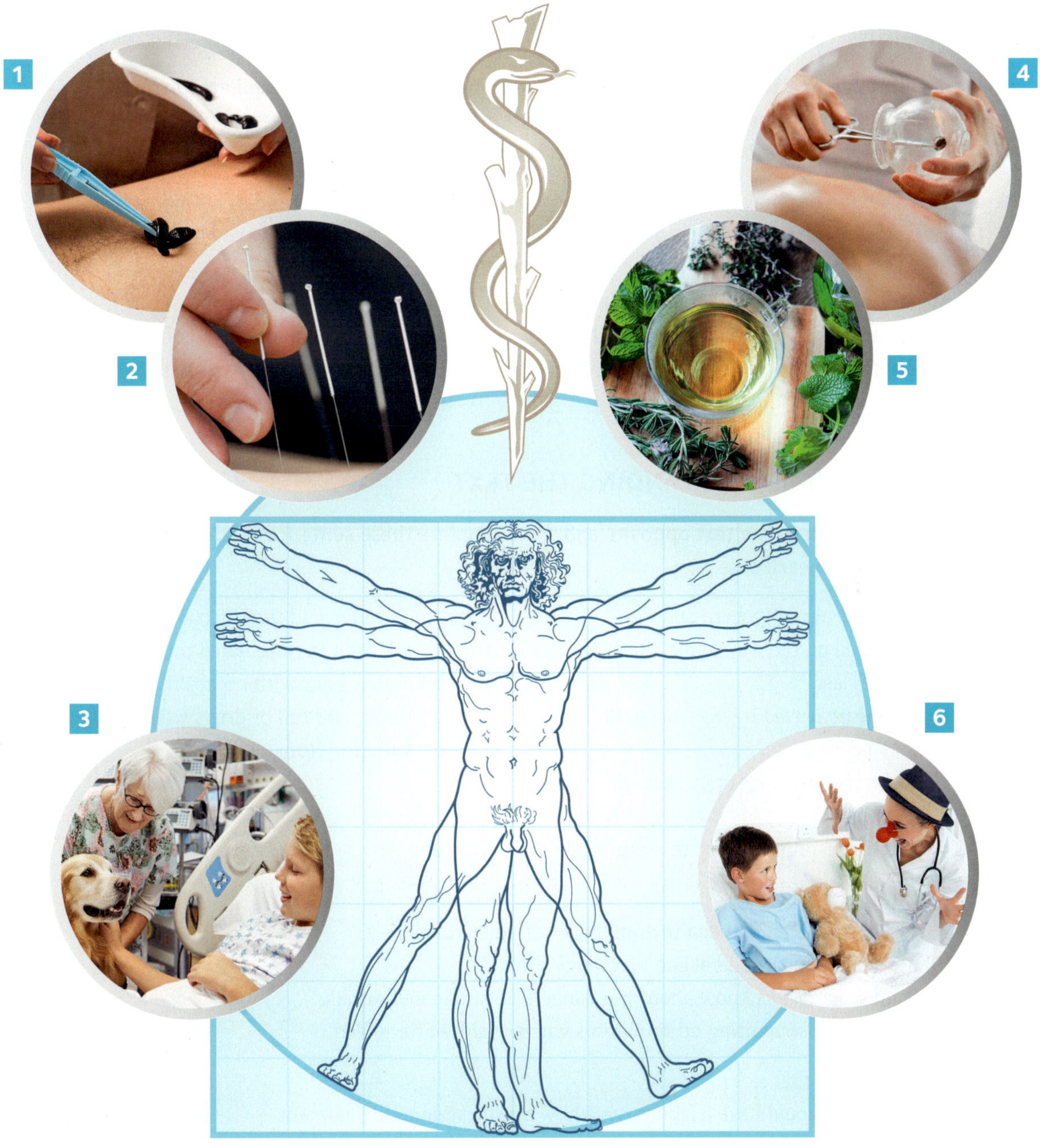

B What similar treatments are you familiar with?

B CAFFEINE: THE HIDDEN DANGER

SITUATION: Caffeine drinks are popular at your school kiosk – not just cold coffee drinks but also energy drinks. But how dangerous can they be? You come across a text about the tragic death of a teenager and decide to use it to inform fellow students about the dangers of caffeine (task 5, p. 59).

1 PREPARING TO READ

Work with a partner. You are going to read a newspaper report with the headline: "Caffeine: The hidden danger". The notes that the journalist made for his report have got jumbled up. With your partner, put the notes in the correct order. (Look up any words you don't know.)

a arrived at the hospital in a coma
b coroner says the young man did not die of a drug overdose
c doctors put him on a life-support system
d follow-up with expert: "Tragic accidents can happen."
e paramedics took R. to hospital
f Richard D. collapsed in his maths class
g R's parents say that they have started a campaign
h teacher called an ambulance
i teen drank too many high-caffeine drinks in a short period of time

2 READING AND UNDERSTANDING THE TEXT

Multiple choice: Read the text opposite and then complete these sentences with the most suitable option in each case.

1 What is true about Richard D.? He …
- **a** collapsed on the way to his afternoon maths class.
- **b** was nearly saved by his teacher and the paramedics.
- **c** had consumed a lot of caffeine in a very short time.
- **d** had had heart problems for some time.

2 The coroner said that Richard was …
- **a** addicted to caffeinated drinks.
- **b** a youngster with no health problems.
- **c** drunk and full of drugs when he died.
- **d** suffering from heart problems.

3 Richard's parents …
- **a** said their son didn't usually drink high-caffeine drinks.
- **b** are demanding a general ban on energy drinks.
- **c** want to let others know about the dangers of caffeinated drinks.
- **d** are actively supporting other parents whose children have died.

4 An expert said that …
- **a** all drinks should have a label saying how much caffeine they contain.
- **b** energy drinks should only be sold to people over 18.
- **c** everyone should be careful about what they drink.
- **d** healthy people can drink a few caffeinated drinks every day without having problems.

15

DAILY NEWS

CAFFEINE: THE HIDDEN DANGER

by Aidan Thomas

A British teenager has died because he drank too many high-caffeine drinks in a short period of time. Richard D. (16), of Bristol, drank a café latte and two energy drinks during the 45-minute school lunch break. He collapsed 15 minutes after he took his seat in the maths class, which was his first class of the afternoon. The class teacher called an ambulance and gave the young man first aid until the paramedics arrived. When they got him to hospital, Richard was in a coma. The doctors put him on a life-support system, but they could not save his life.

At a press conference, the coroner, Dr Ranya Shahen, said the boy had had a heart attack which might have happened as a result of drinking too much caffeine in a very short space of time. Richard's friends and family said that he had always had a coffee or an energy drink in his hand. According to Dr Shahen, it was Richard's love of these caffeinated drinks that might have killed him.

'Richard was a healthy teenager with no heart conditions. There were no drugs or alcohol in his system when he died,' Dr Shahen said. 'It was not the total amount of caffeine in his system that killed him but the fact that he drank so many caffeinated drinks one after the other. People should cut down on the number of drinks they consume,' she said.

Richard's parents have now started a campaign to let young people know that they have to be careful about drinking too many caffeinated drinks too quickly. Richard's father said, 'You shouldn't drink too many on one day and you have to give your body time to recover between each drink.' He went on, 'Every parent worries about their children's health and safety as they're growing up. At the same time, every young person has to be allowed to do what the other kids do. Richard died because he drank too many drinks with caffeine in them, just like so many of his friends. We must make other parents and their children aware of the possible dangers of these drinks. We hope that our campaign will be able to get that message across.'

An expert said, 'Tragic accidents can happen sometimes. After a report like this, many people might worry that caffeine could put them at risk. My advice is, if you don't have heart problems, you may have two to three cups of coffee a day or, if you prefer to get your caffeine in energy drinks, drinking a couple of them is also all right. As long as you don't drink them all at once, you needn't worry.' (446 words)

3 LANGUAGE IN USE: MODAL AUXILIARIES

→ Modal auxiliaries, S. 260

A Find all the modal auxiliaries in the text.

EXAMPLE: *they could not save his life (l. 15)*

REMEMBER ! modal auxiliaries

Modal auxiliaries are used to express permission (**may**), ability (**can**), obligation (**must**), etc.
Here is a list of the main modals (and their substitutes in brackets):
can (be able to), may (be allowed to), might, must (have to), need not (not have to)
Most modals use the substitute form in the future:
Can you come now? → **Will** you **be able to** come tomorrow?

B Replace the German words in the texts below with a modal auxiliary or a suitable substitute.

Our neighbour, Mrs Smith, is 86 years old. She *kann*[1] look after herself but she *kann nicht*[2] lift heavy things, so I go shopping for her. My mum has a key to her house so we *können*[3] get in if anything is wrong. When I took round her shopping yesterday, I *konnte*[4] see that something was wrong. Mrs Smith *konnte nicht*[5] speak properly. I thought she *könnte*[6] be ill, but she *war nicht in der Lage*[7] to tell me what the problem was. I ran home and got mum. She said. "We *müssen*[8] call the doctor." Then she said, "You *sollst*[9] get a glass of water for Mrs Smith while we are waiting." When the doctor came, she said, "I *muss*[10] do a lot of home visits when the weather is warm like this. A lot of my older patients don't drink enough water. That *könnte*[11] be the problem with Mrs Smith." After the doctor examined Mrs Smith, she wrote a prescription for some pills. "You *sollten*[12] take one as soon as you get up in the morning and one before you go to bed," she said to Mrs Smith. "You *sollten nicht*[13] take more than two pills a day. And please drink your water. We *müssen*[14] make sure this doesn't happen again," she said.

C Match the things shown in the safety signs (1–6) on page 59 to the words below (a–f) and then use modal verbs to describe what the signs mean. Sometimes you can use more than one modal verb.

a wash / hands / before / handle food
b first-aid kit / find / in office
c fire / use stairs
d bike helmet / in case / fall off / bike
e bottle / not drink / toxic liquid
f wet floor / take care / not slip (*ausrutschen*)

1

2

3

4

5

6

4 WORKING WITH WORDS

A The expressions below are in the text. Use the verbs from column A and the phrases from column B to make other expressions.

- to make people aware of something (ll. 50–51)
- to get a message across (l. 53)
- to put someone at risk (l. 57)

A	B
make	angry
get	an appointment
put	drunk
	ill
	a mistake
	someone laugh
	someone on a course of treatment
	someone on a drip
	well

B Make sentences using six of the expressions.

5 MEDIATION

→ Mediation, S. 243

Viele Schülerinnen und Schüler an Ihrer Schule trinken Energydrinks. Daher nehmen Sie den Text über Richard D. als Grundlage für einen kurzen Text für die Schulwebsite, um vor den Gefahren von Koffein zu warnen.

C AN EXCITING TECHNOLOGICAL DEVELOPMENT

1 PREPARING TO LISTEN

You are going to listen to a radio interview with Andrew Murray, a researcher into technology which helps with medical problems.

A Before you listen, study the picture and read the short description of the technology. Then choose the best heading for the picture.

- **a** Calling for assistance
- **b** Helping the blind to see
- **c** Pressing a key to save a life

An app that can help people with poor eyesight to lead more independent lives.

B Match these expressions from the text (1–5) with their German equivalent (a–e). The expressions are in the order they appear in the interview.

1	to have poor eyesight	**a**	ein unabhängiges Leben führen
2	to lead an independent life	**b**	etwas weiterleiten
3	to need assistance	**c**	Hilfe brauchen
4	time zone	**d**	schlecht sehen
5	to forward something	**e**	Zeitzone

2 LISTENING: A NEW APP

16

Look at the following list of statements and decide in which order they are made by Andrew Murray. The first one has been marked for you (1). Copy the list and number the others. There are two statements that don't come up in the interview. Put crosses (×) in their boxes instead of numbers.

number	statements
	Your helper is also a person with poor eyesight, so he understands your situation.
1	The app doesn't cost anything.
	You film something that you can't see very well and send the video to your helper.
	The app manages to find suitable helpers very quickly, as it knows which language you are speaking and where in the world you are located.
	The app calls people from a list of possible helpers in all parts of the world.
	The app connects the blind person to someone who is willing to help without getting paid for it.
	The app automatically calls through a list of helpers until one is available.

3 LANGUAGE IN USE: MODAL AUXILIARIES

→ Modal auxiliaries, S. 260

Work with a partner. Decide together where to use *must / must not* and where to use *should / should not*.

EXAMPLES: *The user **must** press a key on their phone.*
*Anyone who is interested in the app **should** check our website.*

REMEMBER ! *must not*

must not = nicht dürfen
You **must not** tell anyone. →
Das dürfen Sie niemandem erzählen.

nicht müssen = not need to
Sie müssen nicht gehen. →
You **don't need to** leave.

1 You ▬ register your details before you are allowed to use the app.
2 You ▬ remember to charge your phone before you use the app.
3 You ▬ make sure that you have internet connection before you try to contact a volunteer. If you don't, the app won't work.
4 You ▬ [a] share any personal information like your credit card number or personal details with a volunteer, even if they ask you to. If they do ask you, you ▬ [b] report them.
5 You ▬ use the app just for fun. The volunteers are not paid for their work.
6 You ▬ thank the volunteer for helping you before you sign off.
7 If you like the app, you ▬ recommend it to others.

4 PRESENTATION

You are going to research, prepare and give a presentation on an interesting piece of technology used in medicine.

TRAIN YOUR SKILLS: Eine Präsentation vorbereiten vgl. auch S. 244

Denken Sie immer daran, dass eine Präsentation ein visuelles Medium ist. Überladen Sie die Präsentation nicht mit Text. Verwenden Sie Illustrationen, um Ihre Ideen zu verdeutlichen.

- Erarbeiten Sie sich das Thema und machen Sie Notizen.
- Finden Sie zum Thema passende Illustrationen online oder machen Sie selbst welche.
- Strukturieren Sie Ihre Notizen unter Überschriften.
- Fügen Sie Details der später zu verwendenden Illustrationen hinzu.
- Verwenden Sie Überschriften für Ihre Grafiken.

A Do research on the internet and find a technological medical development that you find exciting. Make notes, collect your illustrations and write headings.

B Before you give your presentation, decide in class, together with your teacher, how you will get feedback on your content and presentation, as well as your way of presenting it.

C Give your presentation to the class.

5 THE WORLD OF WORK — Working at a spa

The spa where you work has a Ladies' Day once a week. Many of the clients who use the spa cannot speak German.

1 INFORMATION

Study the information from the English page of the website and make notes on the following:

a why people go to the spa
b facilities at the spa
c treatments on offer
d special offers
e general information

http://www.luxus-therme.com

Our ***Luxury Health Spa*** is a place of rest and relaxation in the middle of Frankfurt.
Swim in our outdoor swimming pool every day of the year.
Enjoy our indoor pool with whirlpool.
Relax at our health bar with juice and salads freshly prepared by our chef.
Choose from one of our three saunas.
Monday is Ladies' Day.

Entry prices	
3 hours	€25
5 hours	€40
All day ticket	€60

Open every day of the year:
10:00 a.m. till 10:30 p.m.
Free parking

Please call 069 444 8888 for information and appointments for massage treatments.

Products	Details	Price
Massage	25 mins / 50 mins	€35 / €65
Classic massage	25 mins / 50 mins	€40 / €75
Sport massage	20 mins	€30
Foot massage	20 mins	€30
Aromatherapy massage	50 mins	€65
Hot stone massage	60 mins	€75
Combination offers	Buy 10 tickets and get one free	
Time out • entry to the club (3 hours) • sauna (bring your own bathrobe) • classic massage • one drink of your choice		€70
Take a break • entry to the club (5 hours) • aromatherapy massage • sauna (bathrobe on loan) • freshly mixed fruit cocktail (alcohol free) • one salad of your choice		€90

2 MANAGING SITUATIONS: ADVISING A CLIENT

A visitor to Frankfurt is interested in coming to the spa on Ladies' Day. Take her phone call and give her advice.

Sie: *1 Melden Sie sich auf Deutsch mit dem Namen der Therme und Ihrem Namen.*
Client: Good morning/afternoon. Do you speak English?
Sie: *2 Sagen Sie, dass Sie Englisch sprechen, und fragen Sie, wie Sie helfen können.*
Client: I would like to make an appointment for a massage tomorrow.
Sie: *3 Fragen Sie die Anruferin, ob sie die Therme schon einmal besucht hat.*
Client: No, this will be the first time. It's my first visit to Frankfurt and a colleague recommended your spa to me.
Sie: *4 Fragen Sie, ob eine ganz bestimmte Massageart gewünscht wird.*
Client: Well, I'm here on business and I'm rather stressed, so anything that would make me feel less stressed would be good.

Sie: *5 Bekunden Sie Mitgefühl und Verständnis und sagen Sie, dass Sie sicher sind, dass geholfen werden kann. Fragen Sie nach Terminwünschen.*
Client: I'm free all evening tomorrow. I can be with you at 6 p.m.
Sie: *6 Sagen Sie, dass das bestens passt. Empfehlen Sie die Angebote „Time out" und „Take a break". Beschreiben Sie diese Angebote. Erklären Sie die wichtigsten Unterschiede.*
Client: I think "Take a break" sounds good. How much does it cost?
Sie: *7 Nennen Sie den Preis.*
Client: That sounds fine. I'll take it. Do your colleagues also speak English?
Sie: *8 Bestätigen Sie, dass sämtliche Angestellten gut Englisch sprechen. Fragen Sie nach dem Namen der Anruferin.*
Client: Elena Tschaikowsky.
Sie: *9 Sie verstehen den Nachnamen nicht und bitten darum, ihn zu buchstabieren.*
Client: It's Tschaikowsky. That's T S C H A I K O W S K Y.
Sie: *10 Wiederholen Sie den Namen und bestätigen Sie den Termin um 18 Uhr. Bitten Sie die Klientin, gleich bei der Ankunft zur Rezeption zu kommen und sagen Sie, dass man sich freut, sie morgen zu sehen.*

B Read out the dialogue with a partner.

3 ROLE-PLAY: SCHEDULING AN APPOINMENT

Work with a partner. Use your notes from task 1 to schedule appointments for a massage or a combination offer.

Students often complain that school is too stressful. As part of your school's project week on health and medicine today, you discuss ways to make your school less stressful.

1 STRESS AT SCHOOL

The school has put up a notice on the notice board. The aim is to find out what students find stressful at school.

Some students have already added their notes. Brainstorm more ideas of your own. Make a list.

too much noise
other people
no place to do homework

2 HOW WE ALREADY COMBAT STRESS

What can you already do at school to combat stress? What facilities does your school offer? How often do you use them? How do they help?

EXAMPLE: *We can use the library to do our homework.*

3 BRAINSTORMING IDEAS

Copy and complete the mind map with ideas about how to combat stress at your school.

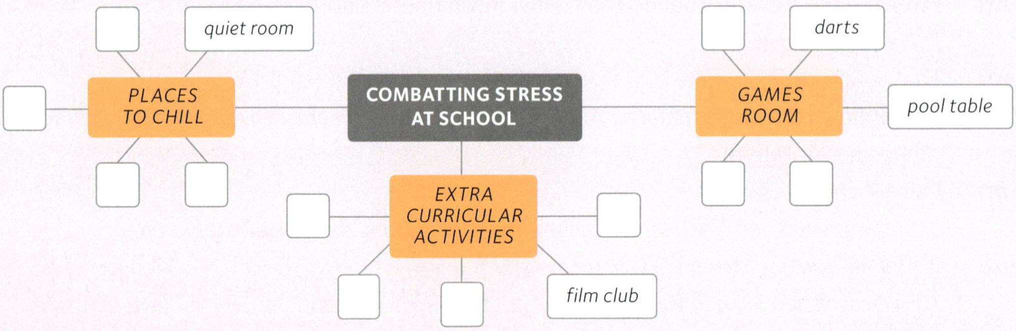

4 CLASS DISCUSSION: REACHING A CONSENSUS

→ Interaktion, S. 245

A **In a group, discuss all your suggestions and choose one to present to the class. Be prepared to explain to the class why it is a good suggestion.**

B **Present your suggestion to the class. Try to reach an agreement on which three suggestions are most suitable. Be prepared to compromise if your suggestion is not accepted.**

Shop, share, swap

6

A WARM-UP: SATISFYING OUR NEEDS

A Sort the photos under these four headings. Think of more examples of where to buy or find what we need.

saving the planet

shopping as an experience

giving and sharing

shopping from home

1

2

3

4

5

6

7

8

B Discuss these questions in groups.

Where do you shop? Who do you shop with?
What do you share? Who do you share with?
What do you swap? Who do you swap with?

B LIVING ON LESS

SITUATION: Your class has been invited to the recording of a TED talk on living on less. TED talks are speeches by experts that are recorded and uploaded onto the internet. They cover new developments in a wide variety of areas. The person who gives the talk believes that we would all be happier if we lived without money. You find the text opposite and decide to write a comment on the TED talk discussion forum (task 6, p. 69).

1 PREPARING TO READ

A You are going to read an interview with a man who lived without money for two years. Skim the text opposite to find the expressions below. Look at the expressions in context and say what they mean. If you are unsure, check your dictionary.

moneyless | strange | to be selfish | to exploit | second-hand | to adapt | consumer goods | smallholder | to challenge | food sharing | to hand in your notice

B Imagine you had to live without money. What problems would you face? What solutions might you find?

2 READING AND UNDERSTANDING THE TEXT

Multiple matching: Read the text. Some of Dylan's statements have been removed from the text. Match the statements (1–8) to the paragraphs (A–F). There are two statements more than you need.

1 I got a lot of criticism at the start.
2 I have a blog and I write articles and books about how to live without money.
3 I just got on with things.
4 I was sick of reading about forests being cut down and people in developing countries making cheap clothes for us.
5 Money rules the world.
6 That you have to build up relationships with the people, plants and animals around you.
7 The first few months were very difficult.
8 You have to trust that it will all work out in the end.

17

LIVING ON LESS

Three years ago, Dylan Frost gave up his job and moved into an old caravan on a smallholding just outside Cambridge. He cooked on a wood-burning stove and got his electricity using a solar panel. Today, Dylan is earning money again. He is using the experience he gained while living a moneyless life to encourage and support other people who want to become less dependent on money.

Evie Rose interviewed him about living on less.

Evie Dylan, what made you decide to live without money for two years?

A ... We exploit people and the planet so that we can buy consumer goods, and I didn't want to be part of that. I wanted to see if it was possible to live without money, and how it would affect me. I heard of a smallholder who was offering free accommodation in exchange for a little help. I went to see him on a Sunday and went into work on the Monday and handed in my notice. Then I cleaned up the caravan, bought a second-hand solar panel and started to live a moneyless life one month later.

Evie How did people react to your decision?

B ... When you challenge money, you challenge the way that other people live. Very few people like that. Support for what I'm doing has grown over the last years, though, and a lot of people want to become less dependent on money. A few of these people want to give up money completely and a few of them are simply interested in how they can spend less.

Evie How easy was it to adapt to living without money?

C ... Everything was new to me. I had to find out how to get food and how to prepare and cook it. I had to figure out how to get from A to B. Simple things, like how to keep myself and my clothes clean, became a challenge. Basically, I had to learn how to survive without money. As it turned out, I needed very little to survive.

Evie So, what did you do?

D ... I grew food and collected mushrooms and herbs in the wood, the smallholder gave me eggs and honey, and I went to a food-sharing place in Cambridge a few times. I walked everywhere or went longer distances by bicycle. I washed my body and my clothes in the river with soap made from a plant called soapwort, and I made toothpaste from salt and baking soda.

Evie What was the most important thing you learned?

E ... Some people couldn't care less about other people or the environment but I realized that if I was selfish, then I would not survive. Of course, living without money has its ups and downs but it showed me that less is more. I've never been happier or healthier in my whole life.

Evie You still live in the caravan and help the smallholder but you've started to earn money again. What are you doing now?

F ... I'm using the money I earn from my articles and books to pay for a little bit of land I bought from the smallholder. I'm building a wooden house with solar panels there. It's probably strange to hear that I'm making money from living a moneyless life-style, but I want to help other people to enjoy that life, too.

(553 words)

3 LANGUAGE IN USE: (A) LITTLE, (A) FEW

→ Quantifiers, S. 264

A Translate the expressions from the text into German.

1 a little help (l. 18)
2 Very few people like that (ll. 25–26)
3 A few of these people want to give up money completely (ll. 29–30)
4 I needed very little to survive (ll. 40–41)

B Choose *(a) little* or *(a) few (of)* to complete the texts.

1 The smallholder was lonely. He had ___[1] friends. He asked Dylan to spend ___[2] time with him in the evenings. Dylan knew that the man had only ___[3] years left to live. He was happy to give him ___[4] hours of his time every week.

2 It is of ___[1] importance how much money you have if you're not happy. ___[2] Dylan's friends thought he was crazy to give up his job. Dylan only needed ___[3] weeks to get used to living without money. Slowly, ___[4] people changed their minds about Dylan's idea. Dylan is working again. He earns only ___[5] money but he is happy.

Go to File 7 on page 185.

C Translation: You told Dylan's story to your parents. They were very interested. Now that you've read more about the smallholder, write down a short text in German about him, translating the information in task 3B 1 above.

4 WORKING WITH WORDS

A Copy the mind map and add words and expressions from the text. Add more words and expressions as you meet them in later tasks.

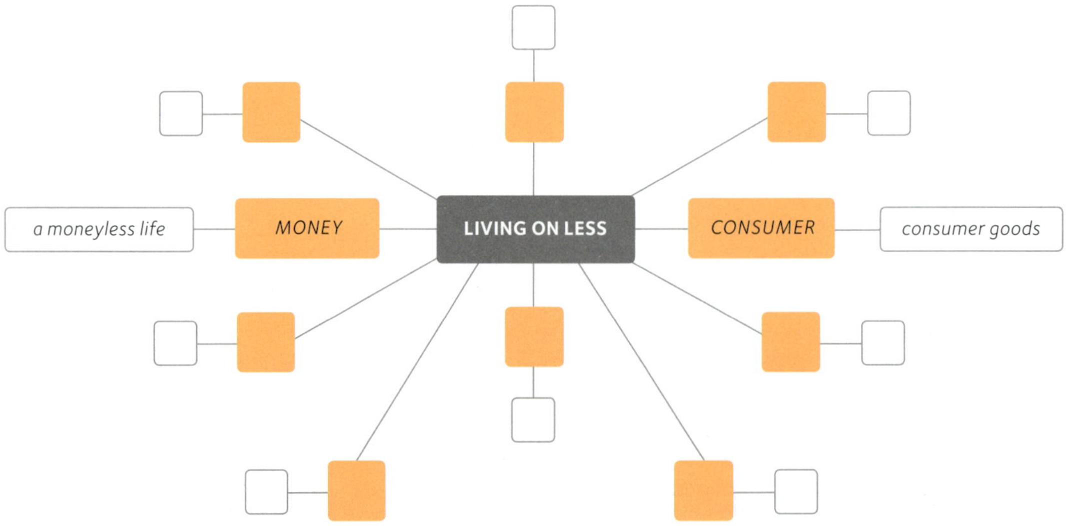

B Dylan uses two idioms and one proverb in the interview. Choose the best sentence ending to express his thoughts in a different way.

1 Some people **couldn't care less about** other people or the environment. (Idiom)

Some people …
- **a** are not at all interested in what happens to other people or the environment.
- **b** don't like other people or the environment.
- **c** should care more about other people or the environment.

2 Living without money **has its ups and downs**. (Idiom)

Living without money …
- **a** is a challenge.
- **b** is good and bad.
- **c** makes you depressed.

3 [Living without money] showed me that **less is more**. (Proverb)

Living without money …
- **a** is better than working.
- **b** makes life complicated.
- **c** makes life more interesting.

C Write three sentences about a situation in your life using the expressions above.

03

5 VIEWING

→ Videos, S. 196

Watch the video called "France ponders opening shops on Sundays despite tradition" and complete the tasks on page 196.

6 WRITING A COMMENT

TRAIN YOUR SKILLS: einen Comment schreiben vgl. auch S. 235

Bei einem Comment müssen Sie Argumente vorlegen, die Ihre Meinung unterstützen.

- Machen Sie zuerst ein Brainstorming, um Argumente und Ideen zu sammeln.
- Es hilft, Argumente in Pro- und Contra-Listen aufzuteilen.
- Es gibt wichtige *connecting words*, die Sie verwenden sollten, um Ihre Argumente einzuleiten und zu unterstützen sowie zum Schluss zu kommen (vgl. hintere Umschlagklappe).

At one point during the TED talk, the speaker says: "Anyone can get used to living without money". Comment on this statement. Write around 150 words.

Go to File 8 on page 186.

C TO SHOP OR NOT TO SHOP

1 PREPARING TO LISTEN

These sayings are used in the audio text. Before you listen, talk in groups and decide what they mean. Do you know the same or similar sayings in German or in another language you speak?

A fool and his money are soon parted.
Money doesn't grow on trees.
You can't take it with you when you go.

2 LISTENING: SHOPPING HABITS

18

A Multiple matching: Decide who says what. There are two statements for each speaker.

speaker	statement
Elias	
Kay	
Will	
Julia	

1 I always want the newest version of any tech equipment.

2 I won't buy a new phone until my old one no longer works.

3 I love my friends but they waste money buying stuff they don't need.

4 I haven't actually worn all the clothes I have.

5 I really love shopping.

6 There's a box of old equipment under my bed.

7 I try to buy as little as possible, as we just don't need so many things.

8 Vintage clothing can be really cool.

B Kay has bought motto t-shirts for herself and her friends. Match one t-shirt (1–4) to each speaker. Give a reason.

1

2

3

4

3 LANGUAGE IN USE: (THE) LESS, AT/THE LEAST, FEWER, THE FEWEST

A Look at these examples from the audio text. Explain when we use *less* and when we use *fewer*.

1 **These T-shirts cost less than** the ones in the shopping mall.
2 **The less stuff** you buy, the better.
3 You have **fewer problems** when you have **less stuff**.
4 I have **the fewest T-shirts** of all of us.

B Translate the German phrases in the sentences below with (*the*) *less*, (*at/the*) *least*, *fewer*, *the fewest*. The first sentence has been done for you.

1 My second-hand printer cost *weniger*[a] less than a new one. Of all my printers, it's the one that's given me *die wenigsten*[b] the fewest problems.
2 Of all the jackets I have, this is the one I wear *am wenigsten*[a]. I like it much *weniger*[b] than the other jackets I own.
3 Shopping is such a waste of time. *Je weniger* time I spend shopping, the more time I have for my hobbies.
4 Boys spend *weniger*[a] money on clothes than girls. That's not because boys buy *weniger*[b] clothes than girls but because boys' clothes cost *mindestens*[c] 25% *weniger*[d] than girls' clothes.

4 DISCUSSION

→ Interaktion, S. 245

A Look at the statements in the speech bubbles on the opposite page. Who do you agree/disagree with?

B Discuss your views with a partner. Give reasons. Make notes.

C Report back to the class. What, (if anything) would people like to change about their shopping habits? Why?

You are doing work experience at an international department store.

1 WHERE CAN I FIND ... ?

A Your supervisor would like you to hang up labels for the various departments in your store. Look at the photos and match them with words from the box.

accessories ▪ children's clothing ▪ cosmetics ▪ food hall ▪ household items ▪ ladies' wear ▪ menswear ▪ sportswear

1

2

3

4

5

6

7

8

B Work with a partner. Brainstorm a list of other departments or places in the store. Draw a sketch of "your" department store and add the names of the departments and places. Do not show your partner your sketch. Take turns to ask and answer questions about where to find goods and places.

Where can I find the restaurant?

It's on the fourth floor. The lift is just over there.

2 WORKING ON THE SHOP FLOOR

A Sort the following phrases into what the shop assistant says and what the customer says.

1 Do you have this in a larger size?
2 Would you like to try it on?
3 That will be thirty-nine euros ninety-nine, please.
4 I'm just looking.
5 Could you put this aside for me?
6 Are you looking for anything in particular?
7 Here's your change.
8 Do you have this in a different colour?
9 What style would you like?
10 Can I pay by credit card?
11 How much does it cost?
12 You can exchange it if it's not the right colour.
13 We can order it for you.
14 How many items can I take into the changing room?

19 **B You listen to a colleague assisting a customer. Before you listen, read the start of the dialogue, then put the remaining parts (A–J) in the correct order. Then listen and check.**

Shop Assistant: Guten Morgen. Wie kann ich Ihnen helfen?
Customer: Hello. Do you speak English?
Shop Assistant: Yes, I do. Can I help you?
Customer: Yes. I'm looking for a jacket.

A **Shop Assistant:** Here we are. Would you like to try this one on?
Customer: Ah. Now that's a much nicer shade.

B **Shop Assistant:** How is it?
Customer: It fits nicely, but I'm not sure about the colour. It's a bit too light.

C **Shop Assistant:** If you'd just come with me, the changing rooms are over here.
Customer: Thank you.

D **Shop Assistant:** I see what you mean. I'll see if we have anything darker.
Customer: That's kind of you.

E **Shop Assistant:** That's a 40 in German. What colour would you like?
Customer: Blue or grey.

F **Shop Assistant:** The jackets are over here. What size are you?
Customer: British size 12.

G **Shop Assistant:** We're actually having a sale at the moment, so there's 20% off.
Customer: Oh. That's great. I'll take it. Can I pay by card?

H **Shop Assistant:** What about this one? It's your size.
Customer: Yes. That's nice. Where can I try it on?

I **Shop Assistant:** Yes, of course. Please come with me to the cash desk.
Remember to keep your receipt in case you have to return it.

J **Shop Assistant:** Yes. That shade suits you much better.
Customer: It does, but it costs a little more than I wanted to spend.

3 ROLE-PLAY: MAKING A SALE

Work with a partner.

Partner A: You are the sales assistant. **Partner B:** You would like to buy a pair of jeans.

Your discussions about shopping and swapping have made you think about holding a bring-and-swap event. Work together to plan the event.

1 INTERNET RESEARCH

Do internet research to find out about swapping events. Make notes.
Use the search words "organize swap".

2 WHAT, WHEN AND HOW

A Decide what you are going to swap.

B Decide where you are going to hold the event.

- Do you need to make any special arrangements, e.g. who do you need to contact for permission?
- Do you need special equipment, e.g. tables, mirrors?

C Decide when you are going to hold the event.

3 RULES

A Set rules for what can be swapped, e.g. only things in good condition.

B Set rules for how to swap, e.g. bring what you can and take what you need.

4 DONATING LEFT-OVER ITEMS

Think about what to do with items that have not been taken. (Do you need to ask people if they want the items back?)

5 ANNOUNCING THE EVENT

Make a poster.

Include:

- an introduction to the event (say why you've decided to hold it)
- date, time, place (mention any important factors, e.g. separate changing rooms for men and women, where people can try on clothes)
- rules (say what can be swapped; say how things can be swapped)
- where the left-over clothes will go

Moving out into the world

7

A WARM-UP: TALKING ABOUT PLANS FOR THE FUTURE

Discuss the following points in small groups.

- What jobs are shown in the photos?
- Where do you see yourself in five years' time?
- How do you think you will use English in your future life or job?
- Can you imagine getting work experience abroad? Why / Why not?
- How are you going to achieve your professional goals?

Report back to the class on what you have discussed.

B GETTING EXPERIENCE IN INDIA

SITUATION: You are thinking about your plans for the future but are unsure of what job you would like to do. You read a job advertisement on the website of the Federal Voluntary Service (*Bundesfreiwilligendienst*), which offers links to voluntary service places abroad. You write a covering letter applying for a position (task 5, p. 79).

1 PREPARING TO READ

A Work with a partner. Study the words from the text opposite (1–5) and match them to the links (a–f). There is one link more than you need.

1 local women and children
2 teach, sew, design clothes
3 speak good English, be able to drive, be good with computers
4 enjoy working with children, fit into the local culture, be creative
5 small villages throughout India

JOBS | RECRUITERS | ABOUT | COMPANIES | SERVICES | LOGIN

- **a** the place you will work
- **b** the voluntary organization
- **c** what you will do
- **d** who needs your help
- **e** your character and personal qualities
- **f** your skills

B Skim the text to check your answers.

2 READING AND UNDERSTANDING THE TEXT

Mediation: Beantworten Sie die folgenden Fragen zur India Charity Foundation auf Deutsch:

1 Wo leben die armen Familien, denen die Organisation hilft?
2 Was müssen die Helfer Frauen beibringen, damit sie sich selbstständig machen können?
3 Nach welchen Kriterien werden die Helfer zu bestimmten Arbeiten eingesetzt?
4 Wie wird das Leben der armen Leute in Indien allgemein und in einem Wort beschrieben?
5 Wer leitet die freiwilligen „Hilfslehrer“ an?
6 Was außer Kreativität, Teamfähigkeit, Bezug zu Kindern und Sprachkenntnissen müssen die Freiwilligen noch mitbringen?

20

TEACHING UNDER THE INDIAN SUN

JOBS | RECRUITERS | ABOUT | COMPANIES | SERVICES | LOGIN

JOB PROFILE: work with poor families

The India Charity Foundation supports and helps poor families who live in small villages and towns throughout India.

Our organization offers various programmes for local women. We teach them how to apply for loans to start small businesses, we also teach them useful skills like sewing, driving and using a computer, so that they can improve their lives.

We also run a school and three kindergartens. We do more than teach the children, we provide meals and supply free school uniforms, and we also offer various free-time activities and games.

JOB DESCRIPTION

You will work with our teachers and support them in class and with the free-time activities. Depending on your interests and competences, you will work in creative areas, sport, languages or computer literacy.

Volunteers who can sew, design clothes, or who are good with computers or can teach people to drive can work with the women's group. Life is a struggle for many poor people. If they can learn new skills to increase their income, this will help families move out of poverty.
You don't need to worry about your teaching skills. Our pedagogical staff will train and support you.

We are looking for volunteers who ...

- are creative.
- enjoy working in a team.
- enjoy working with children.
- will fit into the local culture.

Good English is a must.
You should also be willing to learn the local language, Hindi.
Starting date: 20 September
Length of service: 9 months

AN IMPORTANT MESSAGE

The communities which you will work with are largely agricultural. The people are religious and conservative. We expect our volunteers to be sensitive towards their religion and to respect the local culture.

Send your CV and covering letter to Mr Kumar at contact@InChFo.com (297 words)

3 WORKING WITH WORDS

Complete this short statement using words from the box.

improve ▪ increase ▪ religious ▪ respect ▪ sensitive ▪ struggle ▪ support

Wherever you volunteer, it is important to be ___[1] towards the local people. In India, for example, most of the people are ___[2] and have conservative moral attitudes. You should ___[3] their customs, even if you don't approve of them. As a volunteer, you are in India to ___[4] the local people not to change their beliefs. If you help the locals to learn new skills, you will ___[5] their lives because they will be able to ___[6] their income. For most poor people in India, life is a ___[7], and our hope is to make their lives easier.

4 LANGUAGE IN USE: THE WILL-FUTURE

→ The future, S. 254

REMEMBER ! the will-future

The future with "will" is formed by using "will" + infinitive. **He will, we will** ~~he wills~~

The future with "will" is often used after the following expressions and verbs:
believe, expect, hope, imagine, suppose, think **I hope that she will come.**
It's clear/obvious that …, There's no doubt that … **There's no doubt that you'll get the job.**

A Find and write down all the sentences in the text which use the will-future.

B Complete the dialogue with *will* or *won't* and the verb in brackets.

Mike: When ___[1] (we – know) the results of our exams?
Anne: I don't know. All I know is that they ___[2] (not come out) this week.
Mike: I imagine that you ___[3] (apply) for the job in India before the results come out, won't you? I think that it ___[4] (be) a great experience.
Anne: I don't think so. I think I ___[5] (wait) until I know my grades.
Mike: I'm sure you ___[6] (get) good grades and my grades ___[7] (be) bad.
Anne: Don't be so negative. You ___[8] (not fail). Everybody in our class ___[9] (pass) with good grades.

C Draw a line in your notebook. Complete the line using the words for prediction in the correct order. Two expressions have been added for you.

~~I don't know~~ ▪ I expect ▪ perhaps ▪ probably ▪ ~~I'm sure~~ ▪ I think

– **I don't know** ———————————————— **I'm sure** +

D **Write sentences about yourself. Use expressions from task 4C to answer the questions. Example answers have been given for the first question.**

Where will you be ...

1 ... on Saturday evening?

EXAMPLES: *I don't know where I'll be.*
I imagine I'll be at home playing video games.
I expect I'll be at the club.
I'm not sure, but I won't be at home.

2 ... at the weekend?

3 ... at 6 a.m. tomorrow?

4 ... at this time next week?

5 ... this summer?

6 ... next year?

5 WRITING

→ Einen Brief oder eine E-Mail schreiben, S. 237

A **Another student is applying for a position at the Indian Charity Foundation. Read her covering letter* below and complete it with the phrases from the box.** *covering letter = *Begleitschreiben*

advert ▪ languages ▪ mother tongue ▪ people from different cultures ▪ school-leaving certificate ▪ skills ▪ spoken and written English ▪ voluntary work ▪ volunteer

Dear Mr Kumar

I saw your ___ 1 on your website. I am interested in working as a ___ 2 at your organization because it will help me develop on a personal basis. I am also keen to work in a country where I can use my practical ___ 3.

I will finish my education this year with a German ___ 4 for year 10. My ___ 5 is very good as I have studied the language for five years. My ___ 6 is German.

In the advert you say you are looking for people who can sew and drive. I know how to sew and I have a driving licence.

I believe the experience I am gaining with my ___ 7 with the Freiburg refugee programme will be useful to your organization. I get on well with ___ 8 and I learn ___ 9 quickly and easily.

I hope that you will consider my application and grant me an interview. Names of referees can be supplied. I look forward to hearing from you soon.

Yours sincerely
Laura Schulze

B **Write your own covering letter to Mr Kumar. Use the structure of Laura's letter but use your own details.**

C GAINING EXPERIENCE

1 PREPARING TO LISTEN

Read the introduction, then choose the best title for the podcast.

a Backpacking in English-speaking countries
b How to get an Australian work permit
c An exciting way to experience life in a foreign country
d How taking a year off can change your life

Hello. Here's Helen from Home Counties Radio. This week, I'm going to take you on the trip of a lifetime. But first, I'm going to ask you a question. Are you interested in working abroad and earning money? I'm going to talk to Colin, who did just that. Colin took a year off and travelled through all of Australia's states with a visa which allowed him to work in different jobs.

21 2 LISTENING: WORKING IN AUSTRALIA

Multiple matching: Make up statements that correspond with Colin's story by matching the beginnings of the sentences with appropriate endings. There are four endings that don't match.

1 Colin took a year off so that he could …
2 The visa he applied for …
3 In Australia, Colin …
4 The work he liked most …

a has an age and time limit.
b relax for a while after school.
c is for a minimum stay of one year.
d qualified him to become a chef.
e work out some plans for his future.
f saw a large part of the country.
g was badly paid but interesting.
h did more travelling than working.

3 LANGUAGE IN USE: THE GOING TO-FUTURE

→ The future, S. 254

REMEMBER ! the going to-future

The future with *going to* is used when you are making plans:

What are you going to do?
I'm going to apply to be a chef.

Or when there is a sign that something is going to happen:

It's dark and cloudy. It looks like it is going to rain.

A Complete the sentences with *going to*.

1 What ___ when he leaves school? (John – do)
What is John going to do when he leaves school?
2 We have a class test tomorrow, so ___ this evening. (we – study)
3 ___ backpacking with her friends in the summer? (Hannah – go)
4 My sister is getting married in June. ___ her bridesmaid. (I – be)
5 There's a new series on TV this evening. ___ it? (you – watch)
6 I usually cycle to school but ___[a] tomorrow so ___[b] the bus. (it – rain; I – take)
7 My brother never does any homework. ___ his exams. (he – fail)
8 We're all tired. ___[a] this evening, ___[b] a pizza. (we – not cook; we – order)

B Work in small groups. Talk about what you are going to do at the weekend.

4 MAKING A FLYER

Make a flyer to show what you can do and learn about on a Working Holiday Visa.

A Think: Listen again to the interview and make notes.
What did Colin do? What did he learn?
Pair: Do internet research and find out what other people did and learned. Make notes. (TIP: search for: working + holiday + experience + Australia)
Share: Bring your notes together and sort them into information for a flyer, e.g. how people travelled, the jobs they did, what they learned, etc.

B Use your notes to write short paragraphs for your flyer. If you can, illustrate it with pictures from the internet.

You have applied for a place as a volunteer at the India Charity Foundation. Mr Kumar is coming to Germany to interview applicants, and you are one of them.

1 GET THAT JOB!

You have found these tips online. A friend who is also going to the interview with you asks you to write the tips for him in German. Just tell him the tips but don't translate word for word.

http://www.interview-tip-online.com

Get that job!

You're going to have an interview. Employers want to be sure you will fit into the company so you have to know how to dress and how to behave.
A face-to-face interview is divided into five parts: Greetings and introductions; the main part of the interview; your questions; further arrangements; the end of the interview. You need to prepare yourself for each of these parts.
Here are some tips.

On the day of the interview: Get to the interview on time. Wear smart, clean clothes that are appropriate for the job.

Greetings and introductions: Body language is important. Walk into the room as confidently as possible, shake hands and make eye contact with the interviewer.

Making small talk: There are some topics that you should always avoid when you make small talk, for example, religion, politics and illnesses. Don't worry. The interviewer will stick to safe topics like the weather or how bad the traffic is. Just relax and respond appropriately.

The main part of the interview: Answer the interviewer's questions honestly and appropriately.

Your questions: Always do background research into the company before the interview. Use the information to write down one or two questions.

Further arrangements and the end of the interview: Ask when you can expect to hear from the company again. Smile and shake hands again if the interviewer wants to. Say goodbye.

2 PLANNING FOR YOUR INTERVIEW

A Plan for the main part of the interview with a partner. Brainstorm ideas about the questions the interviewer will ask you.

Here are two ideas:

- Why do you want to work for us?
- What do you know about India?

B In groups, talk about what you would like to know about the India Charity Foundation. Make notes. Then brainstorm a list of questions you can ask.

Here are two ideas:

- How many volunteers work at the foundation?
- What happens to the things the women sew?

3 ROLE-PLAY: A JOB INTERVIEW

Job interview	Job interview

You are **Mr Kumar**, the representative of the Indian Charity Foundation. You interview an applicant for the job as volunteer. Act out the interview with your partner.	**You** attend an interview with Mr Kumar of the Indian Charity Foundation. The interview is in English. Act out the interview with your partner.
→ Begrüßen Sie den/die Bewerber/in und fragen Sie, weshalb er/sie sich als Freiwillige/r bewirbt.	→ Sie grüßen Herrn Kumar ebenfalls und nennen ihm gute Gründe, warum Sie sich bewerben.
→ Fragen Sie nach schulischen und beruflichen Erfahrungen.	→ Erzählen Sie ihm von Ihren schulischen und beruflichen Erfahrungen (Schulfächer, Praktika usw.) und beruflichen Erfahrungen.
→ Fragen Sie nach Stärken und auch nach eventuellen Schwächen.	→ Antworten Sie.
→ Fragen Sie nach Hobbys.	→ Antworten Sie.
→ Fragen Sie, ob es noch offene Fragen gibt.	→ Stellen Sie Fragen an Mr. Kumar (vgl. Beispielfragen unter 2B).
→ Reagieren Sie auf die Fragen.	→ Danken Sie Mr. Kumar.
→ Beenden Sie das Gespräch.	

You are going to take a working holiday in Australia. You research the current conditions for the Working Holiday Visa and plan where you would like to go (Tip: Search "Working Holiday Visa Australia"). You work out a budget for your trip and make a list of things you are going to take with you.

1 THE AUSTRALIAN WORKING HOLIDAY VISA

Read the information and make notes on the most important points. Do you qualify to apply for the visa?

- aims of the visa
- how long it runs
- number of jobs you can have
- age group
- what you need

Information: The Australian Working Holiday Visa is a temporary visa that encourages cultural exchange and closer ties between Australia and eligible countries. The visa runs for 12 months and you can have as many jobs as you want in that time.

Qualifying: The visa is for people between 18 and 30. You need to have a passport for a country or a region that takes part in Australia's Working Holiday Maker programme.

2 DECIDING WHERE TO GO AND WHAT TO DO

Study the map. Which cities or areas would you like to visit? What do you want to see and do? Make notes.

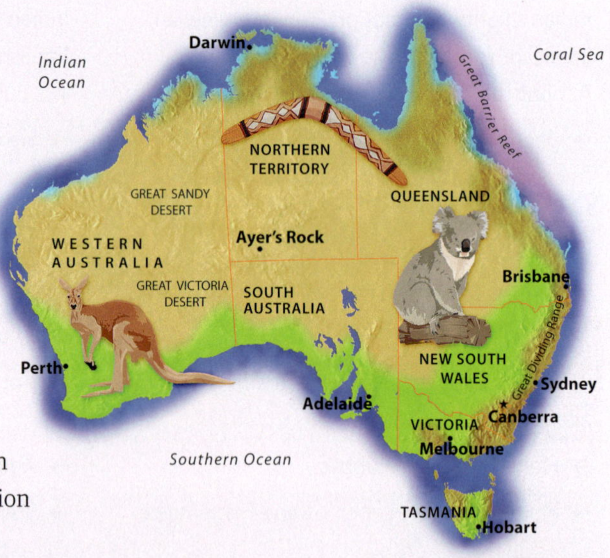

3 INTERNET RESEARCH: HOW MUCH WILL IT COST?

After you have decided where you are going to go, you need to work out how much your trip is going to cost. The most expensive part of your trip to Australia is going to be the flight. When you're there, hostel accommodation is cheap. Sometimes you get accommodation at the place you work.

Search the internet for flights and accommodation. Work out how much money you are going to need for meals, etc.

4 PLANNING YOUR TRIP

A **Make a mind map showing your trip. Use the following branches: where to go, what to do, costs. Add other branches with your own ideas.**

B **Pin your mind map on the wall and do a gallery walk. Whose mind map looks most interesting?**

Screenagers

8

A WARM-UP: ARE YOU A SCREENAGER?

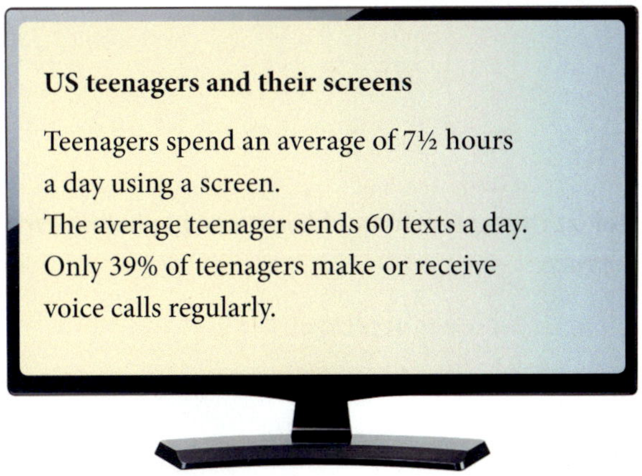

A Look at the figures above. How do you compare with the average US teenager? Think about all the kinds of screens that you use.

B What do you think the people in the pictures are doing with internet technology? What do you use it for? List as many things as you can think of.

C Do a class survey on internet use. Your teacher will give you a questionnaire. Record your findings in a bar chart or pie chart.

B LIVESTREAMING

SITUATION: You are a member of a leisure group (e.g. fitness, beauty, fashion) on social media. Members around the world share tips and advice. The group language is English. The group is considering using livestreaming and has asked members to write their opinions in a comment (task 5, p. 89).

1 PREPARING TO READ

Work with a partner. Look at the screenshots of livestreaming below. Write a description of livestreaming in one sentence.

Livestreaming is when you ... / Internet users can ...

A

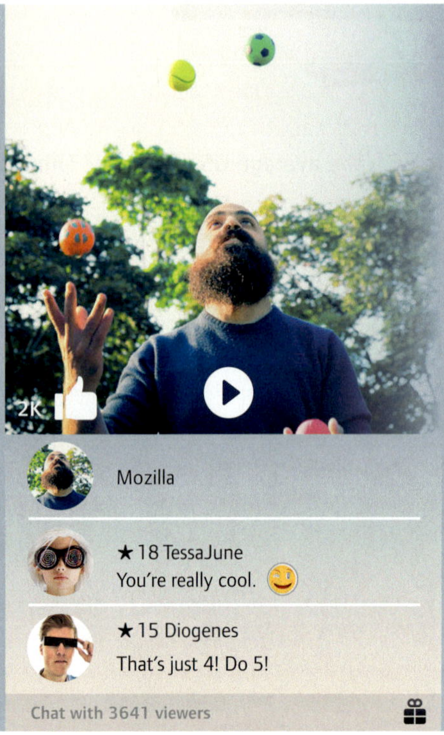

B

2 READING AND UNDERSTANDING THE TEXT

A Skim the text opposite from an e-magazine. Which description fits the text best? Give reasons.

- **a** The article warns readers about the dangers of livestreaming.
- **b** The article gives different opinions about livestreaming.
- **c** The article gives tips about the best ways to use livestreaming.

B Match the screenshots above to the interviewees. One does not have a screenshot. Why not?

22

LIVESTREAMING – FUN, GOOD FOR BUSINESS OR JUST WEIRD?

Millions of people around the world use livestreaming to share their lives online. Why do they do it? We asked three of our regular contributors for their thoughts.

Joey, 19, personal trainer

I've heard about people who make a living from livestreaming. There's one girl, Sammie Firth I think her name is, who earns about $200,000 a year as a livestreaming host. She doesn't do anything special – she just leads a normal life, but chooses to broadcast it to the world. She has 300,000 subscribers. She uses one of those livestreaming apps that allow viewers to send virtual gifts. The livestreaming host can then convert them into real money.

As for me, I don't think my life is that interesting! I livestream sometimes to my close friends on social media because I enjoy sharing my thoughts and feelings with them. About once a week I also livestream with a circus skills group on social media. I show my latest tricks and the other group members ask questions and make comments. Then others take turns at livestreaming too. It's a way to share tips and encourage each other. It's less stressful than making a video and uploading it, because nobody expects you to be perfect when you're livestreaming.

Alex, 21, musician

I started livestreaming from my studio a couple of years ago as a way to help my music career. It's just like a live concert, only more relaxed. People can chat to me online and ask me questions about my music, or request songs that they like. I love having that personal contact with my audience. It's a great way to connect with other people.

I earn about £100 a month from livestreaming. Viewers can send me virtual money if they like what I'm doing. It isn't much, but it helps to pay my bills. The publicity for my music is more important. I like getting feedback about new songs before I release them. I hope to get a song into the charts one day.

Brent, 17, student

I prefer to keep my personal life private. So I would hate sharing my life online. I mean, it's my life – my boring, normal life – not a soap opera. If anyone wants to watch that, they must have problems. It's just weird!

I'm also worried about the lack of security. Experts don't recommend sharing personal information online because of the dangers of stalking and identity theft. With livestreaming, it's easy to share a lot more information than you realize. After all, you can't check the video before you upload it: it's live. (431 words)

C Multiple choice: Choose the most suitable option in each case.

1 Sammie's income comes from …
- **a** companies advertising on her site.
- **b** the host of the website she broadcasts on.
- **c** the people who watch her livestream.
- **d** the developer of the app she uses.

2 Joey uses livestreaming …
- **a** to make friends with people online.
- **b** to earn money.
- **c** to share and improve his circus skills.
- **d** to get publicity for his circus act.

3 Which of the following statements would not be from Joey?
- **a** I show them something and I get shown things in return.
- **b** People don't mind if I make mistakes.
- **c** I choose the people I share my life with.
- **d** I have got a lot to offer to the world.

4 For Alex, a live concert is … than livestreaming.
- **a** more important
- **b** less demanding
- **c** more lucrative
- **d** less intimate

5 Alex likes livestreaming because it …
- **a** is an easy way to earn money.
- **b** is a good way for a musician to get experience.
- **c** helps her to find out what her fans want.
- **d** helps her to sell her songs.

6 Brent doesn't use livestreaming because he …
- **a** tried it and found it boring.
- **b** wants his life to stay private.
- **c** had problems with identity theft.
- **d** thinks there are too many weird people online.

3 LANGUAGE IN USE: -ING FORM OR TO-INFINITIVE?

→ Verb + -ing Form · Verb + to-infinitive, S. 262

A Find verbs in the text which …

1 are followed by *to* + the infinitive. **EXAMPLE:** *choose to broadcast (l. 13)*
2 are followed by *-ing*. **EXAMPLE:** *enjoy sharing (l. 21)*

Write the verbs with the line numbers. Check on page 262 which of the verbs can be followed by both forms.

B Copy and complete these sentences with the correct form of the verb in brackets. If both are correct, write both versions.

1 At what age did you start … (use) social media?
2 Which photo do you recommend … (put) in my profile?
3 Every morning, Mum enjoys … (read) what her friends have written on social media.
4 Matt hopes … (become) famous through livestreaming.
5 Dan hates … (read) long posts on social media.
6 He only wants … (follow) celebrities.
7 Chloe loves … (watch) music videos.
8 Why does anyone like … (watch) videos of cats?

C **Ask your partner about his/her social media use. Find at least one thing that he/she:**

- likes/enjoys doing
- loves doing / to do
- dislikes doing
- recommends doing
- hates doing / to do
- wants to do in the future
- has recently started to do

I love watching funny animal videos.

I want to follow more bands.

4 WORKING WITH WORDS

A **Find these words and expressions relating to social media in the text on page 87.**

1 person who runs a show or social media page (*Joey*)
2 to send information to many people by TV, radio, internet, etc. (*Joey*)
3 person who receives your social media updates (*Joey*)
4 person who watches a TV show, video, etc. (*Joey*)
5 to ask for something (*Alex*)
6 to have a good relationship with somebody (*Alex*)
7 pretending to be somebody else, especially to get money (*Brent*)
8 to put something on the internet (*Brent*)

B **Use words from A to complete the text. You will need to change the form of some words.**

Dan Middleton is the ___ [1] of a video games channel, DanTDM. ___ [2] of his video clips can see Dan play various video games. He ___ [3] a new games video almost every day. He also ___ [4] a vlog about his daily life outside of gaming. DanTDM is one of the most popular channels, perhaps because Dan's sense of fun makes it easy for fans to ___ [5] with him. He has nearly 15 million ___ [6] and earns about $2 million a year.

5 WRITING

Write a comment for your online leisure group about livestreaming. Before you write, make a mind map. Include relevant ideas from the text on page 87, then add your own ideas. Write about 150 words. Include the following points:

- different ways to use livestreaming
- advantages of using livestreaming
- disadvantages of using livestreaming
- reasons why some people are against it

Don't forget to give your own opinion.

Go to File 9 on page 186.

C THE DANGERS OF MOBILE PHONE GAZING

1 PREPARING TO LISTEN

You are going to listen to a radio broadcast about "cell phone gazing" and accidents. Before you listen, look at the photo. What do you think "cell/ mobile phone gazing" is? Think of other situations where it might be a problem. Use these expressions from the recording to talk about the problem of phone gazing.

at the same time ▪ cause an accident ▪ cross the road ▪ look up ▪ phone screen ▪ step out in front of ▪ vehicle

TIP !

Handy = mobile phone (BE)
cell phone (AE)

23 2 LISTENING: STAY SAFE

A Listen and check your answers to task 1. Did you guess correctly?

B Listen again and answer the questions.

When is it dangerous to use a mobile phone? (two situations)
EXAMPLE: It is dangerous when ▬
It is dangerous when you are driving and when you are walking.

1 What do people seem to think about using a phone and walking?
They seem to think that it is ▬
2 What does the interviewer think is a normal thing to do when you get a message or call?
The interviewer thinks that it is normal to ▬
3 What may be the reason for more pedestrian deaths in traffic accidents?
The reason may be that people ▬
4 How have some countries tried to stop this?
In some countries it is illegal to ▬
5 Why hasn't this worked?
It hasn't worked because there are ▬
6 What changes to traffic lights might help?
It might help if there were traffic lights ▬
7 What could mobile phone users download to keep them safe?
They could download an app which warns them about ▬

3 WORKING WITH DIAGRAMS

TRAIN YOUR SKILLS: Schaubilder beschreiben und analysieren vgl. auch S. 242

Diagramme und Kurvenbilder werden verwendet, um Informationen deutlicher zu visualisieren. Machen Sie sich zu folgenden Fragen Notizen:

- Was sagt die Überschrift aus? Welche Beschriftung liegt vor?
- Welche Zahlen und Einheiten werden verwendet, um die Daten darzustellen?
- Wofür steht die x-Achse? Wofür die y-Achse?
- Welche Muster können Sie in den Daten erkennen?
- Welche Schlüsse können Sie aus diesen Mustern ziehen?

Look at the two graphs below. Write a short description of the information in the graphs.

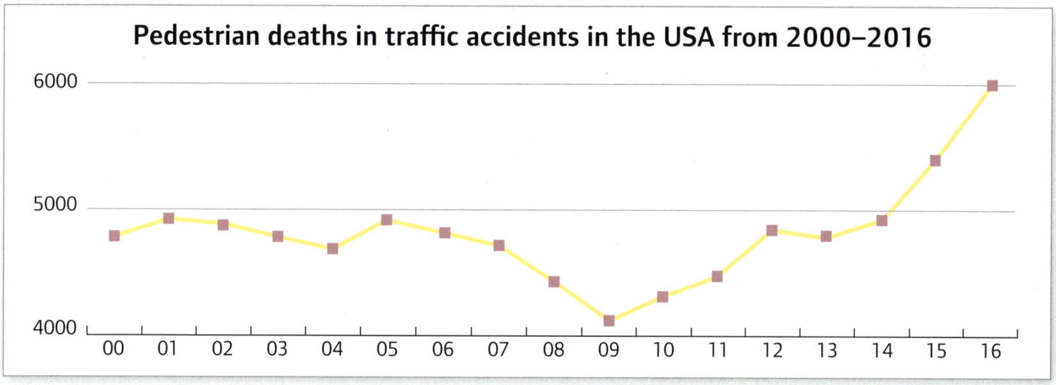

Go to File 10 on page 187.

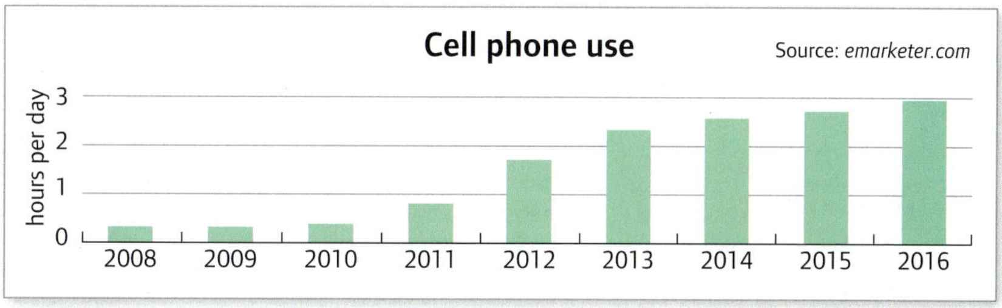

4 PLACEMAT ACTIVITY

Work in a group of four students. Sit around a table with a large sheet of paper in the middle. Write "Safe streets for mobile phone gazers" in the centre as a title. Follow these steps.

1 **Individual note taking.** Think about your local area. What dangers are there for mobile phone gazers who are not looking where they are going? Make notes on your corner of the placemat.
2 **Discussion.** Discuss your ideas with the rest of the group. Write the main dangers around the title. For each danger, brainstorm solutions.
3 **Presentation.** Explain your placemat to the rest of the class.

You are an intern doing work experience in the Frankfurt am Main office of an international insurance company. The main language in the office is English.

1 READING: MOBILE PHONE USE IN THE OFFICE

Read the company policy on mobile phone use below.

Global Insurance AG – Mobile Phone Policy

1 Personal mobile phones can cause problems at work. Employees who use their personal mobile phones might:
   - **a** do less work because they use their phones too much.
   - **b** disturb their colleagues.
   - **c** download company documents on their mobiles.

2 We ask our employees to:
   - **a** use company phones only for work matters.
   - **b** surf the internet, text and talk on a personal mobile phone only for a few minutes per day.
   - **c** turn off or silence their phones in meetings.

3 Employees are not allowed to:
   - **a** use their mobile phone's camera or microphone to record information about the company.
   - **b** make personal calls at their desk or where they might disturb colleagues.
   - **c** log on to the company network using a personal mobile phone.

4 Employees are allowed to use their phones:
   - **a** to receive brief personal calls and messages.
   - **b** during official breaks or the lunch hour.
   - **c** if they speak to their manager first.

Decide whether the employees in the illustrations are following company policy. Which rules apply?

24 2 LISTENING: PHONE RULES IN THE OFFICE

A Listen to the conversations and answer the following questions.

1. What does Bethany need to do?
2. Where does Mr Carter say she can do this?
3. What does Darren want to do for his school project?
4. Why isn't he allowed to do it?
5. What does Mr Carter suggest instead?

B Listen to the recording again. Which of the expressions below do you hear?

1. Excuse me, can I just ask a quick question?
2. Sorry to bother you, but …
3. Just a moment, I'll be right with you.
4. Can it wait until later? I'm very busy.
5. Please may I … ?
6. Is it okay if I …?
7. Yes, that's fine. Go ahead!
8. Yes, alright, but please don't …
9. No, I'm sorry, that's against the rules.

3 ROLE-PLAY: ASKING PERMISSION

Use the format below to role-play a dialogue between an intern and his/her supervisor. Use some of the phrases from task 2B in the dialogue. When you have finished, change roles and play the dialogue again.

Praktikant/in	Vorgesetzte/r
→ Entschuldigen Sie sich für die Störung.	→ Fragen Sie, worum es geht.
→ Fragen Sie etwas, z. B. ob Sie einen privaten Anruf im Büro machen dürfen?	→ Reagieren Sie, z. B. indem Sie ihn/sie darum bitten, bis zur Pause zu warten.
→ Erklären Sie, dass es dringlich ist.	→ Reagieren Sie, z. B. dass es in Ordnung geht, er/sie aber Rücksicht auf die Kolleginnen und Kollegen nehmen soll.
→ Reagieren Sie, z. B. indem Sie sich bedanken.	→ Reagieren Sie.

When fake news goes viral, blame the media, says study

It's true. Don't believe everything you read on the internet.

In fact, according to a study by media researchers, many news organizations fail to do enough to separate fact from fiction, and often help unverified rumours and reports to go viral online. 'Rather than acting as a source of accurate information, online media frequently promote misinformation in an attempt to drive traffic and social engagement,' said the study [...].

While news organizations have always dealt with unverified information, practices at some websites may accelerate the dissemination of fake news, said the report, Lies, Damn Lies and Viral Content.

'Many news sites apply little or no basic verification to the claims they pass on. Instead, they rely on linking-out to other media reports, which themselves often only cite other media reports as well,' the study concluded.

Fake stories are often sexier or more interesting than the real ones, and as such get wider dissemination, said Craig Silverman, who led the study. 'The extent to which a fake news article can get traction was surprising to me.' [...]

For example, a story about a Kurdish woman 'Rehana the ISIS slayer', or the 'Angel of Kobane' purported to have killed 100 Islamic fighters, turned out to have no basis in fact even though reports about her spread for weeks. [...]

Silverman said that even if much of the fake news is spread by 'new media' or tabloid journals, the traditional or 'quality' journalism outlets often sit by, allowing rumours to gain traction. [...]

And many news organizations fail to follow up when a false report is debunked, the report said: 'The explosive claim that ISIS fighters had been apprehended at the US-Mexico border was refuted within 24 hours and yet only 20 percent of news organizations that wrote an initial story came back to it.'

The findings show 'a very disturbing trend', said Bill Adair, a Duke University journalism professor who in 2007 founded [a] fact-checking website [...]. 'It's particularly disturbing when journalists pass along things without knowing whether they are true or not.'

Because of the fast-moving nature of [...] social media, Adair said that 'many people including journalists feel that if it's tweeted, it's out there and it's fair game. But news organizations have always had an obligation to check out what they pass on.'

Sometimes the sheer number of repetitions of false information makes people believe something is true, the researchers said. [...]

The internet's 'crowdsourcing' ability can often bring the truth out, but cannot entirely correct the problem, said Silverman. 'Over time the truth emerges, but the corrections don't tend to be as viral or get as widely distributed. And they don't always reach the same people,' he said.

'I am a believer in the value of the crowd, but the truth is often far less interesting and shareable than the lie.'

Source: *The Daily Mail*, 15 February 2015; 475 words

- ■ **to go viral:** *sich rasant verbreiten*
- 03 **unverified:** *unbestätigt*
- 05 **traffic:** *(Netz-)verkehr*
- 07 **dissemination:** *Verbreitung*
- 10 **to cite:** *zitieren*
- 14 **to get/gain traction:** *an Boden gewinnen*
- 19 **sit by:** do nothing; take no action
- 20 **debunked:** *entlarvt*
- 28 **fair game:** *Freiwild*

Read the text opposite carefully, then do the tasks below.

A Answer the following questions with information from the text.

1 What should news organizations provide, according to the study?
2 Why does fake news often spread more widely than the truth?
3 How do traditional news organizations often react when fake news spreads?
4 What happens when many sources repeat false information?

B Choose the most suitable option in each case.

1 According to the report, online news organizations spread false information …
- a when they make mistakes.
- b to get more visitors to their sites.
- c because they do not have enough journalists.
- d only in a few cases.

2 According to the report, online news organizations …
- a always check that links in their stories are true and relevant.
- b put too many links in their stories.
- c copy other stories instead of writing original material.
- d use links to sources which haven't checked the facts.

3 When someone proves that a news story is untrue, news organizations …
- a often do not correct the mistake.
- b usually correct it within 24 hours.
- c take at least 24 hours to correct it.
- d always check the facts.

4 According to Bill Adair, many journalists …
- a do not trust social media.
- b prefer not to use social media.
- c do not check information they find on social media.
- d use social media to spread fake news.

C Are the following statements true, false or not in the text?

1 Unchecked information is a new problem for news organizations.
2 Many online news organizations pass on information which may be false.
3 People often spread false information online deliberately.
4 Rehana was a Kurdish woman who fought against ISIS in Kobane.
5 Only 20 per cent of people believed the story about ISIS on the US-Mexican border.
6 Many journalists rely on information from social media.

D Finish the sentences using the information from the text. Use your own words.

1 News organizations have a responsibility to publish stories …
2 Bill Adair is particularly concerned about …
3 Although the true story usually comes out in the end, …

A Correct these statements using the information in brackets.

EXAMPLE: Matt uses social media every day. (occasionally)
Matt doesn't use social media every day. He uses it occasionally.

1 Sarah posts on social media several times a day. (a few times a week)
2 I'm writing a text message. (email)
3 Tyler and Joseph run a blog. (livestreaming website)
4 They're having a lot of success. (not attract many users)
5 Alyssa makes a living from livestreaming. (personal training)
6 She is livestreaming at the moment. (run an online training session)
7 Daniel is reading a text message. (looking at an email)
8 It's from his girlfriend. (sister)
9 We're having fun. (do an English grammar exercise)

B Use the prompts to ask questions which go with the answers.

1 What – you – look at ? I'm looking at a video on social media.
2 Who – Jan – work for ? Jan works for a website design company.
3 What – you – do ? I'm waiting for this app to download.
4 What – it – do ? It helps you to avoid accidents while mobile gazing.
5 I – disturb – your work ? Yes, you are disturbing my work.
6 We – be allowed – use our phones here ? No, we aren't allowed to use our phones here.

C You meet a young Chinese tourist on a bus. What do you say – a or b?

1 a Do you enjoy your stay in Germany?
b Are you enjoying your stay in Germany?
2 a Do you speak German?
b Are you speaking German?
3 a What do you do back home in China?
b What are you doing back home in China?
4 a What part of China are you coming from?
b What part of China do you come from?
5 a You are speaking very good English.
b You speak very good English.
6 a Where do you go today?
b Where are you going today?
7 a What sort of music do you listen to now?
b What sort of music are you listening to now?
8 a I'm going to a concert this evening. Would you like to come?
b I go to a concert this evening. Would you like to come?
9 a Lots of my friends are going.
b Lots of my friends go.
10 a I get off now. Have a great day!
b I'm getting off now. Have a great day!

D Which sentence could you use the adverbs in the box with?

1 I'm listening to a new band.
2 I listen to music on the bus.

always ▪ at the moment ▪ every day ▪ never ▪ right now ▪ sometimes ▪ today ▪ usually

A Great British holiday

9

A WARM-UP: QUIZ

How much do you know about the British Isles? Do the quiz to find out.

1 Which map shows England (1), the British Isles (2), the United Kingdom (3)? (3 points)

a

b

c

2 Which of the following uses the Euro as its currency? (1 point)
- **a** the UK
- **b** Scotland
- **c** the Republic of Ireland

3 How much money is this? (2 points)

4 Match the names to the photos of famous attractions. Two are not shown. (6 points)

the Cliffs of Dover ▪ Edinburgh Castle ▪ Ffestiniog Railway ▪ the Highland Games ▪ the London Eye ▪ Stonehenge ▪ Titanic Belfast ▪ the Tower of London

a

b

c

d

e

f

5 Which of the four countries that make up the United Kingdom are the attractions located in? (6 points)
Which of the attractions above would you like to visit?

9 A Great British holiday

C A TRIP TO EDINBURGH

1 PREPARING TO LISTEN

Ruby and Lisa from Chicago are on holiday in Edinburgh. You are going to listen to Ruby's voicemail messages to her parents. Before you listen, do the tasks below.

A Match the reviews to the photos. There are two reviews for two of the photos.

Things to do in Edinburgh – top tips

1 Edinburgh Castle
★★★★★ (15,106 reviews)

2 Escape Room Games
★★★★★ (893 reviews)

3 Camera Obscura & World of Illusions
★★★★★ (1159 reviews)

4 Hop-On Hop-Off Tours
★★★★★ (821 reviews)

5 Edinburgh Old Town
★★★★★ (3059 reviews)

6 Murder and Mystery Tour
★★★★★ (346 reviews)

Reviews

A The location is great, right next to the castle. Lots of amazing illusions. You won't believe your eyes!
B Great game. The puzzles were quite hard. We got out with only two minutes to spare!
C A lovely part of town to walk around and enjoy the architecture and the atmosphere.
D Very entertaining! Not too scary, lots of fun for the kids.
E It's on top of a very steep hill. The Scottish monarchs used to live there.
F A beautiful old building surrounded by wonderful views over the city. So much history!
G A good way to see the city quickly. The driver was friendly and informative.
H Lots of shops, cafés and restaurants, and such colourful buildings!

B Which of the attractions would you visit if you went to Edinburgh? Why?

2 LISTENING: RUBY'S VOICEMAIL MESSAGES

26

A **Listen to the voicemail messages. Put the sights and activities in 1A into the order in which Ruby mentions them. One sight is not mentioned.**

B **Copy the table into your exercise book. Then listen again and complete the table.**

attraction	when visited	details
Hop-On Hop-Off Tour	*Tuesday afternoon*	*Saw the whole city, good fun*
...	...	...

3 VIEWING

04

→ Videos, S.197

Watch the video "Tourist London" and complete the tasks on page 197.

4 MANAGING SITUATIONS

In einem Couchsurfing-Netzwerk bieten Sie eine kostenlose Unterkunft an. Clara aus Edinburgh hat sich als erster Gast gemeldet. Sie hat gerade bei Ihnen geklingelt.

Clara: Hi there! I'm Clara. I hope you were expecting me?

You: *1 Antworten Sie und begrüßen Sie Clara. Stellen Sie sich vor. Bitten Sie sie, hereinzukommen.*

Clara: Thanks … Hey! Nice place you have here!

You: *2 Bedanken Sie sich. Sagen Sie, dass Sie hoffen, Clara wird einen angenehmen Aufenthalt bei Ihnen haben.*

Clara: Thanks, I'm sure I will … Is there somewhere I can put my stuff?

You: *3 Sagen Sie, dass sie ihre Sachen im Gästezimmer (spare bedroom) aufbewahren soll. Dort wird sie auch schlafen.*

Clara: Wow! So I've got my own bedroom. I didn't expect that. That's great!

You: *4 Sagen Sie, dass sie jederzeit die Küche benutzen kann, um Getränke und Snacks zu holen. Fragen Sie, ob sie jetzt Hunger und Durst hat.*

Clara: A cold drink would be nice. I'm not hungry at the moment, thanks.

You: *5 Sie holen ihr ein Glas Wasser. Fragen Sie, ob sie für den Nachmittag bereits Pläne hat.*

Clara: No, I haven't. To be honest, I don't really know this area at all. I've never been here before. I was hoping that you could suggest something.

You: *6 Wenn sie mag, werden Sie ihr die Stadt zeigen. Es gibt einige Sehenswürdigkeiten, die sie unbedingt sehen sollte.*

Clara: That would be lovely! Thanks so much!

You: *7 Schlagen Sie vor, in einer Stunde loszuziehen. Sie kann sich bis dahin ausruhen und ihre Sachen auspacken. Fragen Sie Clara, wie lange sie bleiben wird.*

Clara: Oh, I'd like to stay three nights, if that's alright.

You: *8 Bestätigen Sie, dass das in Ordnung ist. Fragen Sie sie, was sie gerne isst.*

Clara: Anything! I don't mind. But maybe I could cook dinner for you and your family this evening, if you'd like? I do a great curry …

You: *9 Sagen Sie, dass das wunderbar wäre. Sie freuen sich darauf.*

You have just visited a trade fair in London with your company. Now you are waiting at London's Gatwick Airport for your flight home.

1 HAND LUGGAGE RULES

You see this notice as you go into the airport.

HAND LUGGAGE RESTRICTIONS

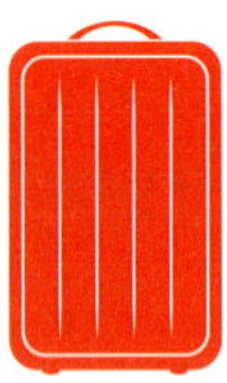

Your bag should be no bigger than 56cm × 45cm × 25cm. Some airlines have maximum weight restrictions. Please check with your airline for details.

Liquids must be no more than 100ml each, making a total of no more than 1 litre. Present all liquids in a clear, resealable bag. Liquids include cream, gel and toothpaste. Medicines are exempt from this rule if you have a prescription.

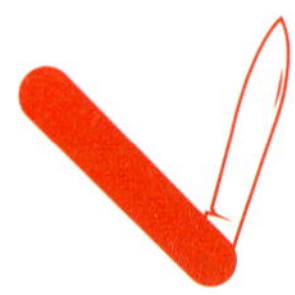

Pack scissors, razor blades and tools in your checked-in luggage. They are not permitted in your hand luggage.

Inflammable and explosive items are not permitted on board the aircraft. They include bleach, camping gas cylinders and some types of battery.

Pack sports equipment in your checked-in luggage. Most items are not permitted in your hand luggage.

Thank you for your assistance!

1 What do you need to know about the bag you carry on to the plane?
2 Which items in your hand luggage should you put in your checked-in luggage instead?
3 Are there any other items which you need to do something special with?

2 UNDERSTANDING YOUR BOARDING PASS

Find the information below on your boarding pass.

1 What flight are you flying on?
2 Where should you go to board your flight?
3 When should you get there?
4 When does the aeroplane leave?

27

3 MEDIATION: SECURITY CHECK

You are going through airport security with a Hungarian colleague who speaks good German but little English. Listen to the security officers and explain in German to your colleague what they want to know and want him to do.

4 ROLE-PLAY: A CONVERSATION ON BOARD

Finally you are on board the aeroplane. Another passenger speaks to you. When you have finished, change roles and act out the dialogue again.

Passenger A	Passenger B
→ Sie müssen kurz stören, um Ihren Fenstersitz (*window seat*) zu erreichen. Entschuldigen Sie sich für die Störung. (*Sorry, can I just … ?*)	→ Reagieren Sie höflich. (*Yes, of course.*)
→ Fragen Sie, ob er/sie in Großbritannien Urlaub gemacht hat.	→ Erklären Sie, dass Sie für die Firma eine Messe (*trade fair*) besucht haben.
→ Äußern Sie höflich Interesse. Fragen Sie, was das für eine Messe war.	→ Nennen Sie eine Messe, z. B. *The IT Support Show, The London Travel Fair*.
→ Erklären Sie, dass Sie eine Geschäftsreise (*business trip*) nach Stuttgart machen.	→ Äußern Sie höflich Interesse. Fragen Sie, ob er/sie öfter nach Deutschland reist.
→ Nein, Sie besuchen Deutschland zum ersten Mal. Leider sprechen Sie kein Deutsch.	→ Sagen Sie, dass die meisten Deutschen Englisch können.
… 90 minutes later, the flight is over. You are all leaving the aeroplane.	→ Wünschen Sie ihm/ihr einen guten Aufenthalt in Deutschland. (*Enjoy your stay …*)
→ Bedanken Sie sich. Wünschen Sie ihm/ihr eine gute Heimreise (*a safe journey home*).	→ Bedanken Sie sich und verabschieden Sie sich.

1 LISTEN AND TAKE NOTES

28

A radio advertisement informs listeners what Buy Nothing Day is all about. Listen to the recording and answer the questions in note form.

1 When is Buy Nothing Day?
2 What will people achieve by taking part in Buy Nothing Day? (three things)
3 In what ways can shopping be harmful? (two ways)
4 How can people help to organize Buy Nothing Day? (three ways)
5 What will taking part teach participants?
6 How will one day without shopping change anything? (two ways)

2 LISTEN AND COMPLETE THE TABLE

29

Amy and Ryan are planning their first holiday together. Ryan wants to go camping in the New Forest, in Hampshire, England. Amy doesn't really want to go.

Copy the table below into your exercise book. Listen to their conversation and take notes.

Ryan: reasons for camping
–
–
–
–
–

Amy: reasons against camping
–
–
–
–
–

Decision
–

3 MULTIPLE CHOICE

30

The German Institute for Economic Research, based in Berlin, has published a report "Leisure Behaviour of Young People". Listen to the radio programme about the findings. Choose the most suitable option in each case.

1 Compared with ten years ago, young people today …
 a use electronic communication and games media more.
 b spend about the same amount of time using electronic media.
 c have reduced their use of games consoles and computers.

2 Extra-curricular educational activities …
 a are less popular than they were ten years ago.
 b have been mostly replaced by informal leisure activities.
 c are more popular than they were ten years ago.

3 Every day, 90 per cent of teenagers …
 a listen to music.
 b spend time with their best friend.
 c watch TV and videos.

4 Compared with ten years ago, …
 a more teenagers visit youth clubs and do voluntary work.
 b fewer teenagers visit youth clubs, but more do voluntary work.
 c fewer teenagers visit youth clubs or do voluntary work.

4 MULTIPLE MATCHING

31

You are going to listen to a broadcast from an outdoor music festival. A reporter is interviewing volunteers. Copy the table below into your exercise book. Then listen to the report and match the statements to the speakers. There are two more statements than needed.

Sarah	
Brendan	
Jane	
Lachlan	

Statements

1 People don't always behave sensibly at festivals.
2 The festival wouldn't go smoothly without us.
3 The work is interesting and varied.
4 It's hard to work when everyone else is having fun.
5 I contact musicians and invite them to play at the festival.
6 Some of the musicians are difficult to deal with.

A Correct these statements using the information in brackets.

EXAMPLE: Anna has been to England three times. (twice)
Anna hasn't been to England three times. She has been there twice.

1 Jude and Lucas went to Scotland on holiday last year. (Wales)
2 They stayed in a hotel. (hostel)
3 It was very comfortable. (dirty and noisy)
4 They had a private room. (two beds in a dormitory)
5 It was expensive. (very cheap)
6 Lucas wanted to spend a lot of money. (spend as little as possible)
7 They have been on holiday together since then. (stay at home)
8 Jude has invited Lucas to Spain this summer. (book a holiday by herself)

B Complete the dialogue with the most suitable forms of the verbs in brackets (simple past or present perfect). Watch out for signal adverbs.

Ashley: Hi, Dylan! I ___ [1] (not see) you for a while.
Dylan: No. I ___ [2] (be) on holiday for two weeks.
Ashley: Wow! I ___ [3] (think) you were looking brown and healthy. Where ___ [4] (you – go)?
Dylan: I ___ [5] (go) to the Inner Hebrides. ___ [6] (you ever – be) there?
Ashley: Yes, my parents ___ [7] (take) me years ago. I ___ [8] (hate) it. It ___ [9] (rain) the whole time.
Dylan: Oh, really? I ___ [10] (love) it. The weather ___ [11] (be) amazing the whole fourteen days.
Ashley: I ___ [12] (have) terrible luck with my holidays this year. I ___ [13] (fly) to Venice at Easter with my boyfriend. As soon as we ___ [14] (arrive), we ___ [15] (have) a massive argument and he ___ [16] (leave) me and ___ [17] (return) home.
Dylan: Oh, no! What ___ [18] (you – do)?
Ashley: I ___ [19] (try) to enjoy the rest of the holiday. But it ___ [20] (not be) the same by myself.
Dylan: Oh, well … You ___ [21] (go) away in the summer, too, didn't you?
Ashley: Yes, my boyfriend and I ___ [22] (ride) around Ireland on our motorbikes.
Dylan: Awesome! So you ___ [23] (get) back together after your argument.
Ashley: No. This ___ [24] (be) a different boyfriend, Liam.
Dylan: Oh. How ___ [25] (that holiday – go)?
Ashley: Really well. Until Liam ___ [26] (meet) another girl in a pub.
Dylan: You really ___ [27] (not have) much luck with holidays this year. Or boyfriends …

C Complete the sentences by translating the expressions in *italics* using *for*, *since* or *ago*.

1 I've been in London *seit zwei Tagen*.
2 We went to Scotland on holiday *vor einem Jahr*.
3 Kelly and Dan have taken part in two hospitality exchanges *seit März*.
4 Renting private homes online became popular *vor ein paar Jahren*.
5 Millions of people have used online holiday rental sites *seitdem*.
6 People have had problems *seit langer Zeit*.

Celebrations and traditions

10

A WARM-UP: CELEBRATIONS AND TRADITIONS

A What are the events in the photos? There are two names you do not need.

Carnival ▪ Christmas market ▪ Eid al-Fitr ▪ Halloween ▪ music festival ▪ New Year's Eve ▪ October beer festival ▪ St Patrick's Day ▪ UEFA Champions League Final ▪ wedding

B Work with a partner. Describe what happens at one of the events in A but do not name the event. Your partner tries to guess which event.

People get together to ...

It's a celebration of ...

They dress up and ...

There are fireworks and ...

C Discuss in a group.

- Why are events like these important to people? Think of as many reasons as you can.
- What other celebrations and traditions can you think of?
- What is your favourite celebration, and why?

B A GREAT AMERICAN TRADITION

SITUATION: You have entered a short story competition in an online youth magazine for English learners. To win the prize of a weekend in New York, you have to write a story about a celebration or tradition (task 5, p. 113). You find an entry in a blog by Sophie from Münster about an American football game that she attended with her exchange family.

1 PREPARING TO READ

A Look at the photos from the game. Brainstorm ideas about the atmosphere.

B Discuss these questions with a partner. Then report back to the class.

- Say what you know about American football.
- Do you think the game should be more popular in Germany? Why (not)?
- Do you think that sports traditions in general are important? Why (not)?

TIP ! Fußball

football (BE) = *Fußball*
football (AE) = *Football*
soccer (AE) = *Fußball*

2 READING AND UNDERSTANDING THE TEXT

32

A GREAT DAY OUT

'It's a great American tradition,' said Mr Duncan mysteriously. 'You'll love it!' The holidays in Colorado with my exchange partner Jess Duncan had been wonderful, but now they were nearly over. It was the start of September, and almost time to fly home and get ready for the start of the new school year. Almost, but not quite. As it turned out, the Duncans had planned one last treat for me.

I was very excited. Then, on the morning of the 'treat', I found out that it was an American football game. 'A really special game: the NFL Kickoff Game,' said Mr Duncan.

Mr Duncan had bought tickets for the first game of the NFL season. The Denver Broncos were playing the Carolina Panthers.

The problem was, I hate sport. All those times when Mr Duncan patiently explained the rules of football to me, and I sat there in front of the TV and looked interested – I just wanted to be polite. Unfortunately, Mr Duncan didn't know that. He thought I was a real sports fan, like him.

So I tried to look pleased, even though I was disappointed. It was too late anyway – he had already bought the tickets. I couldn't disappoint the Duncans, who had been so kind to me. Jess, Mr Duncan and I drove down the Interstate to Denver's Mile High Stadium. It's a huge building – it can hold 76,000 fans, and on the first day of the season, it was full. Our seats were up the back.

It was terrifying. I don't like crowds and I'm scared of heights. As we climbed up the steep steps to our seats high above the playing field, everyone around us started to stamp their feet. It made a deafening sound. Mr Duncan explained that this was the Mile High Thunder. One of the game's 'great traditions', he said.

It was freezing cold, and it started to rain a little bit. Mr Duncan rushed down to the

fast food stands to get us something to eat and drink. He came back with three huge buckets of cola and three-foot-long hotdogs. 'Traditional football food,' laughed Jess.

The opening ceremony was amazing. There were fireworks, and brass band music, the American national anthem, and cheerleaders dancing.

Then the game started. I had seen a couple of football games on TV before, but being there in person was different. It was brutal. When two opposing players ran into each other at full speed, we heard the 'crack!' all the way up the back of the stadium.

The game seemed to be three hours of inactivity and discussion with short bursts of violent action. Someone knocked someone down. Stop. Someone came onto the field and kicked the ball. Stop. And so it went on.

And yet ... about halfway through the second quarter, I realized I was enjoying myself. We were next to a bunch of Broncos fans who were cheering wildly for their team. Soon we too cheered loudly each time the Broncos scored. It was actually a great evening out. 'Our' team won, by one point. It was thrilling.

Jess later said to me, 'You know, Dad doesn't really like football. He just wanted to take you to a game, as you're such a fan.' (545 words)

C THANKSGIVING IN THE USA

1 PREPARING TO LISTEN

Leon from Würzburg is on a school exchange in Boston, Massachusetts. It's mid-November and his hosts, the Jaeger family, are about to celebrate Thanksgiving. You are going to listen to Sally Jaeger talking to Leon about Thanksgiving. Before you listen, do the tasks below.

A Leon is writing a blog in English about his semester in the USA. Summarize the information about Thanksgiving in German: *Was? Wo? Wann? Wie? Warum?*

Thanksgiving

When I went into the kitchen this morning, Sally (my exchange partner Ryan's mom) was getting everything ready for Thanksgiving Day – that's tomorrow. While she was working, she told me all about it.

Thanksgiving Day is a public holiday which is celebrated in the USA on the fourth Thursday in November. It began as a day to give thanks for the harvest. In Canada it is celebrated on the second Monday in October. It usually involves a traditional family meal including turkey, corn, potatoes or sweet potatoes and squash or pumpkin.

Here's a photo of last year's Thanksgiving dinner – it looks delicious, doesn't it? I'm looking forward to tomorrow!

B Write down six key words that you expect to hear in the conversation.

TIP ! holidays

the holidays – *die Ferien*
on holiday (BE) – *im Urlaub*
on vacation (AE) – *im Urlaub*
public holiday – *gesetzlicher Feiertag*

2 LISTENING: THANKSGIVING

33

A Listen to the conversation. Copy and complete the table.

what Thanksgiving celebrates	*food, family and friends*	family reunion	
what happens		sport	
food that is eaten		Black Friday	

B Listen again and make notes about the history of Thanksgiving.

1 Why was life hard for the first English settlers in the 1600s?
2 How did Native Americans help?
3 What do many modern Native Americans think about Thanksgiving?
4 Why are particular foods used for the meal?

3 LANGUAGE IN USE: PAST PROGRESSIVE

→ Past progressive, S. 250

A Find examples of the past progressive in Leon's blog on page 114.

B Complete this extract from Leon's blog using the past progressive of the verbs in brackets.

Thanksgiving Day

When I got up on the morning of Thanksgiving Day, so much *was happening* 1 (happen)! Nathan, Sarah and their children had just arrived. Sally and her daughter-in-law Sarah … 2 (stand) by the car hugging each other. They … 3 (cry) because they were so happy. They hadn't seen each other for a whole year. The kids … 4 (run) around the garden and into the house and out again with their dirty shoes, but nobody minded. Rocky, the Jaegers' dog, … 5 (bark) and … 6 (get) very excited. Delicious smells … 7 (come) from the kitchen, where the turkey … 8 (cook) in the oven. I … 9 (feel) a bit lonely in the middle of this family scene, but then Nathan introduced himself and soon we … 10 (talk) and … 11 (laugh) together and I … 12 (start) to feel like one of the family.

4 VIEWING

05

→ Videos, S. 198

Watch the video "Australians celebrate ancient indigenous culture" and complete the tasks on page 198.

5 PLACEMAT: PLANNING A CELEBRATION

Exchange students are at your school. You have decided to organize a traditional celebration. It could be a German tradition or one from another country. Sit around a table in a group of four with a large sheet of paper in the centre. Write down the event in the centre of the placemat.

1 Each person has one task:
- food and drink
- music
- activities (e.g. games)
- publicity (invitations, etc.)

Make notes about your task on your corner of the placemat.

2 Discuss your ideas and make a plan.
3 Report back to the class with your plan.

10 THE WORLD OF WORK

Working as a tour guide

You have a holiday job as a tour guide in Berlin. On your first day, you're working as an assistant to an experienced tour guide, Nikki.

34

1 TODAY WE'RE GOING TO …

Listen to Nikki and complete the schedule.

09:00	9:45 arrive at Museum Island
10:00	
11:00	
12:00	
13:00	
14:00	
15:00	
16:00	
17:00	
18:00	18:10 bus from Gendarmenmarkt 18:45 drop off at hotel entrance

35

2 AT THE MUSEUM

A **Look at the plan on page 117 and listen to Nikki giving directions. You are at position A on the plan. Complete the key with words from the box. There are two items that you do not need.**

ATM ▪ café ▪ men's toilet ▪ lift ▪ ticket desk ▪ stairs

key
1
2
3
4 women's toilet
5 information desk
6 cloakroom
7 gift shop
8

TIP ! American English versus British English

toilet (BE) =
restroom/bathroom (AE) =] *Toilette*
lift (BE) =
elevator (AE) =] *Aufzug*

B **Help these tourists by giving them directions.**

1 "Can you tell me where the restroom is, please?"
2 "Where can we buy some postcards?"
3 "How do we get to the special exhibition?"
4 "I don't want to carry this big coat around the museum. Can I leave it somewhere?"

Giving directions in a building

- Go straight ahead / through the door.
- Go up the stairs.
- Take the first / second / third door on the left / right.
- Turn left / right / around.
- It's to your left / right.
- It's right in front of you.
- It's on the ground floor / first floor.
- Go out the door onto the street.
- It's about 100 metres away.

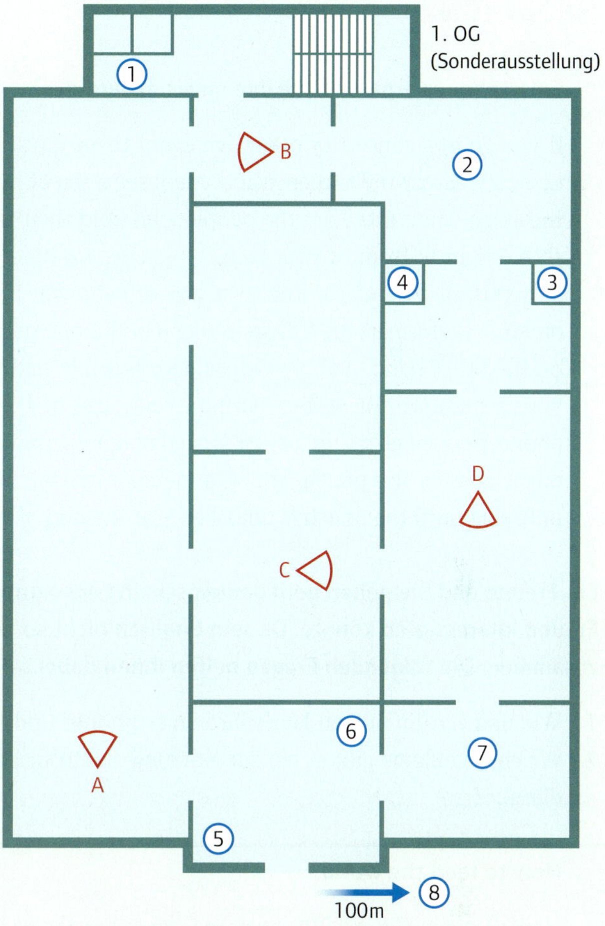

3 YOUR TURN

Now it's your turn to take charge of the tour! Work in a group of 3–4 people. Choose a tour guide. The rest of the group are tourists. Change roles so that you all have a turn as tour guide.

Scene 1: In the hotel lobby

Tour guide: Introduce yourself and explain the schedule for the day. Use attractions in your local area.

Tourists: Ask questions about the schedule.

Scene 2: At the museum

Choose a position on the plan: B, C or D.

Tourists: Ask the tour guide to help you with your problems.

Tour guide: Give the tourists help and directions.

1 MEDIATION

1

Smartphones – part of the live music experience?

If you go to a concert or other live event these days, your smartphone is part of the experience. Look out across the audience and you'll see a sea of brightly lit smartphone screens all the way to the stage. Then there are the people who hold their tablets high above their heads to get a good shot – right in front of your face.

Is this all part of the fun at a gig, or seriously irritating? Opinions of live music lovers are divided. Performers aren't sure either. On the one hand, all publicity is good publicity, right? But on the other hand, wobbly videos with horribly bad sound on YouTube aren't going to improve your reputation for perfect harmony. Because of these concerns, venues are starting to create phone-free zones by the use of locked magnetic pouches. You can bring your phone to the gig – but it goes in the pouch, which a member of staff will lock. The magnetism makes the device unusable until the pouch is unlocked – at the end of the gig. (176 words)

Ein Freund und Sie gehen gern gemeinsam in Live-Konzerte. Sie lesen diesen Artikel, der Ihren Freund interessieren könnte. Da sein Englisch nicht so gut ist, fassen Sie die Hauptpunkte zusammen. Die folgenden Fragen helfen Ihnen dabei.

1 Wie und warum nutzen Leute ihre Smartphones und Tablets bei Live-Konzerten?
2 Welche Probleme gibt es bei der Nutzung elektronischer Aufnahmegeräte und wie kann man diese lösen?

2

How to feed the world?

Harry Jacobs: "I run a 300-hectare farm in Iowa with two full-time employees. The farm has been in my family for four generations. We put good healthy food on thousands of dinner tables every week. Our farm uses modern methods and a lot of expensive machinery. We have only six crops because we sell all our produce to supermarket chains and they need large quantities. Profits are low because consumers expect low prices. We use chemicals to feed our soil and control pests – it's the only way. You can only feed the world's growing population with efficient modern agriculture."

Helen Kowalski: "I farm 15 hectares next door to Harry Jacobs. I bought the land from him 10 years ago. It was just one big, bare field. Now I have hundreds of different crops and lots of farm animals. I use a system called Permaculture – it's all about working with nature, not against it. I use organic methods, no chemicals and only simple machinery. I sell my produce at local markets. It's more expensive than supermarket food, but my customers want clean, safe food. Permaculture is the only sustainable way to feed everyone without destroying the planet." (196 words)

Die Familie einer Freundin betreibt einen Bauernhof. Sie glauben, dass sie dieser Artikel interessieren wird. Fassen Sie die Hauptpunkte des Artikels zusammen. Die folgenden Fragen helfen Ihnen dabei.

1 Wie betreibt Harry Jacobs seinen Bauernhof, und warum?
2 Wie betreibt Helen Kowalski ihren Bauernhof, und warum?

2 GAPPED SUMMARY

Fill in the gaps with words from the corresponding sections of the text "Online shopping – know your rights". Use only one word for each gap. Give the number of the line in which you found the word/expression.

Consumers buying goods, whether online or in a store, enjoy more legal ▬[1] in the EU than you may know of. If you have reason to complain about goods you've ordered, it is your right to ask for a reduction, replacement or ▬[2]. In addition, online customers may simply ▬[3] the goods they are not happy with within two weeks. The ▬[4] you send the goods back to does not need to know your reason. There is a general minimum ▬[5] on goods that you buy in the EU, which even applies to ▬[6] items. However, this is only the case for goods bought from a proper store, not from a ▬[7] ▬[8]. Before giving your payment information to an online store you need to check the security situation. There are well-known organizations and labels that check the ▬[9] of online transactions. They tell you, if your trader ▬[10] to the criteria set by the EU. Similar seals operate ▬[11] and show you if a store outside the EU is the property of a real ▬[12] and if you can entrust it with your ▬[13].

Online shopping – know your rights

Have you ever had a problem with an online purchase? As an EU consumer, you have a lot of protection under the law, so it's worth knowing your rights.

Have you received faulty goods, or goods that do not look or work as advertised? Then it's the retailer's responsibility to repair or replace them, offer you a price reduction or refund the whole purchase price. They cannot simply direct you to the manufacturer instead.

If you bought goods online and you're not happy with them for any reason, you have additional protection: you have the right to return your order within 14 days and get a refund. You do not have to give a reason. You can simply change your mind. However, the retailer is entitled to insist that you pay the postage.

Under EU law you always have the right to a two-year guarantee at no extra cost. It doesn't matter whether you bought your goods online, in a shop or by mail order: the same rules apply. If goods that you bought anywhere in the EU are faulty or do not look or work as advertised, the retailer must repair or replace them free of charge or refund some or all of your money. But beware: if you bought goods from an online store based outside the EU, the laws of that country usually apply.

Do you like to shop second-hand? Good news! Second-hand goods that you buy from a retailer also have a minimum two-year guarantee. On the other hand, goods that you buy from a private individual are not covered, so bear that in mind next time you're using an auction site like eBay: it makes a difference whether you're buying from a store or an individual.

You also need to be sure that an online store protects the security of your credit card or bank details. If you are unsure about whether it is safe to use, look for quality seals such as Euro-Label and Trusted Shops. Where you see them, you can be confident that the store conforms to EU standards. There are also worldwide quality seals such as Thawte, based in South Africa, which show that the store belongs to a genuine company and will protect your data. (376 words)

10 REVISION

Comparison of adjectives, adverbs of manner (S. 266), relative clauses (S. 267)

A Use the comparatives and superlatives of the adjectives and adverbs in brackets to complete the sentences.

1 The weather at Christmas was ⬬ than usual. (bad)
2 I don't like flights usually, but this one went a lot ⬬ than I expected. (well)
3 Soccer is a lot ⬬ than American football in my opinion. (exciting)
4 Mexican food is the ⬬ food that I've ever eaten. (hot)
5 The Broncos fans were a lot ⬬ than the Panthers fans. (noisy)
6 The weather in Colorado was the ⬬ weather I've experienced in September. (cold)
7 Don't queue for tickets at the gate: you can buy tickets ⬬ online. (easily)

B The Denver Broncos are deciding which new player to sign. Compare the players like this, using the adjectives in the box.

EXAMPLE: *Joel is older than Mario but Reuben is the oldest player.*

fast ▪ heavy ▪ ~~old~~ ▪ successful ▪ tall ▪ young

	Statistic	Joel Fleischman	Reuben O'Malley	Mario Maretti
1	Age	24	25	22
2	Speed (secs/100m)	12.14	11.26	11.05
3	Height (cm)	185	180	182
4	Weight (kg)	106	93	90
5	Points (average/season)	158	147	161

C Complete each sentence with *who* or *which*.

1 You won't believe some of the objects ⬬ people have put in their checked-in luggage.
2 The passenger ⬬ packed this bag didn't read the luggage restrictions.
3 The gas cylinders ⬬ were in the bag are explosive items.
4 People ⬬ don't follow the rules cause a lot of problems for airport staff.
5 Many items ⬬ are not permitted in hand luggage can go in checked-in luggage.

D Zoe is writing captions for her holiday photos. Write sentences with relative clauses.

EXAMPLE: These are some photos. I took them on my trip to Canada.
These are some photos which I took on my trip to Canada.

1 Here you can see one of the hosts. We stayed with her in Vancouver.
2 This is the guide. He took us kayaking.
3 We visited an island. It had bears on it.
4 Tourists cause a lot of trouble. They feed the bears.
5 Bears become confident around people. They receive food from tourists.
6 There are lots of signs. They say "Do not feed the bears!"

One world

11

A WARM-UP: IT'S ALL CONNECTED

A **Match the expressions from the box to the pictures.**

climate ▪ consumer goods ▪ energy ▪ environment ▪ natural resources ▪ pollution ▪ transportation

B **Work with a partner. Make connections between pictures that are next to each other. Continue until you have used all the pictures at least once. You may find the words in the box below useful.**

Pollution is bad for our environment.

Our environment provides natural resources.

Natural resources ...

affect ▪ be good/bad for ▪ cause ▪ come from ▪ deliver ▪ provide ▪ require ▪ use up

C **What effect do our daily purchases have on the environment? Think of daily items you use. What environmental dangers can they cause?**

B JOURNEY OF A PAPER CUP

SITUATION: Your class is on a school exchange in Britain. As part of World Environment Day the school wants to come up with a solution for dealing with the large amount of disposable cups the students use each day (task 5, p. 125). You find some information about paper cups.

1 PREPARING TO READ

Find these stages in the illustration and read out the explanations from the key.

1 one stage where natural materials are taken from the environment
2 four stages where materials or goods are transported
3 six stages where industrial processes happen
4 one stage where the consumer is involved

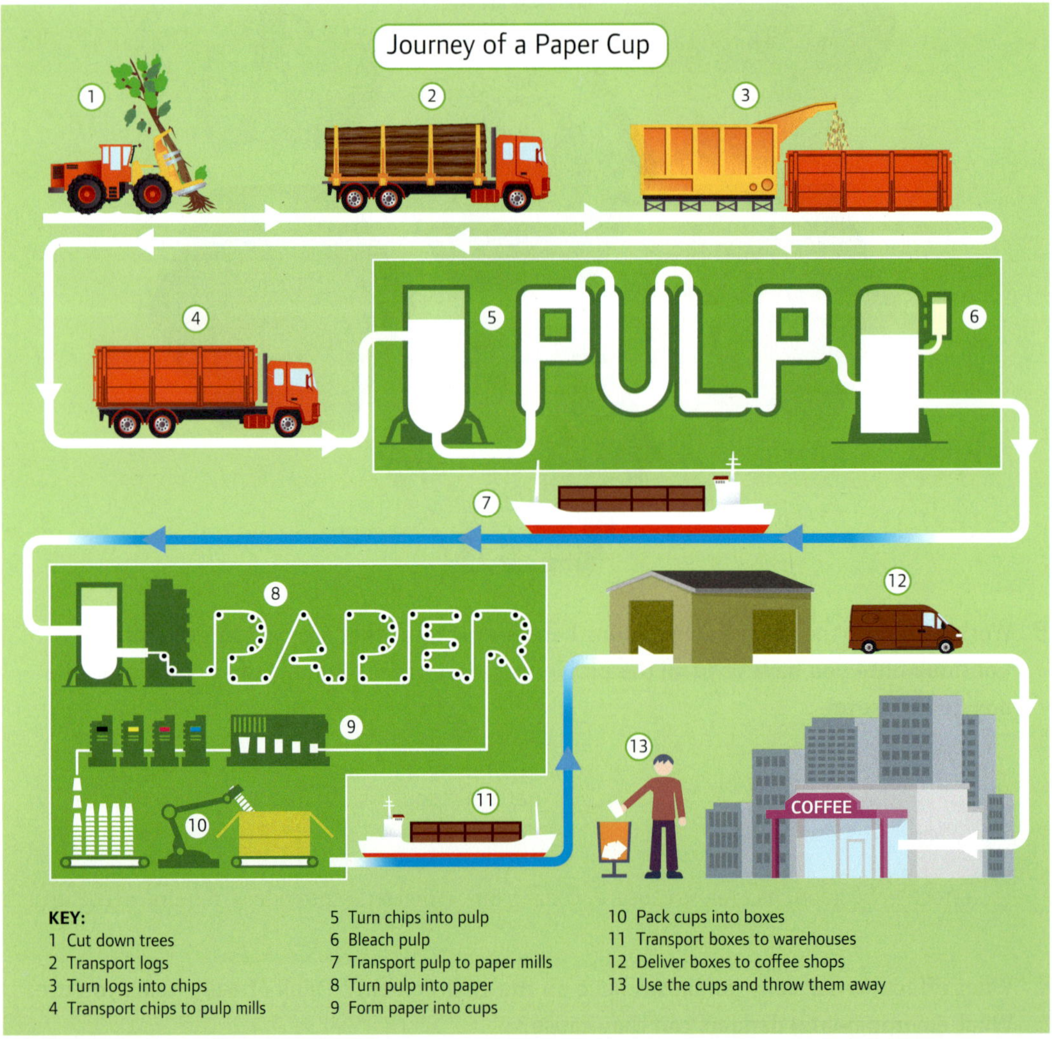

KEY:
1 Cut down trees
2 Transport logs
3 Turn logs into chips
4 Transport chips to pulp mills
5 Turn chips into pulp
6 Bleach pulp
7 Transport pulp to paper mills
8 Turn pulp into paper
9 Form paper into cups
10 Pack cups into boxes
11 Transport boxes to warehouses
12 Deliver boxes to coffee shops
13 Use the cups and throw them away

2 READING AND UNDERSTANDING THE TEXT

36

The Long Journey of a Paper Cup

1 It's just a disposable paper cup – nothing special, nothing complicated. If you go to a fast food restaurant and order a drink with your meal, or stop off at a café or kiosk to have a hot or a cold drink while you're in town, you will probably get your drink in one just like it. Have you ever thought about how the cup is made?

2 It all begins with a natural material: wood. In a **forest** in Australia, trees are cut down. They are put on a truck and transported to a **chipping plant** at the port of Geelong near Melbourne.

3 At the chipping plant, the trees are turned into wood chips. Huge steel disks cut the wood into tiny pieces. Tonnes of wood chips wait at the port until a ship comes to collect them. Ships carry these wood chips all over the world, but the chips for our paper cup are going to Malaysia.

4 At a **pulp plant** near Kuala Lumpur, Malaysia, the wood chips are unloaded from the ship. Here the chips are processed to make pulp. Pulp is a mixture of wood and water – like a thin, grey soup. The pulp is treated with chemicals to make it white. Paper mills all over Asia use this pulp, but the pulp for our cup is going to China.

5 A ship takes the pulp to Ningbo, China, one of the largest ports in the world. The **paper cup factory** is right next to the dock. It's a high-tech factory and a lot of things happen there. First, the pulp is sprayed onto wide metal screens and squeezed between hot rollers to make long rolls of paper. Then a machine forms the paper into cups. The cups are coated with a type of plastic called polyethylene, which means they cannot be recycled as paper. Finally, the cups are put in a cardboard box – 1000 cups per box. The boxes are put into a 12-metre shipping container. About 240 boxes fit into one container – that's 240,000 cups.

6 The cups from Ningbo belong to a company in Portsmouth, in the south of England. The company sells its cups all over the world, but our cup is going to Hamburg, Germany. The container is loaded onto a ship and begins its journey. Twenty-eight days and 22,639 kilometres later, the ship arrives in Hamburg.

7 On arrival, the container is loaded onto a truck and taken to a large **warehouse** near the port. From there, boxes of cups are delivered to **coffee shops** all over Germany – but our cup doesn't have to travel that far. A van takes it with 999 others to a kiosk at Hamburg's main railway station.

8 Someone comes along, feeling thirsty, and buys a coffee. The coffee is served in a paper cup – our cup. After five minutes the customer has drunk his nice, hot coffee. Then our cup is thrown in the rubbish bin. From there it is taken to a landfill, along with the 3 million other paper cups that are thrown away every day in Germany. (509 words)

A **Multiple matching: Match the headings (a–j) to the paragraphs (1–8) in the text. There are two more headings than you need.**

- **a** Production and packaging
- **b** Recycling useful materials
- **c** Just an ordinary item
- **d** Polluting the land and the sea
- **e** A long trip
- **f** Raw material from Down Under
- **g** A mass of white pulp
- **h** Used and thrown away
- **i** Turning trees into chips
- **j** Getting the goods to the shops

B **Finish the sentences using information from the text.**

1. Cups like the one in the photo ___
2. To get from the factory to the warehouse ___
3. Making the cup requires a lot of time, energy and resources, but ___

3 LANGUAGE IN USE: THE PASSIVE

→ The passive, S. 255

A **Find examples of the passive in the text on page 123. Write down the passive form in the text, the infinitives of the verbs and the line numbers.**

passive form	infinitive	line in text
is made	*make*	*8*
___	___	___

B **Copy and complete the flow chart to show the life cycle of a paper coffee cup in eight steps. Use the expressions from the box in the passive.**

coat cups with plastic ▪ ~~cut down trees~~ ▪ deliver boxes of cups to coffee shops ▪ form paper into cups ▪ turn pulp into paper ▪ process wood chips into pulp ▪ send cups to landfills ▪ serve drinks in cups ▪ throw away cups ▪ treat pulp with chemicals ▪ turn trees into wood chips

1. *Trees are cut down* and ___ →
2. Wood chips are ___ →
3. Pulp ___ and ___ →
4. Paper ___ ↓
5. Cups ___ ←
6. Boxes of cups ___ ←
7. Drinks ___ ←
8. Cups ___ and ___

Go to File 15 on page 189.

C **Work with a partner. Ask and answer questions. What is done where?**

What is done in the forest in Australia?

Trees are cut down. What is done in Geelong?

The trees ...

4 WORKING WITH WORDS

A **Complete the sentences with words from the text on page 123.**

1 What ▬ are the cups made from – paper or plastic? (ll. 7–11)
2 The ▬ tree was too big to fit on the truck. (ll. 11–15)
3 Plastic items slowly break into ▬ pieces in the ocean. (ll. 13–17)
4 The water isn't safe to drink because of the ▬ in it. (ll. 16–19)
5 Several ships were loading and unloading goods at the ▬. (ll. 20–24)
6 The company makes TVs and computers in its ▬ in China. (ll. 21–26)
7 If everything you need is ▬ to your home, you don't need to go shopping. (ll. 31–34)
8 We produce a lot of ▬ when we buy disposable things. (ll. 35–39)

B **Explain the following expressions from the text on page 123. Write complete sentences.**

1 natural (l. 9)
2 mixture (l. 17)

5 GROUP DISCUSSION

As part of your partner school's World Environment Day project, you have been asked to discuss ways to reduce the number of disposable cups, which are used in the school's hot drink vending machines and nearby cafés. The cups are not recyclable because they are made of composite materials: paper with a plastic liner.

Presentation phase

Choose one of the suggestions listed in File 2 on page 193 and in one minute say why you favour it.

Interaction phase

Discuss the suggestions and the merits of each one and how it could be implemented. Try to reach an agreement on which one is most suitable. Be prepared to compromise if your suggestion is not accepted.

C REPAIR CAFÉS

1 MEDIATION

In Bradford finden Sie eine Anzeige in der Lokalzeitung für ein neues Repair-Café. Sie glauben, dass sich Ihre Freunde in Deutschland für das Konzept des Repair-Cafés interessieren könnten. Fassen Sie die wichtigsten Punkte zusammen, indem Sie die folgenden beiden Fragen beantworten. Übersetzen Sie nicht Wort für Wort.

- Wie funktioniert ein Repair-Café?
- Wie kann man sich einbringen?

REPAIR CAFÉ
Bradford

In the old days, when things broke, they were repaired. Today, when things break, they are thrown away. Often there isn't much wrong with them, but people don't know how to fix them. Soon, those important repair skills will be lost.
Here at Repair Café Bradford we want to make sure that people have the tools, skills and facilities to repair things.
A Repair Café is a free meeting space where people can get together, have a drink – and repair things. Visitors to a Repair Café find tools and materials to help them make repairs to clothes, furniture, computers, bicycles, electrical goods and other items. The Café is run by expert volunteers with repair skills in all kinds of fields.

Sounds like a good idea? Then get involved!

- DONATE – give us your old tools, materials and spare parts
- VOLUNTEER – teach people your repair skills; welcome visitors; make drinks; tidy up, etc.
- TAKE PART – bring along your broken things and learn to repair or upcycle them

LATEST NEWS

Upcycling Workshops – Come along and learn how to turn rubbish into attractive and useful things!

Tuesday evenings	Broken pallets to furniture
Thursday evenings	Beautiful jewellery from tin cans
Sunday mornings	Old jeans to backpacks, glass bottles to drinking glasses

REPAIR CAFÉ Bradford,
15a Foundry Road, Bradford

Open
Tues–Fri 4–8 p.m.
Sat & Sun 10 a.m.–5 p.m.

2 LISTENING: A REPAIR CAFÉ

37

Multiple matching: Make statements that correspond with the radio interview by matching the beginnings of the sentences with appropriate endings. There are three endings that don't match.

1 Megan doesn't like to
2 With Bob's help she
3 As she was successful, Megan
4 Bob was able to help her because he once
5 Bob loves to be able to

a repaired an old piece of furniture.
b help people to help themselves.
c was active as a volunteer.
d didn't have anything else to do.
e get rid of slightly damaged things.
f make the Repair Café a popular place.
g made furniture on a professional basis.
h developed her own business idea.

3 DISCUSSION

Work with a partner. You want to get involved in a Repair Café. What will you do? Think about:

- skills you have, e.g. sewing, IT, bicycle maintenance, making drinks, welcoming visitors
- tools (e.g. pair of scissors, screwdriver) or materials you have and don't want (e.g. plastic bottles, old bicycle)
- things that you would like to fix
- creative ideas for an upcycling workshop

Make notes, then report back to the class with your best ideas.

4 LANGUAGE IN USE: THE PASSIVE

→ The passive, S. 255

A Find examples of the passive in the text opposite. Identify the tense that is used.

B Use the expressions in the grid to write sentences in the passive. Use the correct tense for each sentence.

EXAMPLE: *In the past, broken things were repaired. Today, ...*

in the past	today	in the future
repair broken things	throw broken things away	repair or upcycle broken things
teach repair skills to the next generation	forget repair skills	learn repair skills at Repair Cafés

5 PRESENTATION

→ Präsentation, S. 244

TRAIN YOUR SKILLS: Recherchieren

Im Internet gibt es fast alles und manchmal ein bisschen zu viel.

- Suchen Sie nach konkreten Stichwörtern. Wenn es um Ideen für Upcycling in Großbritannien geht, dann suchen Sie Wörter/Wortkombinationen wie „upcycling ideas" + Britain.
- Grenzen Sie Ihre Suche zeitlich ein. Ältere Seiten enthalten womöglich bereits überholte Informationen.
- Wenn Sie nach Informationen suchen, überprüfen Sie, ob die Webseite seriös ist. Am besten lesen Sie den Bereich „About" auf der Webseite, um mehr über den Ersteller der Webseite zu erfahren.

You are going to give a presentation at your exchange school in Bradford on cool ideas for upcycling. Read the information in the box before you start.

You have started work in a large hotel in Munich. The Housekeeping Manager tells you that the hotel has a lot of international guests who are not familiar with German environmental practices and rules.

1 EDITING: CORRECTING SIGNS

The manager has asked you to check these signs before they are printed. Find the two mistakes in each sign and rewrite them correctly so that they can be printed and put up in the hotel.

Guests, please note! a

If you will remove the keycard from the holder by the door when you leave your room, the lights and the air conditioning will be turned off to save electricity. While you are in your room, please leaving the key in its holder to activate the power.

Thank you!
Hotel Manager

Toiletries b

To reduce rubbish, our soap, shampoo, conditioner and moisturizer are in one dispenser each. We provide not toiletries in individual disposable containers. If you will like the brand, our hotel shop will be happy to sell you toiletries to take with you on your journey.

Mini-bar c

Please turn on the fridge if you will keep things cold. Please turning it off again at the end of your stay in order to save electricity.

Why isn't my towel clean? d

Towels are not wash every day. This helps us saving water and energy. If you require clean towels, please leave your wet towels on the floor and they will be replaced with clean ones.

Thank you!
Housekeeping

Dear Guest e

Welcome at the breakfast buffet. Please understand that jam and butter are being served in large bowls and not individual disposable containers. This is to avoid unnecessary packaging and rubbish.

Enjoy your meal!
Head Chef

38 2 LISTENING: GUEST COMPLAINTS AND QUESTIONS

Guests don't always read the signs in the hotel. Listen and match the complaints and questions to the signs in task 1.

3 MANAGING SITUATIONS: DEALING WITH HOTEL GUESTS

An American guest phones reception asking for help. Complete the conversation, then practise it with a partner.

Es klingelt.

You: *1 Melden Sie sich mit „Reception" und Ihrem Namen.*

Guest: Hello, it's Brenda O'Brien here, room 311.

You: *2 Begrüßen Sie Frau O'Brien. Fragen Sie, wie Sie helfen können.*

Guest: We've just moved into our room and the lights and the air conditioning aren't working. Can you send someone to fix them, please?

You: *3 Fragen Sie Frau O'Brien, ob sie den Schlüssel in den Behälter neben der Tür gesteckt hat.*

Guest: Next to the door? No, why?

You: *4 Erklären Sie, dass der Schlüssel den Strom anschaltet, wenn er im Behälter steckt. Das ist eine Stromsparmaßnahme.*

Guest: Oh, I see! Thanks for your help … Yes, the lights are working now.

You: *5 Fragen Sie, ob Sie ihr sonst noch behilflich sein können.*

Guest: No, thanks. Bye now!

You: *6 Verabschieden Sie sich und legen auf.*

Frau O'Brien ruft nach kurzer Zeit nochmals an.

Guest: Hello, it's Brenda O'Brien again, room 311.

You: *7 Begrüßen Sie Frau O'Brien. Fragen Sie, wie Sie helfen können.*

Guest: I've just had a look in the bathroom and there aren't any bars of soap or little bottles of shampoo. Just a funny dispenser thing on the wall in the shower and another one next to the basin. Can you ask Housekeeping to send up some proper soap and shampoo, please?

You: *8 Erklären Sie, dass die Seifenspender wieder eine umweltfreundliche Maßnahme des Hotels sind.*

Guest: Really? Well, that does seem strange. It's not what we're used to back home.

You: *9 Es tut Ihnen leid, aber das ist in deutschen Hotels normal. So wird an Seife und an Einwegflaschen gespart. Wenn Frau O'Brien möchte, kann sie extra Seife und Shampoo im Hotelladen kaufen.*

Guest: No, no. That won't be necessary, thanks. We'll manage.

You: *10 Fragen Sie, ob Sie noch etwas für sie tun können.*

Guest: Yes, perhaps you can explain something else for me. There's a notice here in the bathroom about towels not being washed every day. Does that mean that nobody will come in here to clean the bathroom until we leave? We're staying for three nights, that's too long to wait.

You: *11 Beruhigen Sie Frau O'Brien. Erklären Sie, dass alle Hotelzimmer und Badezimmer jeden Tag gereinigt werden, aber die Handtücher werden nur gewechselt, wenn der Gast es will. Im Hotel werden täglich Tausende von Handtüchern gewaschen, das verbraucht viel Strom und Wasser.*

Guest: I see. That sounds very sensible. Thank you so much for your help this afternoon.

You: *12 Gern geschehen (*You're welcome*). Wünschen Sie Frau O'Brien einen angenehmen Aufenthalt im Hotel.*

Guest: Thanks again. Goodbye!

1 WRITING A LETTER

Your Australian friend Anna wants to know what your views are on globalization.

Write a letter of 150 words to Anna about how globalization influences your life. Think about the things you can buy in the shops and supermarkets and how much they cost. You should also write about the influence of globalization on our climate. Make some suggestions how new technologies may help.

Do not forget the structure of a letter:

1 salutation
2 introduction
3 main part
4 close

2 WRITING AN ESSAY

Pick ONE of the following topics. Write about 70 words.

Social
- **a** Would you like to work with children? Explain why / why not.
- **b** What activities can be offered to entertain old people and keep them fit?

Business
- **a** Do you agree with the saying "The Customer is King"? Give reasons.
- **b** Is it possible for a business to be successful without harming the environment? Give examples.

Technical
- **a** What technical advances will change our lives in the next 20 years? Explain how.
- **b** What skills does a good technician need, other than just technical skills? Explain why.

3 WRITING A COMMENT

Write about 150 words.

MONEY CAN BUY HAPPINESS, STUDY FINDS
Time Magazine, April 8, 2016

Comment on the headline. Write about 150 words.

Here are some ideas for your text.

- What things do people need to be happy?
- Is it possible to buy those things?
- What are the consequences of not having money?
- Explain why you agree, partly agree or totally disagree with the statement.

4 COMPLETING A STORY

Pick ONE of the following options. Complete the story. Write 150–180 words.

Option A

I had always wanted to see America. Last summer, my dream finally came true. My best friend and I travelled across the USA by Greyhound bus.

Unfortunately, our trip didn't get off to a smooth start. When we landed at New York JFK, we went to the baggage carousel and waited for our backpacks. As the minutes passed, we realized that …

Ideas for your story:

- Describe what happened.
- Describe how you felt about it.
- Explain what happened next.
- What were the consequences for the rest of your trip.

Option B

It was a cold January afternoon and starting to rain as Jack hurried home from football practice. He was just about to cross the street when he saw a smartly dressed, elderly man nearby acting strangely. The man seemed confused and frightened.

'Is there anything wrong?' asked Jack. 'Yes,' said the man. 'Something terrible has happened.'

Ideas for your story:

- What had happened to the man? Why was he acting strangely?
- How did Jack respond to the situation? How did he feel?
- What happened next?
- Did the situation have a happy, unhappy or a mysterious ending?

5 WRITING A STORY ABOUT A PHOTO

Write a story about one of the photos. Write about 150 words.

A Complete these sentences with a suitable modal auxiliary to replace the German verb.

1. They *dürfen nicht* cut down the trees unless they plant new ones.
2. Environmental experts say that we *müssen* change our way of life.
3. Pollution *darf nicht* be allowed to destroy our environment.
4. We *sollten* talk about solutions, not just environmental problems all the time.
5. People *können nicht* repair things unless they have the tools, skills and facilities.
6. Consumers *müssen nicht* stop buying new items completely.
7. However, companies *könnten* design goods to last longer and be easier to repair.
8. People *sollten* be prepared to pay more for well-made goods.
9. We consumers *sollten nicht* rely on governments to solve the problem.

B You are writing tips for reducing our environmental impact. Suggest actions that people *could, might, should, should not* or *must not* take.

EXAMPLE: drop rubbish in the street – *We must not drop rubbish in the street.*

1. use public transport more often
2. stop buying disposable goods
3. waste valuable natural resources
4. use disposable plastic bags
5. have shorter showers to save water
6. leave the lights on when leaving a room
7. replace old appliances with energy-efficient new ones
8. throw away recyclable materials
9. throw plastic in the paper recycling bin
10. turn up the heating instead of putting on warmer clothes

C Rewrite the sentences using the phrases on the right. Change the tense and use substitutes for the modal auxiliaries if necessary.

EXAMPLE: We must find ways to live sustainably. *In the future,* ...
In the future, we will have to find ways to live sustainably.

1. Industry needn't worry about climate change. *In the 19th century,* ...
2. Business can exploit natural resources. *Until now,* ...
3. Our school can install energy-efficient lights. *In the last two years,* ...
4. Companies must find ways to reduce waste. *In the future,* ...
5. Scientists can work out the amount of plastic in the ocean more accurately. *Last year,* ...
6. We can't eat fish from the ocean because of plastic pollution. *In 50 years' time,* ...
7. Supermarkets must give waste food to poor people. *Soon* ...
8. We can predict the consequences of doing nothing. *Fifty years ago,* ...
9. We can't prevent the situation getting worse. *Since then* ...
10. People cannot understand our attitude to the environment. *Future generations* ...

English for work and leisure

12

A WARM-UP: ENGLISH AROUND THE WORLD

How much do you know about the English language around the world. Do the quiz to find out.

1 What percentage of web pages are in English? (1 point)
a more than 90% **b** about 50% **c** about 10% **d** less than 5%

2 How many countries have English as an official language? (1 point)
a 5 **b** 17 **c** 56 **d** 127

3 Which country has the largest number of English native speakers? (1 point)
a India **b** England **c** China **d** the USA

4 What do Americans celebrate on 4th July? (1 point)
a Thanksgiving **b** Independence Day **c** St Patrick's Day **d** Labor Day

BONUS POINT: Which of the above is not a national holiday in the USA?

5 When does winter begin in Australia? (1 point)
a December **b** March **c** June **d** September

6 Where does the President of the USA live and work? (1 point)
a the Empire State Building **c** the Capitol Building
b the Pentagon **d** the White House

7 Name the countries. (4 points)
a English is just one of 23 official languages in this country. Over a billion people live here.
b This country hosts the most websites in the world.
c This country has 11 official languages, including English and Afrikaans.
d This is the second largest country in the world. It has two official languages: English and French.

8 Match the names of the countries to their shapes. (4 points)

Australia ▪ Canada ▪ India ▪ Republic of Ireland ▪ Jamaica ▪ New Zealand ▪ the USA ▪ Wales

B WHY LEARN ENGLISH?

SITUATION: Your school is holding an open day (*Tag der offenen Tür*) and you have decided to produce a poster explaining why it is important to learn English (task 5, p. 137).

1 PREPARING TO READ

A Brainstorm in a group. How many situations can you think of where English is useful? Note down your ideas. (They will be useful for your poster.)

A tourist stops you in the street and asks you for directions.

You want to understand the lyrics of your favourite song.

B Look at the photos. How do you think these people use English in their daily lives?

1

2

3

4

C Match the photos to the interviewees in the article on the opposite page.

REMEMBER !

interviewer – interviewee
employer – employee

2 READING AND UNDERSTANDING THE TEXT

A Multiple matching: Match the statements below with the people in the article. There are two statements that do not match.

1 This person needs English for travel.
2 This person uses English for his/her education.
3 This person uses English in his/her work and for socializing.
4 This person speaks English at home.
5 This person needs English for communicating with colleagues and customers.
6 This person uses English for his/her hobby.

ENGLISH – the World Language

This month we profile non-native English speakers from different parts of the world. What do they see as the benefits of speaking English?

Janek is an online gamer from Estonia. His great passion is role-playing games (RPGs). The popular stereotype of a gamer is a social misfit who lives alone in a fantasy world. Janek disagrees: 'Non-gamers say that we're unsociable, but that's totally wrong. We spend a lot of our time online discussing strategy, telling stories and swapping tips. It's a social hobby.'
The RPG community is global and gamers need to collaborate with the people in their team (called a 'clan' or 'guild'), so they need a common language. Janek's clan communicates in English. 'We use a lot of game slang and code words,' explains Janek, 'but we still need good English to work well together.'

Adeela lives in Bangalore, an important centre for IT. Like most Indians she's multi-lingual: Adeela speaks Tulu at home, Kannada around town and English at work. She can also read Hindi. When she was at school, Adeela showed an aptitude for computer languages and told her teacher that she wanted to work in IT. 'Keep up your English, then!' replied Mrs Sharma.
Adeela followed her teacher's good advice and now she works as a software engineer. In her company there are colleagues with several different native languages. This isn't unusual, as there are 23 official languages and over 120 major languages in India.
'English is our company language because it's the only language all of us speak well, even though most of us aren't native speakers,' explains Adeela. 'As a world language, English is also essential for dealing with our customers around the world.'

Luuk is from the Netherlands. For the last three years he's been travelling the world. He's lived in Morocco, Brazil, Mexico, Vietnam and at the moment he's in Malaysia. He doesn't have a lot of savings, so he's working his way around the world. He does casual jobs on building sites and farms, but he says that his best job was as a waiter at a beach bar in Rio de Janeiro.
Luuk would like to speak the local language of every place he visits. Unfortunately, that isn't realistic if you travel a lot. That's why English is so useful for nomads. 'You can always find someone who speaks English,' he explains.

Like almost all Swedes, **Elsa** learned English at school. 'You hear so much English in Sweden, it hardly feels like a foreign language,' she says. After Elsa finished school, she wanted to learn something more exotic, so she spent a summer learning basic Portuguese, in preparation for a job as an au pair in Lisbon.
'And guess what? As soon as I started here, the parents said that they wanted me to speak English all the time in the house!' laughs Elsa. They explained that speaking fluent English would be good for their children's education and career prospects. Elsa uses Portuguese a lot outside the home, for things like shopping, so she feels confident speaking Portuguese, but when she meets up with other au pairs – from Denmark, France, Austria and Poland – English is the language they have in common. 'So we speak English, of course!'

(539 words)

B Multiple choice: Choose the most suitable option in each case.

1 Janek needs English to …
- **a** understand the rules of the games he plays.
- **b** work effectively as part of a team.
- **c** write role-playing games.
- **d** chat with his friends.

2 Adeela speaks …
- **a** different languages with family, in shops and at work.
- **b** four foreign languages.
- **c** Hindi better than English.
- **d** the same languages as most other Indians.

3 Luuk thinks that …
- **a** it isn't important to learn a lot of languages.
- **b** English is the only language you need.
- **c** English is useful all around the world.
- **d** most locals can speak English wherever you go.

4 Elsa chose to work in Portugal because …
- **a** her employers told her that she could speak English.
- **b** she found Portuguese more interesting than English.
- **c** her employers wanted a Portuguese speaker.
- **d** her employers promised to teach her Portuguese.

C Mediation: Beantworten Sie die folgenden Fragen auf Deutsch.

1. Gegen welche falsche Vorstellung von Gamers wehrt sich Janek?
2. Warum muss Adeela sogar mit ihren indischen Kollegen oft Englisch sprechen?
3. Welche Art von Arbeiten beschreibt Luuk, wenn er von seiner Arbeit auf dem Bau, dem Bauernhof oder in der Bar spricht?
4. Warum möchten Elsas Arbeitgeber, dass ihre Kinder Englisch lernen?

3 WORKING WITH WORDS

A How many phrases using "language" can you find in the text?

1. Make a list. Write the German translation next to each phrase.
   EXAMPLE: *common language (l. 17): gemeinsame Sprache*
2. Write down one sentence for each phrase.
3. Compare sentences with a partner, then read out your best sentences to the class.

B Find expressions in the text to complete the sentences.

1. People who can speak several languages are ▬. (ll. 18–22)
2. Anything that you cannot manage without is ▬. (ll. 33–38)
3. If German is the first language that you learned, then you are a ▬ ▬ of German. (ll. 33–38)
4. A language which is spoken around the world is a ▬ language. (ll. 33–38)
5. If you can only say a few simple things in English, your English is ▬. (ll. 55–62)
6. If you can speak quickly and without making mistakes, your English is ▬. (ll. 63–68)
7. If you don't worry about making mistakes, you are ▬. (ll. 69–75)
8. If you share a characteristic with other people, you have it ▬ ▬. (ll. 69–75)

4 LANGUAGE IN USE: REPORTED SPEECH

→ Reported speech, S. 258

A Find examples of reported speech in the text. Write what the people said in direct speech.

EXAMPLE: *Non-gamers: "You're unsociable …"*

B Report what these people said. Remember to change the pronouns if necessary. The first one has been done.

1 Janek: "I find it easy to talk about games in English."
Janek said that he found it easy to talk about games in English.
2 Janek's friends: "His English has improved very quickly."
3 Adeela: "I still make some mistakes in English."
4 Mrs Sharma: "Adeela was one of my best students."
5 Luuk: "I'm embarrassed by my strong Dutch accent in English."
6 An American tourist: "Luuk's Dutch accent is cute!"
7 Elsa: "I want to practise Portuguese more."
8 Elsa's employers: "We'll give you time off to take Portuguese lessons."

C Think. Note down your own answers to these questions.

1 When did you start learning English?
2 What have you enjoyed most about English so far?
3 What do you find most difficult about English?
4 How will you use English in your life?

Pair: Tell your partner your answers and listen to theirs. Make notes on what they said.

Share: Tell the rest of the class the most interesting thing your partner told you. Remember to use reported speech.

Sven said that he wanted to work in the USA.

5 MAKING A POSTER

Make a poster (one page DIN-A4) for your school's open day to explain to new students why English is important.

1 Draw a mind map to organize your thoughts. You might want to include the following points:
- importance of English as a world language
- training and higher education
- leisure interests (e.g. reading, music, gaming)
- travel

2 Write a short text. It could be in the form of questions to the reader, or statements, or (invented) quotations from people who have learned English as a foreign language.

Go to File 16 on page 189.

3 Think about pictures to emphasize your message.
4 Give your poster a design that will catch the reader's attention.
5 When you have finished, pin up your poster in the classroom and do a gallery walk.

C DO YOU SPEAK "DENGLISH"?

1 PREPARING TO LISTEN

False friends are words or expressions that look the same in English and German but have different meanings. Get them wrong in English and "Denglish" can be the result! You are going to listen to some British and American people talking about their experiences with Germans speaking English. Before you listen, match the labels to the photos. There are several labels that you do not need.

1

2

body bag ▪ boss ▪ chef ▪ email (v.) ▪ handy ▪ mail (v.) ▪ messenger bag ▪ mobile (phone) ▪ photo shoot ▪ powerwalking ▪ shooting ▪ walking

3

4

5

6

2 LISTENING: WORKING WITH GERMANS

40

A **Listen to the stories, then check your answers in task 1. Write the other words from the box with their German meanings.**

B **Multiple matching: Listen again. Copy the table and match the speakers to the statements. There are two statements that you do not need.**

speaker	Brendan	Colin	Suzy	Helen
statement				

Statements
1 A customer was angry with me because of a language misunderstanding.
2 I had a much more active lunch break than I had expected.
3 I once embarrassed myself by using a false friend.
4 I'm used to Germans speaking English, but sometimes I still misunderstand them.
5 My boss was angry about a misunderstanding, but it was the customer's mistake.
6 My customers' English is much better than my German.

3 FALSE FRIENDS

What other false friends do you know? Make a list. Use a dictionary to check meanings.

German	correct English	false friend
Rente	pension	rent (Miete)

4 MANAGING SITUATIONS: A MOTORING HOLIDAY IN IRELAND

A Sie haben in Dublin ein Auto gemietet. Jetzt sind Sie in der Stadtmitte. Als Sie zum Auto zurückkehren, gehen die Türen nicht auf. Sie rufen die Mietautofirma an.

Hire company: Hello, O'Malley Hire Cars, Leanne speaking. How may I help you?

Sie: *1 Melden Sie sich mit Ihrem Namen. Sie haben vor einer Stunde ein Auto von der Firma gemietet. Sie haben bereits ein Problem mit dem Auto.*

Hire company: Ah, yes, I remember you! I'm sorry to hear that you're having problems already. What seems to be the trouble?

Sie: *2 Sie haben eingekauft und sind gerade zum Wagen zurückgekehrt, aber die Türen öffnen nicht. Sie sind aus dem Auto ausgesperrt* (locked out).

Hire company: Oh, no! Do you have the k****b?

Sie: *3 Sie haben akustisch nicht verstanden. Bitten Sie um Wiederholung.*

Hire company: Do you have the key fob?

Sie: *4 Sie wissen nicht, was ein „key fob" ist.*

Hire company: The key and remote control, to unlock the vehicle and start the engine.

Sie: *5 Ja, Sie haben den Fahrzeugschlüssel. Aber er funktioniert nicht.*

Hire company: Okay. Can you give it another try now, just in case?

Sie: *6 Sie versuchen es nochmals. Er funktioniert immer noch nicht. Die Lichter gehen an, aber die Türen entriegeln nicht* (don't unlock).

Hire company: I see ... It sounds like the keyless entry system may be faulty.

Sie: *7 Sie verstehen „faulty" nicht.*

Hire company: Not working. Broken.

Sie: *8 Sie verstehen jetzt. Was kann man da tun?*

Hire company: I'm not sure, but we'll sort it out. Don't worry. Whereabouts are you?

Sie: *9 Auf dem Parkplatz vom „SuperBuy" Supermarkt in der Liffey Street.*

Hire company: Good ... I'll have to get someone to come out to you, it may take about an hour. I'm really sorry about that.

Sie: *10 Sie fragen, ob es schneller geht, da Sie einen Termin in Cork haben.*

Hire company: Just a moment, please ... I've just spoken to my manager. He'll bring you a new car. He'll be there in about 15 minutes.

Sie: *11 Sie sind einverstanden und bedanken sich höflich.*

Hire company: I hope it all turns out okay for you. Bye now!

B Read the dialogue with a partner.

You work for a small automotive company. Your boss is interested in registering for the UK Motor Show and has asked you to find out some information.

1 READING: MOTOR SHOW WEBSITE

A Your boss has some questions about the fair. Where is the best place to look for answers on the website? (There may be more than one relevant section.)

1 Wie können wir uns als Aussteller anmelden?

2 Wie sieht das Messegelände aus?

3 Wie können wir uns auf dem Laufenden halten?

4 Was kostet der Eintritt?

Home	Information	Exhibiting	Visiting	Media	Contact us
	About us	Exhibitor list	Tickets	Virtual tour of the exhibition village	Send us a message
	FAQs	Exhibitor registration form	Opening hours	Highlights from last year's show	
	Latest news		Getting here	Press registration form	
	Mailing list		Floor plan		
	Activities		Catering		

B Decide to which of the headings in the website the following pieces of information belong.

Over 130 brand new vehicles 1

Over 20 manufacturers and 30 dealerships are represented at this year's show.
Test drive this year's models.
See concept cars with the latest automotive designs and technology.
Special deals for visitors make this the perfect place to buy your next car.

Delicious food and drink 2

20 food trucks cater for all tastes, from freshly made pizza and BBQ sausages to Indian vegetarian food. As well as street food favourites, the show has a sit-down café with a great view of the vehicle displays.

Fantastic entertainment 3
A full programme of talks by motoring celebrities and industry experts.
Thrilling simulator rides for kids and adults alike!

National Exhibition Centre 4
(near Junction 6, M42 motorway)
Birmingham B40 1NT
Ten-minute walk from Birmingham International Railway Station & Airport

2 MEDIATION: SHARING INFORMATION

→ Mediation, S. 243

Your colleague wants to know what the website says. Summarize the main points by answering the following questions in German. Do not translate word for word.

1 Was gibt es auf der Messe Interessantes für Fachleute?
2 Was könnte die ganze Familie interessieren?
3 Wie kommt man dorthin?

3 LISTENING: AT THE TRADE FAIR

41

At the trade fair several visitors come to your company's stand. Listen to what they say and choose the best response to each of them (a, b or c).

1 **a** Yes, we do. Thanks very much.
b I'm not sure. I'll ask my boss.
c Yes, of course. Here's our brochure.

2 **a** Hi, Laura. Are you having fun at the show?
b Hello, I'm (your name) from (your company). Pleased to meet you.
c Hi, Laura. I'm (your name). Why don't we go and get a coffee?

3 **a** Yes, thanks, I'm really enjoying it.
b No, I'm tired and my head hurts. I'm looking forward to closing time.
c Yes, thanks. We've had a lot of interest in our new products.

4 **a** No, sorry. But if you give me your contact details, I'll send you one.
b No, I'm sorry, it's the only one we have on the stand.
c No. Please download one from our website.

5 **a** I don't know. Why don't you have a look at the show guide?
b I recommend the Formula One racing simulator, I'd love to go on that!
c We're going to present our latest product in about ten minutes. I think you'll find it interesting.

TIP !

Meeting people in a professional situation
I'm … from … Pleased to meet you.
I work at (organization) as a (position).
It was nice to meet you / a pleasure talking to you.

4 ROLE-PLAY: MEETING AND GREETING AT A TRADE FAIR

Work with a partner.

Partner A: Your teacher will give you File A.

Partner B: Your teacher will give you File B.

1 GROUP DISCUSSION: A HOLIDAY IN LONDON

You are planning a short holiday in London with friends. You are looking for a fun activity to take up no more than half a day.

Presentation phase

Each of you has found an interesting activity and presents the suggestion in about one minute.

Interaction phase

Discuss the pros and cons of each activity and try to find one activity everybody can agree on.

Agent Chaos
Agent Chaos is a puzzle-solving and adventure spy game set in London during the Cold War. A secret agent assists you in your mission. Enemy agents will try to stop you.

- You have 90 minutes to solve puzzles, identify enemy spies and save London!
- There are five missions to choose from, some indoor and some mostly outdoors.
- To succeed you'll need original thinking, smart teamwork and a good level of fitness.
- Special after-midnight mission!

Time: 2 hours including briefing
Cost: £120 per team

East London Safari
Discover the London you won't find in the guide books. Small group tours give us the flexibility to give you choices – see what you want to see!

- Unique and original walking tours led by locals. Find out all about local history and culture.
- Bike tours along quiet roads, cycle paths and canals deep into the East End.
- Food and drink tours – visit London's most exciting food markets with cuisine from Jamaica to Japan.
- Street art tours and graffiti workshops led by local street artists.

Time: 2–4 hours
Cost: £20 per person (2-hour tours); £30 per person (4-hour workshops)

Wet & Wild Thames Ride
Speed along the River Thames on one of our high-speed jet boat tours.

- See London's famous sights from a unique perspective.
- Get an adrenaline rush as your boat reaches speeds of 56 km/h then suddenly twists and turns.
- Our guide will tell you all sorts of interesting facts about London and its famous river.
- Return to base at a gentler pace so that you have time to take awesome photos of your river trip.

Time: 90 minutes
Cost: £70 per person

Husky Rides in Epping Forest

- Learn to drive a dog team like a professional.
- We only take small groups (2–4 people) so everyone will get a turn driving the huskie team.
- Real hands-on experience: this isn't the sort of ride where you sit back and enjoy the scenery!
- Make friends with our beautiful huskies and learn all about this unique working dog.

Time: Taster session 30 minutes; full husky experience 2 hours
Cost: £30–£120 per person.

2 GROUP DISCUSSION: HEALTHIER SCHOOLS

As part of your school's project week on health and fitness, you have been asked to discuss general ways in which schools could be made healthier places.

Presentation phase

Each of you chooses a different suggestion below and presents it in about one minute.

Interaction phase

Discuss all the suggestions and discuss the merits of each one and how it could be put into action. Try to decide on two suggestions that will be used. Be prepared to compromise.

Ban students from coming to school by car or moped; students should use public transport, cycle or walk.
- Walking just three times a week for 30 minutes can significantly increase your fitness.
- Walking is good for your brain. Walking at an easy pace at least 1.5 hours per week helps to improve brain function.
- Cycling is a good way to control or reduce weight, as it raises your metabolic rate and burns body fat.
- Cycling improves strength, balance and coordination.

Introduce a compulsory sport lesson every day; always to be done at different times on the timetable, not just in the afternoon.
- Sport improves your concentration, particularly if you do sport 3–5 times a week for at least 30 minutes.
- Team sports in particular provide a chance to relax and get rid of stress.
- Sport is an excellent, fun way to improve your fitness.
- Sport has lots of social benefits: allowing you to connect with teammates and friends.

Remove all snack vending machines from the school premises.
- Snack foods contain unhealthy amounts of salt and may lead to high blood pressure.
- Snacking on high-energy foods increases your chances of gaining weight.
- Eating sugar-rich snacks coats your mouth with sugar. This sugar coating attacks your teeth.
- Snack foods often contain little dietary fibre and this may lead to problems with your digestive system.

Introduce a school canteen selling healthy meals, vegetarian meals and a salad buffet.
- Health experts say that we should all eat at least two portions of fruit and five portions of vegetables a day. (A portion = 80g.)
- Healthy eating becomes a life-long habit – as does unhealthy eating.
- Balanced meals improve mental concentration and mood.
- Vegetarian food is generally low in saturated fat and high in dietary fibre. It's good for your heart and digestive system.

Introduce "health and nutrition" as a compulsory school subject for all students.
- Well-designed nutrition education programmes can lead to healthier food choices.
- News stories about the health benefits of particular foods can be confusing and contradictory.
- Knowing the basic facts about health and nutrition helps you to tell real health news from fake news.
- Health education can make students more aware of the dangers of drug and alcohol abuse.

A *Any* or *some*? Choose the correct alternative.

1 If you could live anywhere / somewhere in the world, where would that be?
2 I love travelling – I can't think of anything / something I'd prefer to do.
3 Think of any / some words which look the same in English and German but have different meanings.
4 Do you speak any / some other foreign languages as well as English?
5 There must be anything / something I can do to learn English faster: don't you have any / some tips?
6 Janek isn't unsociable: he will talk to anybody / somebody.
7 I don't think that any / some of the students in my class speak Hindi.
8 In India it's hard to find anybody / somebody who isn't multilingual – except for tourists.
9 I'd love to live anywhere / somewhere warm – Australia, for example.
10 I can't think of any / some reason to leave Germany.

B Complete the sentences with *many, much, a lot (of), (a) little, (a) few* instead of the German words. There may be more than one possible answer.

1 Luuk speaks very good English, but he still makes *einige wenige* mistakes.
2 Relatively *wenige* web pages are in languages other than English.
3 I've tried to find a good course in Dutch but I've had *wenig* success.
4 Why do so *viele* songs have lyrics in English?
5 Is there *viel* casual work for backpackers in Australia?
6 There are *viele* jobs on farms or in restaurants.
7 *Viele* casual farm jobs are hard work for *wenig* money.
8 *Wenige* local people want to work on farms.
9 English is important for *viele* restaurant jobs.
10 There isn't *viel* work you can do in Australia without good English.

C Translate the sentences into English.

1 Wie viele Amtssprachen (official languages) gibt es in der EU?
2 Wie viel Zeit braucht man für eine Weltreise (trip around the world)?
3 Es gibt nicht viele Restaurants in dieser Stadt.
4 Es gibt viel zu sehen auf der Messe.
5 Es gibt nicht viel Arbeit in dieser Stadt.
6 Es gibt wenige Berufe (professions), in denen Englischkenntnisse nicht nützlich sind.
7 Wenige Messebesucher bleiben mehr als eine Nacht in der Stadt.
8 Weiß hier irgendjemand die richtige Lösung zu dieser Aufgabe?
9 Viele Rucksackreisende reisen jedes Jahr nach Thailand.
10 Einige wenige von ihnen werden dort sesshaft (settle down).

Is it art?

13

A WARM-UP: IDEAS ABOUT ART

A Which of these things are "art" for you?

Cadillac Ranch, Amarillo, Texas

bonsai tree

tattoos

abstract painting

"An Experiment on a Bird in the Air Pump" by Joseph Wright (1768); National Gallery, London

graffiti by Eintracht fans

Pop Art

B What do you think of these statements about art? Choose one statement that you agree with and one that you disagree with. Choose a photo above that you think supports your opinion.

1. Art has to be beautiful. If it's ugly, it isn't art.
2. Art makes you look at things in a new way.
3. Anything can be art. It all depends on how you look at it.
4. Art expresses our connection to life.
5. Art expresses the artist's deepest feelings.
6. People pretend to like art because they want to look intellectual.
7. Only artists can create real art.
8. We all have artistic talent.

C Work with a partner.

- What experiences of art have you had?
- Write down a definition of art that you both agree with.

B GRAFFITI AND STREET ART

SITUATION: An international youth magazine has invited contributions about graffiti. You decide to write an essay about graffiti and street art (task 7, p. 149). While you are researching the topic, you find an extract from a graphic novel about a graffiti sprayer, Nat Stone.

1 PREPARING TO READ

Discuss these questions with a partner.

1 Is there much graffiti in your area? Why do you think this is?
2 Is graffiti vandalism or street art? What is the difference?

2 READING AND UNDERSTANDING THE TEXT

Read the graphic novel below. Then put the parts 1–5 on page 148 in the correct order to tell Nat's story.

Nat Stone, Street Artist

If I gave him a criminal conviction, he would only get into more trouble. He deserves another chance...
There is a street art programme for graffiti offenders. It's an alternative to a criminal conviction for vandalism. If I gave you another chance, would you take it?
Yes, of course!
Instead of breaking the law and making our streets ugly, they create beautiful street art... This is Nat, one of our best artists.
If your friends asked you to go back to spraying graffiti, would you do it?
No way!
A few days later...
That's bad. No respect!
EVENING NEWS
"Street art" programme fuels graffiti storm.
...and so, because of the negative publicity, we've decided to cancel the programme and cover up the mural. I know you'll be disappointed, but it's for the best.
So it was all a waste of time!

1 A few days later, Nat had to go to court. Dressed in his smart clothes, Nat tried to look confident and grown up, but he was worried: if he got a criminal record, he would find it difficult to get a job or a training place.
Luckily the magistrate, Mrs Adebayo, was a kind woman. She decided to give Nat a chance to change his life and avoid a conviction. She invited him to join a street art programme. Nat accepted her offer.

2 That night, graffiti vandals sprayed tags in the city centre near to the mural. They vandalized walls and shop windows. It looked ugly and it took a lot of time and money to clean up the mess. Like other local people, Nat was shocked. However, he was even more shocked when he read Selena's big story about the graffiti. In her article, Selena blamed the graffiti on the street art project. She claimed that the murals sent young people the message that graffiti on buildings was 'street art'. The local council held a meeting and decided that there was too much negative publicity about the street art programme. It had to close. A council officer came to tell the participants that the programme was cancelled. Council workers arrived to paint over the mural. Nat was angry and disappointed about the council's decision.

3 Nat started to work on a big, beautiful mural in the city centre with other young people. He enjoyed using his imagination and artistic skills on this project and he wasn't interested in illegal graffiti any more. People who were walking past often commented on the mural. They said that it was great and really brightened up the boring city centre. Nat felt proud of his work.
Reporters from a local newspaper, the *Evening News*, came to see the project and interview the participants. The project leader, Sam, explained to the reporters that the programme gave young people a chance to be creative and keep out of trouble. A young female reporter, Selena, asked Nat some questions about his life and why street art was important to him.

4 Nat Stone lived in an industrial town in England. It was an ugly, anonymous place with lots of concrete walls and rubbish on the streets. It was the sort of place where nobody knew their neighbours. There wasn't much for young people to do.
To pass the time and for a little excitement, Nat used to go 'tagging' with his friends Emma and Dan. They sprayed graffiti tags on surfaces and objects all over town – walls, street signs, posts, anything. It made them feel that the town 'belonged' to them and they belonged to it. They didn't know what the other residents thought about all the graffiti, and they didn't care.

5 One evening Emma and Dan asked Nat to come tagging, but Nat said that he wasn't interested. He had decided that tags were silly and childish. He wanted to draw a much bigger piece of graffiti – something that was more creative and special, something that would get lots of attention. When it was dark, Nat went to a subway in town with a bag full of spray cans and started to sketch his new graffiti design on the wall.
After a while, Nat stood back to look at his work. He was pleased with what he saw. Unfortunately he didn't notice the two police officers until it was too late to run away. They took him to the police station. (584 words)

3 WORKING WITH WORDS

A Find words in the text which match the definitions below.

1 building where decisions about law are made (part 1)
2 the act of finding somebody guilty of breaking the law (part 1)
3 painting on a wall (part 2)
4 people who live in a particular place (part 4)

B Explain what these expressions from the text mean. Write complete sentences.

1 blame something on somebody (part 2)
2 use your imagination (part 3)

4 LANGUAGE IN USE: CONDITIONAL SENTENCES TYPE 2

→ Conditional sentences, S. 256

A Find examples of conditional sentences type 2 in the graphic novel on pages 146–147.

EXAMPLE: *If I gave you another chance, would you take it?*

B Join the sentence halves. There may be more than one answer.

1 If I was in Nat's position,
2 If there was more for young people to do,
3 If there were more murals,
4 It would be better for Nat
5 More people would feel proud of their town
6 Nat could be a professional artist

a concrete walls would be less ugly.
b I wouldn't go back to graffiti spraying.
c if he worked hard to improve his skills.
d if there were more public art.
e if the street art programme started again.
f there would be less graffiti.

C Complete these sentences with your own ideas. Compare sentences with a partner, then share the four best ones with the class.

1 If our town had more street artists, …
2 If I joined a street art programme, …
3 Our area would be more interesting if …
4 Fewer young people would get into trouble if …

5 VIEWING

06

→ Videos, S. 199

Watch the video "Berlin activists turn Nazi hate graffiti into art" and complete the tasks on page 199.

6 MIND MAP: GRAFFITI

Work in a group of about four people. Sit around a table with a large sheet of paper in the middle.

1 Write "Graffiti" as the start of a mind map. Design the mind map as a piece of graffiti.
2 Add relevant ideas from Nat's story to the mind map.
3 Add your own ideas. Use a dictionary if necessary.
4 Pin up your graffiti mind map in the class and do a gallery walk. Write comments and suggestions on other groups' mind maps.

7 WRITING AN ARGUMENTATIVE ESSAY

Write an essay on the topic: "Graffiti – street art or vandalism?" Write about 200 words. Consider both sides of the argument, then give your own opinion and justify it.

Go to File 17 on page 190.

C TAKING BETTER PHOTOS

1 PREPARING TO LISTEN

Even if you just want to take "happy snaps" with friends, it is good to know a few basic photography techniques.

A Talk to your partner. Do you like taking selfies? Do you take good ones?

B Match the tips to the pictures.

a Check your pose.
b Use filters.
c Use natural light, not flash.
d Get the angle right.
e Edit: crop and rotate.
f Be spontaneous.

2 LISTENING: TIPS FOR SELFIES

42

A Listen to Shani Wells's podcast. Put the tips from task 1B into the order in which they are mentioned.

B Listen again. Answer the questions in note form.

1 How does Shani want people to think of her tips?
2 What does the selfie-taker need to do to present him or herself as an interesting person with various sides?
3 What's the best way to light your face?
4 What advice does Shani give about flash?
5 When does a selfie-taker look tense and unrelaxed?
6 How can you make your face more interesting after you've taken a photo?
7 What can you do to highlight the forms of the objects on your photo?

http://www.photo-clinic.co.uk

Shani Wells' PHOTO CLINIC

Thank you Abbie from Stuttgart for sending in this photo. Abbie writes *I think this photo isn't bad, but it could have been better. Any tips?* Here's my reply.

Abbie has made some good artistic choices. She has used the natural light from the window to define her face. She has also chosen an interesting angle. The white background is deliberately overexposed. If it had been darker, it would have distracted us from the main subject – Abbie. It's a lovely photo which expresses her personality. On the other hand …

- If Abbie had smiled less, the photo would have been more mysterious.
- If she hadn't held her arm straight, her pose would have been more natural.
- Her attractive eyes would have been more obvious if she had cropped the picture.
- The picture would have been more unusual if she had cropped and rotated it.
- If she had used a black-and-white filter, it would have highlighted her features.

3 LANGUAGE IN USE: CONDITIONAL SENTENCES TYPE 3

→ Conditional sentences, S. 256

A Find examples of conditional sentences type 3 in the text above.

B Complete the sentences using the key words.

1 If you had kept a copy of your photos, … (you – not lose – them).
2 If I had bought a new phone, … (I – take – better photos).
3 If it hadn't been so sunny, … (photo – not be – overexposed).
4 You wouldn't have had scary red eyes if … (you – use – natural light).
5 The photo would have been more interesting if … (he – crop – it).
6 The faces would have been too dark if … (she – not use – flash).

4 DISCUSSION: IMPROVING YOUR PHOTOS

A Bring in some of your own photos. Discuss with a partner how they could have been better – or just different.

If you had used flash, ...

B Write your own "photo clinic" for one photo.

You have started work experience at a British printing plant. There are several workplace hazards, so safety procedures are an important part of your induction*. *induction = *Einarbeitung*

1 WORKING WITH SIGNS

As part of your induction you have to complete a health and safety test. You have to understand the safety signs in your workplace.

A Match the instructions to the signs. There are more instructions than signs.

- **a** You must wear ear protectors in this noisy area.
- **b** You may not enter this area without a helmet.
- **c** You must not operate this machinery without safety glasses.
- **d** You should beware of forklift trucks here.
- **e** This material could catch fire.
- **f** You should beware of getting an electric shock.
- **g** You must wear protective gloves.
- **h** You must pull down the guard before using the machinery.
- **i** This machinery could crush your fingers.
- **j** You must wear protective clothing in this area.

1

2

3

4

5

6

7

8

B Your colleague is taking you around the plant. You both do as you are told in the signs. Write down what he/she tells you might/could/would happen if you didn't take notice of the signs.

EXAMPLE: *If you didn't wear safety glasses, your eyes could be damaged.*

C Which of the signs would you expect to see in these workplaces, and why?

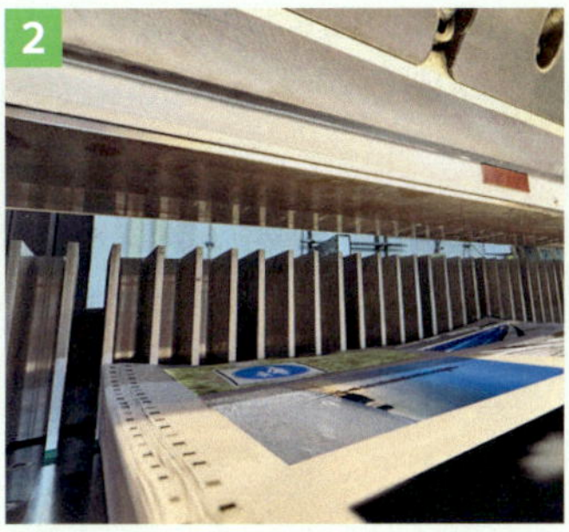

2 PLACEMAT: WORKPLACE SAFETY

Read this case study about an industrial accident at a printing plant, then complete the task below.

Case Study

Jack worked in a magazine printing works. Sometimes there was too much ink on the rollers on the big printing press. Occasionally a whole print run had to be thrown away – thousands of magazines. The company tried to repair the printing press, however the problem always came back. The company couldn't afford a new press: over a million pounds.

The simple solution was to clean the rollers with a cloth every hour. The rules said that the press had to be shut down for this procedure. Jack and his colleagues thought that this wasn't necessary. Besides, it took a lot of time to stop the press and start it again.

One day, Jack was cleaning the rollers on the printing press with a cloth while the press was running. He had done this hundreds of times.

This time, the cloth got stuck between the moving rollers. They pulled the cloth into the press – and Jack didn't have time to let go. His hand was pulled between the rollers. Fortunately his wedding ring got stuck and the rollers didn't pull his whole arm into the press. However his fingers were crushed. Jack spent 13 days in hospital. The doctors took skin from his foot to repair his hand. Unfortunately, they weren't able to save one of his fingers, which had to be removed. Jack spent six months off work.

(Based on a true story, name and details changed.)

Work in a group of four. Sit around a table with a large sheet of paper. Write "Workplace Safety" in the middle as a title.

You are the members of your company's Youth and Trainee Representation (*Jugend- und Auszubildendenvertretung, JAV*). Your task is to write workplace safety recommendations to avoid accidents like the one described above.

Step 1 Make notes on your corner of the sheet.
Step 2 Discuss your ideas with the rest of your group.
Step 3 Take decisions and agree on four workplace safety recommendations. Write them under the title.
Step 4 Show your recommendations to the class.

1 MAKING COMPARISONS

You are planning a trip from Frankfurt to Paris and want to find the best way of getting there, taking time, cost and environmental effects into account. (Use *than* and *as … as*.)

Means of transport	Time (each way)	Cost (return)	CO_2 emissions
air travel	2:30	€89	108kg
road travel	6:30	€75 (per person)	55kg (per person)
rail travel	4:15	€160	11kg

a Air travel is ▬ (expensive) ▬ road travel. Rail travel is ▬ (expensive) means of transport.
b Air travel is ▬ (fast) means of transport. Rail travel is ▬ (fast) ▬ road travel.
c Rail travel is ▬ (good) for the environment ▬ road travel, but road travel is not ▬ (bad) for the environment ▬ air travel. Air travel is ▬ (bad) option if you care about the environment.

2 MODAL AUXILIARIES

Three friends are thinking about starting a Repair Café at their school. Complete the dialogue with the most suitable modals from the box. Use each modal once. Sometimes there is more than one possibility.

can't ▪ don't have to ▪ have to ▪ may ▪ must ▪ must not ▪ should ▪ shouldn't

Alice: Why don't we start a Repair Café at school? It ▬ be very satisfying to do your own repairs.
Zack: Nice idea! But before we start one, we ▬ find out whether there is already one in our area.
Alice: I've already checked. I ▬ find one. So let's ask the school principal for permission.
Dan: Wait a minute! We ▬ rush into it. Let's do more research first.
Zack: That's right. There ▬ be rules to follow.
Dan: You ▬ be a qualified electrician to repair electrical goods, for example.
Zack: And you ▬ encourage people to do their own electrical repairs. That's against the law.
Alice: That's true, but we ▬ repair electrical goods. We can do easier things.

3 TO + INFINITIVE OR -ING?

John Langham gave up money for six months. Cross out the wrong verb form.

a Last summer John decided to live / living for three months without spending money.
b He had always enjoyed to grow / growing his own food.
c So he didn't expect to have / having any difficulties feeding himself.
d He didn't mind to go / going without electricity and running water.
e He had to stop to watch / watching TV and to surf / surfing the internet.
f His friends expected him to give up / giving up after a few days, but he surprised them.
g John recommends to try / trying the moneyless lifestyle yourself.

4 CONDITIONAL SENTENCES (TYPES 1 AND 2)

Zoe has written to a newspaper advice column "Ask Meg". Complete the letter with verbs in the correct tenses.

Dear Meg,

I want to become a vegan, but my parents are making it difficult. Mum says I ___ (damage) my health if I ___ (not have) a balanced diet. Dad says if I ___ (stop) eating meat, I ___ (get) anaemia. I explained to them that millions of people around the world are vegans and are perfectly healthy. If there ___ (be) dangers connected with a vegan diet, we ___ (know) about it by now. In fact, if more people ___ (have) a meat-free diet, it ___ (be) better for their health and better for the planet too. But Mum and Dad still aren't convinced. I don't want to give up, but I'm worried that it ___ (hurt) Mum's feelings if I ___ (not eat) the meals she cooks for me. What ___ (you – do) if you ___ (be) me?

Zoe, 17, Manchester

5 PRESENT PERFECT OR SIMPLE PAST?

Complete the sentences with the correct form of the verb in brackets.

a ___ (you – read) the *Harry Potter* books yet?
b Yes, I ___ (read) the whole series last summer, except for the last one. I ___ (buy) it last month but I ___ (not start) it yet.
c What ___ (you – think) of them?
d I ___ (not like) the first book much but I ___ (find) the others quite good. What about you?
e I ___ (see) all the films so far, but I ___ (not read) any of the books. Do you think I should?
f Maybe not. There isn't much point in reading the book if you ___ (already see) the film.

6 THE PASSIVE

Ruby Welsh recently had problems with her email account. Put the verbs in brackets into the indicated form of the passive.

a Last week Ruby ___ (call; simple past) by her internet service provider (ISP).
b Thousands of spam messages ___ (send; past perfect) from her email address.
c "Obviously the emails ___ by me," (not write; simple past) said Ruby.
d "It looks as if my password ___ (steal; present perfect)."
e "I used the password 'p@ssw0rd'. My ISP explained that passwords like that ___ (guess; simple present) too easily by hackers."
f Ruby ___ (warn; present perfect) to use a better password in future.
g "Otherwise my account ___ (close; will-future)," she said.

13 REVISION The future (S. 254)

A Correct these statements using the information in brackets.

EXAMPLE: I'm going to play computer games this evening. (watch TV)
I'm not going to play computer games this evening. I'm going to watch TV.

1 I'm going to spray tags again. (become a professional artist)
2 I expect the number of industrial accidents will go up. (go down)
3 I think the street art project will stay in the city centre. (move to the industrial estate)
4 The city residents will be happy about that. (sad)
5 The graffiti problem will get better. (worse)
6 Your photo will look better with flash. (natural light from the window)
7 It's going to be cold today. (warm and sunny)
8 The workers will obey the safety signs. (ignore them)
9 We're going to take selfies. (make a video)
10 I'm going to share my photo album online. (keep it private)

B Use the prompts to ask questions which go with the answers.

1 Dan – celebrate his 18th birthday ? Yes. He's going to have a big party.
2 who – remove the graffiti ? The council workers will do it, I expect.
3 the magistrate – give Emma a conviction ? No, she's going to give her a warning.
4 you – wear safety glasses ? Yes, of course. I'm going to wear gloves too.
5 the workers – shut down the machine ? Yes. They aren't going to risk another accident.
6 the machine – cause more accidents ? No, I'm sure the company will replace it now.
7 which unit – do next ? We're going to do Unit 14.
8 how – we do in the exams ? We'll do very well, hopefully.
9 what – do – when you leave school ? I'm going to become a chef.
10 what – do – if you win the lottery ? I'll buy a nice car and go on a road trip around the USA.

C Choose the best future form for each context.

1 Do you believe the local newspaper, etc. ___ (give) publicity to the street art project?
2 I expect the vandals ___ (get) criminal convictions.
3 It's clear that the graffiti problem ___ (get) worse without creative solutions.
4 I hope our town ___ (start) a street art programme.
5 The sky is dark and cloudy: it looks as if it ___ (rain).
6 I imagine Nat ___ (get) a creative job of some kind.
7 When I leave school, I ___ (start) an apprenticeship.
8 Maria ___ (apply) for a New Zealand work permit when she finishes school.
9 I'm sure Jack ___ (be) more careful working on the printing press in future.
10 Jack's family hopes he ___ (look for) a safer job.

How others see us 14

A WARM-UP: DIFFERENCES, SIMILARITIES

A Why do people form negative opinions about people they don't know? Make a sentence to go with each photo.

There are many people who

- are intolerant of
- are scared/afraid of
- are suspicious of
- don't like
- don't understand
- don't feel comfortable with
- won't have anything to do with

- alternative lifestyles.
- different attitudes to sex.
- different religious beliefs.
- other races/cultures.
- people who haven't succeeded in life.
- people who dress differently.
- people who just look different.
- people with disabilities.
- younger/older generations.

B Half the class writes their name on a piece of paper and puts it in the box. The other half draws a name from the box. Sit with the person whose name you have drawn and find five things that you share.

- a fear
- a favourite food or drink
- an ambition
- a place you have been
- a TV show

You have three minutes to complete the task. Report back to the class with what you have found out.

B EVIL ROBOT MONKEY

SITUATION: You have joined an online story-telling group to improve your English. Each month the group writes short stories on a particular theme. This month the theme is "Appearances can be deceptive" (*der Schein trügt manchmal*). You write a story on this theme (task 4, p. 161). You search the internet for inspiration and find a story about Sly, a chimpanzee who has an implant (*Implantat*) which makes him more intelligent than other chimpanzees.

1 PREPARING TO READ

Look at the picture below and the title of the story on the page opposite. Answer these questions with a partner, then report back to the class.

- How would you describe Sly's situation?
- How would you feel if you were Sly?
- How would you feel if you saw Sly in a zoo?

Step away from your cameraphone

Constantly taking photographs STOPS our brains remembering what happened.

From children's birthdays to that long-awaited family holiday, we all want to remember those cherished moments with a photograph. But if you're one of those people who can't stop snapping, beware – you could end up forgetting it all in a flash.

A study has found that taking too many photos may prevent us from forming detailed memories. […]

Researchers led a group of students around a museum and asked them to either photograph or try to remember certain works of art and historical exhibits. The next day, their memory was tested. It showed they were worse at recognising objects they had photographed than those they had only looked at. They were also poorer at recalling details of the objects they had taken pictures of.

Dr Linda Henkel, who conducted the study at Fairfield University in Connecticut, said: 'People so often whip out their cameras almost mindlessly. When people rely on technology to remember for them, it can have a negative impact on how well they remember their experiences.'

Previous studies have suggested that reviewing old photos can help us remember, but only if we spend long enough doing it. 'In order to remember, we have to access and interact with the photos, rather than just amass them,' said Dr Henkel.

Source: *The Daily Mail*, 10 December 2013; 209 words

07 exhibit: *Ausstellungsstück*
12 to whip out: *zücken*
17 to amass: *anhäufen*

2 MEDIATION

Ihr Freund macht Ihrer Meinung nach zu viele Fotos. Sie sehen diesen Zeitungsartikel und erzählen ihm davon. Folgende Fragen helfen Ihnen dabei. Übersetzen Sie nicht Wort für Wort.

1 Warum fotografieren wir Familienereignisse?
2 Welche Auswirkungen hat das Fotografieren auf unser Erinnerungsvermögen?
3 Wie haben Forscher die Auswirkungen festgestellt?
4 Was geschieht, wenn Menschen sich auf Technik verlassen, um sich zu erinnern?
5 Was können wir tun, um unser Erinnerungsvermögen zu stärken?

A Make the active sentences passive. Use *by* only where you are instructed to do so.

EXAMPLES:

They hold the marathon in August.	*The marathon is held in August.*
Refugees in Crisis runs the marathon. (by)	*The marathon is run by Refugees in Crisis.*

Simple present

1 We post information packs to the runners a month before the event.
2 We give each competitor a number.
3 They pin the number on their vest before the race.
4 Race officials check the name and number of each runner at registration. (by)
5 We separate the runners into different groups according to their age, sex and ability.

Simple past

6 They didn't warn Sly about the school visit.
7 Sly's behaviour embarrassed the teacher. (by)
8 They punished Sly for throwing the clay.
9 They took his clay away.
10 Vern put Sly's vase in the kiln. (by)

Present perfect

11 They have tidied the kitchen.
12 Hassan has asked Ryan not to cook bacon in the flat. (by)
13 Ryan's experience has changed his ideas about different cultures. (by)
14 Channel Z has interviewed the flatmates. (by)
15 They haven't washed the dishes yet.

Will-future

16 Our Mainz office will organize the marathon again this year. (by)
17 We will send out press kits in July.
18 You will find more information on our website.
19 Our volunteers will process your registration forms. (by)
20 We won't pass on your contact details to marketing companies.

B Translate the sentences into English. Think carefully about which tense to use.

1 Ein Implantat wurde in Slys Kopf eingesetzt. (put an implant into)
2 Die Vase wurde gegen das Fenster geworfen.
3 Die Schulkinder sind nicht von ihrer Lehrerin bestraft worden.
4 Die Besuchsregeln sind seitdem geändert worden. (rules for visitors)
5 Schulklassen werden davor gewarnt, Sly zu erschrecken. (warn not to startle)
6 Schlechtes Benehmen der Besucher wird nicht mehr toleriert. (tolerate bad behaviour by visitors)
7 Sly wird in Zukunft vor jedem Schulbesuch von Vern informiert.
8 Nächstes Jahr wird ein Dokumentarfilm über Sly gedreht. (make a documentary)

New horizons

15

A WARM-UP: LOOKING AHEAD

A **Look at the photos. Choose one which represents your dreams for the next ten years. Describe the photo to a partner and explain why you chose it.**

B **What do you want to achieve in the next ten years?**

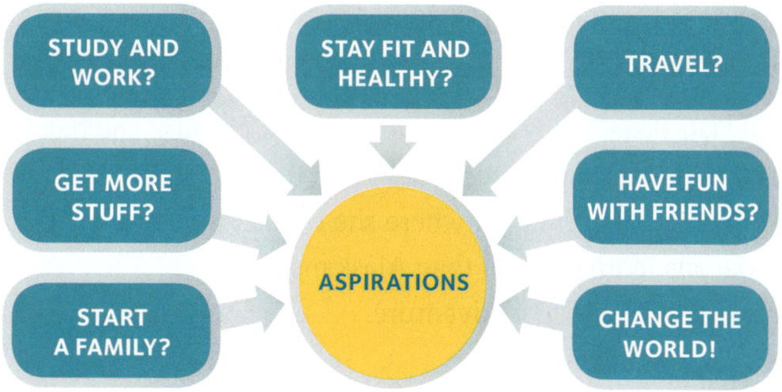

- Use the diagram to organize your ideas.
- Compare ideas with your partner.
- Describe some of your partner's aspirations to the class.

C **How will the world be better when your generation is in charge? Brainstorm ideas in a group and write a "to do" list for 2050.**

B GLOBAL NOMADS

SITUATION: Lots of people make use of their time to travel abroad and live for a while in another country. You've been asked by an Australian website to explain to Australian youngsters why they should spend time in Germany (task 4, p. 172). Before you do so, you read about some people who have decided to explore other countries.

1 PREPARING TO READ

Skim the texts on page 171. Match each blogger profile below to the correct text.

Hitomi Matsumoto is a chef from Alaska. She loves languages and speaks English, Japanese, German and French. She's now living in Freiburg im Breisgau.

Lukas Petersen is a nurse from Bremen. He's living and working in Durban, South Africa, while he saves to continue his journey around the world.

Anna Lehmann and Fabian Müller are a couple from Munich. Anna is a web designer and Fabian is a motor mechanic. They are currently touring Australia in a converted school bus.

2 READING AND UNDERSTANDING THE BLOGS

A Finish the sentences using the information from "Just Jammin'". Use your own words.

1 The blogger of "Just Jammin'" worries that the world will soon become ___
2 Although he would prefer to work as a nurse, most countries ___
3 He was so moved by seeing the Victoria Falls that ___

B True or false: Decide if the following statements about "Off Piste" are true or false. Explain your answers in German.

1 The blogger of "Off Piste" finds it easier to get work because she has completed her training.
2 She works as a ski instructor because she needs the money.
3 People who visit her blog often ask where she feels at home.
4 She finds Europeans more unusual than Alaskans.
5 She now feels ready for a bigger adventure.

C Fill in the gaps with words from "Aussie Bush Bus Adventure". Use only one word for each gap. Give the number of the line in which you found the word.

Fabian and Anna are travelling around Australia. Farmers give Fabian work fixing their ___ [1] and Anna earns money by creating websites. But she also does other jobs on a ___ [2] basis. Anna just got pregnant. They had wanted to gain some ___ [3] ___ [4] first, but they've accepted the new situation and are happy to have ___ [5] ___ [6]. In the outback people are easy-going while the animals can be dangerous. But their main fear is that their old bus will ___ [7] ___ [8].

GLOBETROTTING BLOGGERS

46

Just Jammin'

Whenever people ask me why I gave up my job in Germany to go travelling, I say 'I want to see the world while it's still there!' Globalization is making places more similar to each other and I want to experience our beautiful, diverse planet before it changes too much.

I've been on the road for two years. In that time I've explored Africa from Tangiers to Durban. I do nursing work if my German qualifications are recognized. (In most countries, they aren't.) For fun, I sometimes get out my guitar and try busking. People don't give me much money – I'm really not that good – but they sometimes sing along!

Visitors to my blog often ask me what has been my best experience so far. It's impossible to answer: there have been so many: playing with traditional musicians in Malawi, photographing lions up close in Kruger National Park … But my first visit to Victoria Falls in Zambia was one of the best. It's awesome. I actually cried, I was so emotional.

People want to know whether I've had any bad experiences. Just one: I was robbed here in Durban. That was scary. I was shaking with fear while it happened. There's a lot of poverty and inequality here, and with that comes crime. It makes you realize how lucky we are in Germany.

OFF PISTE

I've been away from home for 18 months. In the summer I work in restaurants and hotels – being a qualified chef means that I can find work quite easily. In the winter, I work as a ski instructor. That's really my dream job. I get a lot of satisfaction from seeing my students' skill and confidence increase.

Commenters on my blog often ask me whether I miss Alaska. Well, I don't miss the dark winter nights, that's for sure! I do miss the eccentric characters, though. There's something about our wide open spaces and harsh climate that attracts unusual people.

What I love about Europe is that everything is so close together. At the moment I'm living near the border between France, Germany and Switzerland. Within a few kilometres there's so much change in language and culture.

All the same, after 18 months in Europe, I think it's time to leave my comfort zone. I'm going to head east to Kazakhstan and Mongolia. That will be different!

Aussie Bush Bus Adventure

Fabian can fix almost any motor, so there's lots of work for him repairing farm machinery. I write our travel blog, design websites and do any kind of casual work I can find. You have to be flexible on the road.

We set off ten months ago, as soon as Fabian had finished his apprenticeship. The plan was to enjoy our freedom and widen our life experience before we settle into a career and start a family. Only it hasn't quite worked out that way.

You guessed it: we're about to start a family! I'm expecting our first baby. She's going to be born here in Australia. They have excellent health care here, and we have health insurance.

If people ask me what has been my favourite moment here in Australia, I say: 'Everything!' People are so open and friendly in these little communities in the bush.

Europeans think that Australia is full of dangerous animals: crocodiles, snakes and sharks. Actually the biggest danger, touring the outback in a 1970s school bus, is mechanical failure. If you break down and can't get mobile phone reception, you're in trouble. It's just as well Fabian's good with motors …

(578 words)

3 LANGUAGE IN USE: TENSE REVISION

A Copy and complete the table. Find at least one example of each of these tenses in the text on page 171.

tense	example	Grund (Deutsch)
simple present	*Whenever people ask me (l. 1)*	*sich wiederholende Handlung in der Gegenwart*
present progressive		
present perfect		
simple past		
will-future		
going to-future		
past progressive		
past perfect		

B Schreiben Sie in Englisch über Ihre Freundin Lena, die in Südostasien unterwegs ist. Der erste Satz wurde schon übertragen.

1 Nachdem meine Freundin Lena ihre Lehre abgeschlossen hatte, ging sie auf Reisen.
After she had finished her apprenticeship, my friend Lena went travelling.
2 Letzte Woche hat sie mir aus Bali geschrieben.
3 Sie hat einen netten Australier kennengelernt, Lachlan.
4 Sie hat ihn sehr gern.
5 Sie verbringen gerade viel Zeit zusammen.
6 Sie arbeitete in einer Bar, als sie ihn kennenlernte.
7 Sie haben vor kurzem entschieden, dass sie noch ein Jahr auf Bali bleiben werden.
8 Im Sommer fliege ich nach Bali, um Lena zu treffen.
9 Es wird interessant sein, Lachlan kennenzulernen.

4 WRITING A WEBPAGE

Just as there is a Working Holiday programme for Germans in Australia (Unit 7, pp. 80–81), so too is there one for Australians in Germany. An Australian website for youngsters has asked young Germans to put together a webpage with information for young Australians.

You should do some research about the sort of jobs they could find and about things they should see or do, and explain to them why the experience will be good for them. Structure your ideas so that the webpage looks attractive.

Go to File 19 on page 191.

C THE FUTURE OF WORK

1 PREPARING TO READ

Read the introduction and look at the picture. What do you think life will be like in this city?

In the late 21st century the Earth's population reaches 31 billion. Most people live in huge "mega-cities" and travel in flying pods. Many spend their whole lives in the same apartment complex and get their experience of the outside world from "proxy broadcasts" – realistic 3D virtual reality experiences which look, feel, smell and even taste like the real thing. Almost all goods and services are provided by robots, so there is little work for humans to do.

2 READING AND UNDERSTANDING THE TEXT

47

First day at work

'Congratulations!' said the Monitor. 'You're going to work today! Your wage will be 52 Credits an hour.'

Jared's heart missed a beat. Work! Great news! The universal income of 2,500 Credits a month was enough to live on, of course, but it would be good to have some extra money – and real work! What fun!

'What's the job?' he asked the large screen, which took up a whole wall in his small flat.

'You're going to be a proxy,' replied the Monitor. 'You'll have a trial period of one week. If feedback from the audience is positive, it could even become a permanent full-time position.'

'That's amazing,' said Jared, 'and I'm really pleased, but … I've never had a job before. I'm only 25, after all. And I don't really know what a proxy –'

'Don't worry! You'll receive the equipment and instructions when the pod arrives to take you to work,' said the Monitor kindly, 'The pod will arrive at 8.37 a.m. – that's in thirty minutes. You can get breakfast at work. Bye now! Have a nice day!'

Forty-five minutes later, Jared was looking out the window of the pod as it approached the mega-city of Frankfurt at 300 kilometres an hour. 'What a city! 27 million residents in skyscrapers 80 storeys high,' said the pod. Some pods weren't very talkative, but this was an unusually chatty one. 'How was the induction? Do you know what you have to do now?' it asked.

'Not really,' said Jared. 'The virtual reality lesson was a bit short – and confusing. I guess I've never really thought about what a proxy does before. I mean, I watch the broadcasts, like everyone else, but I didn't realize –' →

21 **induction:** *Einarbeitung*

'I've driven a few proxies to work,' interrupted the pod. 'You'll love it … anyway, we're here: Gruneburg Park. Have a nice day!'

Jared stepped out of the pod, which gave him a cheerful 'Goodbye!', closed its door and zoomed off. As it was identical to the thousands of other small silver robotic vehicles on the street, Jared lost sight of it in seconds. Jared adjusted the Proxy 360° sensor so that it was a comfortable fit in his ear, with a good connection to his brain, and looked around him.

The sun shone down from a clear blue sky and there was a gentle breeze. Jared looked around at the tall trees. He could hear birds singing. In front of him was a footpath, leading between the trees. From his induction, Jared knew that he had to follow this path to get to work. But what exactly was 'work'?

He walked along the path eagerly, enjoying the beautiful May morning and the fresh air – so unlike the polluted smog outside the city's protective dome. In Jared's home town, the 'park' was a tiny rooftop garden. Gruneburg Park was the only large park in western Germany and most people had to wait years for permission to visit.

He passed other walkers, alone, in pairs and groups. Three people were jogging, in the old-fashioned way! Jared heard them chatting as they passed, and realized with a shock that he didn't understand them. The universal translator microchip in his brain had been turned off! He tried to pick out different languages as he walked and listened. He thought he heard Chinese, English and possibly even a couple speaking German, just like his grandparents used to.

Jared remembered that he hadn't had any breakfast. Luckily, he could see a food dispenser ahead. As he approached it, Jared realized that it wasn't just an automatic food dispenser, it was a traditional sausage stand – with two real human servers cooking and serving the food! There was even real coffee in paper cups. It all smelled and looked delicious. His heart beating quickly, Jared ordered a currywurst and a black coffee.

Sitting on a bench by the small lake, Jared sighed contentedly. He wondered what to do with the empty cup and paper plate. He asked a young woman who was passing, carrying a strange metal object on her shoulder, like a fork for eating with, only much, much bigger. Jared guessed that it must be some sort of gardening tool, and that the young woman was a park gardener. How exciting to work with your hands, and maybe even get dirty!

'Just throw them on the grass,' explained the woman patiently. 'That's what they used to do, in the old days.'

It seemed a bit strange, but Jared did as he was told. He sat on the bench for a while longer, watching people walking by, and occasionally greeting them if they looked nice. It was such a thrill when they replied in some strange foreign language that he couldn't understand.

Jared blinked twice quickly to call up the virtual reality information screen in his left eye. '10.45 a.m. on Monday, 3 May 2067' read the screen. A quarter to eleven – surely he was late for work? Jared tried to remember what the induction programme in the pod had told him. And what was 'work'?

Just then a middle-aged woman sat down next to Jared. 'Hello, Jared,' she said in a soft voice. 'I'm your boss, Celia Hoffman. How was your first day at work? Feedback from the audience is 94% positive. They loved the currywurst! So authentic! It looks like you have a natural talent for proxy work. So – same time tomorrow?' (904 words)

A **It is Jared's first day at work. What will his job involve? How would you feel in Jared's situation? As you read the story, make notes. When you have finished, discuss your notes with a partner and report back to the class.**

B **What predictions does the story make about life in 2067? Copy and complete the mind map with information from the text.**

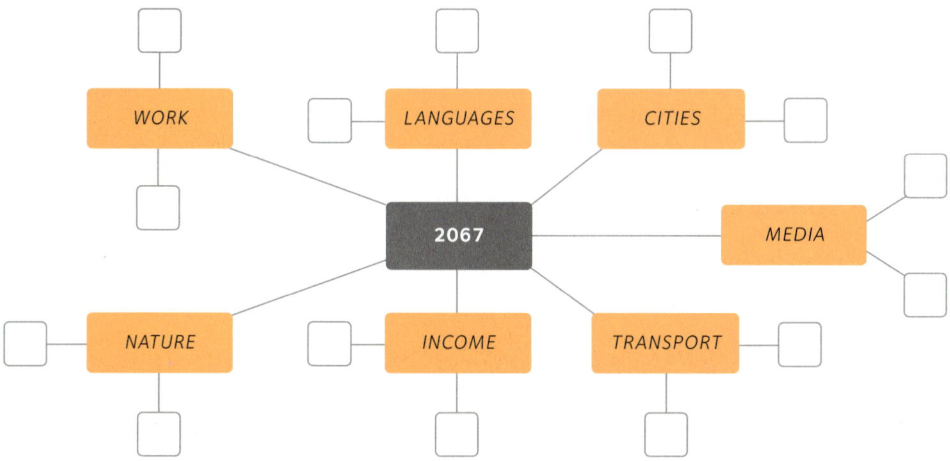

C **Class discussion. Do you think that these predictions are likely to come true? What other things in 2067 might be different to today? What might be the same?**

D **Imagine you can communicate with Jared: what do you want to know about his life?**

1 Write three questions for Jared. Use three different types of verb forms or question words.
2 Give your questions to a partner. Write answers to your partner's questions as if you are Jared.

3 WRITING A SHORT STORY

→ Eine Geschichte zu einem Bild schreiben, S. 240

These two photos show two more of Jared's work assignments. Choose ONE photo and write a story about Jared's next day at work. Write about 150 words.

It is your first day as a trainee. The company's Human Resources Manager, Karen Wade, presents an induction programme for all new employees.

48

1 LISTENING: THE INDUCTION PROGRAMME

Listen as Karen Wade introduces the induction programme. Make notes about the following topics.

1 Contents of the induction
2 When and how you should contact Karen
3 Role of the Human Resources department

2 UNDERSTANDING COMPANY STRUCTURE

You are given a handout with the company's organizational chart. Match the descriptions of functions to the chart. There are two descriptions that you do not need. What might these departments be called?

1 Prepare information about income and spending.
2 Manufacture the company's products.
3 Take decisions about the company's main aims and the allocation of resources.
4 Design and test new products.
5 Maintain and upgrade computer systems, provide computer access to employees.
6 Check the quality of finished products and the efficiency of processes.
7 Communicate with the company's customers.
8 Supply the company's products to its customers.
9 Look after the interests of employees, recruit new employees and organize training.
10 Buy components and raw materials and store them until they are needed.

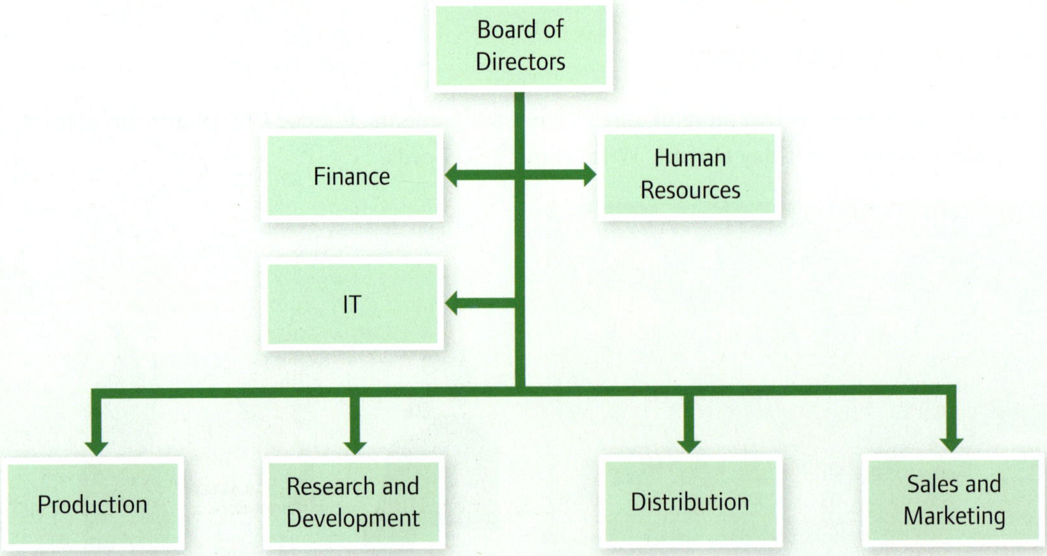

3 LISTENING: UNDERSTANDING HOW YOU FIT IN

49

Listen as Karen Wade explains a typical department structure. Copy and complete the chart using words from the box. You will need some words more than once.

manager ▪ members ▪ mentor ▪ supervisor ▪ team ▪ trainees

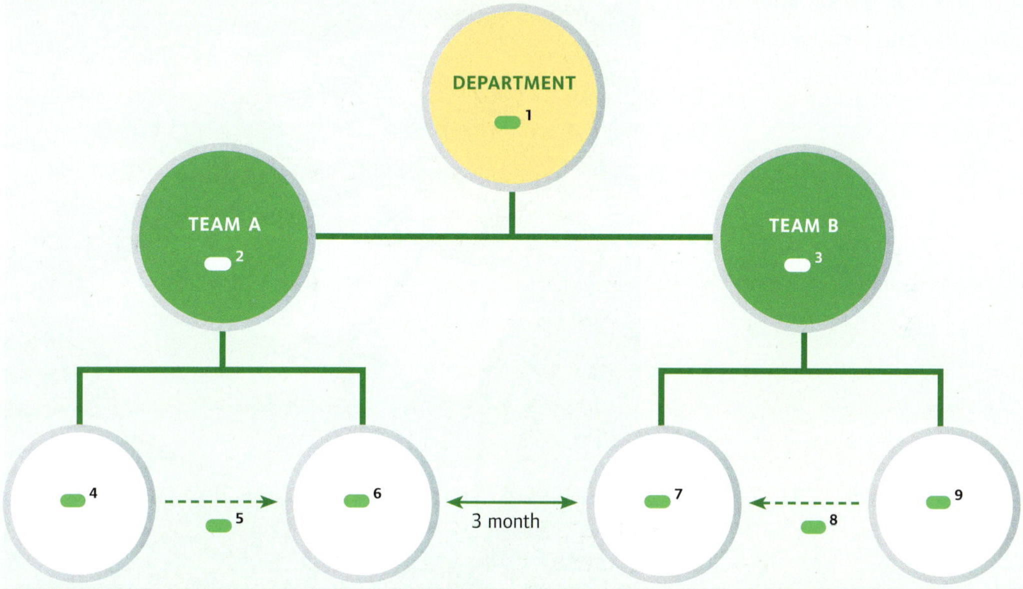

4 THINK – PAIR – SHARE

Think: Look back at tasks 1–3. What other information would you like to have today, as a trainee? Make a list of five questions to ask Karen.
Pair: Compare questions with a partner and choose the three questions that you agree are most important.
Share: Read out your list to the class. How many other pairs have the same questions? Do any have questions which are better than yours?

5 RESEARCH AND PRESENTATION

A Work in a small group. Research an organization that you would like to work for. Find out:

- number of employees
- location of head office
- locations of branches
- main business (services, products, etc.)
- employment opportunities
- other useful information (check your notes for task 4)

B Prepare and present a short introduction to the organization as part of an induction programme.

15 EXAM SKILLS PRACTICE Writing

1 COMMENTING ON A PHOTO

Write about 150 words.

Comment on the photo:

- Describe the photo.
- Give your opinion of it.
- Comment on the situation in Germany and what you think should be done about it.

Fridge and industrial waste dumped on the South Wales coast

2 WRITING

> 'Take risks: if you win, you will be happy; if you lose, you will be wise.'
> Anonymous

Respond to the statement. Write about 150 words.

Here are some ideas for your text.

- Reasons for taking risks
- Possible consequences of risky behaviour
- Healthy and unhealthy risks
- Are you a risk taker? Explain why or why not.

3 LISTEN AND COMPLETE THE TABLE

50

You are going to listen to a youth radio phone-in about leisure time and school work. Copy the table below into your exercise book. Listen to their conversation and take notes.

Jack's experiences and plans regarding school work and leisure	Lucy's experiences last year
...	...
...	...
...	...
...	...
...	...
...	...
...	...
Lucy's advice to Jack	
...	

4 LISTEN AND TAKE NOTES

51

Leoni Krüger has applied for a job with the American company RTA Automotive. She has been invited to an interview. Erica Stevens from RTA leaves a message on Leoni's voicemail about the arrangements for her interview.

Listen to the recording and answer the questions in note form.

1 When and where will the interview take place? (date, place, time)
2 What should Leoni do when she arrives at the hotel?
3 What will happen when she arrives? (four things)
4 What will happen in the group interviews and why?
5 What can Leoni do during lunch?
6 What will happen after lunch and when will it finish?

15 REVISION

Conditionals sentences (S. 256)

A Complete the conditional sentences using the correct forms of the verbs.

Conditional sentences type 1

1 If it *rains* (rain), I ___ (stay) at home today.
2 If our car ___ (break down), we ___ (call) a motor mechanic.
3 If robots ___ (do) most of the work in future, there ___ (not be) many jobs for humans.
4 We *will make* (make) your position permanent if you ___ (complete) the trial period successfully.
5 I ___ (be) happy to help you if you ___ (have) any questions.
6 You ___ (not make) a good impression if you ___ (be) late for work on your first day.

Conditional sentences type 2

7 If I *had* (have) the money to go travelling, I ___ (explore) South America.
8 If I ___ (try) busking, I ___ (earn) lots of money.
9 If there ___ (be) a universal income, some people ___ (not work) at all.
10 I *wouldn't like* (not like) the long winter nights if I ___ (live) in Alaska.
11 Anja ___ (want) to see crocodiles and snakes if she ___ (go) to Australia.
12 I ___ (get) to know all the locals if I ___ (live) in a little community in the bush.

Conditional sentences type 3

13 If Anna *had been* (be) pregnant before their trip, she and Fabian ___ (stay) at home.
14 If Lukas ___ (have) less confidence, he ___ (not go) travelling by himself.
15 If Jared ___ (listen) carefully during the induction, he ___ (know) what to do.
16 Fabian *would have studied* (study) engineering if he ___ (be) better at maths.
17 Hitomi ___ (have) more difficulty getting a job if she ___ (not be) a qualified chef.
18 She ___ (become) bored if she ___ (stay) in her comfort zone.

B Translate the sentences into English. (Remember to use "if", not "when".)

1 Wenn ich ein Visum bekomme, werde ich in Neuseeland arbeiten.
2 Wird Lukas als Krankenpfleger arbeiten, wenn seine Qualifikationen anerkannt werden?
3 Wir werden froh sein, wenn wir eine gute Abschlussnote (final grade) erhalten.
4 Wenn ich Gitarre spielen könnte (be able to play), würde ich mal auf der Straße spielen (try busking).
5 Würdest du nervös sein, wenn heute dein erster Arbeitstag (day at work) wäre?
6 Wenn ich Automechaniker/in wäre, könnte ich mein Auto selber reparieren.
7 Wenn ich Annas Blog nicht gelesen hätte, wäre ich nicht auf die Idee eines Australienaufenthalts gekommen (think of a trip to Australia).
8 Ich wäre sofort nach Hause zurückgekehrt, wenn man mich auf meiner Weltreise (while globetrotting) überfallen hätte.
9 Was hättest du gemacht, wenn dir so etwas passiert wäre?
10 Wenn mir so etwas passiert wäre, wäre ich trotzdem weitergereist. (still carry on travelling)

APPENDIX

FILE 4 Unit 3, Section B, Task 3B

→ page 38

A journalist asked another mother who gave up her child for adoption why she did so. Read the mother's answers and then complete the journalist's questions with the correct form of the verb.

1 Why ▬ (you – give up) the child for adoption?
I gave up the child for adoption because I was very young.
2 How old ▬ (you – be)?
I was 18 years old.
3 ▬ (you – have) anybody to help you with the child?
No, I didn't have anyone help me.
4 ▬ (you – have) a job?
No, I didn't have a job.
5 How ▬ (you – find) the adoption agency?
Someone in my church told me about the adoption agency.
6 Why ▬ (you – refuse) to meet your child?
I refused to meet my child because I have another family now.

FILE 5 Unit 3, The World of Work, Task 3B

→ page 43

In the four columns below you can see the expressions Karin and Andy use in their discussion. Decide which heading to give them:

Agreeing ▪ Asking for an opinion ▪ Disagreeing ▪ Introducing your opinion

▬	▬	▬	▬
That's a good idea. That sounds good. I agree with you that … I think you are right that … That's a good idea.	The problem with that is … I don't think that … I disagree with you.	Let's have your thoughts on the matter. Have you thought about …? Let's discuss …	I think that … is the best option. The main advantage is that … Another point I would like to make is … Can I suggest that …?

FILE 6 Unit 4, The World of Work, Task 1A

→ page 52

Listen to the trainer and complete the notes below using words from the text. Use one word for each gap. The first two gaps have been done for you.

Behaviour	Chinese people	You
1 Greetings	shake hands when they meet people	Wait until the other person holds out his/her *hand*[a], then look in the other person's *eyes*[b] when you shake hands.
2 Clothes	dressed in ___[a] clothes	Wear smart clothes. Do not wear bright colours, ___[b] or T-shirts. Women should not wear low cut ___[c].
3 Body language	do not like ___[a] ___[b]	After you have shaken hands, do not ___[c] them again.
4 Being prepared	it is likely they have done ___[a] on the places they will visit	Make sure you can give basic details of your ___[b] ___[c].
5 Language	probably won't speak good ___[a]	Speak ___[b] and ___[c]. Repeat things if necessary.

FILE 7 Unit 6, Section B, Task 3B

→ page 68

Choose the correct word or phrase from the brackets to complete the texts.

a The smallholder was lonely. He had (few / a little / little)[1] friends. He asked Dylan to spend (a few / a little / a few of)[2] time with him in the evenings. Dylan knew that the man had only (few / a few / little)[3] years left to live. He was happy to give him (a few / little / a little)[4] hours of his time every week.

b It is of (little / a few / a little)[1] importance how much money you have if you're not happy. (A few / A little / A few of)[2] Dylan's friends thought he was crazy to give up his job. Dylan only needed (few / a few / a little)[3] weeks to get used to living without money. Slowly, (a little / a few / few)[4] people changed their minds about Dylan's idea. Dylan is working again. He earns only (few / little / a little)[5] money but he is happy.

FILE 8 Unit 6, Section B, Task 6

→ page 69

At one point during the TED talk, the speaker says: "Anyone can get used to living without money." Comment on this statement in around 150 words.
Another student has made notes for their comment. Work with a partner and put the notes in the correct order.

1 *Among the people who are interested in trying out a moneyless life, putting the idea into practice might be difficult.*
2 *Apart from the challenge of finding food to eat, some people might not be able to give up the comfort of hot and cold running water.*
3 *Even someone who is not a big consumer needs money.*
4 *First of all, not everyone wants to live without money. Second, even people who would like to try the idea might have difficulties adapting to the moneyless way of life.*
5 *I disagree with the statement.*
6 *In my opinion, many people enjoy having money. They like to be able to spend it on clothes and products that suit the life they lead.*
7 *I suggest that the statement "Anyone can get used to living without money" should continue with, "if they want to and feel they are up to the challenge.".*
8 *These are just a few of the reasons why a moneyless life is not for everyone.*

FILE 9 Unit 8, Section B, Task 5

→ page 89

Write a comment for your online leisure group about livestreaming. Before you write, make a mind map. Include relevant ideas from the text on page 87, then add your own ideas. Write about 150 words. Include the following points:

- different ways to use livestreaming
- advantages of using livestreaming
- disadvantages of using livestreaming
- reasons why some people are against it

Don't forget to give your own opinion.

You could start like this:
Hello everyone! I've done some research into livestreaming and I've thought about how we can use it in our group. Here's what I've found out.

Finish these paragraphs with your own ideas:
We can use livestreaming to …
There are several advantages to using livestreaming. People like it because …
On the other hand, some people are against livestreaming. They …
In my opinion, we should …

FILE 10 Unit 8, Section C, Task 3

→ page 91

Look at the two graphs on page 91. Write a short description of the information in the graphs. Use some of these sentences and expressions to structure your description.

The two graphs show … . The top graph gives the number of … each year from … to … .
The lower graph gives … in … per … from … to … .
If we look at the top graph first, we can see that … .
… reached their lowest point in … .
… started to rise after … .
… rose rapidly until … .
… levelled off from … to … .
… started to rise again in … .
… rose rapidly.
Comparing this to the bottom graph we find that … .
… increased rapidly after … .
… levelled off from … to … .
… increased again after … .
The graphs show (similar /different) patterns. This suggests that there (may / may not) be a connection between … and … .

FILE 11 Unit 9, Section B, Task 3B

→ page 100

Match the consequences in the box to the conditions in the *if*-clauses. Write complete sentences. There may be more than one possibility.

find interesting people to stay with ▪ have problems at the campsite ▪ like a Youth Discovery holiday ▪ meet other young tourists ▪ need some British money ▪ not enjoy camping

1 If you go to the UK on holiday, …
2 If you enjoy being outdoors, …
3 If the weather isn't good, …
4 … if you stay in a hostel.
5 … if you look on the Couchsurfing website.
6 … if you go with a big group of teenagers.

FILE 12 Unit 9, Section B, Task 5

→ page 101

Ihre Gruppe besteht aus acht Jugendlichen. Sie sind alle 16–17 Jahre alt. Sie wollen zwei Wochen in Großbritannien verbringen. Die Unterkunft sollte möglichst preiswert sein.

Informieren Sie Ihre Gruppe in einer E-Mail über relevante Möglichkeiten aus dem Text auf Seite 99. Erwähnen Sie dabei die Vor- und Nachteile, die im Text genannt werden. Schreiben Sie ca. 150 Wörter. Fangen Sie so an:

> Hallo Leute!
>
> Ich habe gerade einen Artikel über Unterkünfte in Großbritannien gelesen. Ich habe Folgendes herausgefunden:
>
> Wir können in einer Herberge übernachten. Sie ist …
> Der einzige Nachteil ist, …

FILE 13 Unit 10, Section B, Task 2C, Question 2

→ page 112

How does Sophie's attitude change during the course of the text, and why?
Hint: These important points in the text tell you what Sophie is thinking:

I was very excited.
I was disappointed.
It was terrifying.
The opening ceremony was amazing.
I realized I was enjoying myself.
It was thrilling.

FILE 14 Unit 10, Section B, Task 2C, Question 3

→ page 112

What kind of person is Mr Duncan? Find evidence in the text to support your opinion.
Hint: These important points in the text tell you what Mr Duncan is like.

Mr Duncan had bought tickets for the first game of the NFL season.
Mr Duncan patiently explained the rules of football to me …
I couldn't disappoint the Duncans, who had been so kind to me.
Mr Duncan rushed down to the fast food stands to get us something to eat and drink.
Dad doesn't really like football. He just wanted to take you to a game, as you're such a fan.

FILE 15 Unit 11, Section B, Task 3B

→ page 124

Copy and complete the flow chart to show the life cycle of a paper coffee cup in eight steps. Add the verb in the passive form. Some verbs can be used twice and interchanged.

coat ▪ ~~cut~~ ▪ deliver ▪ make ▪ process ▪ send ▪ serve ▪ throw ▪ treat ▪ turn

1. Trees are *cut* down and are … into wood chips.
2. Wood chips are … into pulp.
3. Pulp is … with chemicals and is … into paper.
4. Paper is … into cups.
5. Cups are … with plastic.
6. Boxes of cups are … to coffee shops.
7. Drinks are … in cups.
8. Cups are … away and are … to landfills.

FILE 16 Unit 12, Section B, Task 5, Part 2

→ page 137

Write a short text. It could be in the form of questions to the reader, or statements, or (invented) quotations from people who have learned English as a foreign language. You can use one or more of these ideas in your short text.

Provocative questions:

Do you want to …?
Do you enjoy …-ing …?
Have you ever dreamed of …-ing …?
Do your career goals include …?
Then you need to learn English!

Personal testimony (with the name of the person):

When I started learning English, I had no idea that …
Now I know that …
I really enjoy …
I plan to …

Persuasive facts:

Did you know that …?
English is spoken …
Companies expect …
… per cent of web pages …
Clearly, it's essential to … if you want to …

FILE 17 Unit 13, Section B, Task 7

→ page 149

Write an essay on the topic: "Graffiti – street art or vandalism?" Write about 200 words. Consider both sides of the argument, then give your own opinion and justify it. You can use the ideas below to structure your essay. Use signposting expressions (*Wegweiser*) to help the reader understand your argument.

Introduction

Graffiti – street art or vandalism? It is a controversial question with strong feelings on both sides. Let's look at …

Main part

On the one hand, …

- make less "anonymous"
- less boring than bare concrete
- creative
- famous graffiti sprayers = artists, e.g. Banksy

On the other hand, …

- damage property
- make people feel unsafe
- make area look "run down" and ugly
- against the law

Conclusion

To sum up, we have looked at …
My personal opinion is …

FILE 18 Unit 14, Section C, Task 4

→ page 163

Describe the cartoon. What can you see? What is happening? What is the cartoon's message? You can use these sentence beginnings to structure your description.

In the foreground, two …
They are looking …
One of the figures is saying to the other …
In the distance, we can see …
This probably refers to the time when …
The cartoon reflects the fact that …
The cartoonist seems to be suggesting that …

Vocabulary that may be useful:

native people ▪ sailing ship ▪ first contact ▪ colonization ▪ exploration ▪ exploitation ▪ immigrant ▪ negative experience

FILE 19 Unit 15, Section B, Task 4

→ page 172

Hier sind einige Informationen, die Sie bei der Recherche herausgefunden haben. Ergänzen Sie noch eine Arbeitsstelle und drei Erlebnisse und schreiben Sie dann Ihre Webseite auf Englisch.

Wo man arbeiten könnte	Was man erleben sollte
in einem Landhotel	das Nachtleben in Berlin
auf einem Bauernhof	das Oktoberfest in München
in einem Call-Center	
in einem Start-up	

Files for group discussion

FILE 1 Unit 3, World of Work, Task 4 → page 43

Music Nights 1

- Youngsters use a game console like "We Sing" to sing their favourite songs. You can sing alone or with a partner. There is a vote for the best singer.
- Adults do not need to help the youngsters.
- Price of a console: £28.95

Smartphone photography course 2

- Every week youngsters learn a new area about digital photography, e.g. how to use different apps, how to frame an object or person so that the photo looks great, how to use light, etc.
- Youngsters know a lot about photography and can tell others about tricks that they know.
- Youngsters need a smartphone for the course.
- An adult with experience will teach the course. He gets some money for his work.
- At the end of the course the youngsters vote on the best photo taken by a member.

Fabulous Fashion Fun 3

- The youngsters learn to sew and alter clothes.
- They visit charity shops to look for clothes that they can improve.
- They have a volunteer from the local art college who shows them how to design and improve old clothes.
- A sewing machine is needed.
- Youngsters need to have pocket money to buy second-hand clothes.

Out on the water! 4

- Once a week youngsters learn to SUP (stand up paddle boarding) or kayak. This is a fun activity. It helps people keep fit.
- The course takes place at Highland Waters, about 10km from town.
- The course lasts 10 weeks and costs £75 (normal price is £250).
- Highland Waters provides all the equipment.

Who we are 5

- Teenagers find out about their community.
- Teenagers visit local shops and talk to the shopkeepers about their business.
- They visit churches, mosques, and temples and discuss problems and issues with local religious leaders.
- They visit old people and help them to cook or shop. The old people talk about their life experiences and the young people tell them what it is like to be young today.

FILE 2 Unit 11, Section B, Task 5

→ page 125

Replace vending machines with capsule-based system
Pod systems use individual capsules of coffee or tea concentrate. Pods can come in the form of aluminium capsules or paper coffee bags, both of which are easily recyclable.
Pods produce better tasting drinks than vending machines and can be used with ceramic cups. Some companies run their own recycling programme, where they pick up used capsules for reuse.

1

Replace vending machines with large filter machines
Even vending machines need to be thrown out at some stage, thereby causing environmental waste. Students can bring in their favourite ceramic cup from home. This reduces waste of natural resources and rubbish which cannot be recycled.

2

Get local cafés or coffee stations involved
Ask cafés to sell reusable plastic cups. When customers bring back the cup for re-use, they get a discount. This reduces the amount of waste going into the environment if enough students take up the offer.

3

Get new vending machines
There are vending machines that use recyclable paper cups or even recyclable plastic cups. The school needs to find a company that will sell one at a reasonable price. While they still use a lot of resources, they are a step in the right direction.

4

Remove vending machines altogether
It is not the school's responsibility to offer drinks to students. Putting up vending machines encourages students to waste more resources. If the students really need a drink, there is water in the taps, or they can bring in a thermos of coffee or tea.

5

01

Unit 1, Section C, Task 5

→ page 21

FIRST VEGETARIAN SCHOOL IN THE US

In America's battle against rising obesity rates, one primary school is trying a new tactic. It's become the nation's first vegetarian public school.

1 Read the information about the video above and then watch the video. Match the statements (1–5) to four people (a–d) who speak in the video. There is one statement more than you need.

1. Children need meat. It makes them strong and it helps them grow.
2. I like the salad bar. They have carrots, and I eat the carrots.
3. I really like this concept because my kids are getting healthy food here, a healthy diet here.
4. Right now, there are kids who are 8 years old on blood pressure lowering medicine and cholesterol lowering medicine.
5. We've grown to work on something so much bigger than just vegetarian meals and to create a healthy lifestyle and teach our kids about healthy living.

a Amie Hamlin, director of the NY Coalition for Healthy School Foods
b Anthony, a student at the school
c a parent
d Robert Groff, school principal

2 Complete the sentences from the video with words and phrases from the box.

100% vegetarian ▪ Asian and Indian ▪ balanced diet ▪ eight other schools ▪ health risks ▪ in the minority ▪ meat and fish ▪ nutrition

1. In this New York primary school, all the meals served are ___.
2. This is the first time a US school has removed ___ from its menus.
3. Students also have lessons on ___[a], where they're taught how to have a ___[b].
4. Child obesity in the US has doubled over the last 30 years, bringing huge ___.
5. 70% of students are from ___ backgrounds, where vegetarianism is more common.
6. Those who can't do without meat are allowed to bring in food from home, but such students are ___.
7. Now, ___ in New York have decided to go vegetarian.

02

Unit 4, Section C, Task 4

→ page 51

MATT DAMON CALLS FOR ACTION ON CLEAN WATER ACCESS

1 A German journalist at Davos mediated some parts of Matt Damon's speech. Match Matt Damon's soundbites (1–6) to the gist of what he says (a–f). The soundbites are in the order that you hear them in the video.

1 Water and sanitation undergirded everything.
2 The magnitude of the problem was mind-blowing.
3 The problem is solvable.
4 It animates their entire lives.
5 It's robbing people of their potential.
6 If we make this comprehensive effort, we can end this crisis.

a Das Problem ist lösbar.
b Die Größe des Problems war atemberaubend.
c Es bestimmt ihr ganzes Leben.
d Es raubt den Menschen Möglichkeiten.
e Wasser und sanitäre Anlagen unterstützten alles.
f Wenn wir diese umfangreiche Aufgabe angehen, können wir diese Krise beenden.

2 Choose one word or phrase from the box to complete the notes. There are two words more than you need. The first answer has been done for you.

are thinking about ▪ complex ▪ get educated ▪ in our lifetime ▪ interested ▪ interesting ▪ learning ▪ shocked ▪ west ▪ USA

1 Some years ago, Matt Damon was *learning*[a] and trying to *get educated*[b] about issues of poverty.
2 He was ___ by how water and sanitation problems surrounded everything.
3 Apart from "mind-blowing", he described the problems as endlessly ___[a] and ___[b].
4 Those of us who live in the ___ solved the problem of clean water and sanitation years ago.
5 When you don't have access to water, it's the only thing you ___.
6 According to Matt Damon, we can end the crisis ___.

03

Unit 6, Section B, Task 5

→ page 69

FRANCE PONDERS OPENING SHOPS ON SUNDAYS DESPITE TRADITION

The French government wants shops to open on more Sundays to boost consumption in an economy in need of a lift.

1 Listen to the opinions of the speakers in the video and complete the following statements with words and expressions from the box. There is one word for each gap.

buy something ▪ buyers ▪ convenient ▪ do your shopping ▪ during the week ▪ family ▪ need ▪ sacred ▪ shop ▪ stays open ▪ to shop ▪ walks ▪ work

The shopper from …

1. Belgium says: "This could make people want [a], even if they didn't plan to. The shop is open, you go in and maybe [b]."
2. the USA says: "I understand why Sunday is so [a] in France and all that, but I think we're at a crossroads now where people [b] to shop and people are busy and Sunday's a great day and it'd be great if the store [c]."
3. Tours (France) says: "It's more [a] for everyone, we're happy to run errands on Sunday because [b] we don't have the time."
4. Portugal says: "I think it's worse for the people who [a], but for the [b] it's good because during the week it's difficult. On Sunday you can [c] more comfortably."
5. China says: "Sunday is a [a] day, we go out for [b]. Besides I work in a [c], I wouldn't like it very much if I had to work."

2 Talk in groups and give your opinion. Use words and expressions from the video if you can. Here are some points to get you started. Report back to the class.

- How often are shops open on Sundays in your area?
- How often do you go shopping when the shops are open on Sundays?
- What do you usually do on Sundays?

04

Unit 9, Section C, Task 3

→ page 103

TOURIST LONDON

1 Watch the video and put these attractions in the order in which the presenter talks about them. Two are not mentioned.

double-decker bus tours ▪ Buckingham Palace ▪ the London Eye ▪ the Monument ▪ the Palace of Westminster ▪ Parliament Clock Tower ▪ Tower Bridge

2 Answer the questions to check how much you remembered. Then watch the video again to check your answers.

1. How long did it take to build Tower Bridge?
2. How high is the High-Level Walkway?
3. Why should you climb to the top of the Monument?
4. What is the more popular name for Parliament Clock Tower?
5. What does that name more accurately refer to?
6. How long has English politics been based in the Palace of Westminster?
7. What happened in 1834?
8. How much do British residents have to pay to visit Parliament?
9. What is special about the London Eye? (two things)
10. What is a good tip to avoid standing in a long queue for the London Eye?

3 Your class is planning a short city break in London. Which THREE of the sights shown in the video would you like to visit? Why?

4 What would you show in a tourist video of your area for British and American visitors? Think of six sights and write brief notes in English for the video production company about each one. Include the following information.

- What it is
- Where it is
- Why it is interesting / worth a visit
- Other details (Do you need to pay to get in? etc.)

05

Unit 10, Section C, Task 4

→ page 115

AUSTRALIANS CELEBRATE ANCIENT INDIGENOUS CULTURE

1 **Read the text from a newspaper and list the activities that visitors to the event can experience.**

NAIDOC in the City is here again!

NAIDOC in the City is an annual event that celebrates the indigenous peoples of Australia. Thousands of people will be attending Sydney's popular annual showcase of indigenous culture in Hyde Park on Monday 2 July.
The city of Sydney event will include a whole range of family-friendly activities and performances, including:

- live music
- dance performances
- kids zones
- a Gunya (a structure for living in made from natural materials)
- a marketplace for arts and crafts
- a sports clinic
- food stalls

The theme for **NAIDOC in the City** is "Our Languages Matter". The theme hopes to draw attention to the importance and richness of indigenous Australian languages.

2 **Watch the video. Which of the activities you listed in task 1 do you see in the video?**

3 **Complete this soundbite from the video:**

Matthew Doyle:
"It gives ___[1] around Australia an opportunity to ___[2] our culture, the ___[3] in the world, and to ___[4] and indeed with ___[5] to our shores."

4 **Use your answers to task 3 to write one sentence explaining to visitors what the celebrations are about.**

5 **Write a short review in German of the event for a travel website. Include the significance of the event, what you can see and do, and what it feels like to be there.**

06

Unit 13, Section B, Task 5

→ page 149

BERLIN ACTIVISTS TURN NAZI HATE GRAFFITI INTO ART

1 Watch the video, then answer the questions.

1 Who are the members of "cultural heirs"?
2 What do they do?
3 Who started the initiative?
4 How often do they go looking for graffiti?
5 What effect have they had so far?
6 When will they stop?

2 Discuss these questions in a small group. Make notes on your answers.

1 Does your area have a graffiti problem? If so: describe the sorts of graffiti you have seen and where it is. If not: why do you think this is the case?
2 What solutions can you think of to deal with a graffiti problem?
3 What approaches do not work, in your opinion?

3 Your English friend Dani lives in a city which has a lot of problems with racist graffiti.

> Hi,
>
> We have a terrible problem with racist graffiti in my area. It used to be a nice area but now there are racist slogans and symbols sprayed on a lot of the walls.
>
> As a young Asian British woman, it makes me feel very unsafe here. That is so unfair! This is my home and I belong here as much as anybody.
>
> The local council has tried various initiatives, but none of them have worked.
>
> Do you have similar problems in your area, and if so, what is being done about them? Do you have any suggestions?
>
> Please write back soon!
>
> Lots of love
> Dani

Write a reply to Dani. Describe to her the aims and methods of "Cultural heirs" group in Berlin and their initiative "Paintback" and assess its effectiveness. Make any other suggestions you discussed in task 2. Write about 150 words.

Further reading

UNIT 1

Canned food or fresh food – which is better for your health?

fresh vegetables

Many people believe that canned foods are less healthy than food that is freshly made. A recent university study compared both types of food and found out that, in a lot of cases, canned foods have similar amounts of vitamins and minerals as the same foods we buy fresh. Food from cans is also often a good source of protein and fibre.

The researchers tested dairy products, fish, fruit, vegetables, meat, pasta and soups. Here are some of the results.

Rice pudding: The canned dessert is lower in fat than homemade rice pudding, even when it's made with semi-skimmed milk. Both homemade and canned rice pudding have about the same amount of calcium, but stuff we buy in cans has three times as much vitamin E and twice as much iodine as the pudding we make at home.

Fish: The researchers found more calcium in canned fish than in fresh fish. This is because the canned fish producers leave some small bones in their products. The bones are soft, so we eat them and take in calcium from them. When they looked at tuna fish canned in salt water, they found it had less saturated fat than fresh tuna. Canned tuna was also a good source of vitamins D, B_{12} and B_6, niacin and phosphorus.

Vegetables: Canned peas give us twice as much beta-carotene as fresh peas and a third more calcium. Even though canned carrots do not have as much beta-carotene, thiamine and folate as fresh carrots, they still give us a similar amount of other vitamins and minerals.

The results of the study showed that you can eat canned foods and get the same amount of goodness as you get from eating fresh foods. As one of the researchers said, 'Canned food takes less time to prepare and cook than fresh foods so people who are too busy to prepare and cook fresh can still have a healthy diet using canned food.' (325 words)

13 semi-skimmed milk: *Halbfettmilch*
15 iodine: *Jod*
22 folate: *Folsäure*

frozen vegetables

canned vegetables

1 PREPARING TO READ

Study the highlighted words and expressions in the text and say which of them you …

- **a** know and how you know them. (For example, it's like a German word.)
- **b** can guess the meaning of. (How did you guess?)
- **c** need to look up in your dictionary. (Look them up now and add them to your vocabulary notebook.)

2 READING AND UNDERSTANDING THE TEXT

1. What did the studies compare? (2 items)
2. What was the result?
3. What types of foods did the researchers look at? (7 items)
4. Which is more nutritious, according to the research?
   - **a** canned rice pudding or homemade rice pudding?
   - **b** canned fish or fresh fish?
   - **c** canned peas or fresh peas?
5. Why should no one feel bad about eating canned foods?

3 WORKING WITH WORDS

Find nouns in the text to match the definitions below. The definitions are in the order the words appear in the text.

1. scientists who study things carefully and write reports about them
2. where we get something from
3. business people who make something …
4. … and the things they make
5. a skeleton (*Skelett*) has many of these
6. a large sea fish

4 A SUMMARY OF THE TEXT

Choose the best summary of the text.

1. According to two studies, fresh food always has more vitamins and minerals than canned food. If you have to, you can eat food from a can, but it won't be as good for you as fresh food.
2. Researchers found out that that canned food is just as good for you as fresh food. In some cases canned foods have more nutrients. If you don't have time to buy and prepare fresh food, you can open a can and still eat a healthy meal.
3. Two studies looked at canned food and fresh food. Canned food is quicker to prepare than homemade food. In some cases canned food contains just as many vitamins and minerals. However, it is not as healthy as fresh food.

UNIT 2

How to improve grades while having fun

A recent US survey of 14–18-year-olds shows that high-school students who play a team sport are likely to get better grades than other students.

Academics from two US universities studied data from 9,700 students from schools in urban, suburban and rural areas. All of the students took part in different types of after-school activities, including music, dance and acting societies, clubs that prepared students for jobs, and team sports.

The academics looked for connections between the types of after-school activities and how the teenagers performed in tests and exams at school.

What they discovered was that students who took part in team sports did better than those who took part in other activities. Three of the most interesting results showed that

- students who play team sports are more successful in day-to-day learning in the classroom;
- young people who take part in sport have the self-esteem and determination that makes them more likely to succeed academically than those who prefer other types of activities;
- teenagers who belong to sports clubs are more likely to complete their high-school years and enter higher education than their peers.

One of the academics on the study said: 'Sport allows young people to develop a mentoring relationship with adults and with other students who have a positive feeling about school. These people encourage the others to become more focused on school work. They may also help people develop time-management skills and the ability to deal with problems. Team sports also help young people learn how to work with others.' (256 words)

03 **academic:** *Wissenschaftler/in*
17 **academically:** *in der Schule, im Studium*
23 **mentoring relationship:** *Mentorverhältnis*
26 **time-management skills:** *Zeitmanagementkompetenz*

1 PREPARING TO READ

Study the headline and the photo. What will the text tell us?

1. After-school activities help students make friends.
2. Doing sports after class helps pupils do better at school.
3. Hanging around with friends makes learning easier.

2 READING AND UNDERSTANDING THE TEXT

True or false. Read the text and decide if the following statements are true or false. Explain your answers in German.

1 The report is about a survey of American university students.
2 Only students who do sports activities after school took part in the survey.
3 According to the study, students who play competitive team sports are good learners.
4 Playing in a team helps students to build up their confidence and will-power.
5 Students who play sport often drop out of school.
6 Students who do sports often help other people improve their business and people skills.

3 WORKING WITH WORDS

Decide which word does not belong in the group. Say why.

1	grade	mark	note	score
2	exercise	games	plays	sport
3	college	education	school	university
4	abilities	competences	energy	skills

4 DESCRIBING A PHOTO

Choose the best description of the photo on page 202.

A The photo shows a group of teenagers sitting with an older man on a football pitch. The teenagers are listening carefully to the man. Everyone looks serious. I think the man is asking the teenagers what they think about the game so far. The other teenagers in the background may be waiting for the man to invite them to join the group.

B The photo shows a group of teenage boys sitting with a man on a football pitch. The teenagers are listening carefully to the man. He may be their coach. I think the man is giving the teenagers tips about how to improve their game. The other teenagers in the background may be members of the opposing team.

C The photo shows a group of students sitting outside in the sunshine with a man who may be their sports teacher. The members of the group are talking to the man. They may be asking him questions about how to play football. In the background, we can see goal posts and a net. There are other teenagers in the background. They are probably waiting for the man to stop talking so that they can start playing.

UNIT 3

Who should your child's role model be?

My daughter has been studying heroes at school this term. She's in Year One, and one day after school she said to me: 'Our teacher asked us to pick a real-life superhero. You know, a person we know who does great things. She said we could choose someone like our mum or dad.'

'Oh?' I said, warming with pride, figuring I might just have the competitive edge on my husband. He taught our daughter how to ride a bike, makes wonderful pizza with her from scratch and runs his own business, all of which is admirable.

But I am, as George W Bush once put it, 'the decider' in our family. I also not-so-long-ago took my daughter with me on a work trip to Kenya, and there were giraffes, which I felt sure would swing the competition in my favour.

'We had to explain who our superhero was, and draw a picture of them using their power,' she said, smiling. 'So, of course, I chose Ellie.'

Ellie is my sister-in-law.

'But it's hard to draw someone being the kindest person in the world, and thinking of other people before themselves and helping me make great art. So I just drew her looking cool – which is also a sort of power,' my daughter mused.

So much for my super-human status. […]

As parents, we want our children to pick good role models. Ellie is a teacher, a businesswoman, a problem-solver extraordinaire. She's a mother, a wife, and a friend to gazillions of people. And she brings an infectious enthusiasm to almost anything she does. She also talks to children as if their opinion matters.

So, ego aside, I'm thrilled that my daughter wants to emulate her aunt. And I hope that, like her aunt, she'll rock the boat a bit, and help diversify the heroes out there – wouldn't it be something if kindness were a superpower that we all wanted to have? And wouldn't it also be grand if, in two years' time, when my son encounters the same school assignment, he also chooses his aunt?

Source: Sally Peck, *The Daily Telegraph*, 13 July 2017; 344 words

- 08 **competitive edge:** *Wettbewerbsvorteil*
- 10 **from scratch:** *ohne Fertigprodukte*
- 12 **the decider:** *der/die Entscheider/in*
- 22 **to muse:** *sinnieren*
- 23 **super-human:** *übermenschlich*
- 25 **problem-solver extraordinaire:** *Problemlöser/in der Extraklasse*
- 25 **gazillions:** *(informal) abertausende*
- 28 **to emulate:** *nacheifern*
- 29 **to rock the boat:** *Staub aufwirbeln*
- 29 **to diversify:** *mannigfaltig machen*

1 READING AND UNDERSTANDING THE TEXT

Make notes on the following questions.

1 What is a superhero?
2 Who did the child choose as her superhero?
3 How many different roles does this "superhero" play in real life? (6 aspects)
4 What are two of the characteristics that make her a good role model, especially for children?
5 How does the writer of the article feel about her daughter's choice, and why?

2 WORKING WITH WORDS: DESCRIBING FAMILY RELATIONSHIPS

Some family relationships are mentioned in the text. Choose words from the box to describe the relationships below. There are more words than you need. The first one has been done for you.

aunt ▪ brother ▪ ~~daughter~~ ▪ husband ▪ nephew ▪ niece ▪ parents ▪ sister-in-law

1 The child who is doing the school project is the *daughter* of the woman who wrote the article.
2 Ellie is the child's ▬.
3 The child's father is the ▬ of the writer.
4 The writer of the article has a son. He's Ellie's ▬.
5 The son of the writer is the child's ▬.
6 The child's mum and dad are her ▬.

3 WHO SHOULD BE THE CHILD'S ROLE MODEL?

List the reasons as to who should be the role model, according to the text.

1 The father, because he ▬ (3 aspects)
2 The mother, because she ▬ (2 aspects)
3 Ellie, because she ▬ (3 aspects)

4 CORRECTING A LETTER

Someone has written a letter to the author of the article. Read the letter carefully and find six mistakes. Without looking back at the text, correct them.

Dear Sally Peck
I enjoyed reading your article about who a child's best friend should be and would like to share my feelings about the subject. Your son's teacher told the class that they could choose their mum or dad, so it's natural that you would think of yourself or your partner. He has taught your child skills, and you both show your child good examples of how to behave. In the end, your child chose your sister as a role model. As a single parent, she clearly knows how to help children. As you say yourself, she is a good role model. It certainly would be good if your son also chooses his aunt Eveyln when the assignment comes around to his class. (132 words)
Yours sincerely

UNIT 4

Malala named youngest ever UN Ambassador of Peace

Malala Yousafzai has been appointed the youngest ever United Nations' Messenger of Peace at a ceremony in New York.

The 19-year-old, who became the youngest person to win the Nobel peace prize in 2014, will take up the role with a special focus on girls' education.

Accepting the accolade on Monday, she said: 'Bringing change starts with us and it should start now. If you want to see your future bright, you have to start working now and not wait for anyone else.'

'The extremists tried their best to stop me, they tried to kill me and they didn't succeed. Now this is a new life, this is a second life and it is for the purpose of education.'

Ms Yousafzai, originally from Pakistan, was shot in the head in October 2012 on her way home from school in the Swat valley for speaking out against the Taliban and its ban on female education.

She [...] remains a prominent activist for female education. UN secretary-general Antonio Guterres said in a statement: 'Even in the face of grave danger, Malala Yousafzai has shown an unwavering commitment to the rights of women, girls and all people.

'Her courageous activism for girls' education has already energized so many people around the world. Now as our youngest ever UN Messenger of Peace, Malala can do even more to help create a more just and peaceful world.'

During the presentation, Mr Guterres described Ms Yousafzai as a 'symbol of perhaps the most important thing in the world – education for all'.

'You are not only a hero, but you are a very committed and generous person,' he added.

Source: Adam Boult, *The Daily Telegraph*, 11 April, 2017; 273 words

01 **Messenger of Peace:** *Friedensbotschafter/in*
05 **accolade:** *Auszeichnung*
11 **ban on female education:** *Verbot der Ausbildung von Frauen*
13 **in the face of grave danger:** *angesichts drohender Gefahr*
14 **unwavering commitment:** *unerschütterlicher Einsatz*
15 **to energize:** *Antrieb gegeben*

1 PREPARING TO READ

Did you know ...? Match names from the text to the facts. The names are in the same order as they appear in the text.

1 Malala Yousafzai ...
2 The United Nations ...
3 Alfred Nobel ...
4 Pakistan ...
5 The Taliban movement ...
6 Antonio Guterres ...

a ... became independent in 1947.
b ... has been working for education for girls since the age of 11.
c ... invented dynamite and other types of explosives.
d ... is from Portugal.
e ... was founded in 1945, after the Second World War.
f ... was founded in 1994.

2 WORKING WITH WORDS

Malala always speaks out about things she believes in. Match what she believes in (1–6) to her statements (a–f).

1 education
2 equality
3 fighting fear
4 standing up against the rulers who destroy our lives
5 taking political action
6 using social media for good

a Don't be afraid. If you are afraid, you can't move forward.
b Don't use Facebook to get "likes" – use it to highlight (*betonen*) women's issues.
c Instead of standing in front of Parliament why don't you go inside and bring the changes you want?
d Our leaders are choosing bombs and bullets over books and bright futures. And we are letting them.
e Pens and books are the weapons (*Waffen*) that defeat (*besiegen*) terrorism.
f We cannot all succeed when half of us are held back.

3 A GOOD MEDIATION

Two students have attempted to mediate the text for the school blog. Read their attempts and choose the better option in each case.

1 Malala wurde neulich zur bisher …
   a jüngsten Friedenbotschafterin der Vereinten Nationen und zur jüngsten Trägerin des Friedensnobelpreises ernannt.
   b jüngsten Friedenbotschafterin der Vereinten Nationen ernannt. 2014 war sie bereits der jüngste Mensch gewesen, der jemals den Friedensnobelpreis erhalten hatte.

2 Bei der Entgegennahme der UN-Auszeichnung erinnerte sie daran, dass …
   a Extremisten 2012 versucht hatten, sie zu ermorden, weil sie sich gegen das Taliban-Verbot der Ausbildung von Frauen ausgesprochen hatte. Ihr „zweites Leben" wolle sie nun Bildungsfragen widmen.
   b die Taliban 2012 versucht hatten, sie zu ermorden, weil sie sich gegen den Taliban-Terrorismus ausgesprochen hatte. Ihr „zweites Leben" wolle sie nun den Rechten für Frauen widmen.

3 UN-Generalsekretär Antonio Guterres betonte …
   a Malalas Einsatz für die Bildung aller Einwohner ihres Landes. Guterres beschrieb Malala als eines der besten Beispiele dafür, was geschehen kann, wenn Menschen Zugang zur Bildung ermöglicht wird.
   b Malalas mutigen und unerschütterlichen Einsatz für die Rechte aller Menschen. Guterres beschrieb Malala als Symbol der Bildung für alle Menschen – vielleicht die wichtigste Sache in der Welt.

UNIT 5

Helping kids without arms

From the outside, it's the most ordinary of garden sheds. But hidden within is a state-of-the-art workshop where a brilliant designer makes prosthetic arms to help scores of children.

Inventor Stephen Davies was himself born without a left lower arm and never forgot the stigma of the NHS prosthetic he wore as a child. After several years of not using one, the 43-year-old, from Swansea, began looking at designs available on the NHS – only to discover they had barely improved in three decades. More sophisticated bionic arms, which are not available on the NHS, can cost upwards of £30,000.

However, having learned how far lighter limbs could be created on a 3D printer, he began to experiment in his garden shed.

He has now set up Team UnLimbited, which creates customised 'cool' limbs for children, featuring their choice of colours and patterns.

The father of three said: '[...] The key is making something the child actually wants to wear and feels is cool enough to show their friends. Sometimes children with prosthetics get bullied at school and something like this can make a huge difference to their confidence.'

[...] Each arm costs about £30 to make, and takes a few days to print and assemble.

All are made in the shed which is insulated with solar-powered air-conditioning to keep it within the very narrow temperature range needed for the 3D printer to work.

Mr Davies – along with his partner, IT consultant Drew Murray [...] – never charge the children for the cost of the limbs, and have instead raised their costs through crowdfunding.

The first recipient was nine-year-old Isabella Jennings, from Bristol, who was born without a lower left arm. A YouTube video of her unwrapping her pink limb has had viewed more than two million times.

Her mother Sarah, 37, said: 'Before we heard about Stephen, Isabella had managed without a prosthetic, but it was always an option if she wanted one. She volunteered to be a guinea pig, but when she saw the arm she fell in love with it and adores wearing it.'

Isabella said the best thing about her prosthetic was she was now able to read heavy books. 'When I wore the arm to school, my friends thought it was so cool,' she added.

Source: Nick Craven, *The Mail on Sunday*, 20 May 2017; 385 words

- **01 garden shed:** *Gartenschuppen*
- **01 state-of-the-art:** *hochmodern, neuester Stand*
- **02 scores:** *viele*
- **04 stigma:** *Makel, Schandfleck*
- **04 NHS = National Health Service:** *staatlicher Gesundheitsdienst*
- **06 sophisticated:** *(technisch) hochentwickelt, ausgereift*
- **08 far lighter limbs:** *viel leichtere Gliedmaßen*
- **16 insulated:** *isoliert*
- **20 recipient:** *Empfänger/in*
- **24 guinea pig:** *(hier) Versuchsperson*

1 READING AND UNDERSTANDING THE TEXT

Who said what? Match the statements (1–6) to the people (a–d). There are two statements more than you need.

1 Every child who needs an arm gets one of the Team UnLimbited prosthetics.
2 Children with artificial limbs sometimes get picked on by other schoolkids.
3 Donations help Stephen and me continue helping kids without arms.
4 This small shed is lined with photos of children the design has helped.
5 Isabella has loved wearing her prosthetic arm since she first got it.
6 With my new arm I can read more easily.

a Drew Murray **b** Isabella Jennings **c** Sarah Jennings **d** Steven Davies

2 WORKING WITH WORDS

Without looking back at the text, match the words in column A with the words in column B to make collocations used in science and technology.

column A	
1	state-of-the-
2	bionic
3	3D
4	solar-
5	air-
7	IT

column B	
a	arms
b	art
c	conditioning
d	consultant
e	printer
f	powered

3 NOTES FOR A PRESENTATION

Someone has made notes for a presentation on Team UnLimbited and their work. Complete the notes using the expressions from the box. There are two expressions more than you need.

a 3D printer ▪ a garden shed ▪ available for free on the NHS ▪ charge their clients ▪ design ▪ donations ▪ films ▪ self-confident ▪ very expensive ▪ was born without the lower part of one arm

1 Steven Davies knows what it is like for a child to wear a prosthetic arm because he ▬.
2 Bionic arms are usually ▬.
3 Steven makes the limbs on ▬.
4 When they order their prosthetics, children can choose their own colour and ▬.
5 Steven uses ideas from ▬ and games the children know and like.
6 The prosthetics help the children feel ▬.
7 Steven and his partner do not ▬ for the prosthetic limbs.
8 The company is supported by ▬.

UNIT 6

Why shopping addiction can cost you more than money

The charity Consumer Credit Counselling Service deals with 50,000 people a year who have got into financial trouble because of their addiction.

So what causes some people to develop full-on buying frenzies? According to Paul Buckley, a consumer psychologist, shopping can be a way to displace negative feelings of sadness, anxiety and depression.

'Owning something new can take your mind off your other problems and give you a temporary lift. It is as if you are buying into a new and better persona,' he says.

But the lift is temporary and soon the depression returns and you are driven to go out to buy more to get that same high.

Kate's story

I can pinpoint the exact beginning of my shopping addiction. It was 10 years ago. […]

I was at the lowest point in my life, I felt worthless and my confidence was in tatters. To cheer me up a friend took me shopping. […]

It was so easy to get credit. I just filled in a form and there was another credit card almost begging me to use it. As I maxed out one card I simply got another one.

However it wasn't long before I started to feel the pinch and it was going into serious debt that was the real tipping point for me.

Last year a menacing letter arrived from a credit card company and the threat of having to go to court was a real wake-up call.

I took a long hard look at myself and managed for the first time in years to admit to myself the real reason why I shopped. I was lonely and objects filled the void.

Once I had said it out loud I felt I could do something about it.

'Acknowledging you have a problem is the first step in starting recovery,' says Paul, who advises that you ask a family friend for help.

I cut up all my credit cards and joined a gym. Now when I feel an urge to splurge I pound off my anxiety on the treadmill. It costs a fraction of the price and my legs have never looked better. I still have the odd weak shopping moment but most of the time my spending is firmly under control.

Source: Kate Mulvey, *The Daily Express*, 12 October 2015; 375 words

01 **to get into financial trouble:** *Geldprobleme bekommen*
03 **a full-on buying frenzy:** *ein Kaufrausch*
04 **displace negative feelings:** *negative Gefühle verdrängen*
06 **temporary lift:** *vorübergehender Auftrieb*
08 **to be driven to sth:** *zu etwas angetrieben werden*
11 **to pinpoint:** *genau bestimmen, lokalisieren*
12 **in tatters:** *in Fetzen, ruiniert*
15 **to max out:** *ausschöpfen*
16 **to feel the pinch:** *den Druck spüren*
17 **tipping point:** *Wendepunkt*
18 **menacing:** *bedrohlich*
19 **wake-up call:** *Weckruf*
21 **to fill the void:** *die Leere füllen*
25 **an urge to splurge:** *ein Verlangen, Geld verschwenderisch auszugeben*

1 READING AND UNDERSTANDING THE TEXT

Choose the most suitable option in each case.

1 The Consumer Credit Counselling Service helps people …
- **a** manage their credit card accounts.
- **b** who want to get loans.
- **c** who have money problems because they cannot stop shopping.
- **d** who don't know what to do with their money.

2 The psychologist says that shopping addicts …
- **a** like to look like other people.
- **b** don't feel good for long after they've been shopping.
- **c** often don't wear the clothes they buy.
- **d** usually feel bad about spending too much money.

3 Kate's shopping addiction started when she …
- **a** was ten years old.
- **b** started to go out with a shopping addict.
- **c** was stressed out at work.
- **d** was having a lot of personal problems.

4 Today, Kate …
- **a** feels lonely and does more sports activities.
- **b** has destroyed her credit cards and goes to therapy.
- **c** has swapped her credit cards for a gym membership card.
- **d** is afraid she will start to shop again.

2 WORKING WITH WORDS

Complete the mind map with words and expressions from the text.

UNIT 7

A recent study looked at the working lives of British employees. Here are some of the results.

Britons in the workplace

A ...

Mr or Ms Average will have three major bust-ups over the years, either with clients, colleagues or the boss; but small disagreements in the workplace will raise their ugly head more frequently at 15 times a year.
And though the typical employee will enjoy one office romance, a busy 6 per cent will rack up five or more.
With this in mind, it's no surprise that the average worker will hear six pieces of juicy gossip through the rumour mill.

B ...

2 bad bosses	94 sick days	9,024 hours of overtime
6 job roles	Late for work 141 times	29,328 cups of tea
9 pay rises	705 minor disagreements	

C ...

Mark Farrar, Chief Executive of the Association of Accounting Technicians, which commissioned the study, said, 'Our working lives see many ups and downs as we move up the ladder, deal with new challenges, or change job completely.
It's revealing to see that the average person will work for at least six different companies over a lifetime, proving that the traditional "job for life" may well be a thing of the past. People should always ensure they take up training opportunities and their skills are up to date, so they can be ready if they need to change job.'

D ...

Mr Farrar said, 'It's more common now to seek a sense of worth at work rather than see a job as just a way to pay the bills. Our surroundings, fellow colleagues and day-to-day tasks also have a huge influence on our job satisfaction. A huge number of adults reach a career point where they feel a change is needed. As the years go by, we learn more and more about what makes us happiest in our working life and the kind of roles and challenges that suit us best. Whether that means entering a whole new field, or aiming for a promotion in your company, there are options which can help your lifetime of employment work for you.'

Source: Lexi Finnigan, *The Daily Telegraph*, 4 November 2015; 326 words

- 02 **major bust-up:** *größere Auseinandersetzung*
- 03 **to raise its ugly head:** *ihr hässliches Haupt erheben*
- 05 **to rack up sth:** *etwas erzielen*
- 07 **juicy gossip:** *pikanter Tratsch*
- 08 **rumour mill:** *Gerüchteküche*
- 15 **to move up the ladder:** *aufsteigen*
- 17 **revealing:** *aufschlussreich*
- 18 **job for life:** *lebenslange Anstellung*
- 22 **sense of worth:** *Wertschätzung*

1 READING AND UNDERSTANDING THE TEXT

A Match the paragraph headings 1–5 to the sections A–D. There is one heading more than you need.

1 A lifetime of work includes …
2 Workplace relationships
3 Why do we work?
4 A lifetime of changing and adapting
5 Job satisfaction

B Make notes on the following points in the text.

1 The personal factor (Section A)
2 A job for life (Section C)
3 Happiness in work (Section D)

2 WORKING WITH WORDS

Find the people described below in the text. Copy the words into your note book. Write the German translation beside each word. Check your dictionary if you have to.

Find a person …
1 who uses the services or advice of a professional person or company.
2 that you work with.
3 who is in charge of other people at work and tells them what to do.
4 who is paid to work for sb.
5 with the highest rank in a company or organization.

3 AN OUTLINE OF THE FINDINGS OF THE STUDY

Complete the text with words and phrases from the box.

atmosphere ▪ challenges ▪ employers ▪ employee ▪ further training ▪ job ▪ job satisfaction ▪ pay rise ▪ position ▪ promotions ▪ skills

The study indicated that the working life of a British ▬[1] changes and develops over the years. People usually get several ▬[2] over the years, allowing them to move up the career ladder. A decent ▬[3] allows them to improve their living standards. An employee could work for six different ▬[4] in their working life. It's no longer the case that a person will stay in the same ▬[5] for ever. For this reason, everyone should make use of the opportunity to do ▬[6] and keep improving their ▬[7]. ▬[8] is an important part of work nowadays: people want to like their work, their work colleagues and the ▬[9] at work. At a certain age, people want a change. Sometimes, that means working to get a better ▬[10] in the company they are in or it can mean looking for new ▬[11].

UNIT 8

Newspapers in the UK

Every day hundreds of different newspapers are published in the UK. The content and layout of each newspaper reflects its target readership.

INFO-BOX

Tabloids and broadsheets

The British press may be separated into **tabloids** (popular press) and **broadsheets** (quality press). Tabloids have shorter articles written in simple language and use more and larger photos. They include a lot of celebrity gossip and scandal. The most popular tabloids in the UK are *The Sun*, *The Daily Mirror* and *The Daily Star*. Broadsheets have a higher news content, longer, more complex articles and fewer photos. They offer analysis of political, social and economic issues. The top broadsheets are *The Times*, *The Telegraph* and *The Guardian*.

Where does news come from?

News stories can be sourced via international news agencies such as the Associated Press and Reuters, but many newspaper stories come from press releases or press conferences. Trusted confidential contacts are often used by journalists to get information, this might be about a person involved in a story or inside information about industries or organisations. Anyone can be a potential source of information from a taxi driver to a company boss.

What is 'news value'?

Newspapers select stories on their value for attracting readers. A newspaper's news agenda will reflect the style, ethos and ideology of the newspaper. The people responsible for deciding on the news agenda are called Gatekeepers, they are usually the newspaper owner, the editor or senior journalists.

Media researchers Galtung and Ruge identified a number of factors that help stories make the headlines. Here are some of the most significant factors they pinpointed:

Factor	Effect
Recency	Important breaking news such as a terror attack is reported with immediacy. Breaking news is very competitive, with newspapers keen to be the first to report things as they happen.
Size	The bigger the story, the more people it affects. A bomb with many casualties is more newsworthy than a hoax bomb alert.
Continuity	An ongoing news event like war will continue to be reported on.
Simplicity	Simple stories which are easy to explain (huge lottery wins, celebrity deaths, road accidents) will be preferred to those which are more complex (foreign wars, economic stories, long-term court cases).

05 to source: *beziehen*
09 confidential: *vertraulich*
24 to pinpoint: *genau bestimmen*
26 recency: *Aktualität*
26 competitive: *umkämpft*
27 with immediacy: *sofort*
27 keen: *begierig*

Elite nations or people	In the UK a story about the American president or an American social issue is more likely to be reported on than a story about less influential countries and their leaders.
Predictability	An anti-war demonstration is likely to be eventful, so journalists will cover the event. This means that it will be reported on, even if it passes off peacefully.
Unexpectedness	Something out of the ordinary has more news value than something that happens every day.
Negativity	Bad news is more likely to make the headlines than good news.
Personality	A story about a celebrity or a heroic member of the general public will have a human interest angle.
Meaningfulness	How close to home is the story, is there a local connection?

In 2005, 13 million newspapers were sold daily; by 2015, this figure fell to 7 million. The availability of newspapers online is partly responsible for this decline, but the popularity of blogs, vlogs (video blogs) and other online content areas have made an impact too.

Source: *the website of the BBC*; 446 words

1 READING FOR DETAIL

Answer the following questions with information from the text.

1 Where do news stories come from, apart from news agencies and organized press events? (two sources)
2 What do newspapers aim to do when they select stories?
3 What does a Gatekeeper in a news organization do?
4 Why do celebrity deaths have a higher news value than foreign wars?
5 What are the main reasons for falling newspaper sales? (two things)

2 OVER TO YOU

A Evaluate the news value of these news stories, using the ten factors which Galtung and Ruge identified. Give them a score of 1 (low) to 3 (high) for each factor.

Government Terrorist Trackers Before 9/11: Bosses Wouldn't Listen
Chicago Man Turns Abandoned Tennis Courts Into Dog Park
Killer Hurricane Predicted To Hit Texas In Next 24 Hours
Civilians Killed In US Drone Attack In Afghanistan
Chinese Man Speaks After 30 Years In Coma
$3.8 Million Disappear From Madonna's School For Girls Project In Malawi

B Now imagine you are the editor of either a broadsheet or a tabloid. Decide which story will make your title page.

UNIT 9

Brexit: All you need to know about the UK leaving the EU

1

It is a word that has become used as a shorthand way of saying the UK leaving the EU – merging the words **Br**itain and **exit** to get **Brexit**.

2

A referendum – a vote in which everyone (or nearly everyone) of voting age can take part – was held on Thursday, 23 June, 2016, to decide whether the UK should leave or remain in the European Union. Leave won by 51.9% to 48.1%. The referendum turnout was 71.8%, with more than 30 million people voting.

3

England voted for Brexit, by 53.4% to 46.6%. Wales also voted for Brexit, with Leave getting 52.5% of the vote and Remain 47.5%. Scotland and Northern Ireland both backed staying in the EU. Scotland backed Remain by 62% to 38%, while 55.8% in Northern Ireland voted Remain and 44.2% Leave.

4

The UK has two years to negotiate its withdrawal. But no one really knows how the Brexit process will work: no country has left the EU before. Some suggest it could take up to six years for the UK to complete exit negotiations. The terms of Britain's exit will have to be agreed by 27 national parliaments, a process which could take some years. EU law still applies in the UK until it ceases being a member. The UK will continue to abide by EU treaties and laws, but not take part in any decision-making.

5

It was said by opponents of the EU that Britain was being held back by the EU, which they said imposed too many rules on business and charged billions of pounds a year in membership fees for little in return. They also wanted the UK to make all of its own laws again, rather than being created through shared decision-making with other EU nations. Immigration was also a big issue for Brexit supporters. They wanted Britain to take back full control of its borders and reduce the number of people coming here to live and/or work. One of the main principles of EU membership is "free movement", which means you don't need to get a visa to go and live in another EU country.

6

Those campaigning for Britain to stay in the EU said it got a big boost from membership – it makes selling things to other EU countries easier and, they argued, the flow of immigrants, most of whom are young and keen to work, fuels economic growth and helps pay for public services. They also said Britain's status in the world would be damaged by leaving and that we are more secure as part of the 28-nation club, rather than going it alone.

7

Big business – with a few exceptions – tended to be in favour of Britain staying in the EU because it makes it easier for them to move money, people and products around the world.

Source: Alex Hunt & Brian Wheeler, *the website of the BBC*, 1 August 2017; 464 words

02 **shorthand:** *als Kurzbezeichnung*
11 **to back:** *unterstützen*
15 **withdrawal:** *Rückzug*
18 **to cease:** *aufhören*
19 **to abide by:** *einhalten*
23 **to impose:** *auferlegen*
24 **in return:** *als Gegenleistung*
30 **boost:** *Aufschwung*

1 READING FOR GIST

Match the headings to the sections 1–8 in the text. There are two headings that you do not need.

- a Why is Britain leaving the European Union?
- b What were the reasons for wanting the UK to stay?
- c What does Brexit mean?
- d How do other EU countries feel about Brexit?
- e How long will it take for Britain to leave the EU?
- f How will it affect EU citizens living in the UK?
- g What were the reasons for wanting the UK to leave?
- h What about businesses?
- i What was the breakdown across the UK?

2 READING FOR DETAIL

Decide which of these statements are true (T), false (F) or not in the text (N).

1 Over a quarter of UK voters did not take part in the vote.
2 Ireland and Scotland wanted to leave the EU, but England and Wales wanted to remain.
3 The timetable for the Brexit process is clear.
4 The campaign to leave the EU was based on incorrect information.
5 Brexit campaigners wanted fewer people to come to live in the UK.
6 People who argued in favour of staying in the EU claimed that it was good for business.
7 Most large British companies wanted the UK to leave the EU.

3 WORKING WITH WORDS

Find words in the text which match the definitions.

1 vote taken by all the people on an important question (ll. 5–8)
2 the proportion of people who participate in a vote (ll. 5–8)
3 try to reach a deal or agreement (ll. 15–20)
4 group of people that makes the laws of a country (ll. 15–20)
5 formal agreement between countries (ll. 15–20)
6 payment, usually in exchange for services or for membership (ll. 22–28)
7 problem or question (ll. 22–28)
8 place where two countries meet (ll. 22–28)

4 OVER TO YOU

In 50–80 words write down your reaction to the fact that the UK is leaving the EU as part of the comments section at the end of the article.

UNIT 10

Bonfire night in the UK

Guy Fawkes Day (5 November) is celebrated in the United Kingdom, and in a number of countries that were formerly part of the British Empire, with fireworks, bonfires and parades. Straw dummies representing Fawkes are tossed on the bonfire, as well as those of contemporary political figures. Dummies have been burned on bonfires since as long ago as the 13th century, initially to drive away evil spirits. Following the Gunpowder Plot, the focus of the sacrifices switched to Guy Fawkes' treason. Traditionally, these effigies called 'guys', are carried through the streets in the days leading up to Guy Fawkes Day and children ask passers-by for 'a penny for the guy'. The fireworks represent the explosives that were never used by the plotters.

In Ottery St Mary, south Devon, in a tradition dating from the 17th century, barrels soaked in tar are set alight and carried aloft through parts of the town by residents. Only Ottregians – those born in the town, or who have lived there for most of their lives – may carry a barrel. Lewes, in south-eastern England, is also the site of annual celebration. Guy Fawkes Day there has a distinctly local flavour, involving six bonfire societies whose memberships are grounded in family history stretching back for generations. The only place in the UK that does not celebrate Guy Fawkes Night is his former school St. Peter's in York. They refuse to burn a guy out of respect for one of their own.

What are the key events on November 5?

Flaming Tar Barrels, Devon
Ottery St. Mary's famous Tar Barrels festival is not for the faint-hearted. Don't like crowds or being close to flames? This event isn't for you.

Lewes, Sussex
Six individual processions, 17 burning crosses, and plenty of costumed revelry and fireworks – this is the biggest and the only proper bonfire night celebration left of its kind in the UK.

Alexandra Palace, London
Ally Pally's annual Fireworks Festival marks Bonfire Night with a bang and attracts around 50,000 visitors.

INFO-BOX

The Gunpowder Plot. A group of men tried to kill King James I of England by exploding barrels of gunpowder under Parliament on 5 November 1605. The attempt failed and the leaders of the plot, including Guy Fawkes, were executed.

'Anonymous' protests

November 5th has become an important date globally now that political activists all over the world are wearing Guy Fawkes masks to protect their identity. These masks were inspired by Alan Moore's dystopian *V for Vendetta* […]. In recent years, supporters of anti-Capitalist group Anonymous have taken to the streets in cities and towns worldwide in the so-called 'Million Mask March' against political oppression.

Source: Cameron Macphail and Keely Lockhart, *The Daily Telegraph*, 6 November 2016; 401 words

03 **to toss:** *(achtlos) werfen, schmeißen*
06 **treason:** *Hochverrat*
10 **to carry aloft:** *hochtragen*
13 **to be grounded in:** *fundieren auf*
18 **not for the faint-hearted:** *nichts für schwache Nerven*
23 **revelry:** *Vergnügen, Festlichkeiten*

1 READING FOR GIST

Which of these is the best summary of the text?

a After the Gunpowder Plot in 1605, citizens celebrated Guy Fawkes's brave attempt to kill the unpopular King James 1 with firework displays and large outdoor fires. This tradition continues today in several parts of the United Kingdom.

b British people have always enjoyed burning effigies of politicians on large outdoor fires. After 1605, fireworks became part of this tradition, because they represent the explosives that Guy Fawkes used to kill the English King James I. Guy Fawkes is a symbol of the fight against political oppression.

c Burning effigies on large outdoor fires has been an English tradition from the 13th century onwards. After 1605 the tradition became connected with the Gunpowder Plot and Guy Fawkes. Today there are several regional events involving fireworks and bonfires on 5 November.

2 READING FOR DETAIL

What do these pictures represent? Find references in the text and write short descriptions for the pictures.

3 WORKING WITH WORDS

Which word is the odd one out? Explain why in German.

1 bonfire ▪ oppression ▪ parade ▪ procession
2 procession ▪ history ▪ celebration ▪ festival
3 dummy ▪ effigy ▪ guy ▪ spirit
4 supporter ▪ activist ▪ character ▪ plotter
5 crowds ▪ bonfire ▪ masks ▪ fireworks

4 OVER TO YOU

You are on a school exchange in the UK in early November. Which of the celebrations described in the text would you most like to attend? Why? Write a short description of the celebrations in German to persuade the teacher who is leading the exchange.

UNIT 11

The UK's first food waste supermarket opens

The UK's first food waste supermarket has opened in Pudsey, near Leeds. Food waste campaigners from the Real Junk Food Project have opened 'the warehouse', a store on the Grangefield Industrial Estate.

Customers are invited to shop for food thrown out by supermarkets and other businesses. The food is priced on a 'pay as you feel' basis and has already helped desperate families struggling to feed their children.

'The warehouse has absolutely been our lifeline over the past month or so,' Kirsty Rhodes told *The Independent*.

Kirsty was recently diagnosed with a chronic pain condition, leaving her husband with no choice but to leave work to take over most of the care of the couple's three children. Overnight the couple's household income was reduced to almost nothing.

'With three young children and two adults to feed we started to struggle straight away. Luckily we took the plunge to go to the warehouse and it was amazing!' Kirsty said.

So far the family have bought fresh pasta, juice, pasta sauce, desserts, fruit, vegetables and lots of salad. 'We've even had baby milk on one occasion and our baby is 7 months so it was perfect,' she said.

Kirsty has plans to run a workshop to teach people how to make jam after she used fruit from the warehouse to make her own.

Adam Smith, founder of the Real Junk Food Project, which is behind the food waste supermarket, told *The Independent* that there are plans to open a warehouse selling surplus produce in every city in the UK. The initiative started as 'boutiques' or food waste stalls selling produce in Real Junk Food Project cafés.

'We're about to start in Sheffield and Bradford,' he said. 'Every city will now obtain central storage and run a "people's supermarket" as well as Fuel for School.'

Fuel for School is the work of a group of food activists from The Real Junk Food Project who deliver surplus bread, fruit, vegetables and dairy products from supermarkets to schools, where it is used to feed hungry schoolchildren. The food, which may otherwise have found its way to landfill, is used to feed 12,000 children a week.

The Real Junk Food Project is also working to expand its 'pay as you feel café' movement. There are now hundreds of cafés around the country feeding people on food waste. As with all the initiatives, customers are invited to pay for their meal in money, time and skills.

'We need volunteers,' Adam says of the new food waste supermarket. 'Driving, weighing, sorting, stacking shelves, cleaning and much more. Lots of opportunities for people to get involved and give back.'

According to an investigation by the *Evening Standard* newspaper, supermarkets in the UK are throwing away £230m of edible food. Source: Hazel Sheffield, *The Independent*, 20 September 2016, 460 words

03 **industrial estate:** *Gewerbegebiet*
07 **lifeline:** *Rettungsanker*
13 **to take the plunge:** *den Sprung wagen*
33 **to stack shelves:** *Regale bestücken*

1 READING FOR GIST

Match the statements to the speakers: Kirsty or Adam? One statement does not match.

1 Without the warehouse, I don't know how we would manage.
2 Supermarkets shouldn't be allowed to throw good food away.
3 I'm going to teach other people how to make good use of cheap fruit.
4 This is something we need to have in every city in Britain.
5 There are lots of ways in which people can be a part of this initiative.

food waste from a supermarket

2 READING FOR DETAIL

Answer the following questions with information from the text.

1 Who decides how much the shoppers at the "warehouse" pay for the food?
2 Why did Kirsty's husband have to leave his job?
3 Where will the Real Junk Food Project open more food waste supermarkets?
4 Why is Fuel for School delivering supermarket produce to schools?
5 How can customers at 'pay as you feel' cafés pay for their meals?

3 WORKING WITH WORDS

Find words or expressions in the text which match the definitions.

1 person who works to achieve a social or political aim (ll. 1–3)
2 do something only with a lot of difficulty and effort (ll. 4–6)
3 money received over a certain period (ll. 9–11)
4 things that farmers have grown or made (ll. 19–22)
5 group of people trying to achieve a social or political aim (ll. 29–31)
6 person who does a job without pay (ll. 32–36)

4 OVER TO YOU

You are on holiday in England. A local supermarket is about to throw its food waste away. Outline alternatives to sending the food to a landfill in an email to the supermarket manager. Write 80–100 words.

UNIT 12

The international companies switching to English

Nearly every meeting Keiko Claassen must attend at work is held in English. No big deal – except that her company is based in Italy and she's Dutch. [...] At ITT Motion Technologies, an Italy-based engineering company where Classen is executive director of communications, every senior staffer is expected to speak English and most communications are delivered in English. While it's not considered an official corporate language, with 4,500 employees working in several countries, including Japan, China, India and Germany, it's the only language that everyone can generally speak in common – even if speaking doesn't mean always fully understanding. In other firms, such as France-based food services company Sodexo, English is being adopted as an official language. [...] German electronics company Siemens also made English its official language years ago. [...]

For most of these companies, the aim is simple: by communicating exclusively in a single language, leaders in South America can collaborate with colleagues in France or the US. It's also part of a larger cultural shift for the company, says Kim Beddard-Fontaine, Sodexo's group vice-president of employee and change communication. 'Business is organised globally and not regionally these days,' she says. 'We want to become more efficient by collaborating across geographies. English is an enabler of that.'

[...] In Europe, nearly 80% of children in their primary years are learning English, while a 2013 survey by the 21st Century Education Research Institute in Beijing found that 70% of Chinese parents want their children to learn the language to help them get into better schools. [...]

Sodexo, in theory, could have made its official language French – it is a 50-year old French company, after all – but only 35,000 of its staff work in France, while 125,000 live in the US. Says Beddard-Fontaine: 'I think if we decided to make French the company's global language we would have had a revolt on our hands.'

Since the change is primarily for the company's 200 executives and its 1,600 senior leaders [...], lower level staffers, many of who don't speak English, will continue to receive communications in different languages. Still, that may change at some point, too, she says. As well, materials might be translated into fewer languages in future.

'It's an absolute must that we move to English,' says Beddard-Fontaine. [...] Both Sodexo and ITT Motion Technologies offer English courses to some staffers who want to get a better grasp of the language. [...] Even so, when an entire language changes, a dose of compassion is necessary – imagine having to suddenly speak in a language that isn't your own or which you don't quite speak fluently.

'Bosses and peers alike should realize that others might not fully understand what's being said,' says Claassen. That could lead to misunderstandings or feelings of awkwardness. She's been on plant tours where the person showing her around began the conversation by apologising for not speaking English well, even though the employee had an impeccable grasp of the language. 'They have to cross this wall for themselves because they don't feel their confidence is high,' she says.

01 **no big deal:** *kein Grund zur Aufregung*
04 **staffer:** *Mitarbeiter/in*
15 **enabler:** *Wegbereiter*
28 **grasp:** *Verständnis*
29 **a dose of sth:** *ein gewisses Maß an etwas*
35 **impeccable:** *tadellos*

In some cases, the perceived language barrier holds employees back. When Claassen has group meetings with Chinese colleagues, many of them remain quiet until they're asked directly for their input. They don't want to lose face by using the wrong word or accidentally saying something funny, she says.

'You have to be conscious of that and really invite them in,' Claassen says. [...] But the move to English as a corporate language just make sense, she says: 'If a Chinese person meets someone from the Middle East, they will speak English. They don't expect to know each other's language.'

Source: Bryan Borzykowski, *the website of the BBC*, 20 March 2017; 601 words

1 READING FOR GIST

Which is the best summary of the text?

a Large international companies need a single language for corporate communications. English is chosen because it is widely spoken. The requirement does not affect all employees. The need to speak English can cause communication problems for employees.

b Large international companies need a single language for corporate communications. English is chosen because of the economic importance of English-speaking countries. All employees in these companies must speak English, which is causing communication problems.

c Large international companies need a variety of languages for corporate communications. English is often one of those languages. Only senior managers have to learn English, not lower level employees. Many of the managers are finding it difficult.

2 READING FOR DETAIL

Copy and complete the table, using the information in the text.

employee	title	company	country based in	number of employees	status of English
Keiko Claassen	*executive director of communications*				
Kim Beddard-Fontaine					

3 OVER TO YOU

How would you feel about speaking only English at work? Write a short comment (50–80 words) on the article, discussing the advantages and disadvantages from the employee's point of view.

UNIT 13

Now please pay attention everybody. I'm about to tell you what art is.

A week ago I confused 1,500 sixth-formers by attempting to answer the non-question: 'What is art?' The students found a lot of what I said surprising. I hope too many of them didn't ditch their portfolios and start new ones on Lady Gaga, because I rather think their teachers found what I said even more confusing than they did. So here is another go at the same thing. Pass it on.

What is art? Art is anything an artist calls art. An artist is someone who makes or does something she or he thinks of as art. Making pictures can be called graphic art, but it is quite likely to have nothing to do with art whatsoever. Take the pictures that hang every weekend on the railings of London's Hyde Park, hundreds of them. No art involved. A graffito on a railway bridge is more likely to be art, most probably bad art, but art just the same. Most art is bad, but you don't get the good art without the bad. Our best artists make stuff they know is bad; the difference is that they destroy it themselves. [...]

Art is a part of life, but in order to be art it has to create for itself a separate zone, what we might call the art space or the art time. A urinal is not an art object as long as it is carrying out its essential function. To make it art we detach it from the plumbing, tip it on its end and set it on a plinth. The beholder then has to entertain a galaxy of new and unfamiliar thoughts about the object, redefining it and herself in relation to it. The original object, which Marcel Duchamp called Fountain, signing it R Mutt, was rejected by the Society of Independent Artists at whose New York gallery it was supposed to be exhibited in 1917 because, they said, it was not art. In 2004, 500 British 'art experts' selected it as 'the most influential artwork of the 20th century'.

Human beings have always done art. They have set aside time to carry out activities that did nothing obviously useful. They made images, transformed their bodies with painted marks, told stories, sang and danced. Nowadays, we imagine that these activities were 'timeless'; it would be truer to say that they were 'timeful', sometimes taking days for preparation, and days for performance. The times and the places they happened in were set aside. [...]

The kids who get up at midnight and head out to a derelict wall to begin working on a graffito are working within a demanding tradition that requires the sequence of execution to have been worked out in detail in advance, before any mark can be made. They can make no money out of what they do. There are no prizes for them. They could go to jail. There is no truer example of the sacredness of the art enterprise than this.

Source: Germaine Greer, *The Guardian*, 6 March 2011; 494 words

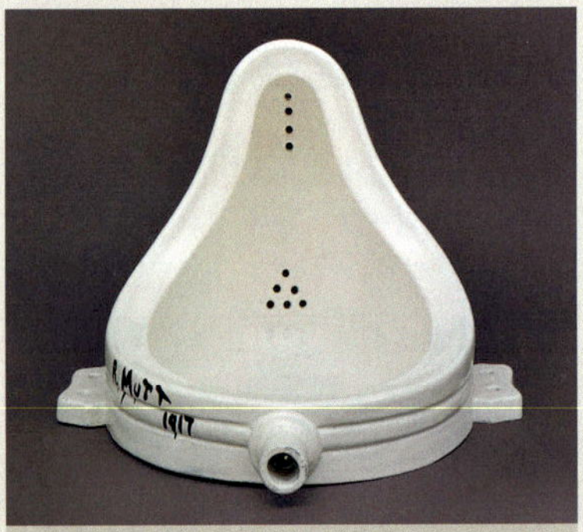

Fountain, by Marcel Duchamp, courtesy of Tate Gallery

- 01 **sixth-former:** *Schüler/in in der Oberstufe*
- 02 **to ditch:** *wegschmeißen*
- 08 **railing:** *Geländer*
- 14 **plumbing:** *Rohrleitungen*
- 15 **plinth:** *Sockel*
- 15 **beholder:** *Betracher/in*
- 15 **to entertain thoughts:** *Gedanken hegen*
- 25 **derelict:** *verfallen*
- 30 **sacredness:** *Heiligkeit*

1 READING FOR GIST

Put these ideas in the order in which they occur in the text. Two ideas are not in the text.

a Art requires careful planning.
b Anything which a person does is art, if the person considers it to be art.
c Art experts do not know what they are talking about.
d Everyone should create art, rather than leaving art to professional artists.
e Objects which once had a practical function can become art.
f People have always created art in one form or another.

2 READING FOR DETAIL

Are these objects art or not, according to the author? Justify your answers by quoting from the text.

a

b

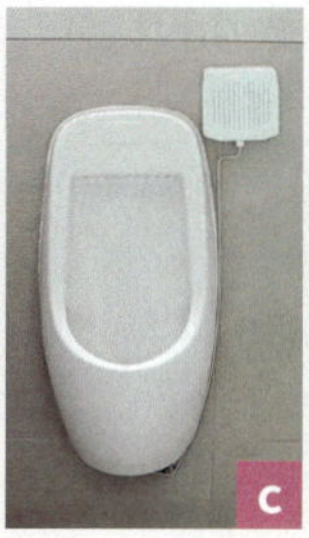
c

d

3 READING BETWEEN THE LINES

What do you think Germaine Greer means? Interpret these statements from the text.

1 "Making pictures can be called graphic art, but it is quite likely to have nothing to do with art whatsoever." (ll. 6–7)
2 "You don't get the good art without the bad." (l. 10)
3 "Nowadays, we imagine that these activities were 'timeless'; it would be truer to say that they were 'timeful' …" (ll. 22–23)

4 WORKING WITH WORDS

Find words in the text which have the opposite meaning. The number of the paragraph in which the word can be found is in brackets after the word.

1 similarity (2)
2 create (2)
3 connect sth to sth (3)
4 well-known (3)
5 accept (3)
6 hide (3)
7 easy (5)
8 afterwards (5)

5 OVER TO YOU

Describe something that is "art" to you but may not be art to other people. Give reasons for your opinion. Write 50–80 words.

UNIT 14

Mother of four to be deported to Mexico in sign of Trump policy shift

The mother of four American children, the youngest of whom is three years old, has been picked up by federal agents at her home in Fairfield, Ohio, and taken into detention ahead of imminent deportation back to her native Mexico. Maribel Trujillo has been told that her deportation is set for next Tuesday from the US, where she has lived for the past 15 years. Her rushed removal is one of the starkest examples yet of Donald Trump's push to catch and deport undocumented immigrants who previously were tolerated by the authorities as law-abiding and peaceful members of society. Though early figures suggest that Trump has not yet increased deportation numbers substantially over the levels sustained by Barack Obama, there is considerable anecdotal evidence that Immigration and Customs Enforcement (ICE) agents are more willing to pick up individuals without a record of major crime.

People who were until recently regarded as of such low priority that it would inflict more harm than good on communities to wrench them from their families are now finding themselves in the deportation pipeline. Trujillo falls firmly into that category. ICE has indicated that she is a priority for removal even though she has no criminal record and last year was granted government permission to work in a local candy factory. Deportation would present Trujillo with a 'Sophie's choice': either she abandons her four US-born, American-citizen children – aged three, 10, 12 and 14 – leaving them to grow up without a mother, or she takes them back to Mexico to an uncertain and potentially perilous future. The children have never set foot outside the US.

In an interview with *The Guardian* conducted before she was detained, she said she was finding the decision extremely painful. 'I don't understand the reason to separate my family. I have no criminal record, I'm here working to support my family, so that my kids can study and have a better life for themselves. Why does President Trump want to divide my family and make me leave my kids behind – what are they going to do without their mama?' [...]

A spokesman for ICE told *The Guardian* that Trujillo's case had been reviewed several times by the courts and she was found to have 'no legal basis to remain in the US'. Asked about the dilemma her detention posed with her children, the spokesman said: 'For parents who are ordered removed, it is their decision whether or not to relocate their children with them.' [...]

She told *The Guardian* that she could not conceive of leaving the children behind, though she also struggles with the idea of taking them with her to Michoacán, a state in central Mexico that she abandoned in 2002 in search of a better life. [...]

The children are also bemused by the idea of going to live in a country that they know scarcely anything about. The elder daughter Alexa, 12, lamented recently: '*Mami*, I can't go to Mexico, I can't go to school there, I don't know how to speak Spanish properly, I have no friends.'

Source: Ed Pilkington, *The Guardian*, 6 April 2017; 508 words

02 federal agent: *FBI-Agent/in*
02 to take into detention: *verhaften*
05 undocumented immigrant: *illegale/r Einwander/in*
06 law-abiding: *gesetzestreu*
12 to wrench from: *entreißen*
13 pipeline: *Wartekiste*
15 candy (AE): *Süßigkeiten*
18 perilous: *gefährlich*
28 to conceive of: *sich vorstellen*
31 bemused: *verwirrt*

1 READING FOR GIST

Which of these things is Maribel Trujillo not allowed to do?

- **a** Leave her children in the USA and return to Mexico.
- **b** Stay in the USA until her children are old enough to look after themselves.
- **c** Return to Mexico and take her children.

2 READING FOR DETAIL

Choose the most suitable option in each case.

1 Before the Trump government's new policy, …
   - **a** immigrants could stay in the USA if they had family there.
   - **b** undocumented immigrants with no criminal record were generally allowed to stay in the USA.
   - **c** it was impossible to make undocumented immigrants return home.
   - **d** the authorities didn't know about people like the Trujillos.

2 Immigration and Customs Enforcement …
   - **a** believes that Mrs Trujillo has committed a major crime.
   - **b** is unwilling to deport Mrs Trujillo because it would do more harm than good.
   - **c** has granted Mrs Trujillo permission to work until she leaves the USA.
   - **d** is deporting Mrs Trujillo as quickly as possible.

3 Mrs Trujillo …
   - **a** plans to leave her children in the USA.
   - **b** doesn't know what to do.
   - **c** has asked President Trump to review her case.
   - **d** thinks that her children will have a better life in Mexico.

3 WORKING WITH WORDS

Find the (abstract) nouns for the following verbs in the text:

deport ▪ detain ▪ immigrate ▪ increase ▪ permit ▪ remove ▪ separate ▪ support

4 OVER TO YOU

As part of an online campaign for the Trujillo family, describe in no more than 100 words what might happen to the family if Meribel is deported.

Skills files

Diese *Skills files* helfen Ihnen, Ihre Sprachfertigkeiten zu trainieren, damit Sie Erfolg in der Prüfung haben. Wenn Sie sich regelmäßig mit dem Lernprozess beschäftigen, fällt Ihnen der Umgang mit der englischen Sprache jeden Tag leichter. Hier bekommen Sie viele hilfreiche Tipps, wie Sie Ihre Fähigkeiten verbessern können.

1 MIT WÖRTERN UMGEHEN

A Ein Wörterbuch benutzen

→ Vokabeln lernen, S. 229

Ein Wörterbuch ist ein hilfreiches Werkzeug. Es hilft Ihnen, einen Text zu verstehen und Ihr Vokabular zu erweitern. Unabhängig von der Art des Wörterbuchs, das Sie nutzen – zwei- oder einsprachig –, ist Folgendes zu beachten:

- Lassen Sie bei Online-Wörterbüchern Vorsicht walten. Wörter haben in verschiedenen Zusammenhängen verschiedene Bedeutungen, und Computer sind nicht schlau genug, um zu erfassen, welchen Zusammenhang Sie brauchen.
- Arabische Zahlen weisen darauf hin, dass es mehrere Bedeutungen gibt. Wählen Sie nicht die erstbeste Bedeutung aus, sondern lesen Sie alle Definitionen und überprüfen Sie sie ein zweites Mal, indem Sie die neu gefundenen Wörter nachschlagen.
- Stellen Sie sicher, dass Sie nach der richtigen Wortart suchen (Verb, Substantiv, Adjektiv, Adverb).

Bevor Sie mit Ihrem Wörterbuch zu arbeiten beginnen:

- Lesen Sie die Inhaltsübersicht, um herauszufinden, was Ihr Wörterbuch neben Definitionen noch alles zu bieten hat. Lesen Sie die Nutzungshinweise sorgfältig durch – sie sind wichtig.
- Sehen Sie sich die Liste der Abkürzungen und Symbole sowie die Legende zur Verbbildung an und stellen Sie sicher, dass Sie deren Bedeutungen verstehen.
- Vergewissern Sie sich, dass Sie die verschiedenen Wortarten kennen. Wenn Sie, zum Beispiel, die Funktion eines Adverbs nicht kennen, wird es Ihnen kaum helfen, ein Adverb nachzuschlagen.

Nutzen Sie ein Wörterbuch, um:

- **mit einem Text zu arbeiten.** Wenn Sie nach Anwendung aller Ihrer Fertigkeiten unbekannte Wörter immer noch nicht verstehen, schlagen Sie sie nach.
- **Ihr Vokabular zu erweitern.** Wenn Sie ein Ihnen unbekanntes Wort nachschlagen, nehmen Sie sich die Zeit, auch verwandte Wörter nachzuschlagen und eine Liste mit Wortfamilien anzulegen.
- ***Idioms*/Redensarten zu erlernen.** In einer Redensart wird ein Wort in einem feststehenden Satz verwendet und ist seiner eigentlichen Bedeutung nur entfernt ähnlich, z. B.: *to get the wrong end of the stick*. Wenn Sie wissen, was *the wrong end* und *stick* bedeuten, verstehen Sie möglicherweise immer noch nicht die Redewendung („etwas in den falschen Hals bekommen“).

B Vokabeln lernen

→ Ein Wörterbuch benutzen, S. 228

Das richtige Erlernen und Benutzen von Wörtern einer Fremdsprache macht Spaß, ist aber zeitaufwendig. Es gibt viele Arten, Vokabeln zu lernen. Sie können dies mithilfe von *Work with English* tun und diese Art des Lernens mit englischen Lese- und Hörverständnisübungen außerhalb des Unterrichts ergänzen. Es gibt natürlich auch eine Vielzahl von Onlineprogrammen und -spielen, um Vokabeln zu lernen, doch sie sind nicht so effektiv wie die Lernmethoden, die Sie sich selbst erarbeiten.

Listen und Zettel

- **Vokabellisten (nicht nur in einem Buch)**
  Vokabellisten, die in einem Notizbuch eingetragen werden, stellen einen leichten Weg dar, neue Wörter während des Unterrichts festzuhalten. Zuhause können Sie weitere Listen erstellen, z. B. von Lebensmitteln, die im Kühlschrank aufbewahrt werden, oder Sie schreiben Ihre Einkaufsliste auf Englisch oder Sie listen die Kleidungsstücke in Ihrem Kleiderschrank auf, nach Art, Farbe und Material sortiert.

- **Lernkarten**
  Schreiben Sie die Wörter, die Sie gern lernen möchten, auf Karteikarten. Schreiben Sie das englische Wort auf die eine Seite und die Übersetzung auf die andere. Fügen Sie eine Zeichnung, eine Definition bzw. einen Beispielsatz auf Englisch unter die deutsche Übersetzung hinzu.

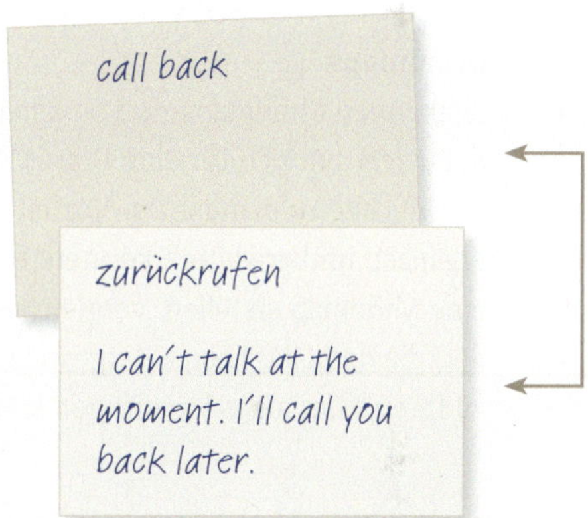

- **Klebezettel**
  Schreiben Sie die Bezeichnung eines Gegenstandes auf einen Notizzettel und kleben Sie ihn an den Gegenstand. Sie können nach Belieben Adjektive hinzufügen, z. B. *pretty picture*, *dirty laundry*.

Wortgitter und Wortgruppen

Während Ihrer Arbeit mit *Work with English* füllen Sie viele Wortgitter mit Wortfamilien aus. In den meisten Fällen werden Sie aufgefordert, ein Wortgitter mit unterschiedlichen Wortarten zu vervollständigen.

noun	verb	adjective
enjoyment	enjoy	enjoyable
entertainment	entertain	entertaining

Wenn Sie sich auf eine Prüfung vorbereiten, können Sie Ihre Wortfamiliengitter um weitere Informationen verändern und ergänzen, z. B. indem Sie Sätze hinzufügen, in denen die Wörter im Kontext benutzt werden.

word	part of speech	opposite(s)	synonym	word in context
large	adjective	small	big	My mum comes from a large family. She has six sisters.
producer	noun	destroyer consumer	manufacturer	Japan is a major producer of cars.

Verknüpfungen herstellen

- **Wortgabeln**

  Wortgabeln eignen sich gut zum Erlernen von Adjektiven und Verben.

delicious	
quick	
home-made	meal
lovely	
tasty	

find	
have	
make	friends
meet	
visit	

- **Mindmaps**

  Sie können Mindmaps zum Sammeln und Verknüpfen von Vokabeln wie auch von Ideen benutzen, um sich für eine Präsentation vorzubereiten oder einen Aufsatz und andere Schriftsätze zu planen. Der Vorteil von Mindmaps ist, dass Sie sie in jede beliebige Richtung ergänzen und erweitern können. Heben Sie bestimmte Aspekte farblich hervor. Wenn Sie eine Mindmap erstellen, vergleichen Sie Ihre mit der eines Mitstreiters / einer Mitstreiterin, der/die dasselbe Thema dargestellt hat. Es ist wahrscheinlich, dass Sie beide weitere Wörter zu Ihren Mindmaps hinzufügen können.

2 REZEPTION: LESEVERSTEHEN

A Vorbereitung auf das Lesen

Eine Vorhersage bedeutet, dass Sie versuchen, den Inhalt des Textes zu erraten, bevor Sie ihn lesen. Wenn Sie sich hierzu Zeit nehmen, bevor Sie mit dem Lesen des Texts beginnen, können Sie den Text besser verstehen.

- Sehen Sie sich den Aufbau des Textes genau an und lesen Sie die Überschrift und Unterzeile bzw. die Einleitung, sofern es eine gibt. Das sollte Ihnen Hinweise liefern, worum es in dem Text geht.
- Sehen Sie sich die dazugehörigen Bilder bzw. Zeichnungen an und lesen Sie deren Unterschriften. Dies wird Ihnen helfen, sich vom Text „ein Bild zu machen".

B Den Sinn eines Textes erfassen

Lesen, um den Sinn zu erfassen oder einen Text überfliegen bedeutet, die wichtigsten Punkte schnell zu lesen.

- Lesen Sie den ersten Satz jeden Absatzes (und den letzten Satz, wenn der Absatz lang ist), denn dort können Sie häufig das Wesentliche des Textes entnehmen.
- Konzentrieren Sie sich auf die Schlüsselwörter, die Ihnen den Sinn des Textes vermitteln, z. B. Substantive, Verben und (häufig) die dazugehörigen Adjektive und Adverbien. Wörter, die unterstrichen bzw. **fett** gedruckt oder *kursiv* gestellt sind, sind i.d.R. wichtig.
- Überspringen Sie jene Wörter, die Sie nicht verstehen. Meist wird die Bedeutung dieser Wörter aus dem Zusammenhang heraus klar, und manchmal taucht etwas später ein Synonym auf. Zum Schluss finden Sie wahrscheinlich heraus, dass Sie den Text verstehen, ohne diese Wörter zu kennen.
- Lesen Sie den ganzen letzten Absatz, da dieser häufig eine Zusammenfassung des Textes darstellt.

C Gezielt Informationen im Text finden

Beim Überfliegen eines Textes geht es um das schnelle Finden von bestimmten Informationen. In Texten wie Stellenanzeigen oder Infobroschüren müssen Sie bestimmte Informationen schnell herausfinden. Sie müssen den Text nicht in aller Tiefe lesen, doch Sie müssen sich den gesamten Text ansehen. Hierzu wenden Sie folgende Strategien an:

- Lesen Sie die Aufgaben sorgfältig durch und stellen Sie sicher, dass Sie verstehen, was zu tun ist.
- Lesen Sie den Text schnell durch und halten Sie an, wenn Sie ein Schlüsselwort gefunden haben. Wenn Sie ein Schlüsselwort gefunden haben, lesen Sie um es herum, um die Aufgabe zu lösen.
- Wenn Sie ein Wort oder eine Redewendung nicht verstehen, halten Sie sich nicht damit auf. Lesen Sie den Text weiter, bis Sie am Ende angelangt sind. Sollte sich herausstellen, dass Sie das Wort benötigen, können Sie sich später noch darum kümmern.

Normalerweise werden die Aufgaben zum Text in der Reihenfolge gestellt, in der die Informationen im Text zu finden sind. In einer Prüfung können Sie den Text markieren bzw. sich die benötigten Details notieren, sobald Sie die Informationen finden, die Sie suchen.

Wenn Sie gefragt werden, *Wh*-Fragen zum Text zu beantworten, denken Sie daran, dass:

Who nach Menschen fragt. Suchen Sie Informationen über die Hauptperson des Textes.
Where nach einem Ort fragt.
When nach einer Zeit fragt. Suchen Sie nach Wochentagen, Daten oder Uhrzeiten.
What nach Objekten und Ereignissen fragt. Suchen Sie nach Informationen darüber oder Andeutungen, warum etwas passiert (ist).

Why nach einem Grund fragt. Suchen Sie nach Erklärungen, warum etwas passiert (ist).
How nach einer Methode fragt. Suchen Sie Beschreibungen, wie etwas gemacht wird.

D Gründliches Lesen

Gründliches Lesen bedeutet, einen Text Satz für Satz zu lesen. Hierzu gibt es folgende Strategien:

- Suchen Sie Schlüsselwörter, die Ihnen helfen, die Aufgaben zu lösen. Werden Sie z. B. nach der Meinung des Autors / der Autorin gefragt, suchen Sie nach Wörtern wie *think*, *believe*, *opinion* usw.; das hilft Ihnen, dem Gedankengang des Autors / der Autorin zu folgen.
- Lesen Sie nun den Text Satz für Satz und erledigen Sie die Aufgaben.
- Wenn Sie fertig sind, lesen Sie sich Ihre Antworten durch und vergleichen Sie sie mit dem Text.

E Mit unbekannten Wörtern umgehen

→ Vokabeln lernen, S. 229

Wenn Sie während des Lesens einem Wort begegnen, das Sie nicht kennen, sollten Sie sich fragen, ob es notwendig ist, das Wort zu verstehen. Wenn Sie das Wort tatsächlich benötigen, versuchen Sie, bevor Sie nach dem Wörterbuch greifen (bzw. online nachschlagen), die Bedeutung des Wortes selbst herauszufinden. Manchmal verstehen Sie die Bedeutung eines Wortes, ohne es bewusst zu „kennen". Wenn dem nicht so ist, nutzen Sie folgende Strategien:

- Erarbeiten Sie es sich aus dem Zusammenhang heraus. Sehen Sie sich genau an, wie das Wort im Satz benutzt wird und wie es mit dem Inhalt dieser Textstelle zusammenhängt.
- Nutzen Sie Ihr Wissen über die deutsche Sprache. Viele englische Wörter haben ähnliche deutsche Entsprechungen bzw. stammen sie von derselben Wurzel ab, z. B.: *ten/zehn*, *light/Licht*, *night/Nacht*, *biology*/Biologie, *democracy*/Demokratie.
- Bringen Sie mehr über Wortbildung in Erfahrung (wie man Wörter aus anderen Wörtern bilden kann).

Vorsilben (*prefixes*)

Vorsilben können die Bedeutung eines Wortes verändern.

anti-	'against'	freeze → antifreeze
co-	'together'	operate → cooperate
inter-	'between'	national → international
sub-	'under' / 'below'	standard → substandard
super-	'above' / 'over'	power → superpower
trans-	'across'	form → transform

dis-	'not' / 'opposite'	agree → disagree
in-		correct → incorrect
im-		possible → impossible
ir-		responsible → irresponsible
un-		friendly → unfriendly
mis-	'not correctly'	understand → misunderstand
re-	'again'	discover → rediscover

Nachsilben (*suffixes*)

Nachsilben können die Wortart eines Wortes verändern.

verbs → nouns

verb	suffix	noun
organize	-ation	organization
express	-ion	expression
begin	-ing	beginning
argue	-ment	argument
bake	-er	baker

nouns → adjectives

noun	suffix	adjective
continent	-al	continental
beauty	-ful	beautiful
day	-ly	daily
hunger	-ry	hungry

verbs → adjectives

verb	suffix	adjective
advise	-able	advisable
rain	-y	rainy
care	-ing	caring

adjectives → nouns

adjective	suffix	noun
stupid	-ity	stupidity
happy	-ness	happiness

adjectives → adverbs

adjective	suffix	adverb
awful	-ly	awfully
democratic	-ally	democratically

3 REZEPTION: HÖRVERSTEHEN

A Vorbereitung auf das Hören

Sich auf die Hörübung vorzubereiten, verstärkt das Hörverständnis. Nutzen Sie hierzu alle Informationen, die sich auf der Seite befinden. Bevor Sie zuhören:

- Lesen Sie alle Ihnen zur Verfügung gestellten Hintergrundinformationen, z. B. eine Einleitung, die die Situation beschreibt und Auskunft darüber gibt, wie viele Personen Sie hören werden.
- Lesen Sie die Aufgabenstellung sorgfältig durch. Denken Sie daran, dass die Fragen, die Sie beantworten müssen, häufig der Reihenfolge entsprechen, in der die Informationen auf der Aufzeichnung vorkommen.

B Während des ersten Hörens

Ein Grobverständnis zu erhalten bedeutet, eine Ahnung zu bekommen, worum es in der Aufzeichnung geht. Während des ersten Hörens brauchen Sie nicht jedes Wort zu verstehen. Entwickeln Sie für das Hören möglichst folgende Fertigkeiten:

- Übergehen Sie Wörter, die Sie nicht verstehen.
- Konzentrieren Sie sich auf Schlüsselwörter.
- Machen Sie sich Notizen auf Englisch. Verwenden Sie Abkürzungen. Schreiben Sie so viel wie möglich auf, während Sie zuhören. Sie können Ihre Notizen zu einem späteren Zeitpunkt übersetzen.

Ordnen Sie Ihre Notizen sofort nach dem Ende der Hörübung. Sie können sie später möglicherweise nicht mehr lesen.

Bemühen Sie sich, alle Aufgaben zu lösen. Aufgaben sind chronologisch angeordnet. Wenn Sie einen Teil der Informationen nicht verstanden haben, raten Sie, ausgehend von dem, was Sie verstanden haben.

C Während des zweiten Hörens

Es ist schwierig, während des Zuhörens Notizen zu machen, weil die Aufzeichnung weiterläuft, während Sie schreiben. Daher verpassen Sie möglicherweise wichtige Informationen. Sie haben sich jedoch bereits beim ersten Hören ein Grobverständnis angeeignet und notiert, was Sie verstehen konnten. Beim zweiten Hören versuchen Sie, sich so viel wie möglich an das zu erinnern, was Sie beim ersten Mal gehört haben. Wenn Sie es sich zur Gewohnheit machen, bei jedem Hören Stichpunkte aufzuschreiben, haben Sie bald den Bogen heraus.

4 PRODUKTION: SCHREIBEN

A Einen Text zusammenfassen

Einen Text zusammenzufassen bedeutet, ihn auf seine wesentlichen Informationen zu reduzieren. Sie werden möglicherweise aufgefordert, einen Text zusammenzufassen, um zu zeigen, dass Sie ihn verstanden haben. Bevor Sie beginnen:

- Stellen Sie sicher, dass Sie den Text verstehen. → Rezeption: Leseverstehen, S. 230
- Lesen Sie die Anweisungen aufmerksam durch und vergewissern Sie sich, dass Sie wissen, welche Informationen aus dem Text für den Leser / die Leserin wichtig sind. Sie können dies tun, indem Sie sich *Wh*-Fragen stellen. → Gezielt Informationen im Text finden, S. 231
- Machen Sie sich auf Schmierpapier stichpunktartige Notizen.

Nun beginnen Sie, Ihre Zusammenfassung zu schreiben.

- Nehmen Sie in der Regel als Zeitform das *simple present*.
- Beschreiben Sie in ein oder zwei einleitenden Sätzen, wovon der Text handelt.
- Lassen Sie alles Unnötige weg. Dies schließt Beispiele, ausführliche Listen, Namen, usw. ein.
- Verwenden Sie, soweit es geht, Ihre eigenen Worte. Verwenden Sie Synonyme für Wörter aus dem Text, z. B. *think* → *believe*, und formulieren Sie um, z. B. *recently* → *in recent years*.
- Wandeln Sie Zitate in die indirekte Rede um, z. B. *The author states that …*
- Verlinken Sie Ideen und lassen Sie sie in der Reihenfolge, in der sie im Text erscheinen.
- Sie dürfen in einer Zusammenfassung eines Textes nicht Ihre eigene Meinung äußern.

Wenn Sie fertig sind, überprüfen Sie Ihre Rechtschreibung und Grammatik.

B Einen Aufsatz oder eine Stellungnahme (*comment*) schreiben

Einen längeren Text in einer Englischprüfung zu schreiben, stellt Ihr Sprachverständnis und Ihre Schaffenskraft auf die Probe. Wenn Sie aufgefordert sind, einen Aufsatz zu schreiben, müssen Sie eine objektive Haltung zu dem Thema einnehmen. Um dies zu erreichen, müssen Sie Argumente sammeln, die die in der Aufgabenstellung enthaltene These stützen und widerlegen. Wenn Sie „kommentieren" bzw. „diskutieren" sollen, wird erwartet, dass Sie Ihre Meinung zum Thema äußern. Hier ist es wichtig, dass Sie zur Untermauerung Ihrer Meinung Beispiele angeben.

Bevor Sie mit dem Schreiben beginnen

- Lesen Sie die Einleitung zu den Aufgaben mehrmals durch und stellen Sie sicher, dass Sie ganz genau verstehen, worüber Sie schreiben sollen.
- Achten Sie auf den genauen Wortlaut der Anweisungen. Suchen Sie nach Schlüsselwörtern in der Aufgabenstellung, die Ihnen sagen, was zu tun ist, z. B.: *identify*, *analyse*, *comment* usw.

Mindmaps zum Inhalt eines Aufsatzes erstellen

Wenn Sie einen Aufsatz schreiben sollen, ist es sinnvoll, Ihre Ideen in Form einer Mindmap festzuhalten.

Hier ist der Anfang einer Mindmap zum Thema „the benefits and dangers of social media“. Sehen Sie, wie die drei Unterpunkte *benefits, dangers, questions* genutzt werden, um Argumente zu sammeln und Fragen aufzulisten, die im Aufsatz abgedeckt werden sollen.

TASK: **Comment on the benefits and the dangers of using social media.**

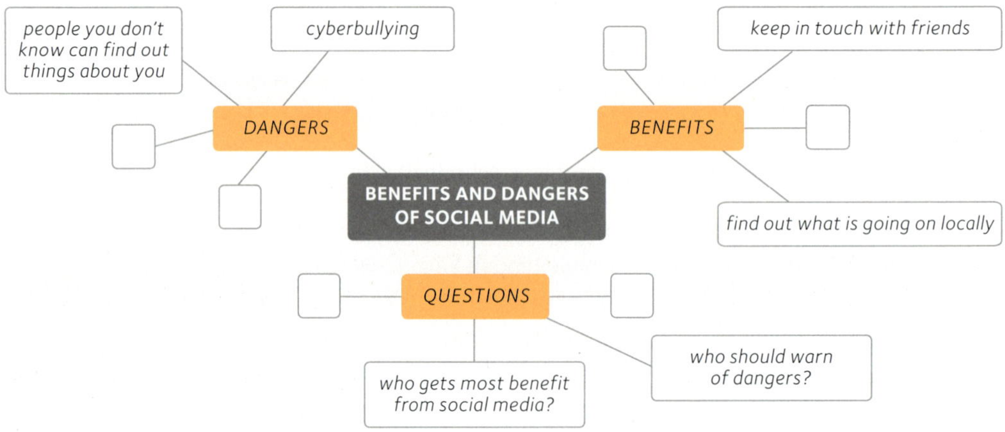

Einen Text sinnvoll gliedern

→ *Language for writing*, hintere Umschlagklappe

Wenn Sie etwas schriftlich verfassen, müssen Sie Ihren Text klar und logisch strukturieren.

Jedes längere Schriftstück bedarf eines Anfangs (Einleitung), eines Mittelteils (Hauptteil) und eines Endes (Abschluss).

Einleitung	Stellen Sie das Thema vor und legen Sie dar, wie Sie es angehen wollen.
Hauptteil	Verwenden Sie für jedes Argument einen Absatz. Sie können erst alle Argumente dafür und dann alle Argumente dagegen darlegen. Verwenden Sie Bindeglieder wie: *However, …, That said, …*, um klarzustellen, dass Sie im folgenden Absatz eine gegenteilige Meinung darlegen werden. Verwenden Sie Ausdrücke wie: *In my opinion, …, My feeling is that …* usw., wenn Sie Ihre Meinung äußern.
Abschluss	Wiederholen Sie Ihre Einleitung. Sagen Sie, ob Sie eine der zwei Seiten befürworten.

Damit der Leser / die Leserin den roten Faden nicht verliert, können Sie die Sprachelemente der hinteren Umschlagklappe dieses Buches nutzen. Hier sind einige Beispiele, wie man mithilfe dieser Elemente einen Aufsatz strukturieren kann.

Argumente gliedern	*In the text we see how three pupils used social media to hurt another pupil.* ***First****, they … *****Secondly/Then****, they …*
Eine Begründung anführen	***Due to / Because of / As a result of*** *this behaviour, the girl became isolated.*
Aspekte ergänzen	***In addition, / Moreover****, the girl didn't get the job she wanted.*
Einen Gegensatz ausdrücken	***Although/While*** *examples like these illustrate the dangers, social media has its benefits, too. Being active on social media can …*
Beispiele anführen	*A young man,* ***for example****, who was diagnosed with terminal cancer aged 15, used social media …*
Ein Fazit ziehen	***To sum up / To conclude****, social media has its good and its bad sides.* ***On the one hand, … On the other hand, …***

Wenn Sie mit dem Schreiben fertig sind:

- Überprüfen Sie Ihre Rechtschreibung, Grammatik und Zeichensetzung sowie Ihren Satzbau.
- Lesen Sie sich das, was Sie geschrieben haben, genau durch und verbessern Sie den Aufsatz dort, wo es der Lesefluss erfordert.

Versuchen Sie in einer Prüfung, rechtzeitig mit dem Schreiben aufzuhören, um genau das tun zu können. Fünf bis zehn Minuten sollten hierfür ausreichend sein.

C Einen Brief (oder eine E-Mail) schreiben

Aufbau

- **Anrede**

  Der Stil der Anrede richtet sich danach, wer der Empfänger / die Empfängerin ist. Anbei einige Beispiele:

  - sehr förmlich (unbekannter Empfänger / unbekannte Empfängerin in einem Geschäftsbrief): *Dear Sir or Madam*
  - förmlich (Geschäftsbrief, in dem die Name bekannt ist): *Dear Mr/Mrs/Ms Smith*
  - freundlich (privater Brief): *Dear Paul/Paula*
  - betont locker (privater Brief): *Hi Paul/Paula*

- **Einleitung**

  - Beginnen Sie den ersten Satz nach der Anrede mit einem Großbuchstaben.
  - Danken Sie ggf. dem Empfänger / der Empfängerin für seinen oder ihren letzten Brief.
  - Entschuldigen Sie sich ggf. dafür, nicht schon früher geschrieben zu haben, und nennen Sie die Gründe.
  - Gehen Sie kurz auf den wichtigsten Punkt im vorangegangenen Brief des Empfängers / der Empfängerin ein.

- **Hauptteil**

  – Nennen Sie den Grund oder aktuellen Anlass für Ihren Brief.
  – Erzählen Sie, was Sie mitzuteilen haben, und machen Sie das gegebenenfalls mit Beispielen oder Erläuterungen anschaulich.

- **Ende**

  – Schreiben Sie, dass (und vielleicht auch warum) Sie jetzt zu einem Ende kommen müssen.
  – Schreiben Sie, dass Sie hoffen, bald wieder von dem Empfänger / der Empfängerin zu hören.

- **Abschließender Gruß**

  Der Schlussgruß richtet sich danach, wie gut man den Empfänger kennt, entsprechend der Anrede.

  – sehr förmlich (unbekannter Empfänger in einem Geschäftsbrief): *Yours faithfully*
  – förmlich (Geschäftsbrief, in dem der Name bekannt ist): *Yours sincerely / Sincerely yours*
  – allgemein freundlich (Geschäftsbrief oder Privatbrief): *Regards / Best regards / Best wishes*
  – Privater Brief: *Yours / All the best / Love*

D Kreatives Schreiben

Kreatives Schreiben ist in vielfältigen Formen möglich: als Blog-Eintrag, als Vervollständigung des schon bestehenden Anfangs einer Erzählung oder in Form einer selbst erfundenen Kurzgeschichte, oder vielleicht werden Sie auch aufgefordert, eine Geschichte zu einem Bild zu verfassen. Auch die Aufgabe, einen Zeitungsbeitrag zu verfassen, kann in den Bereich „Kreatives Schreiben" gehören.
Unabhängig von der genauen Aufgabenstellung gelten beim Kreativen Schreiben grundlegende Regeln.

Planen

Beschließen Sie, wie Sie sich dem Thema nähern wollen, und machen Sie Notizen. Bringen Sie eine Struktur in diese Notizen (Mindmap oder Liste). Schreiben Sie Schlüsselwörter auf, die Sie verwenden wollen.

Schreiben

- Schreiben Sie einen Einführungssatz.
- Verfassen Sie den Hauptteil. Achten Sie auf verbindende Wörter und Satzglieder, die den Leser durch den Text führen.
- Schreiben Sie den abschließenden Satz.

Überprüfen

Beim schnellen Durchlesen entgehen Ihnen leicht ungenaue Wortverwendungen und andere ungeschickte Formulierungen sowie Tippfehler. Wenn die Aufgabe als Hausaufgabe gegeben wurde, können Sie nach Möglichkeit einen Freund oder eine Freundin bitten, Ihren Text zu lesen und Verbesserungsvorschläge zu machen. Sich selbst den Text laut vorzulesen hilft ebenfalls, auf Unstimmigkeiten aufmerksam zu werden.
Drucken Sie Ihren Text nach Möglichkeit aus. Auf Papier entdeckt man oft Dinge, die einem beim Lesen am Bildschirm entgangen sind. Vor allem aber kann man den Text als Ganzes so besser bewerten.

Formen

Einen Blog schreiben

- Lesen Sie alles, was bereits zum Thema gesagt wurde. Stellen Sie sicher, dass Sie das Thema und seine bisherige Behandlung richtig erfasst haben.
- Ihr erster Satz sollte sich bereits direkt auf das Thema beziehen.
- Widmen Sie jedem Aspekt einen eigenen Absatz. Verwenden Sie sinnverbindende Wörter und Satzteile.
- Betonen Sie Ihre Stellungnahme durch einen prägnanten Schlusssatz.
- Auch wenn ein Blog-Beitrag weniger förmlich ist als andere schriftliche Kommentare, sollten Sie sich um einen höflichen Ton bemühen. Versuchen Sie nicht, um jeden Preis witzig zu sein.

Eine Geschichte fortsetzen

- Lesen Sie den Anfangssatz der bestehenden Geschichte. Er gibt oft bereits Auskunft über den Ort der Handlung und enthält Hinweise zum Thema der Geschichte.
- Studieren Sie dann den Rest der Geschichte sorgfältig.
- Machen Sie sich mit der Form der Geschichte vertraut. Wird in der Ich-Form erzählt? Wie werden Dialoge eingesetzt? Achten Sie auf Hinweise, die auf den Ausgang der Geschichte hinweisen könnten.
- Notieren Sie sich die Namen der handelnden Personen. Achten Sie darauf, sie korrekt zu schreiben. Machen Sie Notizen zu den Charakteren, damit Sie wissen, was für Menschen sie sind und wie sie sich in Ihrer Fortsetzung benehmen und agieren werden.
- Kopieren Sie den bisherigen Schlusssatz. Nutzen Sie dann Ihre Notizen zur Weiterführung der Geschichte.
- Achten Sie darauf, dass Ihr Schlusssatz die Geschichte zu einem überzeugenden Ende bringt.

6 PRODUKTION: SCHAUBILDER UND STATISTIKEN BESCHREIBEN UND ANALYSIEREN

Diagramme und Kurvenbilder werden verwendet, um Informationen visuell darzustellen.

TYPES OF DIAGRAMS

Table

	Germany	UK
2010	568	261
2018	822	98

Bar chart

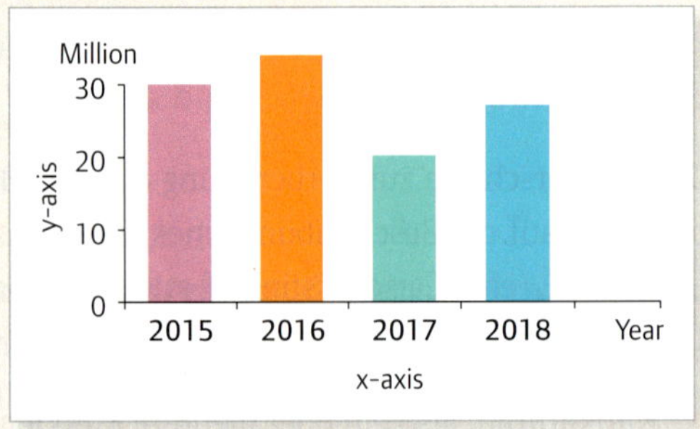

Pie chart

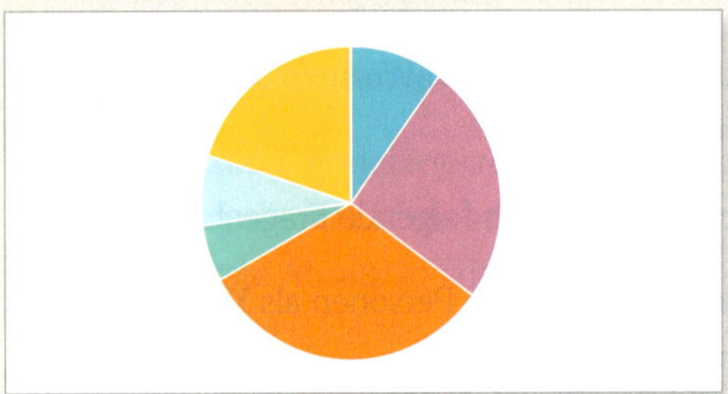

Graph, line graph

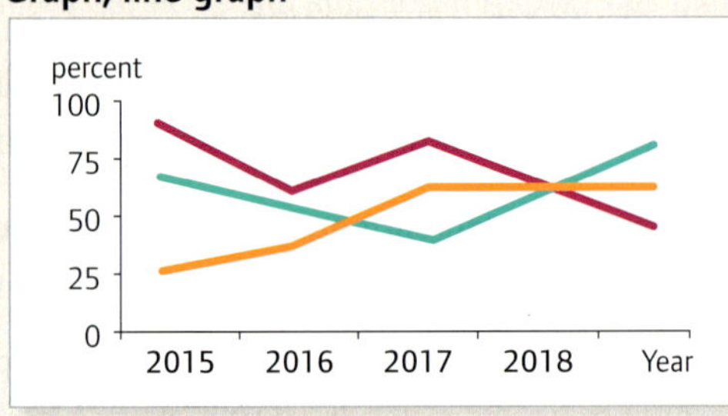

Bevor Sie mit dem Schreiben beginnen, nehmen Sie Schmierpapier zur Hand, sehen sich die Abbildung genau an und machen sich zu folgenden Fragen Notizen:

- Was sagt die Überschrift aus? Welche Beschriftung liegt vor?
- Welche Zahlen und Einheiten werden verwendet, um die Daten darzustellen?
- Wenn ein Balkendiagramm / eine Kurve vorliegt, wofür steht die x-Achse? Wofür die y-Achse?
- Welche Muster können Sie in den Daten erkennen?
- Welche Schlüsse können Sie aus diesen Mustern ziehen?

Um Ihre Beschreibung und Analyse der Abbildung zu ordnen, nutzen Sie Ihre Notizen folgendermaßen:

■ eine Einleitung zum Diagramm bzw. Kurvenbild (Überschrift)	*The diagram/graph shows … / refers to …*
■ ein Überblick dessen, was es darstellt	*The figures in the table show …* *The x-axis shows …, the y-axis shows …*
■ eine ausführliche Beschreibung der Informationen	*The graph shows a huge increase in …*
■ die Beziehung zwischen den Kategorien	*Germany produces twice as much … as the UK.*
■ eine Auswertung des Diagramms bzw. Kurvenbilds	*The figures indicate that …*

7 MEDIATION

Mediation ist das Übertragen wesentlicher Textelemente von einer Sprache in eine andere. Mediation ist nicht mit dem Wort „Übersetzung" austauschbar. Sie sollen nur den Sinn des Textes übertragen und bestimmte Informationen wiedergeben.

A Vorbereitung

- Lesen Sie sich die Anweisungen sorgfältig durch. Vergewissern Sie sich, dass Sie wissen:
  - warum die Informationen in einer anderen Sprache wiedergegeben werden.
  - für wen die Mediation gedacht ist, z. B. für andere Schüler/innen, Ihr Chef / Ihre Chefin.
  - welche Textart gefordert wird, z. B. eine E-Mail, eine Informationsbroschüre.
- Lesen Sie den Text zügig, um den groben Sinn zu erfassen. Verschwenden Sie keine Zeit mit einzelnen Wörtern, die Sie nicht verstehen.
- Lesen Sie die Anweisungen noch einmal, dann gehen Sie den Text ein weiteres Mal durch und suchen nach Textpassagen, die jene Informationen enthalten, die Sie zur Lösung der Aufgabe benötigen. Notieren Sie wichtige Informationen aus dem Text (z. B. Wer? Wann? Wo? Wieso?). In einer Prüfung können Sie die betreffenden Stellen unterstreichen oder farblich hervorheben. Folgende Textstellen können als unwesentlich betrachtet werden: Wiederholungen (oft eingeleitet durch *in other words, to put it another way*) und Anekdoten und Exkurse (*by the way, incidentally*).

B Einen Mediationstext schreiben

Schreiben Sie die wichtigsten Punkte des Textes in klarem, einfachem Deutsch auf. Halten Sie sich an das, was im Originaltext gesagt wurde. Wenn Sie damit fertig sind:

- Lesen Sie sich Ihren Text durch und stellen Sie sicher, dass der Inhalt des Originals klar und verständlich übertragen wurde.
- Überprüfen Sie, dass Sie nur solche Informationen übernommen haben, die für die Aufgabe relevant sind.
- Überprüfen Sie, dass Sie für die Zielgruppe Ihres Textes angemessen formuliert haben.
- Lesen Sie Ihren Text Korrektur, d. h. überprüfen Sie die Rechtschreibung und Grammatik.

8 ÜBERSETZEN

Einen Text oder Textauszug zu übersetzen verlangt Sorgfalt und Geduld. Im Gegensatz zur Mediation ist für eine Übersetzung jedes Wort des Originaltextes wichtig. Ihre Aufgabe als Übersetzer/in ist es, den Sinn des Textes mit deutschen Entsprechungen zu reproduzieren. Merken Sie sich folgende Regeln:

- Übersetzer/innen haben keine eigene „Stimme". Selbst wenn Sie mit der Aussage nicht einverstanden sind, dürfen Sie weder den Text an sich noch den Ton verändern.

- Von Ihnen werden weder Bewertungen noch Meinungsäußerungen erwartet.
- Streben Sie keine wortgetreue Übersetzung an, denn das ist unmöglich. Stattdessen konzentrieren Sie sich beim Lesen auf Informationsblöcke, die Sie dann als Ganzes übersetzen.

Bevor Sie mit dem Schreiben beginnen:

- Schreiben Sie sich Wörter und Strukturen auf, die Sie nicht verstehen.
- Wenden Sie Ihre Fertigkeiten zur Worterkennung an, um sich die Bedeutung von unbekannten Wörtern und Satzstrukturen zu erarbeiten. Verwenden Sie dabei auch Ihr Wörterbuch, wenn es die Zeit erlaubt.

Wenn Sie mit Ihrer Übersetzung fertig sind:

- Vergleichen Sie Ihren Text und das Original Satz für Satz, um sicherzustellen, dass Sie nichts ausgelassen haben.
- Lesen Sie Ihren Text durch und vergewissern Sie sich, dass er klar und verständlich ist.
- Überprüfen Sie Ihre Rechtschreibung und Grammatik.

9 PRÄSENTATION

Im Verlauf Ihres Schuljahres könnten Sie aufgefordert werden, eine Präsentation vorzubereiten und zu geben. Die Fertigkeit des Präsentierens können Sie in der Schule üben; das gibt Ihnen die nötige Sicherheit, um später erfolgreich eine Präsentation im Berufsleben/Studium zu geben.

A Vorbereitung

- Sammeln Sie möglichst viele Informationen und Ideen zu dem Thema, indem Sie im Internet und in Büchern recherchieren, ein Brainstorming machen, usw.
- Wählen Sie jene Ideen aus, die Ihr Thema am sinnvollsten widerspiegeln, und machen Sie sich Notizen.
- Verwenden Sie Ihre Notizen, um Ihre Ideen in logische Einheiten einzuteilen.
- Ordnen Sie diese Einheiten so, dass ein roter Faden klar erkennbar ist.
- Stellen Sie Ihre Präsentation zusammen und benutzen Sie eine grobe Gliederung.
- Wenn Sie das geschrieben haben, was Sie sagen wollten, lesen Sie Ihre Präsentation durch. Suchen Sie nach Stellen, wo Sie etwas kürzen oder löschen können. Fragen Sie sich immer wieder: Kann ich das noch kürzer, präziser ausdrücken?
- Erstellen Sie sich nun Stichwortkarten als Erinnerungshilfe für die wichtigsten Informationen. Schreiben Sie auf Karteikarten; schreiben Sie deutlich und in Großbuchstaben und möglichst keine ganzen Sätze außer den ersten und den letzten – Sie benötigen nur Stichwörter.
- Es hilft, Ihre Präsentation als Trockenübung zu geben, besonders vor einem Publikum.

B Eine Präsentation halten

- Beginnen Sie mit einer Begrüßung Ihrer Zuhörer/innen und stellen Sie anschließend sich und Ihr Thema vor. Versuchen Sie, das Interesse und die Aufmerksamkeit Ihrer Zuhörerschaft von Anfang an zu wecken. Sagen Sie, wie lang Sie über etwas reden werden, z. B.: *In the next 10 minutes, I will share my ideas about …*
- Teilen Sie Ihrem Hörerkreis mit, wie Sie Ihre Präsentation unterteilt haben bzw. wie viele Punkte Sie abdecken wollen, z. B.: *I've divided my talk into three sections: first … second …*
- Nachdem Sie das Ende Ihrer Präsentation eingeläutet haben, fassen Sie sich kurz und kommen Sie zum Ende. Ermutigen Sie Ihre Zuhörer/innen, Fragen zu stellen.

10 INTERAKTION

Sie werden möglicherweise im Unterricht aufgefordert, an einer Diskussion bzw. einem Rollenspiel mitzuwirken. Beide dieser Aufgaben schließen einen Austausch mit anderen Menschen ein. Folgen Sie den u.s. allgemeinen Tipps.

Tipps für einen guten Austausch

- Verinnerlichen Sie die Ausdrücke auf der hinteren Umschlagklappe und verwenden Sie sie im Unterricht, sooft Sie können. → *Language for speaking*, hintere Umschlagklappe
- Halten Sie sich an das Thema.
- Bleiben Sie locker und denken Sie, bevor Sie sprechen.
- Bleiben Sie immer höflich und geben Sie auch anderen die Möglichkeit zu reden. Hören Sie aktiv zu und gehen Sie auf die anderen Teilnehmer/innen ein. Nehmen Sie Augenkontakt auf und zeigen Sie Interesse, Überraschung, usw. Stellen Sie Fragen.
- Werten Sie andere niemals ab. Wenn ein anderer Teilnehmer / eine andere Teilnehmerin Probleme zu haben scheint, helfen Sie ihm/ihr, indem Sie in Worte fassen, was (Sie glauben, was) er/sie ausdrücken möchte, z. B.: *So, you mean that … I think I understand what you're getting at. You're saying that …*

An Diskussionen teilnehmen

In einer Diskussion sollten Sie Ihre Meinung zum Ausdruck bringen.

- Lesen Sie die Anweisungen sorgfältig durch und entscheiden Sie, was Sie sagen möchten.
- Machen Sie sich Notizen und schreiben Sie einige Schlüsselwörter bzw. -ausdrücke auf Englisch auf.
- Versuchen Sie vorauszusehen, was die anderen Teilnehmer/innen sagen könnten. Überlegen Sie sich, wie Sie hierzu reagieren würden, und fügen Sie Ihren Notizen englische Ausdrücke der Zustimmung bzw. Widerrede hinzu. → *Language for speaking*, hintere Umschlagklappe

11 PRÜFUNGSSTRATEGIEN

Alles, was Sie während Ihres Schuljahres gelernt haben, wird Ihnen zu guten Prüfungsergebnissen verhelfen. Die folgenden Tipps helfen Ihnen, in jedem Test bzw. in jeder Prüfung Ihr Bestes zu geben.

A Die schriftliche Prüfung

- Lesen Sie sich alle Aufgaben sorgfältig durch und stellen Sie sicher, dass Sie wissen, was zu tun ist.
- In Bezug auf textbezogene Aufgaben fragen Sie sich: Welche Textstelle/n benötige ich zur Lösung der Aufgabe?
- In Bezug auf Aufgaben zum Hörverständnis fragen Sie sich: Worauf muss ich achten?
- In Bezug auf schriftliche Aufgaben fragen Sie sich: Welche Art von Text muss ich schreiben? Dann machen Sie sich Notizen und ordnen Sie Ihren Text, bevor Sie die Endfassung schreiben. Zum Schluss überprüfen Sie Rechtschreibung und Grammatik.
- Wenn Sie mit den Prüfungsaufgaben fertig sind und bevor Sie Ihre Aufgaben abgeben, überprüfen Sie, dass Sie alle Anweisungen und jede Aufgabe ordentlich erfüllt haben. Vergewissern Sie sich, dass Sie nichts ausgelassen haben.

B Die mündliche Prüfung

- Lesen Sie sich den Text und die Aufgabenstellung durch, sofern vorhanden.
- Sofern es erlaubt ist, machen Sie sich Notizen zu dem, was Sie sagen möchten, und zwar bevor Sie zu reden beginnen (Stichpunkte reichen aus).
- Denken Sie an die Redewendungen, die Sie gelernt haben, sowie die Strategie, sich abzuwechseln.
- Wenn Sie plötzlich einen Gedächtnisausfall haben und sich an kein einziges Wort erinnern können, umschreiben Sie, was Sie sagen möchten. Reden Sie weiter!

Wenden Sie diese Tipps bei nächster Gelegenheit an, z. B. bei einem Klassenarbeit oder einer Prüfung. Die Rückmeldungen, die Sie auf Ihre Darbietung von Ihrer Klasse bekommen, zeigen Ihnen, in welchen Bereichen Sie sich noch verbessern können.

THE SIMPLE PRESENT

FORM: Das *simple present* wird so gebildet:

Aussage	*I **play** football every day.* *He play**s** football at school.* *He go**es** to school at 8 a.m.* *She push**es** her bike uphill.*	*I/we/you/they*: Grundform *he/she/it*: Grundform + *s* *he/she/it*: Grundform + *es* (nach einem „*o*" oder einen Zischlaut wie „*sh*")
Verneinungen	*They **don't play** football.* *She **doesn't play** football.*	*I/we/you/they don't* + Grundform *he/she/it doesn't* + Grundform
Fragen	***Do** you **play** football?* ***Does** she **play** football?*	*Do I/we/you/they* + Grundform *...?* *Does he/she/it* + Grundform *...?*
Kurzantwort	*Yes, I **do**.* *Yes, she **does**.* *No, I **don't**.* *No, she **doesn't**.*	*I/we/you/they do* *he/she/it does* *I/we/you/they don't* *he/she/it doesn't*

GEBRAUCH: Das *simple present* wird verwendet für:

gleich bleibende Zustände	*I **come** from Germany.*
regelmäßige, wiederholte Handlungen	*She **eats** a lot of fruit.*
was zum Tagesablauf gehört	*I **wake** up at 7 a.m.*
was man beruflich und in der Freizeit macht	*I **work** in a hospital.*

SIGNALWÖRTER: Das *simple present* verwendet man häufig mit den folgenden typischen Zeitangaben:

- always, usually, often, sometimes, rarely, never
- every morning/day/year
- at ... o'clock, in the morning, at lunchtime, after school
- on Monday(s), at the weekend, in June, in the summer

THE PRESENT PROGRESSIVE

FORM: Das *present progressive* wird so gebildet:

Aussage	***I'm playing** football.* *He **is playing** football.* *He is tak**ing** a photo.* *You are si**tt**ing in my chair.* *He is ru**nn**ing around the house.*	*am/is/are ('m/'s/'re)* + *-ing*-Form des Verbs Verben auf *-e*: das *-e* entfällt einsilbige Verben mit Konsonant am Ende, die kurz gesprochen werden: Konsonant verdoppelt

Verneinungen	*I'm **not playing** football* *She **isn't playing** football.*	*'m not/isn't/'s not/aren't/'re not* + *-ing*-Form des Verbs
Fragen	***Are** you **playing** football?* ***Is** she **playing** football?*	*am/is/are* wird mit dem Subjekt getauscht
Kurzantwort	***Yes, I am.*** ***Yes, she is.*** ***No, I'm not.*** ***No, she isn't.***	*simple present* des Verbs „*to be*"

GEBRAUCH: Das *present progressive* wird verwendet für:

vorübergehende oder im Moment des Sprechens ablaufende Handlungen und Situationen	*I'**m playing** football right now.* *Shhh! I'**m talking** to my mum.*

SIGNALWÖRTER: Das *present progressive* verwendet man häufig mit den folgenden typischen Zeitangaben:

- at the moment, now
- just, still
- today, this week, this month, this summer

1 Complete the sentences with simple present forms of the verbs in brackets.

EXAMPLE: ▬ 1 (you – know) Emma Gordon? — *Do you know Emma Gordon?*
No, ▬ 2. I ▬ 3 (not know) her. — *No, I don't. I don't know her.*

1 ▬ 1 (you – speak) English?
Yes, ▬ 2. But I ▬ 3 (not use) it very often.
2 ▬ 1 (your friend Mike – have) a car?
No, ▬ 2. But he ▬ 3 (own) a motorbike.
3 ▬ 1 (English people – watch) German films?
No, ▬ 2. They ▬ 3 (not watch) many foreign language films.
4 ▬ 1 (your coffee – taste) good?
Yes, ▬ 2. It ▬ 3 (taste) bitter, which is how I like it.

2 Complete the sentences with present progressive forms of the verbs in brackets.

1 What ▬ 1 (you – do) at the moment? ▬ 2 (you – work)?
No, ▬ 3. I ▬ 4 (check) my private emails.
2 What language ▬ 1 (that woman – speak)? ▬ 2 (she – speak) Spanish?
No, ▬ 3. She ▬ 4 (speak) Portuguese.

3 Sorry, ⬬ [1] (I – phone) in the middle of your meal?
No, ⬬ [2]. We ⬬ [3] (not eat) at the moment.
4 ⬬ [1] (your friends – play) basketball in the sports hall?
Yes, ⬬ [2]. They ⬬ [3] (practise) for the game next week.

3 Complete the sentences with the correct simple present or present progressive forms of the verbs in brackets.

1 I ⬬ [1] (try out) a new internet provider. I ⬬ [2] (think) that it's better than my old one.
2 Where ⬬ [1] (you – come) from? Are you Canadian?
3 What ⬬ [1] (Manuela – do)? ⬬ [2] (she – work) as a radio journalist too?
4 What ⬬ [1] (Manuela – do) today? ⬬ [2] (she – work) in the studio?
5 Tunisia is a hot country. It ⬬ [1] (not rain) much.
6 Oh no! It ⬬ [1] (rain). We can forget our barbecue.

THE SIMPLE PAST

FORM: Das *simple past* wird so gebildet:

Aussage	*I **played** football yesterday.* *She **liked** the match.*	regelmäßige Verben: Grundform + *-ed* Verben auf *-e*: nur *-d*
	*They sto**pp**ed the fight.*	einsilbige Verben mit Konsonant am Ende, die kurz gesprochen werden: Konsonant verdoppelt
	*She **bought** a bike last week.* *I **was** at the party.*	unregelmäßige Verben: → S. 275
Verneinungen	*They **didn't play** football.* *He **didn't buy** a bike.*	*did not (didn't)* + Grundform
	*She **wasn't** at the party.*	*to be: was not (wasn't)* und *were not (weren't)*
Fragen	***Did** you **play** football?* ***Did** she **buy** a bike?*	*did* + Grundform
	***Were** you at the party?*	*to be: was* und *were*
Kurzantwort	*Yes, I **did**.* *No, they **didn't**.*	*I/you/he/she/it/we/they did* *I/you/he/she/it/we/they didn't*

GEBRAUCH: Das *simple past* wird verwendet für:

abgeschlossene Ereignisse und Zustände	*I **saw** him yesterday.*

SIGNALWÖRTER: Das *simple past* verwendet man häufig mit den folgenden typischen Zeitangaben:

- yesterday
- last week/year
- three days ago
- in 2010
- When …?

4 Complete the sentences with simple past forms of the verbs in brackets.

1 …[1] (you – make) a pizza last weekend?
No, I …[2]. I …[3] (buy) one.
2 When …[1] (you – last – speak) to your friend in England?
I …[2] (skype) with her last weekend.
3 …[1] (your brother – fly) to Zurich yesterday?
No, he …[2]. He …[3] (not fly). He …[4] (go) by car. He …[5] (drive) there.
4 Why …[1] (you – not come) to Amy's party last weekend?
I …[2] (want) to go, but I …[3] (spend) the whole day in bed.

THE PAST PROGRESSIVE

FORM: Das *past progressive* wird so gebildet:

Aussage	*I **was playing** football.* *They **were playing** football.*	*was/were* + *-ing*-Form des Verbs
	He was taking a photo. *You were sitting in my chair.* *He was running around the house.*	Verben auf *-e*: das *-e* entfällt einsilbige Verben mit Konsonant am Ende, die kurz gesprochen werden: Konsonant verdoppelt
Verneinungen	*I **was not playing** football* *They **weren't playing** football.*	*was/were not/wasn't/weren't* + *-ing*-Form des Verbs
Fragen	***Were** you **playing** football?* ***Was** she **playing** football?*	*was/were* wird mit dem Subjekt getauscht
Kurzantwort	*Yes, I **was**.* *Yes, you **were**.* *No, I **wasn't**.* *No, you **weren't**.*	*I/he/she/it was* *you/we/they were* *I/he/she/it wasn't* *you/we/they weren't*

GEBRAUCH: Das *past progressive* wird verwendet für:

einen länger andauernden Vorgang, der durch ein Ereignis von kurzer Dauer unterbrochen wird. Dieses kurze Ereignis steht im *simple past*.	*I **was doing** my homework when I saw the terrible news on the TV.* *We **were walking** home when Martina passed us on her moped.*
Ereignisse, die in der Vergangenheit zu einem bestimmten Zeitpunkt gerade im Gange waren.	*I didn't see my boyfriend last week, as he **was studying** all week.*

5 In each sentence there is one simple past and one past progressive form. Complete the sentences with the correct forms of the verbs in brackets.

1 Where ⬬ [1] (you – go) when I ⬬ [2] (see) you yesterday?
2 I ⬬ [1] (answer) the last question in the test when the teacher ⬬ [2] (tell) us to stop writing.
3 I ⬬ [1] (not be) in town yesterday evening. I ⬬ [2] (play) a computer game at home.
4 My friends and I ⬬ [1] (just – leave) when it ⬬ [2] (start) to rain.
5 It ⬬ [1] (not rain) when I ⬬ [2] (get – on) the bus.
6 She ⬬ [1] (drink) a cup of coffee in the café when she suddenly ⬬ [2] (remember) that she had an appointment at the dentist.

THE PRESENT PERFECT

FORM: Das *present perfect* wird so gebildet:

Aussage	*I**'ve played** football all my life.* *She**'s gone** to see her friend.*	*have/has ('ve/'s)* + Partizip Perfekt unregelmäßige Verben: → S. 275
Verneinungen	*They **haven't played** football all day.* *He **hasn't bought** a bike yet.*	*haven't/hasn't* + Partizip Perfekt unregelmäßige Verben: → S. 275
Fragen	***Have** you **played** football today?* ***Has** she **bought** a new bike?* ***Have** you ever **been** to China?*	*have/has* wird mit dem Subjekt getauscht
Kurzantwort	*Yes, I **have**.* *No, he **hasn't**.*	*I/we/you/they have* *he/she/it has* *I/we/you/they haven't* *he/she/it hasn't*

GEBRAUCH: Das *present perfect* wird verwendet für:

Ereignisse, die in der Vergangenheit begonnen haben und bis in die Gegenwart andauern	*I **have lived** in this town all my life.* *I**'ve** just **finished** work.*
Ereignisse, die irgendwann einmal – oder noch nie – stattgefunden haben, ohne Angabe des Zeitpunkts	***Have** you ever **been** to London?* *Yes, I**'ve been** to London many times.*

SIGNALWÖRTER: Das *present perfect* verwendet man häufig, aber nicht immer, mit den folgenden typischen Zeitangaben:

- already, just, before, (not) yet
- for (*seit*) three weeks/months/years
- since Monday/2010
- How long …?
- ever …?
- lately, recently
- up till now

6 Complete the sentences with present perfect forms of the verbs in brackets.

1 I ___[1] (just – see) the new movie. ___[2] (you – see) it yet?
2 Susanne ___ (make) copies for everyone, so please take one.
3 My parcel ___[1] (still – not arrive). What about yours? ___[2] (yours – arrive) yet?
4 Hi, I'm Andy. We ___[1] (not meet) before, but I ___[2] (hear) a lot about you from Claire.
5 ___[1] (you – have) lunch? I ___[2] (not eat) and I'm starving.

7 Look at the box "Signalwörter" on p. 251 and decide whether you should use "for" or "since" with the following expressions.

1 I've lived here (for/since) eighteen months.
2 I haven't been to the doctor (for/since) a year and a half.
3 My dog has been sick (for/since) Tuesday morning.
4 I haven't spoken to my parents (for/since) last January.
5 I haven't seen you (for/since) ages.
7 I've played in the orchestra (for/since) 2015.
8 I've been on a diet (for/since) New Year's Day.

8 Complete these sentences with the simple present or the present perfect forms of the verbs in brackets.

1 I ___[1] (live) in London for six years. I now ___[2] (feel) at home there.
2 We ___[1] (know) each other for a long time and you ___[2] (become) my closest friend!
3 Marina ___[1] (be) ill all this week. I ___[2] (hope) that she will soon be back at work.
4 This computer never ___[1] (work). We ___[2] (have) it for years. We ___[3] (need) to get a new one.
5 How long ___[1] (you – be) a member of this sports club? ___[2] (you – like) it?

9 Make dialogues as in the example.

EXAMPLE: ___[1] (you – ever – watch) an international football match live?
Yes, I ___[2]. I ___[3] (see) the match between Germany and Denmark last year.
Have you ever watched an international football match live?
Yes, I have. I saw the match between Germany and Denmark last year.

1 ___[1] (you – ever – meet) a celebrity?
No, I ___[2]. But I ___[3] (see) a reality TV star in a café in Berlin last month.
2 ___[1] (you – make) notes for your presentation yet?
No, I ___[2]. But I ___[3] (select) the graphs that I want to talk about.
3 ___[1] (you – ever – have) an accident?
No, I ___[2]. But my brother ___[3] (break) his leg on a skiing trip in January.
4 ___[1] (you – buy) your new phone yet?
Yes, I ___[2]. I ___[3] (find) a great offer on the internet.

10 Complete the sentences with the correct verb form: present perfect or simple past.

1 Last year I ▬ (take) a trip to Ireland.
2 I ▬ (be) there twice now.
3 I ▬ (make) some good friends when I was there. We chat nearly every week.
4 Last time I ▬ (fly) with a new airline.
5 Flying ▬ (become) much cheaper in recent years.

THE PAST PERFECT

FORM: Das *past perfect* wird so gebildet:

Aussage	*I **had** only **visited** London once before I moved there.*	*had* + Partizip Perfekt
Verneinungen	*I got a bad mark because I **hadn't learned** enough.*	*had not (hadn't)* + Partizip Perfekt
Fragen	***Had** you **been** to London before you moved there?*	*had* wird mit dem Subjekt getauscht

GEBRAUCH: Das *past perfect* wird verwendet:

wenn etwas beschrieben wird, das bereits vor einem Zeitpunkt in der Vergangenheit geschah	*I arrived at the station two minutes late and the train **had** already **left**!*

11 Which happened first, A or B?

	A	B
1	We went out	after it had stopped raining.
2	I was short of cash	because I had spent so much on presents.
3	Jack had already arrived	when I got there.
4	The policewoman explained to me	that my car had been stolen.
5	There I was at the bank	and I had left my wallet at home.

12 In each sentence there is one verb in the simple past and one in the past perfect. Complete the sentences with the correct forms.

1 The road ▬ [1] (be) blocked, as there ▬ [2] (be) an accident.
2 We ▬ [1] (not drive) far, when a warning light ▬ [2] (come) on.
3 I ▬ [1] (run) to the gate, but the flight ▬ [2] (already/close).
4 I ▬ [1] (not remember) the man, although I ▬ [2] (actually/meet) him the year before.
5 Maggie ▬ [1] (invite) Tony to her party, but he ▬ [2] (already make) other plans.

THE FUTURE

FORM UND GEBRAUCH:

going to-future	*This **is going to** be a great year!* ***Are** you **going to** move flat?*	logische Schlussfolgerungen Pläne und Absichten
will-future	*It **won't** rain tomorrow.* *Your bag looks heavy! I'**ll** carry it for you!* *Don't worry, I'**ll** do it tomorrow.*	Vorhersagen spontane Entscheidungen Versprechen, Angebote
present progressive	*Carrie **is travelling** around Australia in July.*	konkrete Pläne und Verabredungen (mit Zeitangabe)
simple present	*Our plane **leaves** at six o'clock.*	Fahrpläne, Programme

Nach den folgenden Verben im *simple present* verwendet man häufig *will-future*:

think, promise, hope, be sure, expect	*I promise that I'll come.*

13 Complete the sentences with "will/won't".

1 Holidays on the moon ⬬ (not happen) in my lifetime.
2 Sorry, kids, but there ⬬ (not be) enough time for a visit to Disneyland.
3 Why ⬬ (there – not be) enough time?
4 When ⬬ (we – find out) how much it's going to cost?
5 Next year is our school's anniversary. This school ⬬ (be) 25 years old.

14 Complete the sentences with "going to".

1 We've got so many interesting things planned. The project week ⬬ (be) a big success.
2 I ⬬ (ask) Tom if he can help me with this maths homework.
3 ⬬ (the police officer – arrest) that man? He stole that woman's purse!
4 We don't need a hotel. We ⬬ (stay) with friends.
5 He's given us a really difficult task for the weekend. It ⬬ (not be) easy.

15 Complete the translation.

1	Du musst uns nicht fahren. Wir nehmen ein Taxi.	You don't have to drive us. We ⬬ a taxi.
2	Ich helfe Ihnen mit Ihrer Tasche.	I ⬬ you with your bag.
3	Ich hole dir ein Pflaster.	I ⬬ you a plaster.
4	Wir nehmen eine große Pizza und zwei Cola, bitte.	We ⬬ a pizza and two colas, please.
5	Lass mal, ich bezahle.	Leave it, I ⬬.

THE PASSIVE

FORM: Das *passive* wird so gebildet:

	Aktiv	Passiv	
		entsprechender Form vom Verb *to be*	**+ Partizip Perfekt**
simple present	*I help*	*I* ***am***	*help**ed***
present progressive	*I am helping*	*I* ***am being***	*help**ed***
simple past	*I helped*	*I* ***was***	*help**ed***
present perfect	*I have helped*	*I* ***have been***	*help**ed***
will-future	*I will help*	*I* ***will be***	*help**ed***
going to-future	*I am going to help*	*I* ***am going to be***	*help**ed***
modals	*I must help*	*I* ***must be***	*help**ed***

GEBRAUCH: Das *passive* wird verwendet:

wenn es nicht nötig (oder nicht möglich) ist zu sagen, wer etwas tut oder getan hat	*Bikes* ***are stolen*** *every day in London.* *My bike* ***was stolen*** *yesterday.* *English* ***is spoken*** *in many African countries.*
wenn der Schwerpunkt auf dem Objekt liegt (mit *by* können wir sagen, von wem etwas gemacht wird)	*The US president* ***was welcomed*** *at the airport.* *Shots* ***were fired*** *(by the police).* *This article* ***was written*** *by a friend of mine.*

16 Complete the sentences with passive forms of the verbs in brackets. Be careful of the tenses.

1 The hotel ⬬ (sell) to a Russian company last January.
2 Whenever someone enters the building at night, the alarm ⬬ (activate) by the CCTV system.
3 The windows ⬬ (not clean) very often. The window cleaner only comes twice a year.
4 The forest ⬬ (destroy) in the last few years by the mining company. There's very little left.
5 Mr Thomas's talk will last 20 minutes. Questions ⬬ (can ask) at the end.
6 All windows ⬬ (must close) at the end of the day.
7 I'm warning you: if anything like this happens again, the police ⬬ (inform).
8 The text is perfect now. All the mistakes ⬬ (correct).
9 When we got to the house, it was clear that we ⬬ (not expect).

17 Say the same thing in the passive, using the underlined word(s) as the subject.

EXAMPLES: *Nobody gave my friend an invitation.*
My friend wasn't given an invitation.

1 They fired me.
2 Someone has stolen my mobile phone!
3 They paid him €500.
4 Somebody taught the intern how to operate the new system.
5 They've offered Tony the position.
6 Make sure that someone writes all this down.
7 Has anyone asked the manager to help?

CONDITIONAL SENTENCES

Conditional sentences (*if*-Sätze) drücken Bedingungen aus.

	if-Teil	Hauptsatz
Type 1 für reale Bedingungen	***simple present*** *If it **rains**,*	***will-future*** *I **will stay** inside today.*
Type 2 für unwahrscheinliche Bedingungen	***simple past*** *If I **had** time,*	***would*** **+ Infinitiv** *I **would see** the film.*
Type 3 für Situationen, die in der Vergangenheit geschehen sein könnten, aber nicht geschehen sind	***past perfect*** *If she **had taken** a taxi,*	***would have*** **+ Partizip Perfekt** *she **wouldn't have missed** the plane.*

ZU BEACHTEN

Anstelle von *will* kann auch ein Modalverb wie *can*, *might* oder *should* im Hauptsatz stehen. Anstelle von *would* kann auch das Modalverb *could* im Hauptsatz stehen.	*If it rains, I **can** stay in bed all day.* *If I wanted more money, I **could** get a second job.*
Im *If*-Satz stehen nie ***will*** oder ***would***.	*If you ~~will~~ come, …*
Wenn der *if*-Satz am Satzanfang steht, wird er meist mit einem Komma vom Hauptsatz getrennt. Steht der Hauptsatz am Satzanfang, verwendet man meist kein Komma.	*If it rains today, I'll go shopping.* *I'll go shopping if it rains today.*

18 In each sentence one verb is in the simple present, one verb in the future with "will". Complete the sentences with the correct forms of the verbs in brackets.

1 If the parcel ▬[1] (arrive) by Friday, that ▬[2] (be) OK.
2 If Manni ▬[1] (say) that one more time, I ▬[2] (explode)!
3 She ▬[1] (not understand) you if you ▬[2] (not speak) more slowly.
4 What ▬[1] (you/do) if they ▬[2] (not offer) you the job?
5 If we ▬[1] (not take) a break soon, I ▬[2] (die) of hunger.
6 If they ▬[1] (invite) you, ▬[2] (you/go)?

19 Complete the translation. All the sentences are type 2 conditional sentences.

1 Wenn ich Zeit hätte, würde ich Ihnen helfen.
If I ▬[1] time, I ▬[2] you.
2 Wenn ich Max besser kennen würde, wüsste ich, wie ich ihm helfen könnte.
If I ▬[1] Max better, I ▬[2] how to help him.
3 Wenn du Francesca fragen würdest, was würde sie sagen?
If you ▬[1] Francesca, what ▬[2]?
4 Was würde passieren, wenn wir einfach nichts tun würden?
What ▬[1] if we simply ▬[2] nothing?
5 Es wäre besser, wenn Sie später noch einmal anrufen könnten.
It ▬[1] better if you ▬[2] again later.
6 Was tätest du, wenn die andere Firma mehr Geld bieten würde?
What ▬[1] if the other firm ▬[2] more money?

20 Say the same thing with a conditional sentence type 3.

EXAMPLE: I didn't know about the meeting so I didn't come. If I ▬
If I had known about the meeting, I would have come.

1 Jenny didn't hear about the job so she didn't apply. If Jenny ▬
2 They didn't have enough money so they didn't buy any souvenirs. If they ▬
3 I didn't have my mobile with me so I didn't call you. If I ▬

EXAMPLE: Jack had to work on Saturday. That's why he didn't come swimming with us.
If Jack ▬
If Jack hadn't had to work on Saturday, he would have come swimming with us.

4 I left my mobile at home. That's why I didn't take any photos. If I ▬
5 I stopped to talk to Martin. That's why I was late. If I ▬
6 They drove too fast. That's why they had an accident. If they ▬

REPORTED SPEECH

Man verwendet die indirekte Rede, um zu berichten, was jemand gesagt hat. Steht das einleitende Verb (*ask, say* usw.) in der Vergangenheit, verschieben sich die Zeiten im Satz entsprechend.

direkte Rede	indirekte Rede
simple present *Susan: "I often play tennis."*	***simple past*** *Susan said that she often played tennis.*
present progressive *Susan: "I am playing tennis."*	***past progressive*** *Susan said that she was playing tennis.*
simple past *Susan: "I played tennis."*	***past perfect*** (*simple past* auch möglich) *Susan said that she had played tennis.*
present perfect *Susan: "I have played tennis."*	***past perfect*** *Susan said that she had played tennis.*
will *Susan: "I will play tennis."*	***would*** *Susan said that she would play tennis.*
can *Susan: "I can play tennis."*	***could*** *Susan said that she could play tennis.*

ZU BEACHTEN

Wenn das Berichtete immer oder immer noch gültig ist, muss keine Zeitverschiebung erfolgen.	*Susan: "My brother lives with my parents." Susan told us that her brother **lives** with her parents.*

REPORTED QUESTIONS

Die Zeitverschiebung bei Fragen findet genauso statt wie bei Aussagen.
Bei Fragen mit Fragewörtern werden die Fragewörter (*where, who, why* usw.) behalten. Bei Fragen, die mit *do, did* usw. anfangen, wird *if/whether* statt *that* (wie bei *reported speech*) verwendet.
Bei Bitten und Befehlen werden *to* + infinitive verwendet.

Fragen	
Susan: "Where is Tom?"	*Susan asked where Tom **was**.*
Susan: "Do you speak English?"	*Susan asked me if I **spoke** English.*
Susan: "Are you coming with me?"	*Susan asked whether I **was coming** with her.*
Susan: "When did you last see Tom?"	*Susan asked me when I **had** last **seen** Tom.*
Bitten	
Susan: "Can you help me, please?"	*Susan asked me **to help** her.*
Susan: "Please don't tell anyone."	*Susan asked me not **to tell** anyone.*
Befehle	
Susan: "Shut up!"	*Susan told me **to shut up**.*
Susan: "Don't talk!"	*Susan told us not **to talk**.*

21 Complete the second sentence as in the example.

EXAMPLE: "They won't agree." (Earlier: "They will accept the offer.") But you said ▬
But you said that they would accept the offer.

1 "We can't get into the system." (Earlier: We have the password.)
But you said ▬
2 "I'm afraid I don't have time." (Earlier: I'll discuss it with you today.)
But you said ▬
3 "I'm not going to the class meeting." (Earlier: I don't want to miss the class meeting.)
But you said ▬
4 "I'm too tired." (Earlier: I'll go to the gym with you.)
But you said ▬
5 "I don't know where to go." (Earlier: I know the way.)
But you said ▬
6 "I believe Michael." (Earlier: "He is lying.")
But you said ▬

22 Complete the second sentence as in the example.

EXAMPLE: Tony: "Did anyone call while I was away?"
Tony wanted to know if *anyone had called while he was away*.

1 Penny: "Do you know the address?"
Penny asked me if I ▬
2 The neighbours: "Please don't park there."
They told me ▬
3 A colleague: "Who drives that red car?"
A colleague wanted to know ▬
4 Sean: "What did you do with all those spare copies?"
Sean wanted to know ▬
5 Our boss: "Who used the room last?"
Our boss demanded to know ▬
6 The receptionist: "Please wait outside."
The receptionist asked ▬

MODAL AUXILIARIES

Funktion	Modale Hilfsverben	
Fähigkeit	*He **can** speak several languages.* *My dad **could** only speak English.*	
Möglichkeit	*With your qualifications you **could** work abroad.* *The boss **may** come in at any moment.* *He **might** ask you what you are doing.*	
Bitte	***Can** I have a word with Ms Sims, please?* ***Could** I speak to Ms Sims, please?* ***May** I interrupt you?* ***Might** I ask you a personal question?*	(neutral) (höflich) (betont höflich) (äußerst höflich)
Erlaubnis	*You **can** go in now.* *The boss is free. You **may** go in now.*	(neutral) (gefällig)
Verbot	*We **mustn't** be late for work tomorrow.*	
Pflicht	*You **must** wear a hard hat in the factory.*	
Wahl	*Most people **don't have to** work on Sundays.* *You **needn't** come.*	
Empfehlung	*You **should** try harder.* *You **ought to** try harder.* *You **must** try harder.*	(neutral) (betont) (streng)

can, could, be able to

simple present	*I **can** see you.*	Ich kann dich sehen.
simple past	*I **could** swim at the age of six.*	Ich konnte mit sechs schwimmen.
present perfect	*I **haven't been able to** contact Harry yet.*	Ich konnte Harry bislang nicht erreichen.
future	*I **can** pay you tomorrow.* *I'**ll be able to** pay you tomorrow.*	Ich kann dich morgen bezahlen.
conditional	***Could** you give a presentation tomorrow?* ***Would you be able to** give a presentation tomorrow?*	Könnten Sie morgen eine Präsentation halten?

must, mustn't, needn't, don't/doesn't have to, had to

Gegenwart		
Aussage	*We **must** meet more often.* *We **have to** meet more often.*	*Wir müssen uns öfters treffen.*
Verneinung	*I **mustn't** forget his birthday.* *You really **don't have to** wait for me.* *You **needn't** come.*	*Ich darf seinen Geburtstag nicht vergessen.* *Du musst wirklich nicht auf mich warten.* *Du musst nicht kommen.*
Frage	*How many tests **do you have to** do?*	*Wie viele Tests musst du machen?*

Vergangenheit		
Aussage	*I **had to** work late yesterday evening.*	*Ich musste gestern abend länger arbeiten.*
Verneinung	*Nina **didn't have to** pay for the ticket.*	*Nina musste nicht für die Karte zahlen.*
Frage	*How much **did** you **have to** pay for the tickets?*	*Wie viel mussten Sie für die Karte bezahlen?*

Zukunft		
Aussage	*I'**ll have to** talk to the boss.*	*Ich werde mit dem Chef sprechen müssen.*
Verneinung	*He **won't have to** go to prison.*	*Er wird nicht ins Gefängnis müssen.*
Frage	***Will** she **have to** go to hospital?*	*Wird sie ins Krankenhaus müssen?*

23 Decide which of the two options is correct.

1 I (mustn't / don't have to) forget to pay for the tickets.
2 You (mustn't / don't have to) come if you don't want to.
3 When was your flight? (Must you / Did you have to) get up very early?
4 You (mustn't / needn't) forget your passport.
5 We (needn't / mustn't) check in till 40 minutes before the flight.
6 He (mustn't / doesn't have to) park there. That's the police car park.

24 Decide which of the sentences are not correct.

1 **a** The problem should have something to do with the battery.
b The problem might have something to do with the battery.
c The problem could have something to do with the battery.

2 **a** The train may be late this morning.
b The train can be late this morning.
c The train might be late this morning.
3 **a** Sue could be trying to skype me. I'll switch the computer on.
b Sue can be trying to skype me. I'll switch the computer on.
c Sue might be trying to skype me. I'll switch the computer on.
4 **a** Ask Jerry. He can know.
b Ask Jerry. He could know.
c Ask Jerry. He might know.

25 Which is correct: "should" or "must"?

1 Employers ▬ pay their employees.
2 We ▬ meet for coffee one day.
3 Homeowners ▬ report thefts to the police.
4 In order to vote you ▬ fill in a form.
5 Waiters ▬ be pleasant to customers.
6 You ▬ be nicer to your sister – she's done a lot for you!

VERB + -ING FORM • VERB + TO-INFINITIVE

Auf bestimmte Verben folgt eine *-ing*-Form, während auf andere ein Infinitiv folgt.

Verb + *-ing* Form	Verb + *to*-Infinitiv	Verb + *-ing* Form oder *to*-Infinitiv
*I **enjoy playing** video games.*	*They **wanted to go** on holiday.*	*We **love cooking**.* *We **love to cook**.*
admit, avoid, dislike, enjoy, finish, involve, not mind, recommend, stop, suggest	agree, choose, decide, expect, hope, learn, manage, seem, want, would like	begin, continue, hate, like, love, prefer, start

Einige Verben haben unterschiedliche Bedeutungen, je nachdem, ob ein Gerundium oder ein Infinitiv folgt.

remember	*Do you remember **telling** me about Ashley?* *Please remember **to tell** Ashley.*	*sich erinnern, etwas getan zu haben* *daran denken, etwas zu tun*
stop	*I wish you would stop **smoking**.* *On the way we stopped **to pick up** Eric.*	*aufhören, etwas zu tun* *anhalten, um etwas (anderes) zu tun*
try	*I tried **to stop** him.* *Why don't you try **jogging** once a week?*	*versuchen, etwas zu tun* *etwas ausprobieren*

26 Complete the sentences with the infinitive or gerund of the verb in brackets.

1 Have you finished … (make) the video yet?
2 She chose … (fly), although it is cheaper to drive.
3 I don't mind … (show) you around.
4 They suggest … (call) the police.
5 We must avoid … (make) the same mistake again.
6 I'd like … (stay) at home.
7 I like … (hang out) with my friends.
8 Why did you stop … (go) to the gym?
9 Rachel seems … (need) some help.
10 Did you remember … (do) your homework? The teacher wants it today.

PLURALS

Die allermeisten Pluralformen werden mit *-s* gebildet.	computer → computers
Bei Substantiven auf *-y* nach einem Konsonant wird *-y* zu *-ies*.	family → families
Substantive auf *-ch*, *-sh*, *-s* und *-x* bilden die Pluralform mit *-es*.	bus → buses beach → beaches
Substantive auf *-f* oder *-fe* bilden die Pluralform meist mit *-ves*.	thief → thieves
Substantive auf *-o* bilden gelegentlich die Pluralform mit *-es*.	potato → potatoes *aber:* photo → photos
Einige Substantive haben unregelmäßige Pluralformen.	man/woman → men/women tooth → teeth child → children person → people
Einige Substantive werden immer im Plural verwendet.	glasses, jeans, trousers, scissors

COUNTABLE AND UNCOUNTABLE NOUNS

Nicht zählbare Substantive haben keine Mehrzahlform, und man kann weder *a/an* noch eine Zahl davorsetzen.

zählbar	one book, two books, three books
nicht zählbar	weather, money, traffic ~~a weather, two moneys, three traffics~~

Bestimmte Substantive sind im Deutschen zählbar, im Englischen aber nicht.

advice	Rat, Ratschlag, Ratschläge	homework	Hausaufgabe, Hausaufgaben
equipment	Ausrüstung, Geräte	information	Information, Informationen
furniture	Möbel	knowledge	Kenntnis, Kenntnisse
hair	Haar, Haare	paper	Papier, Papiere
help	Hilfe, Hilfen, Hilfestellungen	progress	Fortschritt, Fortschritte

Das Verb steht nach einem nicht zählbaren Substantiv immer im Singular	*This information is interesting.* (Diese Information ist/Diese Informationen sind interessant.)
Nicht zählbare Substantive verwendet man mit *this/that* und *much*.	*There's not much information here.*
Mit Ausdrücken wie *a piece of* oder *a bit of* kann man Ersatzsingular- und Pluralformen bilden:	*Can I have a piece of paper, please?* *Let me give you a piece of advice.* *I need a bit of help.*

QUANTIFIERS

some/any

Some und *any* bezeichnen eine unbestimmte Menge oder Zahl. *Some* wird vor allem in bejahten Aussagesätzen, Angeboten und Bitten verwendet. *Any* steht meist in verneinten Aussagesätzen und in Fragen.

Aussagen	*I downloaded **some** music.* ***Somebody** sent me a message.*
Verneinungen	*I didn't download **any** videos.* *I don't know **anybody** here.*
Fragen	*Have you received **any** emails today?* *Has **anybody** seen Emma today?*
Bitten/Angebote	*Could you send me **some** information?* *Would you like **something** to drink?*

many/much/a lot of/little/a little/few/a few

Das Einsetzen von *many/much/a lot of/little/a little/few/a few* hängt davon ab, ob sie in Zusammenhang mit einem zählbaren oder unzählbaren Substantiv verwendet werden.

many	viel	wird mit zählbaren Substantiven verwendet, besonders in Verneinungen und Fragen	*I don't have **many** friends.* *How **many** pets do you have?*

much	viel	wird mit unzählbaren Substantiven verwendet, besonders in Verneinungen und Fragen	*I don't have **much** money.* *How **much** time do you have?*
a lot of	viel	wird statt *many* und *much* in gesprochenem Englisch oft verwendet, besonders in Aussagen.	*I have **a lot of** friends and **a lot of** money!*
few	wenig	wird mit zählbaren Substantiven verwendet	*I have **few** friends.*
little	wenig	wird mit unzählbaren Substantiven verwendet	*We have very **little** time!*
a few	einige / ein paar	wird mit zählbaren Substantiven verwendet	*I spent **a few** days in London.*
a little	etwas / ein wenig	wird mit unzählbaren Substantiven verwendet	*I need **a little** help.*

27 Decide whether "any" or "some" is correct.

1 I don't have (any/some) brothers or sisters.
2 I'm going out to buy (any/some) things from the supermarket. Do you need (anything/something)?
3 I heard that John said (anything/something) horrible to Jan. Do you have (any/some) idea what he said?
4 Do you know (any/some) good bars around here?
5 I would like (any/some) chips and (any/some) water, please!
6 I need (any/some) change (*Kleingeld*) to tip the waiter but I haven't got (any/some) coins.

28 Find the correct quantifier for the German word.

1 They have had ▬ (viel) homework recently.
2 How ▬ (viel) time do you need to get ready?
3 There are ▬ (viele) people in the pool – it's crowded!
4 I've been to ▬ (wenige) foreign countries. I don't like travelling.
5 Just take ▬ (einige) drops of this medicine – it's really strong!
6 Very ▬ (wenige) people managed to pass the exam.
7 I have ▬ (wenig) patience for such people.
8 It is often said that ▬ (etwas) knowledge is a dangerous thing.
9 ▬ (viele) people fail their driving test the first time.
10 There aren't ▬ (viele) students in class today.

COMPARISON OF ADJECTIVES

FORM: Adjektive werden wie folgt gesteigert:

	Adjektiv	Komparativ	Superlativ
einsilbiges Adjektiv	long big	long**er** bigg**er**	(the) long**est** (the) bigg**est**
zweisilbiges Adjektiv, das auf *-y* endet	pretty lucky	prett**ier** luck**ier**	(the) prett**iest** (the) luck**iest**
Adjektiv mit zwei oder mehr Silben	famous important	**more** famous **more** important	(the) **most** famous (the) **most** important
unregelmäßige Adjektive	good bad	better worse	(the) best (the) worst

Wenn zwei Sachen verglichen werden, muss man *than* oder *as … as* verwenden. (niemals *then* = dann)	*He is taller **than** his brother.* *He is **as** tall **as** his father.*
Wenn man den Superlativ in ein größeres Verhältnis setzen möchte, verwendet man die Präposition *in* oder *of*.	*He is the tallest person **in** the world.* *She is the cleverest student **in** her class.* ***Of** all the people I know he is the tallest.* *She is the cleverest **of** all her friends.*

ADVERBS OF MANNER

Mit Adverbien beschreibt man, wie etwas geschieht.
FORM: Adverbien werden wie folgt gebildet:

	Adjektiv		Adverb	
Adjektiv + *ly*	quick slow		quick**ly** slow**ly**	
Adjektiv auf *-y* → *-ily*	happy easy		happ**ily** eas**ily**	
Adverb bleibt formgleich mit Adjektiv	fast hard	early late	fast hard	early late
unregelmäßige Adverbien	good		well	

FORM: Adverbien werden wie folgt gesteigert:

	Adverb	Komparativ	Superlativ
Adverb formgleich mit Adjektiv: *-er*/*-est* anhängen	fast hard	fast**er** hard**er**	fast**est** hard**est**
Adverb auf *-ly*: *more*/*most* voranstellen	carefully	**more** carefully	**most** carefully

29 Make comparisons with the adjectives in brackets. In some sentences you need to add "than".

EXAMPLE: In the summer I have a *longer* (long) working day *than* in the winter.

1 This is one of the … (complicated) systems I have ever had to use.
2 Reading in a foreign language is normally … (easy) listening.
3 The old instruction manual was much … (thin) this one.
4 My cough (*Husten*) is … (bad) yesterday.
5 The tickets aren't … (cheap) last year. They're … (expensive).

30 Complete the sentences with the comparative or superlative form of the adverb.

1 You have to work … (hard) if you want to get a pay rise.
2 The new member of the team is doing … (good) now that he's had some training.
3 Four companies suggested solutions, but the German company solved the problem … (efficient).
4 My team is playing … (bad) than all the other teams.
5 The changes are happening … (gradual) than we had expected.
6 John drives … [1] (fast) than me but he also drives … [2] (careful) than me.

PERSONAL PRONOUNS AND POSSESSIVE ADJECTIVES

FORM:

subject pronouns		object pronouns	possessive adjectives
	Wer?	Wen? Wem?	Wessen?
ich	I	me	my
du/ihr/Sie	you	you	your
er/sie/es	he/she/it	him/her/it	his/her/its
wir	we	us	our
sie	they	them	their

RELATIVE CLAUSES

Relativsätze sind Nebensätze, die ein Substantiv näher definieren. Sie werden mit Relativpronomen eingeleitet. Ein Relativpronomen kann weggelassen werden, wenn der Nebensatz ein anderes Subjekt hat.

Personen	*who* oder (seltener) *that*	*People* ***who/that*** *don't eat meat are vegetarians.* *That's the girl* ***(who/that)*** *I saw at school.*
Dinge	*which* oder *that*	*He bought the bike* ***which/that*** *cost 500 euros.* *This is the house* ***(which/that)*** *I live in.*

Chronological word list

Dieses Wörterverzeichnis enthält alle Wörter, die nicht in der Liste des Grundwortschatzes enthalten sind, d. h. die nicht als bekannt vorausgesetzt werden. Wörter aus den *Audiotexten* sind mit einem gelben Balken, Wörter aus den *Videotexten* mit einem orangenen Balken, Wörter aus den *Differentiation files* mit einem blauen Balken und Wörter aus den *Group discussion files* mit einem grünen Balken gekennzeichnet. Die neuen Wörter aus den *Further reading*-Texten sind am Ende des Verzeichnisses. Vorausgesetzt wird jeweils der Wortschatz aus dem Hauptteil des Buches einschließlich der entsprechenden Unit.

AE = American English	*v* = verb	*phr* = phrase (*feststehende Wendung)*
BE = British English	*adj* = adjective	*pl* = plural
AusE = Australian Englisch	*adv* = adverb	*esp* = especially
n = noun (*Substantiv*)	*inf* = informal (*Umgangssprache*)	<> = opposite (*Gegensatz*)

GETTING STARTED

page 6

to **get started**	[get ˈstɑːtɪd]	to begin	loslegen, anfangen
to **match**	[mætʃ]	to put two things together	zuordnen
to **take turns to do sth**	[ˌteɪk ˈtɜːnz tə duː]	e.g. We took it in turns to look after the children.	etw abwechselnd tun
to **practise**	[ˈpræktɪs]	*n* practice	üben
to **understand**	[ˌʌndəˈstænd]	to know what sth means	verstehen
to **speak up**	[ˌspiːk ˈʌp]	to say sth louder	lauter sprechen
to **pronounce**	[prəˈnaʊns]	*n* pronunciation	aussprechen
to **slow down**	[ˌsləʊ ˈdaʊn]	to say sth slower	langsamer sprechen
to **mean**	[miːn]	e.g. What does this word mean?	bedeuten
to **start off**	[ˌstɑːt ˈɒf]	<> to finish	anfangen
to **add**	[æd]	*n addition*	hinzufügen
next to	[ˈnekst tə]	beside	neben
column	[ˈkɒləm]	vertical row or list	*(Text:)* Spalte
to **be short on sth**	[bi ˈʃɔːt ɒn]	to not have enough of sth	zu wenig von etw haben
to **try**	[traɪ]	to do your best to do sth	versuchen
to **fill**	[fɪl]	to make sth full of sth	füllen
statement	[ˈsteɪtmənt]	*v* to state	Aussage, Aussagesatz

page 7

waiter	[ˈweɪtə]	sb who works in a cafe or restaurant	Kellner
call centre agent	[ˈkɔːl sentər eɪdʒənt]	sb who takes/makes phone calls for a business	Telefonagent/in, Callcenteragent/in
flight attendant	[ˈflaɪt ətendənt]	sb who works on an aircraft	Flugbegleiter/in
safety regulations *pl*	[ˈseɪfti regjuleɪʃnz]	rules to make a place/thing safe	Sicherheitsvorschriften, -vorkehrungen
receptionist	[rɪˈsepʃənɪst]	sb who welcomes guests, answers phones	Empfangsmitarbeiter/in, Rezeptionist/in
guest	[gest]	*esp*sb staying in a hotel	Gast
personal	[ˈpɜːsənl]	private, about yourself	persönlich, privat
fantasy	[ˈfæntəsi]	*here:* made up	Phantasie-
engineer	[ˌendʒɪˈnɪə]	sb who designs technical/mechanical things	Ingenieur/in, Techniker/in
to **introduce sb to sb**	[ˌɪntrəˈdjuːs]	e.g. Steve introduced me to Helen.	jdn jdm vorstellen

page 8

in front of	[ɪn ˈfrʌnt əv]	<> behind	vor
board	[bɔːd]	e.g. The teacher wrote the vocabulary on the board.	(Wand-)Tafel
dictionary	[ˈdɪkʃənri]	book with lists of words and their meanings	Wörterbuch
trolley	[ˈtrɒli]	small vehicle with wheels	Wagen
to **brainstorm**	[ˈbreɪnstɔːm]	to think of new ideas	Ideen sammeln
pencil	[ˈpensl]	e.g. Please use a pen, not a pencil.	Bleistift
mobile (phone) *BE*	[ˈməʊbaɪl]	e.g. Please turn off your mobile phone in class.	Handy
schoolbag	[ˈskuːlbæg]	bag for carrying books, etc. to school	Schultasche
iced tea	[aɪst ˈtiː]	sweet, cold tea	Eistee
positive	[ˈpɒzətɪv]	<> negative	bejahend, positiv
negative	[ˈnegətɪv]	<> positive	verneinend, negativ
to **report back to sb**	[rɪˌpɔːt ˈbæk tə]	to give sb information	jdm berichten, jdm Bericht erstatten
pen	[pen]	e.g. He signed the letter with a pen.	Stift

page 9

dream	[driːm]	images in your mind while you are asleep	Traum
facilities *pl*	[fəˈsɪlətiz]	buildings, equipment, services	Einrichtung(en), Ausstattung
cinema	[ˈsɪnəmə]	place to watch films	Kino
to **sleep**	[sliːp]	e.g. I sleep eight hours a night.	schlafen
student	[ˈstjuːdnt]	sb learning at school, college, university	Schüler/in, Student/in
to **arrive**	[əˈraɪv]	<> to leave	eintreffen, ankommen
rule	[ruːl]	the way sth should be done	Regel, Vorschrift

vowel	[ˈvaʊəl]	e.g. a, e, i, o, u	Vokal
consonant	[ˈkɒnsənənt]	<> vowel (a, e, i, o, u)	Konsonant
church	[tʃɜːtʃ]	building for Christian religion	Kirche
shelf, shelves	[ʃelf, ʃelfvz]	sth that you place books on	Regal, Regale
piano	[piˈænəʊ]	large musical instrument with black and white keys	Klavier
hero	[ˈhɪərəʊ]	brave, good person	Held

page 10

exception (to sth)	[ɪkˈsepʃn]	sth that does not follow a rule	Ausnahme (von etw)
certain	[ˈsɜːtn]	special, particular	bestimmte/r/s, gewisse/r/s
sound	[saʊnd]	sth you can hear	Laut, Klang
to **become (sth)**	[bɪˈkʌm]	to later be	(etw / zu etw) werden
sheep, sheep	[ʃiːp]	e.g. one sheep, two sheep	Schaf, Schafe
tooth, teeth	[tuːθ, tiːθ]	e.g. one tooth, two teeth	Zahn, Zähne
scissors *pl*	[ˈsɪzəz]	used for cutting paper, etc.	Schere
sentence	[ˈsentəns]	e.g. Please answer using full sentences.	Satz
to **decide**	[dɪˈsaɪd]	*n* decision	(sich) entscheiden
parking space	[ˈpɑːkɪŋ speɪs]	place to park a car	Parkplatz
capital	[ˈkæpɪtl]	main city in a country or region	Hauptstadt
bowl	[bəʊl]	e.g. a bowl of soup	Schale, Schüssel, Napf
cupboard	[ˈkʌbəd]	piece of furniture with doors and shelves used to keep food, clothes, etc.	Schrank

page 11

bracket	[ˈbrækɪt]	*phr* in brackets	Klammer
dirty	[ˈdɜːti]	<> clean	schmutzig, dreckig
scooter	[ˈskuːtə]	a light motorcycle with small wheels	Tretroller, Motorroller
speech bubble	[ˈspiːtʃ bʌbl]	circle around words that sb says, especially in a cartoon	Sprechblase
maths	[mæθs]	school subject in which you learn how to count	Mathe
to **translate**	[trænsˈleɪt]	to change words into a different language	übersetzen
to **make sb do sth**	[meɪk ˈduː]	e.g. The teacher makes us do our homework.	jdn dazu bringen, etw zu tun

page 12

to **be afraid of sb/sth**	[bi əˈfreɪd əv]	e.g. I am afraid of dogs.	vor jdm/etw Angst haben, sich vor jdm/etw fürchten
wallet	[ˈwɒlɪt]	where you keep your money	Brieftasche, (Herren-)Portemonnaie
to **lend**	[lend]	e.g. The library lends books.	leihen, borgen
to **hurry up**	[ˌhʌri ˈʌp]	to do sth more quickly	sich beeilen
present	[ˈpreznt]	gift	Geschenk
to **send**	[send]	e.g. to send an email/letter/parcel	schicken, senden
to **be lost**	[bi ˈlɒst]	to not know where you are	sich verlaufen haben
spoken language	[ˌspəʊkən ˈlæŋgwɪdʒ]	<> written language	gesprochene Sprache
to **count**	[kaʊnt]	e.g. He counted all the books on the shelf.	zählen
uncountable	[ˌʌnˈkaʊntəbl]	not able to be counted	unzählbar
countable	[ˈkaʊntəbl]	able to be counted	zählbar
usually	[ˈjuːʒuəli]	<> seldom, rarely	normalerweise, gewöhnlich
fridge	[frɪdʒ]	refrigerator *AE*	Kühlschrank

page 13

choice	[tʃɔɪs]	*v* to choose	Wahl
to **spend**	[spend]	e.g. I spent a year in Los Angeles learning English.	*(Zeit:)* verbringen
homework	[ˈhəʊmwɜːk]	e.g. We have to fill in this worksheet for homework.	Hausaufgaben
reason	[ˈriːzn]	*v to reason*	Grund, Begründung
pocket money	[ˈpɒkɪt mʌni]	money parents give to their children	Taschengeld
worried	[ˈwʌrid]	*v* to worry	besorgt, beunruhigt
beer	[bɪə]	e.g. There are many types of beer in Germany.	Bier
muscle	[ˈmʌsl]	e.g. Doing sport helps you build muscles.	Muskel
chicken	[ˈtʃɪkɪn]	bird that is cooked and eaten	Huhn, Hühnchen
timetable	[ˈtaɪmteɪbl]	plan that shows when things happen	Fahrplan
to **be careful with sth**	[bi ˈkeəfl wɪð]	e.g. Be careful with the glasses!	bei etw aufpassen, vorsichtig bei/mit etw sein
weekday	[ˈwiːkdeɪ]	e.g. Monday, Tuesday, Wednesday, Thursday, Friday	Wochentag, Werktag
TV show	[ˌtiː ˈviː ʃəʊ]	e.g. The Big Bang Theory, American Idol, etc.	Fernsehsendung

page 14

nationality	[ˌnæʃəˈnæləti]	e.g. German, British, American	Staatsangehörigkeit, Nationalität
to **combine**	[kəmˈbaɪn]	*n* combination	verbinden, kombinieren
item	[ˈaɪtəm]	a thing, a piece	Gegenstand, Artikel, Ding
once	[wʌns]	one single time	einmal
chart	[tʃɑːt]	e.g. table, bar chart, flow chart, pie chart, etc.	Tabelle
cathedral	[kəˈθiːdrəl]	large church in a city	Dom, Kathedrale
holiday resort	[ˈhɒlədeɪ rɪzɔːt]	place to go on vacation	Urlaubsort, Ferienort
island	[ˈaɪlənd]	land surrounded by water	Insel
mountain	[ˈmaʊntən]	e.g. Matterhorn, Everest, Kilamanjaro	Berg
monument	[ˈmɒnjumənt]	a statue/place to remember a special person or time	Denkmal

Chronological word list

river	['rɪvə]	e.g. Danube, Amazon, Nile, etc.	Fluss
state	[steɪt]	part of a country	Staat
photocopy	['fəʊtəʊkɒpi]	e.g. Bring a photocopy of your passport.	Fotokopie
to fill in	[ˌfɪl 'ɪn]	e.g. Could you please fill in this form?	eintragen, ausfüllen

UNIT 1

page 15

to identify	[aɪ'dentɪfaɪ]	*n* identification	identifizieren
to taste (of sth)	[teɪst]	*n* taste	(nach etw) schmecken
to order	['ɔ:də]	e.g. Let's order a pizza	bestellen
to deliver	[dɪ'lɪvə]	*n* delivery	liefern
to give reasons	[ˌgɪv 'ri:znz]	to say why you do sth	begründen

page 16

task	[tɑ:sk]	*phr* to give sb a task	Aufgabe
to feed	[fi:d]	*n* food	ernähren
to take part in sth	[teɪk 'pɑ:t ɪn]	*n* participant	an etw teilnehmen
global	['gləʊbl]	all around the world	global, weltumspannend
issue	['ɪʃu:]	question, problem	Frage, Streitpunkt, Problem
to inform	[ɪn'fɔ:m]	to let sb know	informieren
to prepare	[prɪ'peə]	*n* preparation	(sich) vorbereiten
translation	[træns'leɪʃn]	*v* to translate	Übersetzung
skill	[skɪl]	*adj* skilled	Fähigkeit, Fertigkeit, Kompetenz
opposite	['ɒpəzɪt]	on the other side	gegenüber
to fit sth	[fɪt]	to be right for sth	zu etw passen
context	['kɒntekst]	*phr* in context	Zusammenhang, Kontext

page 17

to grow	[grəʊ]	to increase	wachsen, zunehmen
billion	['bɪliən]	one thousand million	Milliarde
agriculture	['ægrɪkʌltʃə]	*adj* agricultural	Landwirtschaft
United Nations *pl*	[juˌnaɪtɪd 'neɪʃnz]	an international peace organization	Vereinte Nationen
to suffer from sth	['sʌfə frəm]	e.g. to suffer from an illness	an etw *(Krankheit usw.)* leiden
to produce	[prə'dju:s]	*n* production	produzieren
protein	['prəʊti:n]	e.g. You get a lot of protein from meat.	Eiweiß, Protein(e)
to destroy	[dɪ'strɔɪ]	*n* destruction	zerstören
environment	[ɪn'vaɪrənmənt]	the atmosphere and things around us	Umwelt
to create	[kri'eɪt]	*n* creation	erzeugen, schaffen
greenhouse gas	[ˌgri:nhaʊs 'gæs]	e.g. carbon dioxide, methane, etc.	Treibhausgas
nutritionist	[nju'trɪʃənɪst]	a healthy food expert	Ernährungswissenschaftler/in
insect	['ɪnsekt]	e.g. scorpion, beetle, ant	Insekt
famine	['fæmɪn]	e.g. The famine caused 10,000 deaths.	Hungersnot
health	[helθ]	*adj* healthy	Gesundheit
powdered milk	[ˌpaʊdəd 'mɪlk]	dried milk	Milchpulver
to mix	[mɪks]	*n* mixture	mischen, vermischen, anrühren
doctor	['dɒktə]	sb you go to if you are not well	Arzt/Ärztin
to reach for sth	['ri:tʃ fə]	to try and get sth	nach etw greifen
to melt	[melt]	e.g. The ice is melting in Antarctica.	schmelzen
chocolate bar	['tʃɒklət bɑ:]	e.g. This chocolate bar may contain nuts.	Schokoriegel
mineral	['mɪnərəl]	e.g. calcium, iron, etc.	Mineral
result	[rɪ'zʌlt]	outcome, consequence	Ergebnis, Resultat
mixture	['mɪkstʃə]	a combination of things	Mischung
nutrient	['nju:triənt]	*adj* nutritious	Nährstoff
package	['pækɪdʒ]	bag, box, parcel, etc.	Packung
to gain	[geɪn]	to get heavier	*(Gewicht)* zunehmen
gram	[græm]	e.g. A thousand grams is one kilogram.	Gramm
sub-Saharan	[ˌsʌb sə'hærən]	the places south of the Sahara desert	südlich der Sahara
healthy	['helθi]	<> ill, sick	gesund
average	['ævərɪdʒ]	normal	Durchschnitt(s-), durchschnittlich
to compare well with sth	[kəmˌpeə 'wel wɪð]	e.g. German schools compare well with Austrian schools.	im Vergleich mit etw gut abschneiden
source	[sɔ:s]	where sth comes from	Quelle
fibre	['faɪbə]	e.g. There is a lot of fibre in whole-grain bread.	Ballaststoffe
antibiotics *pl*	[ˌæntibaɪ'ɒtɪks]	medicine used against bacteria	Antibiotika
hormone	['hɔˌməʊn]	chemicals in the body	Hormon
natural	['nætʃrəl]	<> unnatural	natürlich
flour	['flaʊə]	used to make bread, cake, etc.	Mehl
to be on sale	[bi ɒn 'seɪl]	to be sold for a lower price	(zum Verkauf) angeboten werden

page 18

sub-heading	[ˌsʌb 'hedɪŋ]	an extra title after the main title	Zwischenüberschrift
paragraph	['pærəgrɑ:f]	e.g. Write a paragraph about the environment.	*(Text:) Absatz*

expert	['ekspɜ:t]	sb with special knowledge	Fachmann/-frau, Experte/-in
to **focus on sth**	['fəʊkəs ɒn]	to concentrate on sth	sich auf etw konzentrieren
spread	[spred]	e.g. butter, etc.	(Brot-)Aufstrich
technology	[tek'nɒlədʒi]	*adj* technological	Technologie, Technik
on earth	[ɒn 'ɜ:θ]	e.g. There are 7 billion people on earth.	auf der Welt
safe	[seɪf]	<> dangerous	sicher, unbedenklich, ungefährlich
slice	[slaɪs]	a piece of sth (e.g. cake)	(Kuchen-)Stück
based on	['beɪst ɒn]	e.g. She wrote a story based on her life.	auf Grundlage von

page 19

to **appear**	[ə'pɪə]	*n* appearance	vorkommen, auftauchen
print	[prɪnt]	e.g. I prefer print to sth online.	gedruckt, Druck-
benefit	['benɪfɪt]	e.g. Try to enjoy the benefits of being a student.	Nutzen, Vorteil
article	['ɑ:tɪkl]	*esp* text in a newspaper	Artikel
interesting	['ɪntrəstɪŋ]	<> boring	interessant

page 20

habit	['hæbɪt]	sth you do often	Gewohnheit
particular	[pə'tɪkjələ]	certain	spezielle/r/s, bestimmt
diet	['daɪət]	food, nutrition	Kost, Ernährung
variety	[və'raɪəti]	a range of different things	Vielfalt, Abwechslung
vegan	['vi:gən]	sb who doesn't eat animal products	Veganer/in; vegan
never	['nevə]	<> always	nie
order	['ɔ:də]	sequence	Reihenfolge
to **survive**	[sə'vaɪv]	to live through	überleben
to **cause**	[kɔ:z]	*n* cause	verursachen
anaemia	[ə'ni:miə]	*adj* anaemic	Blutarmut, Anämie
to **persuade**	[pə'sweɪd]	to talk sb into doing sth	überzeugen, überreden
to **happen**	['hæpən]	to occur	geschehen, passieren
to **make sth happen**	[ˌmeɪk 'hæpən]	e.g. Positive thinking can make good things happen.	dafür sorgen, dass etw geschieht
red blood cells *pl*	[ˌred 'blʌd selz]	e.g Red blood cells carry oxygen through the body.	rote Blutkörperchen
to **continue to do sth**	[kən'tɪnju: tə]	<> to stop doing sth	etw weiterhin tun
vegetarian	[ˌvedʒə'teəriən]	someone who doesn't eat meat	Vegetarier/in; vegetarisch
allergy	['ælədʒi]	e.g. He has an allergy to dogs and nuts.	Allergie
human	['hju:mən]	e.g. If you wouldn't eat a human, why eat an animal?	Mensch
product	['prɒdʌkt]	*v* to produce	Produkt, Erzeugnis
to **kill**	[kɪl]	e.g. The fire killed 10 people.	töten, umbringen
dietician	[ˌdaɪə'tɪʃn]	an expert in food and eating	Ernährungswissenschaftler/in
as long as	[əz 'lɒŋ əz]	e.g. I'll remember that day as long as I live.	solange
lentil	['lentl]	e.g. lentil soup	Linse
soya	['sɔɪə]	protein made from beans	Soja
pork	[pɔ:k]	a type of meat	Schweinefleisch
taste	[teɪst]	how sth tastes	Geschmack
to **lead**	[li:d]	e.g. to lead sb in the right direction	führen, bringen
final	['faɪnl]	last	letzte/r/s
in my opinion	[ɪn maɪ ə'pɪniən]	I think …, I believe …	meiner Meinung nach

page 21

to **respect**	[rɪ'spekt]	to think a lot of	respektieren
to **draw**	[drɔ:]	e.g. to draw a picture/graph	zeichnen
battle	['bætl]	a fight, a war	Kampf, Schlacht
rising	['raɪzɪŋ]	getting higher	steigend
obesity	[əʊ'bi:səti]	*adj* obese	Fettleibigkeit
rate	[reɪt]	e.g. a high crime rate	Quote
primary school *BE*	['praɪməri sku:l]	*AE* elementary school	Grundschule
tactic	['tæktɪk]	game plan	Taktik
nation	['neɪʃn]	e.g. Germany, Turkey, Russia	Land, Nation
public school *AE*	[ˌpʌblɪk 'sku:l]	a free school for everyone	staatliche Schule
menu	['menju:]	e.g. The restaurant has a big menu.	Speisekarte, Speiseplan
dessert	[dɪ'zɜ:t]	sweet food you eat at the end of a meal	Nachtisch, Dessert
surprisingly	[sə'praɪzɪŋli]	e.g. Food prices are surprisingly low.	erstaunlicherweise
to **remove**	[rɪ'mu:v]	to take sth away	entfernen
nutrition	[nju'trɪʃn]	food, nourishment	Nahrung, Ernährung
balanced	['bælənst]	*v* to balance	ausgewogen
to **grow to do sth**	[ˌgrəʊ tə 'du:]	to develop	(allmählich) dahin kommen, etw zu tun
lifestyle	['laɪfstaɪl]	the way sb lives	Lebensweise
to **respond to sth**	[rɪ'spɒnd tə]	to react to sth	auf etw reagieren
to **double**	['dʌbl]	to be twice the amount	sich verdoppeln
risk	[rɪsk]	*adj* risky	Risiko
blood pressure	['blʌd preʃə]	e.g. High blood pressure can lead to health problems.	Blutdruck
to **lower**	['ləʊə]	to reduce	senken
medicine	['medsn]	e.g. The doctor gave medicine to the patient.	Medikament(e)
cholesterol	[kə'lestərɒl]	a fatty substance in the body	Cholesterin
fatty streaks *pl*	[ˌfæti 'stri:ks]	early signs of heart disease	Schaumzellen, Verkalkungen

Chronological word list

artery	[ˈɑːtəri]	takes blood from the heart to the body	Ader, Arterie
literally	[ˈlɪtərəli]	e.g. there were literally 1000 people	buchstäblich
early stage	[ˌɜːli ˈsteɪdʒ]	<> late stage	Frühstadium
heart disease	[ˈhɑːt dɪziːz]	e.g. The old man died from heart disease.	Herzerkrankung
scary	[ˈskeəri]	e.g. The horror film was too scary.	erschreckend, beängstigend
background	[ˈbækgraʊnd]	origin	Herkunft
vegetarianism	[ˌvedʒəˈteəriənɪzm]	a lifestyle without eating meat	vegetarische Lebensweise
common	[ˈkɒmən]	popular	verbreitet, häufig, üblich
supportive	[səˈpɔːtɪv]	e.g. My parents are very supportive of my plans.	unterstützend
concept	[ˈkɒnsept]	idea, plan	Idee, Plan, Konzept
to **pick sth up**	[ˌpɪk ˈʌp]	to take	etw nehmen, etw holen
to **do without sth**	[ˌduː wɪˈðaʊt]	e.g. I can't do without coffee.	ohne etw auskommen
to **be allowed to do sth**	[bi əˈlaʊd tə duː]	to be permitted to do sth	etw tun dürfen
minority	[maɪˈnɒrəti]	<> majority	Minderheit
test-case	[ˈtest keɪs]	the first time sth is tested	Probelauf
to **be off to a promising start**	[bi ˌɒf tu ə ˌprɒmɪsɪŋ ˈstɑːt]	to start well	vielversprechend angelaufen sein
greens *pl*	[griːnz]	vegetables (often green)	Grünzeug, Gemüse
principal	[ˈprɪnsəpl]	headteacher	Schuldirektor/in
low-carb	[ˌləʊ ˈkɑːb]	food with few carbohydrates, e.g. celery	kohlenhydratarm

page 22

suitable	[ˈsuːtəbl]	<> unsuitable	geeignet
cereal	[ˈsɪəriəl]	muesli, corn, grains	Müsli, Getreideflocken
to **contain**	[kənˈteɪn]	e.g. Wine contains alcohol.	enthalten
variety	[vəˈraɪəti]	many different things	Auswahl
plain	[pleɪn]	without sth added	einfach, Natur
jam	[dʒæm]	e.g. toast with strawberry jam	Marmelade
starter	[ˈstɑːtə]	what you eat before your main meal	Vorspeise
course	[kɔːs]	e.g. starter, main course, dessert	*(Menü:)* Gang
stir-fried	[ˈstɜː fraɪd]	cooked in a pan with oil	pfannengerührt
ice cream	[ˌaɪs ˈkriːm]	cold, sweet food made from cream	Eis, Eiskrem
various	[ˈveəriəs]	different types of	verschiedene/r/s
flavour	[ˈfleɪvə]	taste	Geschmacksrichtung, Aroma
cheesecake	[ˈtʃiːzkeɪk]	e.g. New York baked cheesecake	Käsekuchen
colleague	[ˈkɒliːg]	sb you work with	Kollege/-in
gapped	[gæpt]	spaces to write in	mit Lücken
to **recommend**	[ˌrekəˈmend]	*n* recommendation	empfehlen

page 23

bill	[bɪl]	document the waiter brings at the end of a meal which says how much the food cost	Rechnung
Enjoy your meal!	[ɪnˈdʒɔɪ jə miːl]	what you say before you eat	Guten Appetit!
tasty	[ˈteɪsti]	delicious	schmackhaft, lecker
role	[rəʊl]	*phr* to play a role	Rolle
to **act sth out**	[ˌækt ˈaʊt]	to play out a scenario	etw (mit verteilten Rollen) spielen

page 24

canteen	[kænˈtiːn]	place where people eat at work	Kantine
to **improve**	[ɪmˈpruːv]	to make sth better	verbessern
to **present**	[prɪˈzent]	*n* presentation	vorstellen, präsentieren
notice	[ˈnəʊtɪs]	information on display	Ankündigung, Mitteilung, Aushang
competition	[ˌkɒmpəˈtɪʃn]	*v* to compete	Wettbewerb
price	[praɪs]	how much sth costs	Preis
target group	[ˈtɑːgɪt gruːp]	e.g. Teenagers are one of the main target groups for gaming.	Zielgruppe
to **write up sth**	[ˌraɪt ˈʌp]	to prepare a text	etw formulieren, etw ausarbeiten
to **illustrate**	[ˈɪləstreɪt]	to make a picture	illustrieren
drawing	[ˈdrɔːɪŋ]	*v* to draw	Zeichnung
nourishing	[ˈnʌrɪʃɪŋ]	*n* nourishment	nahrhaft
to **pin**	[pɪn]	e.g. pin the photo to the wall	(mit einer Nadel) anheften
to **study sth**	[ˈstʌdi]	to read carefully	sich etw genau ansehen/durchlesen
to **rank**	[ræŋk]	to put in order	einstufen, (nach Rang) ordnen
category	[ˈkætəgəri]	group of similar things	Rubrik, Kategorie
design	[dɪˈzaɪn]	e.g. Graffiti has interesting designs.	Gestaltung, Entwurf
attractiveness	[əˈtræktɪvnəs]	*v* to attract	Attraktivität
overall	[əʊvərˈɔːl]	e.g. the overall effect, the overall performance	Gesamt-, insgesamt

UNIT 2

page 25

to **notice**	[ˈnəʊtɪs]	to see sth	bemerken, feststellen
to **do sport**	[du ˈspɔːt]	e.g. football, fitness, etc.	Sport treiben

page 26

diary	[ˈdaɪəri]	journal *(esp AE)*	Tagebuch
winner	[ˈwɪnə]	*v* to win	Gewinner/in, Sieger/in
importance	[ɪmˈpɔːtns]	*adj* important	Bedeutung, Wichtigkeit
to provide	[prəˈvaɪd]	to give	liefen, bieten
trip	[trɪp]	*phr* to take a trip	Reise
to share	[ʃeə]	to divide into parts	teilen, mitteilen
activity	[ækˈtɪvəti]	*adj* active	Tätigkeit, Beschäftigung, Äktivität
to get sth in order	[ˌget ɪn ˈɔːdə]	to organize sth	etw auf die Reihe kriegen
athlete	[ˈæθliːt]	*adj* athletic	Sportler/in
run	[rʌn]	e.g. They went on a run in the park every morning.	Lauf
no matter	[ˌnəʊ ˈmætə]	not important	egal, ganz gleich
runner	[ˈrʌnə]	*v* to run	Läufer/in
to make friends	[meɪk ˈfrendz]	to find friends	Freunde finden/gewinnen

page 27

to keep a diary	[kiːp ə ˈdaɪəri]	to write about your life every day	ein Tagebuch führen
to record	[rɪˈkɔːd]	*n* record	aufzeichnen, protokollieren
progress	[ˈprəʊgres]	*v* to progress	Fortschritt(e), Entwicklung, Vorankommen
entry	[ˈentri]	*v* to enter	Eintrag
to take a photo	[ˌteɪk ə ˈfəʊtəʊ]	e.g. I took a photo of my best friend.	ein Bild machen
lazy	[ˈleɪzi]	<> hard-working	faul
to get a life	[get ə ˈlaɪf]	e.g. Get off the sofa, turn off the internet and get a life!	mit seinem Leben (endlich) etwas anfangen
gym	[dʒɪm]	a place to do sport	Fitness-Studio
twice	[twaɪs]	two times	zweimal
mental	[ˈmentl]	<> physical	geistig, mental
confidence	[ˈkɒnfɪdəns]	*adj* confident	Selbstvertrauen, Selbstbewusstsein
weight	[weɪt]	*v* to weigh	Gewicht
to lose weight	[ˌluːz ˈweɪt]	<> to gain weight	abnehmen
to develop	[dɪˈveləp]	*n* development	(sich) entwickeln
energetic	[ˌenəˈdʒetɪk]	*n* energy	voller Energie, tatkräftig
to give up	[ˌgɪv ˈʌp]	to stop doing sth	aufgeben
motivated	[ˈməʊtɪveɪtɪd]	*n* motivation	motiviert

page 28

account	[əˈkaʊnt]	e.g. Facebook account or profile	Konto
tag line	[ˈtæg laɪn]	caption	Bildunterschrift, Slogan
to get ready	[get ˈredi]	to prepare oneself	sich fertigmachen, sich zurechtmachen
local	[ˈləʊkl]	<> foreign	örtlich, lokal
kind	[kaɪnd]	type, sort	Art
to turn up	[ˌtɜːn ˈʌp]	to show up	kommen, auftauchen
pressure	[ˈpreʃə]	*phr* to put sb under pressure	Druck
to accept	[əkˈsept]	*n* acceptance	akzeptieren, annehmen
atmosphere	[ˈætməsfɪə]	the feeling of a place or situation	Atmosphäre
record	[ˈrekɔːd]	*v to record*	Aufzeichnung(en), Protokoll
lonely	[ˈləʊnli]	alone	einsam
aspect	[ˈæspekt]	side	Gesichtspunkt, Aspekt, Seite

page 29

summary	[ˈsʌməri]	*v* to summarize	Zusammenfassung
gap	[gæp]	hole	Lücke
however	[haʊˈevə]	but, on the other hand	allerdings, doch, jedoch
to sort out sth	[ˌsɔːt ˈaʊt]	to make sth clear, to organize sth	etw klären, etw regeln
to increase sth	[ɪnˈkriːs]	to improve	etw steigern, etw erhöhen
popular	[ˈpɒpjələ]	<> unpopular	beliebt
suggestion	[səˈdʒestʃən]	*v* to suggest	Vorschlag
living room	[ˈlɪvɪŋ ruːm]	a room for relaxing and socializing	Wohnzimmer
to hold sth up	[ˌhəʊld ˈʌp]	to lift sth up high	etw hochhalten
remote control	[rɪˌməʊt kənˈtrəʊl]	what you use to change the program on TV	Fernbedienung
to clutch sth	[klʌtʃ]	to hold sth tightly	etw umklammern, etw festhalten
grandparents *pl*	[ˈgrænpeərənts]	e.g. grandmother, grandfather	Großeltern

page 30

league	[liːg]	e.g. football league	Liga
match	[mætʃ]	e.g. A football match lasts 90 minutes.	Spiel, Partie
season	[ˈsiːzn]	e.g. The football season kicks off in September	Saison
equipment	[ɪˈkwɪpmənt]	things you need to do a certain sport	Ausrüstung, Geräte
challenge	[ˈtʃælɪndʒ]	*adj* challenging	Herausforderung, (schwierige) Aufgabe
strength	[streŋθ]	*adj* strong	Stärke, Kraft
coach	[kəʊtʃ]	team trainer	Trainer/in
to win	[wɪn]	e.g. I want my team to win!	gewinnen
to move up	[ˌmuːv ˈʌp]	to get to a higher place	aufsteigen

Chronological word list

to bet	[bet]	e.g. I bet money our team will win.	wetten
team spirit	[ˌtiːm ˈspɪrɪt]	good feeling in a team	Mannschaftsgeist
interested in sth	[ˈɪntrəstɪd ɪn]	*adj* interesting	an etw interessiert
traditionally	[trəˈdɪʃənəli]	*n tradition*	üblicherweise, traditionell
skillful	[ˈskɪlfl]	good at doing sth	geschickt
parkour	[ˌpɑːˈkɔː]	running, jumping, climbing through an area	Parkour
obstacle	[ˈɒbstəkl]	an object in your way	Hindernis
Just a minute.	[ˌdʒʌst ə ˈmɪnɪt]	Hold on.	Einen Moment!
basically	[ˈbeɪsɪkli]	most importantly	im Prinzip, grundsätzlich

page 31

mostly	[ˈməʊstli]	generally, mainly	hauptsächlich, meistens
normally	[ˈnɔːməli]	e.g. I normally eat breakfast before going to work.	normalerweise
rarely	[ˈreəli]	*adj* rare	selten, kaum
right now	[raɪt ˈnaʊ]	in this moment	gerade (jetzt)
thought	[θɔːt]	*v* to think	Gedanke
attention	[əˈtenʃn]	*adj* attentive	Aufmerksamkeit
to **pay attention to sth**	[ˌpeɪ əˈtenʃn tə]	to notice sth	auf etw achten
to **agree**	[əˈɡriː]	e.g. I agree with you.	zustimmen, einverstanden sein
to **split up**	[ˌsplɪt ˈʌp]	to go separate ways	sich trennen
treadmill	[ˈtredmɪl]	a machine at a gym that you run on	Laufband
instead	[ɪnˈsted]	e.g. We didn't want to go out and stayed home instead.	stattdessen
guy	[ɡaɪ]	man	Typ, Kerl
juice	[dʒuːs]	e.g. orange juice, apple juice	Saft
presentation	[ˌpreznˈteɪʃn]	*v to present*	Präsentation
leisure	[ˈleʒə]	free time	Freizeit

page 32

to **volunteer**	[ˌvɒlənˈtɪə]	to do sth without getting paid	ehrenamtlich arbeiten, (freiwillig) helfen
career	[kəˈrɪə]	*phr* to start a career	Karriere, Laufbahn
advertisment	[ədˈvɜːtɪsmənt]	*inf* ad, advert	Anzeige, Werbung
heading	[ˈhedɪŋ]	title	Überschrift
characteristic	[ˌkærəktəˈrɪstɪk]	feature	Merkmal, Eigenschaft
volunteer	[ˌvɒlənˈtɪə]	*adj* voluntary	(freiwilliger/ehrenamtlicher) Helfer/in
event	[ɪˈvent]	happening	Veranstaltung
to **manage sth**	[ˈmænɪdʒ]	*n* management	etw verwalten, etw organisieren, etw managen
behind the scenes	[bɪˌhaɪnd ðə ˈsiːnz]	things that are not seen	hinter den Kulissen
to **join up**	[ˌdʒɔɪn ˈʌp]	to become part of sth	sich anmelden
team leader	[ˈtiːm liːdə]	sb who organizes the work of a team	Teamleiter/in
schedule	[ˈʃedjuːl]	timetable	Zeitplan, Ablaufplan
missing	[ˈmɪsɪŋ]	*v* to miss	fehlend
to **be missing**	[bi ˈmɪsɪŋ]	not there	fehlen
distance	[ˈdɪstəns]	the space between two places	Strecke
participant	[pɑːˈtɪsɪpənt]	*v* to participate	Teilnehmer/in
wheelchair	[ˈwiːltʃeə]	a special chair for sb who cannot walk	Rollstuhl
aged …	[eɪdʒd]	at the age of …	im Alter von … Jahren
adult	[ˈædʌlt]	<> child	Erwachsene/r
highlight	[ˈhaɪlaɪt]	the best moment	Höhepunkt
course	[kɔːs]	e.g. She ran the course in 30 minutes.	Verlauf, Lauf
series	[ˈsɪəriːz]	row, line	Reihe
obviously	[ˈɒbviəsli]	clearly	natürlich, offensichtlich

page 33

frequently asked questions (FAQs)	[ˌfriːkwəntli ɑːskt ˈkwestʃənz]	most popular questions and answers	häufig gestellte Fragen
to **update**	[ˌʌpˈdeɪt]	*n* update	aktualisieren, auf den neuesten Stand bringen
area	[ˈeəriə]	e.g. You need a special pass for this area.	Bereich, Zone
to **change (into sth)**	[tʃeɪndʒ]	to put on different clothes	sich umziehen, sich etw anziehen
gear	[ɡɪə]	sports clothes	(Sport-)Kleidung
to **have a shower**	[həv ə ˈʃaʊə]	e.g. I always have a shower in the morning.	duschen
race	[reɪs]	e.g. I finished first in the race.	Rennen
during	[ˈdjʊərɪŋ]	while sth else is happening	während
tent	[tent]	e.g. When we go camping we sleep in a tent.	Zelt
changing tent	[ˈtʃeɪndʒɪŋ tent]	a place to put on/take off clothes	Umkleidezelt
first aid	[ˌfɜːst ˈeɪd]	help you give sb who has had an accident	Erste Hilfe
along	[əˈlɒŋ]	e.g. We walked along thr river.	entlang
route	[ruːt]	way	Strecke, Route
refreshment point	[rɪˈfreʃmənt pɔɪnt]	a stop for sth to drink	Verpflegungspunkt
finish	[ˈfɪnɪʃ]	the end of the race	Ziel
drop-off	[ˈdrɒpɒf]	place to leave sth	Abgabe, Aufbewahrung
to **register**	[ˈredʒɪstə]	to sign up for a race	sich anmelden
registration	[ˌredʒɪˈstreɪʃn]	e.g. Registration closes at 5 p.m.	Anmeldung

noon	[nu:n]	midday, 12 p.m.	Mittag
entry fee	[ˈentri: fi:]	money to enter a race	Anmeldegebühr
credit card	[ˈkredɪt kɑ:d]	e.g. I used my credit card to pay for some new clothes.	Kreditkarte
confirmation	[ˌkɒnfəˈmeɪʃn]	*v* to confirm	Bestätigung
immediately	[ɪˈmi:diətli]	right away	sofort
via	[ˈvaɪə]	e.g. to fly to London via Hamburg	mittels, über
job interview	[ˈdʒɒb ɪntəvju:]	e.g. I was invited for a job interview at the London office.	Vorstellungsgespräch
employer	[ɪmˈplɔɪə]	<> employee	Arbeitgeber/in
profession	[prəˈfeʃn]	job	Beruf
relevant	[ˈreləvənt]	<> irrelevevant	relevant, wichtig (für etw)
CV *BE*	[ˌsi: ˈvi:]	*AE* résumé	Lebenslauf
to **imagine sth**	[ɪˈmædʒɪn]	*adj* imaginary	sich etw vorstellen
interviewer	[ˈɪntəvju:ə]	<> interviewee	*Person, die ein Vorstellungsgespräch führt*
experience	[ɪkˈspɪəriəns]	*v* to experience	Erlebnis(se), Erfahrung(en)
prompt	[prɒmpt]	hint, clue	Stichwort

page 34

flyer	[ˈflaɪə]	advertising brochure	Handzettel, Broschüre
exchange student	[ɪksˈtʃeɪndʒ stju:dnt]	a student from another country	Austauschschüler/in
area	[ˈeəriə]	district, region	Gegend, Gebiet
to **research sth**	[rɪˈsɜ:tʃ]	to look for information about sth	etw recherchieren, Nachforschungen über etw anstellen
opportunity	[ˌɒpəˈtju:nəti]	possibility	Möglichkeit, Gelegenheit
precise	[prɪˈsaɪs]	exact	genau, präzise
research	[rɪˈsɜ:tʃ]	*v* to research	Recherche, Nachforschungen
attractive	[əˈtræktɪv]	nice to look at	ansprechend, attraktiv
map	[mæp]	atlas	Landkarte, Karte
to **comment on sth**	[ˈkɒment ɒn]	to say sth about sth	etw kommentieren
to **vote (on sb/sth)**	[vəʊt]	*n* vote	abstimmen, (jdn/etw) wählen

UNIT 3

page 35

relationship	[rɪˈleɪʃnʃɪp]	connection you have with sb	Beziehung
member	[ˈmembə]	*phr* to become a member of sth	Mitglied
wife	[waɪf]	married woman	Ehefrau
blended family	[ˌblendɪd ˈfæmli]	a family made from two or more families	Patchworkfamilie
extended	[ɪkˈstendɪd]	e.g. My extended family includes my aunts, uncles and cousins.	erweitert
intercultural	[ˌɪntəˈkʌltʃərəl]	from different cultures	kulturübergreifend, interkulturell
single parent	[ˌsɪŋgl ˈpeərənt]	parent without a partner	Alleinerziehende/r
single-parent family	[ˌsɪŋgl peərənt ˈfæməli]	family with one parent	Einelternfamilie
nuclear family	[ˌnju:kliə ˈfæməli]	family with two parents and children	Kernfamilie, Kleinfamilie
to **be made up of sth**	[bi ˌmeɪd ˈʌp əv]	to consist of	aus etw bestehen
cultural	[ˈkʌltʃərəl]	*n* culture	kulturell
generation	[ˌdʒenəˈreɪʃn]	people born around the same time	Generation
to **bring sb up**	[ˌbrɪŋ ˈʌp]	e.g. They are bringing up three children.	jdn großziehen, jdn aufziehen
to **consist of sth**	[kənˈsɪst əv]	e.g. Their family consists of one child, one parent and a dog.	aus etw bestehen
to **be familiar with sth**	[bi fəˈmɪliə wɪð]	to know about sth	mit etw vertraut sein, etw kennen

page 36

focus	[ˈfəʊkəs]	*v* to focus	Schwerpunkt, Hauptaugenmerk
to **set up sth**	[ˌset ˈʌp]	to start sth	etw einrichten, etw gründen
to **mention**	[ˈmenʃn]	to name	erwähnen, nennen
meaning	[ˈmi:nɪŋ]	*v* to mean	Bedeutung
to **look sth up**	[ˌlʊk ˈʌp]	to look in a dictionary	etw *(in einem Wörterbuch)* nachschlagen
at all	[ət ˈɔ:l]	e.g. That was no fun at all.	überhaupt
twin	[twɪn]	one of two children from the same birth	Zwilling
journey	[ˈdʒɜ:ni]	trip	Fahrt, Reise
birth mother	[ˈbɜ:θ mʌðə]	biological mother	leibliche Mutter

page 37

to **freak out**	[ˌfri:k ˈaʊt]	to become emotional, to lose control	ausrasten, durchdrehen
to **adopt**	[əˈdɒpt]	*n* adoption	adoptieren
adoption	[əˈdɒpʃn]	e.g. She gave her child up for adoption	Adoption
agency	[ˈeɪdʒənsi]	business or organization	Agentur
to **study**	[ˈstʌdi]	to learn about sth	studieren
fashion	[ˈfæʃn]	*adj* fashionable	Mode
actress	[ˈæktrəs]	a woman who acts in films, TV, theatre	Schauspielerin
to **sound**	[saʊnd]	e.g. That sounds like a great plan!	klingen
double	[ˈdʌbl]	sb who looks exactly the same as another	Double, Doppelgänger/in

Chronological word list

port	[pɔːt]	a safe place for boats	Hafen
to **contact** sb	[ˈkɒntækt]	to get in touch with	Kontakt zu jdm aufnehmen
details *pl*	[ˈdiːteɪlz]	*phr* contact details	Angaben, Daten, Einzelheiten
to **have** sth **in common**	[həv ɪn ˈkɒmən]	to like the same things as sb	etw gemeinsam haben
to **adore** sb/sth	[əˈdɔː]	to really love sb/sth	jdn/etw über alles lieben
friendship	[ˈfrendʃɪp]	being friends with sb	Freundschaft
to **grow up**	[ˌɡrəʊ ˈʌp]	to get older, to become an adult	aufwachsen
only child	[ˈəʊnlɪ tʃaɪld]	child without brothers or sisters	Einzelkind
to **receive**	[rɪˈsiːv]	*n* receipt	erhalten, bekommen
surprised	[səˈpraɪzd]	shocked, amazed	überrascht, erstaunt
excited	[ɪkˈsaɪtɪd]	enthusiastic	aufgeregt, begeistert, gespannt
while	[waɪl]	e.g. While I was in Paris, I visited the museums.	Weile
to **suspect**	[səˈspekt]	to guess, to have a feeling	vermuten
identical twins *pl*	[aɪˌdentɪkl ˈtwɪnz]	two babies that grew from one egg	eineiige Zwillinge
to **give** sb **up for adoption**	[ɡɪv ˌʌp fər əˈdɒpʃn]	to give a child to another family	jdn zur Adoption freigeben
separately	[ˈseprətli]	<> together	getrennt, separat
set of parents	[ˌset əf ˈpɜːrənts]	mother and father	Elternpaar
adoptive family	[əˌdɒptɪv ˈfæmli]	a family that adopts a child	Adoptivfamilie
thousand	[ˈθaʊznd]	e.g. on vacation, I took one thousand photos	tausend, Tausend
to **grow closer**	[ˌɡrəʊ ˈkləʊsə]	to have a more intense relationship with sb	sich näherkommen, die Beziehung intensivieren
to **raise funds**	[ˌreɪz ˈfʌndz]	to collect money	Spenden sammeln
documentary	[ˌdɒkjuˈmentri]	TV programme about things that really happened	Dokumentation, Dokumentarfilm
to **track** sth	[træk]	to find/locate sth	etw nachverfolgen, etw nachzeichnen
discovery	[dɪˈskʌvəri]	*v* to discover	Entdeckung
release	[rɪˈliːs]	*v* to release	Mitteilung, Veröffentlichung
to **prove**	[pruːv]	*n* proof	beweisen, nachweisen
indeed	[ɪnˈdiːd]	in fact	tatsächlich, in der Tat

page 38

to **mention**	[ˈmenʃn]	to name	erwähnen, nennen
to **match**	[mætʃ]	to fit together	zusammenpassen
to **keep in touch**	[ˌkiːp ɪn ˈtʌtʃ]	to stay in contact	in Verbindung bleiben
to **get to know** sb	[ɡet tə ˈnəʊ]	to learn about sb new in your life	jdn kennenlernen
in person	[ɪn ˈpɜːsn]	face to face	persönlich
journalist	[ˈdʒɜːnəlɪst]	a writer for the media	Journalist/in
married to sb	[ˈmærid tə]	e.g. My father is married to my stepmother.	mit jdm verheiratet
to **refuse** to do sth	[rɪˈfjuːz tə duː]	to say you will not do sth	sich weigern, etw zu tun

page 39

to **mind**	[maɪnd]	not to be okay	etw dagegen haben
childhood	[ˈtʃaɪldhʊd]	<> adulthood	Kindheit
to **take the time** to do sth	[ˌteɪk ðe ˈtaɪm tə duː]	to do sth slowly and with care	sich die Zeit nehmen, etw zu tun
to **look forward to** sth	[ˌlʊk ˈfɔːwəd tə]	to be excited about sth in the future	sich auf etw freuen
wish	[wɪʃ]	*v* to wish	Wunsch
Best wishes	[best ˈwɪʃɪz]	greetings at the end of a letter or email	*(Brief:)* Mit besten Grüßen
signature	[ˈsɪɡnətʃə]	*v* to sign	Unterschrift

page 40

to **hurt**	[hɜːt]	to make sb feel pain	wehtun, schmerzen, verletzen
jealous	[ˈdʒeləs]	e.g. He was jealous when he saw his ex-girlfriend with another man.	eifersüchtig
cheating	[ˈtʃiːtɪŋ]	to go out with sb else behind your partner's back	Fremdgehen
to **have an argument**	[həv ən ˈɑːɡjumənt]	to fight with sb	sich streiten
for ages	[fər ˈeɪdʒɪz]	a long time	eine Ewigkeit
serious(ly)	[ˈsɪəriəs]	e.g. Why are you laughing? Please take what I say seriously!	ernst, ernsthaft
What's up?	[ˌwɒts ˈʌp]	Are you OK?	Was ist los?
to **go out with** sb	[ˌɡəʊ ˈaʊt wɪð]	to date/be in relationship with sb	mit jdm ausgehen
to **affect** sb/sth	[əˈfekt]	to influence sb/sth	jdn/etw beeinflussen, sich auf jdn/etw auswirken
to **be glad**	[bi ˈɡlæd]	to be happy	sich freuen, froh sein
to **cheat on** sb **with** sb	[tʃiːt]	e.g. He cheated on me with my best friend!	jdn mit jdm betrügen
of course	[əf ˈkɔːs]	naturally, for sure	natürlich, selbstverständlich
hurt	[hɜːt]	pain	verletzt
Never mind.	[ˌnevə ˈmaɪnd]	Oh well.	Das macht nichts.
to **cry**	[kraɪ]	e.g. Don't cry, it will be all right!	weinen
shoulder	[ˈʃəʊldə]	part of the body at top of arm	Schulter
programmer	[ˈprəʊɡræmə]	*v* to progamme	Programmierer/in

page 41

princess	[ˌprɪnˈses]	<> prince	Prinzessin
kind(ly)	[kaɪnd]	nice, friendly	nett, freundlich, liebenswürdig

royal	[ˈrɔɪəl]	king, queen, prince, princess, etc.	königlich, Königs-
car crash	[ˈkɑː kræʃ]	e.g. Their mother died in a car crash.	Autounfall
to **suffer**	[ˈsʌfə]	e.g. He suffers from migraines.	leiden
to support sb	[səˈpɔːt]	*n* support	jdm helfen, jdn unterstützen
terrible	[ˈterəbl]	bad, awful	furchtbar
press	[pres]	the media and their journalists and reporters	Presse
wild	[waɪld]	<> tame	wild
media *pl*	[ˈmiːdiə]	TV, radio, internet, newspaper, etc.	Medien
to **report**	[rɪˈpɔːt]	*n* report	berichten, Bericht erstatten
stable	[ˈsteɪbl]	steady, solid	stabil
thread	[θred]	online conversation	Thema, Forumsthread
to **contribute**	[kənˈtrɪbjuːt]	*n* contribution	mitwirken, (etw) beitragen
comment	[ˈkɒment]	*v* to comment	Kommentar, Bemerkung
to **be intended to sth**	[bi ɪnˈtendɪd tə]	e.g. Books are intended to be read.	etw sollen
page 42			
intern	[ˈɪntɜːn]	sb doing a work experience	Praktikant/In
youth centre	[ˈjuːθ sentə]	place for young people	Jugendzentrum
opening times *pl*	[ˈəʊpənɪŋ taɪmz]	e.g. Opening hours are Mon–Fri 9 a.m.–5 p.m.	Öffnungszeiten
youngster	[ˈjʌŋstə]	young person	Jugendliche/r
quality	[ˈkwɒləti]	character	Eigenschaft
essential	[ɪˈsenʃl]	absolutely important	wesentlich, unerlässlich
youth worker	[ˈjuːθ wɜːkə]	sb who works with young people	Jugendarbeiter/in, Erzieher/in
energy	[ˈenədʒi]	*adj* energetic	Energie
patience	[ˈpeɪʃns]	*adj* patient	Geduld
creativity	[ˌkriːeɪˈtɪvəti]	*adj* creative	Kreativität
optimistic	[ˌɒptɪˈmɪstɪk]	*n* optimism	optimistisch
enthusiastic	[ɪnˌθjuːziˈæstɪk]	*n* enthusiasm	begeisterungsfähig
attitude	[ˈætɪtjuːd]	belief, view	Einstellung, Haltung
role model	[ˈrəʊl mɒdl]	sb you want to be like	Vorbild
view	[vjuː]	*phr* point of view	Ansicht, Meinung
to **communicate**	[kəˈmjuːnɪkeɪt]	*n* communication	kommunizieren
sense	[sens]	e.g. touch, taste, smell, etc.	Sinn
humour	[ˈhjuːmə]	e.g. Sb with a sense of humour finds life amusing.	Humor
budget	[ˈbʌdʒɪt]	e.g. The budget for this project is €1000.	Budget, Etat, Haushalt
most of all	[ˌməʊst əv ˈɔːl]	most importantly	vor allem
mentor	[ˈmentɔː]	sb who helps a younger person	Mentor/in
to **apply for sth**	[əˈplaɪ fə]	*n* application	sich um etw bewerben
page 43			
manager	[ˈmænɪdʒə]	leader	Leiter/in
advantage	[ədˈvɑːntɪdʒ]	<> disadvantage	Vorteil
ramp	[ræmp]	sloping surface	Rampe
jump	[dʒʌmp]	obstacle	Sprunghindernis
matter	[ˈmætə]	subject, business	Sache, Angelegenheit
option	[ˈɒpʃn]	possibilty, alternative	Möglichkeit, Alternative
to **join in**	[ˌdʒɔɪn ˈɪn]	to be part of sth	mitmachen
basics *pl*	[ˈbeɪsɪks]	most important information	Grundlagen
pound	[paʊnd]	British currency	Pfund
free of charge	[ˌfriː əf ˈtʃɑːdʒ]	at no cost	gebührenfrei, kostenlos
glove	[glʌv]	sth to keep your hands warm	Handschuh
anger	[ˈæŋgə]	*adj* angry	Wut
beauty	[ˈbjuːti]	*adj* beautiful	Schönheit
to **disagree with sb**	[ˌdɪsəˈgriː wɪð]	*n* disagreement	jdm widersprechen, anderer Meinung als jd sein
violence	[ˈvaɪələns]	*adj* violent	Gewalt
control	[kənˈtrəʊl]	*phr* to keep things under control	Kontrolle
community	[kəˈmjuːnəti]	people in a place	Gemeinschaft, Gemeinde
to **introduce**	[ˌɪntrəˈdjuːs]	*n* introduction	einführen, vorstellen
ranking list	[ˈræŋkɪŋ lɪst]	a list organized by level	Rangliste
vote	[vəʊt]	e.g. We won 80% of the vote.	Wahl, Abstimmung, Stimmen
photography	[fəˈtɒgrəfi]	the art of taking photos	Fotografie
to **frame**	[freɪm]	*phr* picture frame	*(Bildmotiv)* gestalten, Bildausschnitt wählen
light	[laɪt]	<> dark	Licht
to **sew**	[səʊ]	to join material together	nähen
to **alter**	[ˈɔːltə]	to change	*(Kleidung)* ändern
charity shop	[ˈtʃærəti ʃɒp]	shop selling second hand items	Second-Hand-Laden *(für wohltätige Zwecke)*
art college	[ˈɑːt kɒlɪdʒ]	school to learn about art and design	Kunstakademie, Kunsthochschule
to **design**	[dɪˈzaɪn]	*n* design	gestalten, entwerfen
sewing machine	[ˈsəʊɪŋ məʃiːn]	machine used to make clothes	Nähmaschine
stand up paddle boarding	[ˌstænd ʌp ˈpædl bɔːdɪŋ]	sport similar to canoeing, only done standing up	Stehpaddeln

to **provide**	[prəˈvaɪd]	to let sb have sth	zur Verfügung stellen
shopkeeper	[ˈʃɒp kiːpə]	sb who owns a shop	Ladenbesitzer/in
mosque	[mɒsk]	religious meeting place for muslims	Moschee
temple	[ˈtempl]	religious meeting place	Tempel
religious leader	[rɪˌlɪdʒəs ˈliːdə]	priest, imam, rabbi, etc.	Religionsführer/in
phase	[feɪz]	period of time	Phase
speech	[spiːtʃ]	*v* to speak	Vortrag, Rede
to **exchange**	[ɪksˈtʃeɪndʒ]	*n* exchange	austauschen
to **convince**	[kənˈvɪns]	e.g. We convinced them to join us.	überzeugen
at least	[ət ˈliːst]	e.g. My idea should at least be in second place!	zumindest, wenigstens
willing	[ˈwɪlɪŋ]	happy to do sth	bereit, willens
to **compromise**	[ˈkɒmprəmaɪz]	e.g. If we can't agree, let's find a compromise.	einen Kompromiss eingehen

page 44

series	[ˈsɪəriːz]	e.g. I watched all six episodes of the series in one go!	(TV-, Roman-)Serie
script	[skrɪpt]	text of a film or TV program	Drehbuch
to **perform**	[pəˈfɔːm]	*n* performance	aufführen, spielen
scene	[siːn]	one part of a film or TV program	Szene
to **portray**	[pɔːˈtreɪ]	*n* portrayal	darstellen, zeigen, porträtieren
to **cover**	[ˈkʌvə]	to deal with	*(Thema)* behandeln
character	[ˈkærəktə]	figure in a film, book, etc.	(Roman-/Film-)Figur, Charakter
audience	[ˈɔːdiəns]	the people who watch sth	Publikum
viewer	[ˈvjuːə]	sb who watches sth (often on TV)	Zuschauer/in
to hand sth out	[ˈhænd ˌaʊt]	e.g. The teacher hands out the test.	etw verteilen
to **announce**	[əˈnaʊns]	to tell	verkünden

UNIT 4

page 45

courageous	[kəˈreɪdʒəs]	*n* courage	mutig
rights *pl*	[raɪts]	e.g. the right to vote	Rechte
education	[ˌedʒuˈkeɪʃn]	*adj* educational	Schulbildung, Ausbildung
to **award**	[əˈwɔːd]	*n* award	*(Preis)* verleihen
peace	[piːs]	*phr* peace and quiet	Frieden
Nobel Peace Prize	[nəʊˌbel ˈpiːs praɪz]	an award for promoting peace in the world	Friedensnobelpreis
to appoint sb sth	[əˈpɔɪnt]	to give sb an official position	jdn zu etw ernennen
messenger	[ˈmesɪndʒə]	sb who brings news	Botschafter/in
besides	[bɪˈsaɪdz]	except	außer
to **donate**	[dəʊˈneɪt]	to give money	spenden
charity	[ˈtʃærəti]	non-profit organization that helps people	Wohltätigkeitsorganisation(en), wohltätige Zwecke
foundation	[faʊnˈdeɪʃn]	an organization that gives money to projects	Stiftung
underprivileged	[ˌʌndəˈprɪvəlɪdʒd]	e.g. We want to make sure all underprivileged children can go to school.	benachteiligt, unterprivilegiert
to **treat**	[triːt]	to deal with	behandeln
equal(ly)	[ˈiːkwəl]	e.g. All men are created equal.	gleich
firefighter	[ˈfaɪəfaɪtə]	the politically correct term for 'fireman'	Feuerwehrmann/-frau
to **save**	[seɪv]	e.g. He saved my life after the car accident.	retten
to achieve sth	[əˈtʃiːv]	*n* achievement	etw erreichen
even though	[ˈiːvn ðəʊ]	although	obwohl
to **behave**	[bɪˈheɪv]	*n* behaviour	sich verhalten, sich benehmen
to look up to sb	[ˌlʊk ˈʌp tə]	to have respect for sb	zu jdm aufsehen, jdn bewundern

page 46

to **get back on track**	[get ˌbæk ɒn ˈtræk]	to go in the right direction once again	wieder in die Spur kommen
to overcome sth	[ˌəʊvəˈkʌm]	to get over sth	etw überwinden
to turn one's life around	[ˌtɜːn wʌnz ˈlaɪf əraʊnd]	to change and become better	das eigene Leben umkrempeln
appropriate	[əˈprəʊpriət]	suitable	passend
responsibility	[rɪˌspɒnsəˈbɪləti]	*adj* responsible	Verantwortung, Verantwortlichkeit
counsellor	[ˈkaʊnsələ]	sb who listens and gives advice	Berater/in

page 47

to drop out of school	[ˌdrɒp aʊt əf ˈskuːl]	to leave school suddenly	die Schule abbrechen
sb realizes sth	[ˈrɪəlaɪzɪz]	e.g. I realized that he was talking to me.	jdm wird/ist etw klar, jdm wird/ist etw bewusst
to live rough	[lɪv ˈrʌf]	to live on the streets with no money	auf der Straße leben, Platte machen
to go off with sb	[ˌgəʊ ˈɒf wɪð]	to start a new relationship with sb	mit jdm ein Verhältnis anfangen
housework	[ˈhaʊswɜːk]	e.g. cleaning, cooking, washing, etc.	Hausarbeit(en)
to look after sb/sth	[ˈlʊk ɑːftə]	e.g. The babysitter looked after the children.	sich um jdn/etw kümmern
to fall behind	[ˌfɔːl bɪˈhaɪnd]	to make less progress	zurückbleiben, zurückfallen
to be supposed to do sth	[bi səˈpəʊzd tə du]	e.g. I am sorry, but don't understand what I am supposed to do.	etw (eigentlich) tun sollen
to go on	[ˌgəʊ ˈɒn]	e.g. I don't want to go on like this anymore	*(Dinge:)* laufen, gehen

trouble	[ˈtrʌbl]	difficulties, problems	Ärger, Schwierigkeiten, Probleme
to **move in**	[ˌmuːv ˈɪn]	e.g. The couple moved in together after just a few months.	einziehen
to **make the most of sth**	[ˌmeɪk ðə ˈməʊst əv]	to use and enjoy sth as much as possible	das Beste aus etw machen, etw ausnutzen
to **throw sb out**	[ˌθrəʊ ˈaʊt]	to tell sb to leave	jdn hinauswerfen
to **camp**	[kæmp]	to live outdoors	kampieren
to **be free to do sth**	[bi ˈfriː tə duː]	to be allowed to do sth	etw tun dürfen
to **beg**	[beg]	to ask for money from strangers	betteln
to **wake up**	[ˌweɪk ˈʌp]	e.g. I woke up from a dream.	aufwachen
goal	[gəʊl]	aim, target	Ziel
to **harm**	[hɑːm]	to hurt, to injure	verletzen
to **throw sth away**	[ˌθrəʊ əˈweɪ]	to dump sth	etw wegwerfen
drop-in centre	[ˈdrɒp ɪn sentə]	a place for homeless people to get help	offenes Beratungszentrum
social worker	[ˈsəʊʃl wɜːkə]	sb who helps people and communities	Sozialarbeiter/in
to **be grateful to sb**	[bi ˈgreɪtfl tə]	e.g. I am so grateful to the doctor who saved my life!	jdm dankbar sein
since	[sɪns]	e.g. Since it happened, I have been …	seit
to **do resits**	[ˌduː ˈriːsɪts]	to do exams again	Prüfungen wiederholen
not … yet	[nɒt ˈjet]	<> already	noch nicht
talk	[tɔːk]	speech, presentation	Vortrag
to **turn out**	[ˌtɜːn ˈaʊt]	e.g. Things turned out well in the end.	*(Dinge:)* sich ergeben
impressed	[ɪmˈprest]	*v* to impress	beeindruckt

page 48

to **sort**	[sɔːt]	to put sth in order	einordnen, einsortieren
neighbour	[ˈneɪbə]	sb next to or near you	Nachbar/in

page 49

to **drop sth**	[drɒp]	e.g. She dropped her book.	etw fallen lassen
period	[ˈpɪəriəd]	length of time	Zeitabschnitt, Zeit
ambitious	[æmˈbɪʃəs]	wanting to be successful, famous, etc.	ehrgeizig
society	[səˈsaɪəti]	*adj* social	Gesellschaft

page 50

to **influence**	[ˈɪnfluəns]	*n* influence	beeinflussen
influence	[ˈɪnfluəns]	sth that changes sb/sth	Einfluss
introduction	[ˌɪntrəˈdʌkʃn]	the beginning of a text	*(Text:)* Einleitung
to **highlight**	[ˈhaɪlaɪt]	to show that sth is important	hervorheben
successful	[səkˈsesfl]	<> unsuccessful	erfolgreich
talented	[ˈtæləntɪd]	*n* talent	talentiert
to **set an example**	[ˈset ən ɪgˈzɑːmpl]	e.g. Smoking sets a bad example for children.	ein Beispiel geben
ambassador	[æmˈbæsədə]	sb who represents a country	Botschafter/in
cause	[kɔːz]	e.g. The money went to a good cause.	(gute) Sache, Anliegen
to **encourage**	[ɪnˈkʌrɪdʒ]	*n* encouragement	ermutigen, fördern
to **inspire**	[ɪnˈspaɪə]	*adj* inspirational	anregen, inspirieren
similar	[ˈsɪmələ]	nearly the same	ähnlich
to **be able to do sth**	[bi ˈeɪbl tə duː]	to have the possibility to do sth	in der Lage sein, etw zu tun
effect	[ɪˈfekt]	result	Wirkung, Effekt
to **represent**	[ˌreprɪˈzent]	*n* representation	vertreten, repräsentieren
to **educate**	[ˈedʒukeɪt]	to teach	unterrichten, informieren, bilden
listener	[ˈlɪsnə]	*v* to listen	Hörer/in, Zuhörer/in
season	[ˈsiːzn]	e.g. I bought season 1 of a box set.	*(TV-Serie:)* Staffel
nasty	[ˈnɑːsti]	cruel, bad	gemein, böse
to **appear on TV**	[əˌpɪər ɒn tiːˈviː]	to be on a TV program	im Fernsehen auftreten
to **host**	[həʊst]	*n* host	moderieren
to **admire**	[ədˈmaɪə]	*n* admiration	bewundern
aid group	[ˈeɪd gruːp]	organization for help	Hilfsorganisation
educational programme	[edʒuˌkeɪʃənl ˈprəʊgræm]	structured way to learn	Bildungsprogramm
to **make sb aware of sth**	[ˌmeɪk əˈweər əv]	to show sb that sth is important	jdm etw bewusst machen, jdn auf etw hinweisen
to **join sth**	[dʒɔɪn]	to become part of sth	einer Sache beitreten
actor	[ˈæktə]	man who acts in films, theatre, TV	Schauspieler
to **impress**	[ɪmˈpres]	*adj* impressive	beeindrucken
passionate(ly)	[ˈpæʃənət]	*n* passion	leidenschaftlich
climate	[ˈklaɪmət]	*phr* climate change	Klima
climate change	[ˈklaɪmət tʃeɪndʒ]	e.g. Scientists from around the world met to discuss climate change.	Klimawandel
well known	[ˌwel ˈnəʊn]	e.g. Mesut Özil is a well-known football player.	bekannt
active(ly)	[ˈæktɪv]	<> inactive, passive	aktiv
involved in sth	[ɪnˈvɒlvd ɪn]	*n* involvement	an etw beteiligt
environmental	[ɪnˌvaɪrənˈmentl]	to do with the environment	Umwelt-
earthquake relief	[ˈɜːθkweɪk rɪˌliːf]	teams that give help after an earthquake	Erdbebenhilfe
to **criticize**	[ˈkrɪtɪsaɪz]	*n* criticism	kritisieren

Chronological word list

agreement	[əˈɡriːmənt]	*v* to agree	Abkommen, Vereinbarung
to **hand sth in**	[ˌhænd ˈɪn]	e.g. You have three days left to hand in your work.	etw abgeben
embassy	[ˈembəsi]	e.g. the German Embassy in the UK	Botschaft
disaster	[dɪˈzɑːstə]	catastrophe	Katastrophe
judgement	[ˈdʒʌdʒmənt]	*v* to judge	Urteil, Urteilsvermögen

page 51

among	[əˈmʌŋ]	in the middle of	unter, bei
celebrity	[səˈlebrəti]	famous person	Prominente/r, Promi
to **get drunk**	[ˌɡet ˈdrʌŋk]	to drink too much alcohol	sich betrinken
law	[lɔː]	*adj* legal	Gesetz(e), Recht
mistake	[mɪˈsteɪk]	error	Fehler
weakness	[ˈwiːknəs]	*adj* weak	Schwäche
evil	[ˈiːvl]	<> good	böse
sadistic	[səˈdɪstɪk]	sb who enjoys cruelty	sadistisch
throne	[θrəʊn]	chair for a king/queen	Thron
chances are	[ˈtʃɑːnsɪz ɑː]	e.g. Chances are it will rain tomorrow.	aller Wahrscheinlichkeit nach
to **turn out to be sb/sth**	[ˌtɜːn ˈaʊt tə bi]	to become sb/sth	sich als jd/etw herausstellen
to **call for action**	[ˌkɔːl fər ˈækʃn]	to ask people to help with sth	zu Maßnahmen aufrufen, Maßnahmen fordern
access	[ˈækses]	e.g. I need high-speed internet access for watching films online.	Zugang, Zugriff
poverty	[ˈpɒvəti]	*adj* poor	Armut
shocked	[ʃɒkt]	surprised in a bad way	schockiert
sanitation	[ˌsænɪˈteɪʃn]	canalization, drinking water system	Abwasserkanalisation, Frischwasserversorgung
to **undergird**	[ʌndəˈɡɜːd]	to reinforce	untermauern
magnitude	[ˈmæɡnɪtjuːd]	e.g. the magnitude of the tsunami	Größe
mind-blowing	[ˈmaɪnd bləʊɪŋ]	unbelievable	irre, überwältigend
kind of	[ˈkaɪnd əv]	somehow	irgendwie
endless(ly)	[ˈendləs]	without an end	unendlich
complex	[ˈkɒmpleks]	complicated	komplex, kompliziert
solvable	[ˈsɒlvəbl]	*v* to solve	lösbar
to **solve**	[sɒlv]	*n* solution	lösen
to **animate**	[ˈænɪmeɪt]	to bring to life	antreiben, mit Leben erfüllen
to **mean**	[miːn]	to have the opinion/idea	meinen
to **rob sb of sth**	[ˈrɒb əv]	to take sth away from sb	jdn einer Sache berauben
to **make an effort**	[ˌmeɪk ən ˈefət]	to try hard	sich anstrengen, sich Mühe geben
comprehensive	[ˌkɒmprɪˈhensɪv]	<> simple, partial	umfassend
crisis	[ˈkraɪsɪs]	big emergency	Krise
in our lifetime	[ɪn aʊə ˈlaɪftaɪm]	during the time we are alive	zu unseren Lebzeiten
to **mediate**	[ˈmiːdieɪt]	to find an agreement	vermitteln, übersetzen
the gist	[ðə ˈdʒɪst]	the general, most important meaning	das Wesentliche, die Hauptpunkte
to **surround**	[səˈraʊnd]	to be around sth	umgeben
to **reflect on sth**	[rɪˈflekt ɒn]	to think about sth	über etw nachdenken

page 52

to **greet**	[ɡriːt]	e.g. by saying 'Hello!'	begrüßen
visitor	[ˈvɪzɪtə]	<> host/hostess	Besucher/in
to **point out sth**	[ˌpɔɪnt ˈaʊt]	to make sb see sth	auf etw hinweisen
announcement	[əˈnaʊnsmənt]	*v* to announce	Ankündigung, Mitteilung
twin town	[ˌtwɪn ˈtaʊn]	partner city in another country	Partnerstadt
vocational training	[vəʊˌkeɪʃənl ˈtreɪnɪŋ]	job training	Berufsausbildung
exciting	[ɪkˈsaɪtɪŋ]	*n* excitement	aufregend, spannend
workshop	[ˈwɜːkʃɒp]	place where things are made	Werkstatt
further education	[ˌfɜːðə edʒuˈkeɪʃn]	e.g. college, university, etc.	Weiterbildung
personality	[ˌpɜːsəˈnæləti]	a person's character	Persönlichkeit
a must	[ə ˈmʌst]	sth you have to do	ein Muss
application	[ˌæplɪˈkeɪʃn]	*v* to apply	Bewerbung
training session	[ˈtreɪnɪŋ seʃn]	a short class in which you learn new skills	Schulungseinheit
trainer	[ˈtreɪnə]	teacher, leader	Dozent/in, Ausbilder/in
to **settle down**	[ˌsetl ˈdaʊn]	to get calm, to become quiet	die Plätze einnehmen, zur Ruhe kommen
consultant	[kənˈsʌltənt]	sb who gives advice	Berater/in
affairs *pl*	[əˈfeəz]	business	Geschäfte, geschäftliche Angelegenheiten
town council	[ˌtaʊn ˈkaʊnsl]	local government	Stadtrat, Stadtverwaltung
dos and don'ts	[ˌduːz ən ˈdəʊnts]	what you should and shouldn't to	Dinge, die man tun und lassen sollte
smooth(ly)	[smuːð]	<> rough	reibungslos, glatt
to **be aware of sth**	[bi əˈweər əv]	to know about sth	etw kennen, sich einer Sache bewusst sein
to **shake hands**	[ʃeɪk ˈhændz]	e.g. It's polite to shake hands when you meet somebody for the first time.	die Hand geben, die Hände schütteln

to **go on**	[ˌgəʊ ˈɒn]	to continue	weitermachen, fortfahren
smart(ly)	[smɑːt]	stylish, chic	*(Kleidung:)* schick
bright	[braɪt]	colourful	*(Farbe:)* kräftig, bunt
low-cut top	[ˌləʊ kʌt ˈtɒp]	She was wearing a very low-cut top.	tief ausgeschnittenes Oberteil
to **move on (to sth)**	[ˌmuːv ˈɒn]	e.g. shake hands, then move on to the next person	(mit etw) weitermachen
body language	[ˈbɒdi læŋgwɪdʒ]	communication using the body	Körpersprache
body contact	[ˈbɒdi kɒntækt]	physical contact with another person	Körperkontakt
to **touch**	[tʌtʃ]	*n* touch	berühren
to **be prepared** to **do sth**	[bi prɪˈpeəd tə duː]	*n* preparation	bereit sein, etw zu tun
likely	[ˈlaɪkli]	probably	wahrscheinlich
basic	[ˈbeɪsɪk]	simple	einfach, grundlegend, elementar
to **deal with sb**	[ˈdiːl wɪð]	to handle sb	mit jdm zu tun haben
customer	[ˈkʌstəmə]	person who buys sth	Kunde/-in
gentleman	[ˈdʒentlmən]	<> lady	Herr
respect	[rɪˈspekt]	e.g. It is important to show respect for older people.	Respekt
polite	[pəˈlaɪt]	*n* politeness	höflich
ordinary	[ˈɔːdnri]	normal	gewöhnlich, normal
page 53			
delay	[dɪˈleɪ]	e.g. The train had a delay of one hour.	Verzögerung, Verspätung
to **train for sth**	[ˈtreɪn fə]	e.g. to train for a profession	eine Ausbildung zu etw machen
flight	[flaɪt]	*v* to fly	Flug
page 54			
background	[ˈbækgraʊnd]	the story behind the situation	Hintergrund, Vorgeschichte
to **structure**	[ˈstrʌktʃə]	to put sth in the correct order	strukturieren
to **conclude**	[kənˈkluːd]	to finish, to end	schließen
handout	[ˈhændaʊt]	e.g. The woman prepared a handout for the meeting.	Arbeitsblatt, Handzettel
structure	[ˈstrʌktʃə]	the way sth is made	Aufbau

UNIT 5

page 55			
treatment	[ˈtriːtmənt]	*v* to treat	Behandlung
to **deal with sth**	[ˈdiːl wɪð]	to handle sth	mit etw zurechtkommen, mit etw umgehen
illness	[ˈɪlnəs]	*adj* ill	Krankheit
page 56			
caffeine	[ˈkæfiːn]	e.g. Caffeine can be found in drinks, e.g. in coffee and tea.	Koffein
hidden	[ˈhɪdn]	*v* to hide	verborgen, versteckt
to **come across sth**	[ˌkʌm əˈkrɒs]	to find sth	auf etw stoßen
tragic	[ˈtrædʒɪk]	very sad	tragisch
fellow student	[ˌfeləʊ ˈstjuːdnt]	sb in your class	Mitschüler/in
report	[rɪˈpɔːt]	e.g. a sports report	Reportage, Bericht
headline	[ˈhedlaɪn]	large title of a paragraph or newspaper article	Überschrift
coma	[ˈkəʊmə]	*phr* to fall into a coma	Koma
coroner	[ˈkɒrənə]	a doctor who explains why/how sb died	Gerichtsmediziner/in
overdose	[ˈəʊvədəʊs]	too many drugs taken at the same time	Überdosis
life-support system	[ˈlaɪf səpɔːt sɪstəm]	a machine to keep sb alive	Lebenserhaltungssystem
follow-up	[ˈfɒləʊ ʌp]	e.g. After the operation, I had a follow-up meeting with my doctor.	Nachfassen
accident	[ˈæksɪdənt]	e.g. a traffic accident	Unfall
paramedic	[ˌpærəˈmedɪk]	healthcare worker for emergencies	Rettungssanitäter/in
to **collapse**	[kəˈlæps]	e.g. The old man collapsed in the heat.	zusammenbrechen
campaign	[kæmˈpeɪn]	movement, action	Kampagne, Aktion
ambulance	[ˈæmbjələns]	used for transporting sb to hospital	Rettungswagen
to **consume**	[kənˈsjuːm]	*n* consumption	zu sich nehmen, konsumieren
to **be addicted to sth**	[bi əˈdɪktɪd tə]	e.g. The rock star was addicted to drugs.	nach etw süchtig sein, von etw abhängig sein
to **demand sth**	[dɪˈmɑːnd]	*adj* demanding	etw fordern
ban (on sth)	[bæn]	*v* to ban	Verbot (von etw)
caffeinated	[ˈkæfiːneɪtɪd]	with caffeine	koffeinhaltig
to **support**	[səˈpɔːt]	to help, to aid	unterstützen
page 57			
lunch break	[ˈlʌntʃ breɪk]	time to have lunch	Mittagspause
to **take one's seat**	[ˌteɪk wʌnz ˈsiːt]	to sit down	seinen Platz einnehmen
heart attack	[ˈhɑːt ətæk]	*phr* to suffer from a heart attack	Herzinfarkt
space of time	[ˌspeɪs əf ˈtaɪm]	e.g. an hour, a day, etc.	Zeitspanne
condition	[kənˈdɪʃn]	illness, sickness	(chronische) Krankheit, Leiden
system	[ˈsɪstəm]	organism	Organismus

Chronological word list

amount	[ə'maʊnt]	quantity	Menge
total	['təʊtl]	e.g. the total amount	Gesamt-, Gesamtmenge/-betrag
to **cut down on sth**	[ˌkʌt 'daʊn ɒn]	to have less of sth	etw reduzieren
to **recover**	[rɪ'kʌvə]	to get well again	sich erholen
to **worry about sb/sth**	['wʌri əbaʊt]	e.g. My mum worries about me a lot.	sich um jdn/etw Sorgen machen
safety	['seɪfti]	*adj* safe	Sicherheit
as	[əz]	during, while	während
to **get sth across**	[ˌget ə'krɒs]	*phr* to get the message across	etw vermitteln
to **put sb at risk**	[ˌput ət 'rɪsk]	to put sb in danger	jdn gefährden
advice	[əd'vaɪs]	*v* to advise	Rat, Ratschlag
at once	[ət 'wʌns]	immediately	auf einmal

page 58

to **express**	[ɪk'spres]	*n* expression	ausdrücken
permission	[pə'mɪʃn]	e.g. My parents gave me permission to stay out late.	Erlaubnis
ability	[ə'bɪləti]	<> inability	Fähigkeit, Möglichkeit
obligation	[ˌɒblɪ'geɪʃn]	sth you must do	Verpflichtung
to **replace**	[rɪ'pleɪs]	to exchange	ersetzen, austauschen
substitute	['sʌbstɪtju:t]	replacement	Ersatz, Ersetzung
to **lift sth**	[lɪft]	to pick sth up	etw heben, etw hochheben
to **go shopping**	[gəʊ 'ʃɒpɪŋ]	e.g. I like to go shopping on Saturdays.	einkaufen gehen
to **take sth round**	[ˌteɪk 'raʊnd]	to bring sth to sb	etw vorbeibringen
shopping	['ʃɒpɪŋ]	food, groceries, clothes, etc.	Einkäufe
proper(ly)	['prɒpə]	correct(ly)	richtig, ordentlich
home visit	['həʊm vɪzɪt]	when a doctor goes to sb's home	Hausbesuch
to **examine**	[ɪg'zæmɪn]	*n* examination	untersuchen
prescription	[prɪ'skrɪpʃn]	a piece of paper the doctor gives you to get medicine	(ärztliches) Rezept
to **make sure**	[ˌmeɪk 'ʃʊə]	to ensure	dafür sorgen, sicherstellen
to **handle sth**	['hændl]	to deal with sth	etw anfassen
first-aid kit	[ˌfɜ:st'eɪd kɪt]	box with medical equipment	Erste-Hilfe-Kasten, Verbandskasten
stairs *pl*	[steəz]	e.g. Don't run on the stairs!	Treppe
helmet	['helmɪt]	protection for the head	Helm
in case	[ɪn 'keɪs]	if/when sth happens	falls; für den Fall, dass
toxic	['tɒksɪk]	poisonous	giftig
liquid	['lɪkwɪd]	fluid	Flüssigkeit
wet	[wet]	<> dry	feucht, nass
to **slip**	[slɪp]	*adj* slippery	ausrutschen

page 59

appointment	[ə'pɔɪntmənt]	e.g. an appointment with the doctor	Termin
course of treatment	[ˌkɔ:s əf 'tri:tmənt]	medicine/therapy	Therapie, Behandlung
drip	[drɪp]	infusion	Infusion

page 60

technological	[ˌteknə'lɒdʒɪkl]	*n* technology	technologisch, technisch
development	[dɪ'veləpmənt]	*v* to develop	Entwicklung
researcher	[rɪ'sɜ:tʃə]	*v* to research	Forscher/in
medical	['medɪkl]	*n* medicine	medizinisch
assistance	[ə'sɪstəns]	help, support	Hilfe, Unterstützung
to call for assistance	[ˌkɔ:l fər ə'sɪstəns]	to ask sb to help	um Hilfe ersuchen
blind	[blaɪnd]	unable to see	Blinde/r, blind
to **press**	[pres]	e.g. to press a button	drücken
equivalent	[ɪ'kwɪvələnt]	*phr* to be the equivalent of …	Entsprechung, Äquivalent
instead of sth	[ɪn'sted əv]	e.g. Mum gave me pieces of fruit instead of biscuits.	anstelle von etw
solution	[sə'lu:ʃn]	answer	Lösung
poor eyesight	['aɪsaɪt]	e.g. If you have poor eyesight, you might need glasses.	Sehschwäche
independent	[ˌɪndɪ'pendənt]	<> dependent	unabhängig
user	['ju:zə]	*v* to use	Nutzer/in, Benutzer/in
connection	[kə'nekʃn]	*v* to connect	Verbindung
to **connect (to sb)**	[kə'nekt]	*n* connection	(sich mit jdm) verbinden
to **point sth at sth**	['pɔɪnt ət]	e.g. Don't point your finger at me!	etw auf etw richten
street sign	['stri:t saɪn]	board with the street name on it	Straßenschild
instruction	[ɪn'strʌkʃn]	*v* to instruct	Anleitung, Anweisung
to **take a call**	[ˌteɪk ə 'kɔ:l]	to answer a phone	einen Anruf entgegennehmen
to **forward sth**	['fɔ:wəd]	to send sth on to sb	etw weiterleiten
within	[wɪ'ðɪn]	inside	innerhalb von, binnen
helper	['helpə]	sb who helps	Helfer/in
to **be located**	[bi ləʊ'keɪtɪd]	*n* location	sich befinden, sich aufhalten
automatic(ally)	[ˌɔ:tə'mætɪk]	by itself	automatisch
label	['leɪbl]	tag	Etikett

page 61

to **register**	['redʒɪstə]	e.g. Please register your address.	anmelden, eintragen
to **charge**	[tʃɑ:dʒ]	e.g. My battery is flat, I'll have to charge my phone.	aufladen

to report sb/sth	[rɪˈpɔːt]	e.g. You must report the crime to the police.	jdn/etw melden
just for fun	[dʒʌst fə ˈfʌn]	<> serious	nur zum Spaß
to sign off	[ˌsaɪn ˈɒf]	to say goodbye	sich abmelden, *(Telefonat)* beenden
medicine	[ˈmedsn]	*adj* medicinal	Medizin
feedback	[ˈfiːdbæk]	reaction	Rückmeldung, Reaktion(en)
content	[ˈkɒntent]	*v* to contain	Inhalt

page 62

lady	[ˈleɪdi]	<> gentleman	Dame
client	[ˈklaɪənt]	customer	Kunde/-in
offer	[ˈɒfə]	*v* to offer	Angebot
on offer	[ɒn ˈɒfə]	available	im Angebot, angeboten
special offer	[ˌspeʃl ˈɒfə]	sth available at a lower price	Sonderangebot
luxury	[ˈlʌkʃəri]	*adj* luxurious	Luxus
rest	[rest]	e.g. After work, I had a rest for an hour.	Erholung, Ruhe
relaxation	[ˌriːlækˈseɪʃn]	<> tension	Entspannung, Erholung
middle	[ˈmɪdl]	*phr* in the middle	Mitte
indoor pool	[ˌɪndoː ˈpuːl]	a place to swim indoors	Hallenbad
fresh	[freʃ]	<> old, stale	frisch
to prepare	[prɪˈpeə]	*n* preparation	*(Essen)* zubereiten
chef	[ʃef]	sb who cooks food professionally	(Chef-)Koch/Köchin
entry	[ˈentri]	e.g. The entry fee to the health club is £25.	Eintritt
stone	[stəʊn]	small rock	Stein
combination offer	[ˌkɒmbɪˈneɪʃn ɒfə]	many things for special price	Kombi-Angebot
time out	[ˌtaɪm ˈaʊt]	a break from normal life	Auszeit
bathrobe	[ˈbɑːθrəʊb]	e.g. After swimming, I put on my bathrobe.	Bademantel
to take a break	[ˌteɪk ə ˈbreɪk]	to stop doing sth for a while	eine Pause machen
on loan	[ɒn ˈləʊn]	borrowed	leihweise

page 63

to manage sth	[ˈmænɪdʒ]	to handle, to deal with sth	etw bewältigen
to advise sb	[ədˈvaɪz]	*n* advice	jdn beraten
to give sb advice	[gɪv ədˈvaɪs]	to advise	jdn beraten
stressed	[strest]	<> relaxed	gestresst
to be free	[bi ˈfriː]	to have time for sth	Zeit haben
to schedule	[ˈʃedjuːl]	to plan, to make an appointment	*(Termin)* planen, festlegen

page 64

stressful	[ˈstresfl]	hard, difficult	anstrengend, stressig
notice board	[ˈnəʊtɪsbɔːd]	place for advertisements, information, etc.	Schwarzes Brett
aim	[eɪm]	goal, purpose	Ziel
to combat sth	[ˈkɒmbæt]	to fight sth and win	etw bekämpfen
to offer	[ˈɒfə]	*n* offer	bieten, anbieten
library	[ˈlaɪbrəri]	place where you can borrow books for a short time	Bibliothek
to chill	[tʃɪl]	to relax, to do nothing	chillen, relaxen
extracurricular	[ekstrəkəˈrɪkjʊlə]	outside school	außerhalb des Stundenplans, außerschulisch
pool table	[ˈpuːl teɪbl]	table to play billiards	Billardtisch
to reach	[riːtʃ]	*phr* to reach a decision	erreichen
consensus	[kənˈsensəs]	everyone has the same opinion	Übereinstimmung, Konsens
agreement	[əˈgriːmənt]	*v* to agree	Übereinkunft, Übereinstimmung

UNIT 6

page 65

to swap	[swɒp]	to change with sb	tauschen
to satisfy one's needs	[ˌsætɪsfaɪ wʌnz ˈniːdz]	to have enough to make you happy	jds Bedürfnisse befriedigen

page 66

to live on sth	[ˌlɪv ˈɒn]	e.g. I live on almost no money.	von etw leben
recording	[rɪˈkɔːdɪŋ]	e.g. a recording of music	Aufzeichnung, Aufnahme
to record sth	[rɪˈkɔːd]	e.g. I recorded the band on my phone.	etw aufzeichnen, etw aufnehmen
to upload	[ˌʌpˈləʊd]	to put information on the internet	hochladen
variety	[vəˈraɪəti]	many different things	Vielfalt, Vielzahl
to skim	[skɪm]	to read something quickly	*(Text)* überfliegen
unsure	[ˌʌnˈʃʊə]	not certain	unsicher
criticism	[ˈkrɪtɪsɪzəm]	*v* to criticize	Kritik
to be sick of sth	[bi ˈsɪk əv]	e.g. I am sick of hearing that terrible song all the time!	etw satt haben
forest	[ˈfɒrɪst]	many trees together	Wald
to cut down	[ˌkʌt ˈdaʊn]	e.g. Too many forests are cut down every year.	*(Wald)* roden, *(Baum)* fällen
developing country	[dɪˌveləpɪŋ ˈkʌntri]	a country with poor industry and economy	Entwicklungsland
to rule	[ruːl]	to control people, governments, countries	(be)herrschen, regieren
to trust	[trʌst]	e.g. Don't trust this man!	(darauf) vertrauen
to work out	[ˌwɜːk ˈaʊt]	e.g. It all worked out in the end.	gut ausgehen

Chronological word list

page 67

caravan	[ˈkærəvæn]	mobile home	Wohnwagen
smallholding	[ˈsmɔːlhəʊldɪŋ]	very small farm	Kleinbauernhof
wood-burning stove	[ˌwʊd bɜːnɪŋ ˈstəʊv]	oven that burns wood for heat	Holzofen
electricity	[ɪˌlekˈtrɪsəti]	*adj* electrical	Strom, Elektrizität
solar panel	[ˌsəʊlə ˈpænl]	e.g. We get our electricity from solar panels.	Solarzelle, Solarmodul
to **earn**	[ɜːn]	to get money for doing work	verdienen
to **gain**	[geɪn]	to get	erwerben, erlangen
moneyless	[ˈmʌnɪləs]	without money	ohne Geld
dependent (on sth)	[dɪˈpendənt]	<> independent	abhängig (von etw)
to **exploit**	[ɪkˈsplɔɪt]	to use sb in an unfair way	ausbeuten
consumer goods *pl*	[kənˈsjuːmə gʊdz]	things to buy	Konsumgüter
smallholder	[ˈsmɔːlhəʊldə]	sb who owns a small farm	Kleinbauer/-bäuerin
accommodation	[əˌkɒməˈdeɪʃn]	place to stay	Unterkunft
exchange	[ɪksˈtʃeɪndʒ]	swap, trade	Austausch
to **hand in one's notice**	[ˌhænd ˈɪn wʌnz ˈnəʊtɪs]	to quit a job	die Kündigung einreichen, kündigen
second-hand	[ˌsekənd ˈhænd]	used, owned by sb already	gebraucht, aus zweiter Hand
to **react to sth**	[riˈækt tə]	e.g. We reacted badly to the news.	auf etw reagieren
to **challenge sth**	[ˈtʃælɪndʒ]	to test sth	etw infrage stellen
simply	[ˈsɪmpli]	e.g. He was simply interested in making money.	einfach, schlichtweg, nur
to **spend**	[spend]	to use money to buy sth	*(Geld)* ausgeben
to **adapt to sth**	[əˈdæpt tə]	to change to fit sth	sich an etw anpassen, sich an etw gewöhnen
to **figure sth out**	[ˌfɪgər ˈaʊt]	to find an answer	etw herausfinden
to **turn out**	[ˌtɜːn ˈaʊt]	e.g. He turned out to be a liar – he didn't tell the truth.	sich herausstellen
to **grow**	[grəʊ]	e.g. I like to grow herbs on my balcony.	*(Pflanzen)* anbauen
mushroom	[ˈmʌʃrʊm]	fungus you can eat	Pilz
herbs *pl*	[hɜːbz]	e.g. oregano, rosemary, basil	Kräuter
soap	[səʊp]	e.g. Wash your hands with soap and water.	Seife
soapwort	[ˈsəʊpwɜːt]	a plant for making soap	Seifenkraut
toothpaste	[ˈtuːθpeɪst]	e.g. Brush your teeth with toothpaste.	Zahncreme
baking soda	[ˈbeɪkɪŋ səʊdə]	chemical substance used for cleaning or cooking	Natron
to **care about sth**	[ˈkeər əbaʊt]	e.g. many people don't care about the environment	sich um etw kümmern, jdm ist an etw gelegen
selfish	[ˈselfɪʃ]	only think of oneself	egoistisch
ups and downs *pl*	[ˌʌps ən ˈdaʊnz]	good and bad moments	Höhen und Tiefen
wooden house	[ˌwʊdn ˈhaʊs]	house made out of wood	Holzhaus

page 68

to **be happy to do sth**	[bi ˈhæpi tə duː]	e.g. I'm happy to help you with your work.	etw gern tun
crazy	[ˈkreɪzi]	<> sane, normal	verrückt
to **get used to sth**	[get ˈjuːst tə]	e.g. I'll never get used to living in the city.	sich an etw gewöhnen
to **change one's mind**	[ˌtʃeɪndʒ wʌnz ˈmaɪnd]	e.g. I liked it at first, but then changed my mind.	seine Meinung ändern
consumer	[kənˈsjuːmə]	*v* to consume	Verbraucher/in, Konsument/in

page 69

idiom	[ˈɪdiəm]	a form of expression	Redensart
proverb	[ˈprɒvɜːb]	a short sentence stating truth or a piece of advice	Sprichwort
depressed	[dɪˈprest]	*n* depression	deprimiert
complicated	[ˈkɒmplɪkeɪtɪd]	<> simple	kompliziert
to **ponder sth**	[ˈpɒndə]	to think about sth	über etw nachdenken
despite	[dɪˈspaɪt]	e.g. Despite the many problems, the project was a big success!	trotz
to **boost consumption**	[ˌbuːst kənˈsʌmpʃn]	to get people to spend more money, buy more	den Konsum ankurbeln
economy	[ɪˈkɒnəmi]	*adj* economic	Wirtschaft
to **be in need of sth**	[bi ɪn ˈniːd əv]	to not have enough of sth	etw brauchen, etw benötigen
lift	[lɪft]	<> drop	*(Wirtschaft:)* Aufschwung
sacred	[ˈseɪkrɪd]	holy, from God	heilig
to **be at a crossroads**	[bi ət ə ˈkrɒsrəʊdz]	to have to choose between two things	am Scheideweg sein
convenient	[kənˈviːniənt]	<> inconvenient	praktisch, bequem
to **run errands**	[ˌrʌn ˈerəndz]	e.g. to do the shopping, to go to the post office, etc.	Besorgungen machen
buyer	[ˈbaɪə]	<> seller	Käufer/in
comfortably	[ˈkʌmftəbl]	in a free, relaxed way	bequem
to **go for walks**	[ˌgəʊ fə ˈwɔːks]	e.g. I like to go for long walks.	spazieren gehen
besides	[bɪˈsaɪdz]	also, additionally	außerdem
at one point	[ət wʌn ˈpɔɪnt]	e.g. We were walking and at one point we stopped.	an einer Stelle
to **put sth into practice**	[ˌpʊt ɪntə ˈpræktɪs]	to use sth in reality	etw in die Praxis umsetzen
apart from	[əˈpɑːt frəm]	except for	abgesehen von, außer
comfort	[ˈkʌmfət]	*adj* comfortable	Komfort, Annehmlichkeit
to **disagree with sth**	[ˌdɪsəˈgriː wɪð]	to have a different opinion about sth	einer Sache nicht zustimmen
to **suit sth**	[suːt]	e.g. That colour doesn't suit you.	zu etw passen
to **be up to sth**	[bi ˈʌp tə]	to be able to do sth	einer Sache gewachsen sein

page 70

saying	[ˈseɪɪŋ]	a short expression that offers advice or wisdom	Sprichwort
fool	[fuːl]	idiot, joker	Narr
to **part**	[pɑːt]	to break, to separate	auseinandergehen, (sich) trennen
catalogue	[ˈkætəlɒg]	a book with a list of products you can buy	Katalog
piece of equipment	[ˌpiːs əv ɪˈkwɪpmənt]	a device, part of a machine	Gerät
to **get by with sth**	[ˌget ˈbaɪ wɪð]	e.g. I get by with the little money I earn.	mit etw auskommen
to **break down**	[ˌbreɪk ˈdaʊn]	to stop working	kaputtgehen
there's no point in doing sth	[ðeəz ˌnəʊ ˈpɔɪnt ɪn duːɪŋ]	e.g. There's no point talking to him, he never listens.	es hat keinen Sinn, etw zu tun
to **admit**	[ədˈmɪt]	e.g He admitted the truth in the end.	zugeben, eingestehen
addict	[ˈædɪkt]	sb who is addicted to sth	Süchtige/r
stuff	[stʌf]	things	Zeug
a ton of	[ə ˈtʌn əv]	a lot of	jede Menge
to **save**	[seɪv]	<> to spend (money)	*(Geld usw.)* sparen
store	[stɔː]	shop	Laden, Geschäft
to **fall in love with sb/sth**	[ˌfɔːl ɪn ˈlʌv wɪð]	e.g. I can't help falling in love with you!	sich in jdn/etw verlieben
unlikely	[ʌnˈlaɪkli]	e.g. It is unlikely to snow in summer.	unwahrscheinlich
dust	[dʌst]	*adj* dusty	Staub
to **waste**	[weɪst]	e.g. to waste money, time	verschwenden, vergeuden

page 71

to **drop**	[drɒp]	to die exhausted	(tot) umfallen
printer	[ˈprɪntə]	*v* to print	Drucker
jacket	[ˈdʒækɪt]	light coat	Jacke, Jackett
to **own**	[əʊn]	to have sth which is yours	besitzen
waste of time	[ˌweɪst əf ˈtaɪm]	e.g. Watching that film was a waste of time.	Zeitverschwendung

page 72

retail	[ˈriːteɪl]	*phr* to work in retail	Einzelhandel
work experience	[ˈwɜːk ɪkspɪəriəns]	*phr* to do work experience	Praktikum
department store		a large shop that sells many different things	Kaufhaus
supervisor	[ˈsuːpəvaɪzə]	boss	Vorgesetzte/r
department	[dɪˈpɑːtmənt]	part of a business	Abteilung
accessory	[əkˈsesəri]	e.g. earrings, scarves, etc.	Accessoire
clothing	[ˈkləʊðɪŋ]	what people wear	Kleidung, Bekleidung, Kleider
cosmetics *pl*	[kɒzˈmetɪks]	e.g. mascara, lipstick, etc.	Kosmetik
food hall	[ˈfuːd hɔːl]	department for food	Lebensmittelabteilung
household items *pl*	[ˈhaʊshəʊld aɪtəmz]	things for your home	Haushaltsartikel
ladies' wear	[ˈleɪdiz weə]	clothes for women	Damenbekleidung
menswear	[ˈmenzweə]	clothes for men	Herrenbekleidung
sportswear	[ˈspɔːtsweə]	clothes for sports	Sportbekleidung
sketch	[sketʃ]	drawing of sth	Skizze
shop floor	[ˌʃɒp ˈflɔː]	where things are sold	Verkaufsfläche
shop assistant	[ˈʃɒp əsɪstənt]	sb who works in a shop	Verkäufer/in
size	[saɪz]	e.g. S, M, L, XL	Größe
to **try sth on**	[ˌtraɪ ˈɒn]	to put on clothes to see if you like them	etw anprobieren
to **put sth aside**	[ˌpʊt əˈsaɪd]	to keep/save sth for sb	etw zurücklegen
sth in particular	[ɪn pəˈtɪkjələ]	sth special	etw Spezielles
change	[tʃeɪndʒ]	money you get back	Wechselgeld
style	[staɪl]	*adj* stylish	Stil, Art
to **exchange**	[ɪksˈtʃeɪndʒ]	to replace sth	umtauschen

page 73

shade	[ʃeɪd]	colour nuance	Farbton
to **fit**	[fɪt]	e.g. This is too big. It doesn't fit me.	passen
light	[laɪt]	<> dark	*(Farbe:)* hell
changing room	[ˈtʃeɪndʒɪŋ ruːm]	place to try on clothes in a shop	Umkleidekabine
sale	[seɪl]	when products are cheaper than normal	Ausverkauf
cash desk	[ˈkæʃ desk]	place in a shop where you pay	Kasse
receipt	[rɪˈsiːt]	piece of paper you get when you buy sth	Quittung, Beleg, Kassenbon
to **return sth**	[rɪˈtɜːn]	to bring sth back to the shop	etw zurückgeben
sale	[seɪl]	*v* to sell	Verkauf

page 74

arrangements *pl*	[əˈreɪndʒmənts]	preparations	Vorbereitungen
mirror	[ˈmɪrə]	e.g. Look at yourself in the mirror.	Spiegel
condition	[kənˈdɪʃn]	*phr* in good/bad condition	Zustand
left over	[left ˈəʊvə]	sth not used	übrig geblieben
factor	[ˈfæktə]	sth to think about	Faktor
separate	[ˈseprət]	<> together	getrennt, separat

Chronological word list

UNIT 7

page 75

abroad	[ə'brɔ:d]	in/to another country	im/ins Ausland
professional	[prə'feʃənl]	related to your job	beruflich

page 76

job advertisement	['dʒɒb ədvɜ:tɪsmənt]	text a company writes when they are looking for employees	Stellenanzeige
federal	['fedərəl]	governmental	Bundes-
voluntary service	[ˌvɒləntri 'sɜ:vɪs]	civil work without pay	Freiwilligendienst
covering letter	['kʌvərɪŋ letə]	letter you send with a job application	Anschreiben, Begleitschreiben
position	[pə'zɪʃn]	place, job	Stelle, Stellung, Position
to **fit into sth**	['fɪt ɪntə]	e.g. It took me a long time to fit into my new school.	sich in etw einfügen
creative	[kri'eɪtɪv]	*v* to create	kreativ, schöpferisch
throughout ...	[θru:'aʊt]	the whole way	in ganz ...
recruiter	[rɪ'kru:tə]	sb who finds jobs for people	einstellendes Unternehmen, Personal-vermittler/in

page 77

loan	[ləʊn]	money a bank lends you	Darlehen, Kredit
to **run**	[rʌn]	to manage, to operate	*(Betrieb)* führen, betreiben
to **supply sth**	[sə'plaɪ]	to give sb sth they need	etw zur Verfügung stellen
depending on	[dɪ'pendɪŋ ɒn]	e.g. Depending on the weather, we could go to the park.	je nach
competence	['kɒmpɪtəns]	skill	Kompetenz
computer literacy	[kəmˌpju:tə 'lɪtərəsi]	ability to use a computer	Computerkenntnisse
struggle	['strʌgl]	difficulty	Kampf
to **increase sth**	[ɪn'kri:s]	to improve	etw steigern, etw erhöhen
income	['ɪnkʌm]	money you get from work	Einkommen
staff	[stɑ:f]	the people who work in a company	Personal
pedagogical staff	[pedəˌgɒdʒɪkl 'stɑ:f]	teachers in a company	Lehrpersonal
to **train sb**	[treɪn]	to teach sb how to do a job	jdn schulen
length of service	[leŋθ əv 'sɜ:vɪs]	how long sb has worked for a company	Beschäftigungsdauer
largely	['lɑ:dʒli]	mostly	überwiegend, größtenteils
agricultural	[ˌægrɪ'kʌltʃərəl]	*n* agriculture	landwirtschaftlich
religious	[rɪ'lɪdʒəs]	*n* religion	religiös
conservative	[kən'sɜ:vətɪv]	<> liberal	konservativ
to **be sensitive towards sb/sth**	[bi 'sensətɪv təwɔ:dz]	to be understanding about sb/sth	für jdn/etw Verständnis haben, verständnisvoll mit jdm/etw umgehen

page 78

custom	['kʌstəm]	a traditional way of doing sth	Sitte, Brauch
to **approve of sth**	[ə'pru:v əv]	to think sth is a good idea	etw gutheißen, etw billigen
belief	[bɪ'li:f]	*v* to believe	Überzeugung, Glaube
the locals *pl*	[ðə 'ləʊklz]	people who live in a particular place	die Einheimischen
to **form**	[fɔ:m]	to build, to shape	bilden
to **suppose**	[sə'pəʊz]	to think	annehmen, glauben
obvious	['ɒbviəs]	clear	klar (erkennbar), offensichtlich
doubt	[daʊt]	e.g. I have my doubts that this is a good idea.	Zweifel
grade	[greɪd]	result from a test or an exam	Note
to **fail**	[feɪl]	e.g. She failed three exams because she didn't study.	*(Prüfung)* nicht bestehen, durchfallen
to **pass**	[pɑ:s]	e.g. Do you think you've passed?	*(Prüfung)* bestehen

page 79

advert	['ædvɜ:t]	short for 'advertisment'	Anzeige
mother tongue	['mʌðə tʌŋ]	native language	Muttersprache
school leaving certificate	[ˌsku:l li:vɪŋ sə'tɪfɪkət]	qualification you get at the end of school	Schulabgangszeugnis
to **be keen to do sth**	[bɪ 'ki:n tə]	to really want to do sth	etw unbedingt tun wollen
driving licence	['draɪvɪŋ laɪsns]	document which allows you to drive a car	Führerschein
refugee	[ˌrefju'dʒi:]	sb who had to leave his/her country	Flüchtling
to **get on well with sb**	[ˌget ɒn 'wel wɪð]	e.g. I get on well with all my classmates.	gut mit jdm auskommen
to **consider**	[kən'sɪdə]	to think about	in Betracht/Erwägung ziehen
to **grant**	[grɑ:nt]	to give sb sth they want	gewähren
referee	[ˌrefə'ri:]	sb who recommends you for a job	Referenz
Yours sincerely	[ˌjɔ:z sɪn'sɪəli]	what you write at the end of a formal letter	Mit freundlichen Grüßen

page 80

backpacking	['bækpækɪŋ]	travelling with only a rucksack	Rucksackreisen
English-speaking	['ɪŋglɪʃ spi:kɪŋ]	e.g. New Zealand is an English-speaking country.	englischsprachig
work permit	[ˌwɜ:k 'pɜ:mɪt]	document which allows you to work	Arbeitserlaubnis
foreign	['fɒrən]	from another country	ausländisch, fremd
to **take time off**	[teɪk ˌtaɪm 'ɒf]	not go to school/work for a period of time	sich frei nehmen
of a lifetime	[əv ə 'laɪftaɪm]	*phr* chance of a lifetime	einmalig
visa	['vi:zə]	travel document	Visum

to **correspond with sth**	[ˌkɒrɪˈspɒnd wɪð]	to match sth	einer Sache entsprechen
to **fasten one's seat belt**	[ˌfɑːsn wʌnz ˈsiːt belt]	e.g. In a car, you must fasten your seat belt.	sich anschnallen
Off we go.	[ˈɒf wiː ɡəʊ]	Let's begin.	Los geht's!
temporary	[ˈtemprəri]	<> permanent	befristet
backpacker	[ˈbækpækə]	traveller	Rucksackreisende/r
qualification	[ˌkwɒlɪfɪˈkeɪʃn]	sth you get at the end of a course of study	Abschluss, Ausbildung
towards the end	[təˌwɔːdz ði ˈend]	e.g. The film was boring so I fell asleep towards the end.	gegen Ende
stay	[steɪ]	time spent somewhere	Aufenthalt
pay	[peɪ]	money from a job	Lohn, Bezahlung
to **fulfil**	[fʊlˈfɪl]	e.g. He fulfilled the requirements and got the job.	erfüllen
limit	[ˈlɪmɪt]	e.g. age limit	Beschränkung
minimum	[ˈmɪnɪməm]	<> maximum	Mindest-
to **qualify**	[ˈkwɒlɪfaɪ]	*n* qualification	(sich) qualifizieren
to **work sth out**	[ˌwɜːk ˈaʊt]	to prepare sth, to draw sth up	etw ausarbeiten, etw erarbeiten

page 81

sign	[saɪn]	e.g. The clouds are a sign that it will rain.	Anzeichen
cloudy	[ˈklaʊdi]	with clouds in the sky	bewölkt
to **get married**	[ˌɡet ˈmærid]	<> to get divorced	heiraten
bridesmaid	[ˈbraɪdzmeɪd]	friend or sister of the woman getting married	Brautjungfer
to **cycle**	[ˈsaɪkl]	to go by bicycle	radeln

page 82

applicant	[ˈæplɪkənt]	*n* application	Bewerber/in
to **interview sb**	[ˈɪntəvjuː]	*n* interviewer, interviewee	mit jdm ein Vorstellungsgespräch führen
to **divide**	[dɪˈvaɪd]	to share, to split	teilen
greeting	[ˈɡriːtɪŋ]	*v* to greet	Begrüßung
introduction	[ˌɪntrəˈdʌkʃn]	*v* to introduce	Vorstellung, Bekanntmachen
further	[ˈfɜːðə]	e.g. We can make further arrangements via email.	weiter, weitergehend
on time	[ɒn ˈtaɪm]	punctual	pünktlich
confident(ly)	[ˈkɒnfɪdənt]	*n* confidence	selbstbewusst
eye contact	[ˈaɪ kɒntækt]	when you look sb in the eye	Blickkontakt
to **avoid**	[əˈvɔɪd]	to try not to do sth	vermeiden, meiden
to **stick to sth**	[ˈstɪk tə]	to stay with sth	sich an etw halten
to **respond**	[rɪˈspɒnd]	to answer	antworten
honest(ly)	[ˈɒnɪst]	truthful(ly)	ehrlich, aufrichtig

page 83

to **attend sth**	[əˈtend]	to take part in sth	an etw teilnehmen
to **act out**	[ˌækt ˈaʊt]	to roleplay sth	spielen, aufführen
representative	[ˌreprɪˈzentətɪv]	*v* to represent	Vertreter/in, Repräsentant/in

page 84

current	[ˈkʌrənt]	<> out-of-date	aktuell
condition	[kənˈdɪʃn]	e.g. Student visa conditions include not working more than 40 hours.	Bedingung
tie	[taɪ]	relationship	Bindung, Beziehung
passport	[ˈpɑːspɔːt]	document which allows you to travel between countries	Pass, Reisepass
to **work sth out**	[ˌwɜːk ˈaʊt]	to find sth out, to calculate sth	etw herausfinden, etw ausrechnen
branch	[brɑːntʃ]	e.g. the branch of a tree	Zweig

UNIT 8

page 85

screen	[skriːn]	display of an electronic device	Bildschirm
text (message)	[tekst]	short message sent on a mobile phone	SMS
voice call	[ˈvɔɪs kɔːl]	speaking to sb on the phone	Sprachanruf
regularly	[ˈreɡjələli]	often	regelmäßig
figures *pl*	[ˈfɪɡəz]	numbers	Zahlen
survey	[ˈsɜːveɪ]	researching public opinion by a series of questions	Umfrage
questionnaire	[ˌkwestʃəˈneə]	list of questions for a survey	Fragebogen
findings *pl*	[ˈfaɪndɪŋz]	results	Ergebnisse
bar chart	[ˈbɑː tʃɑːt]	type of graph with columns	Säulendiagramm
pie chart	[ˈpaɪ tʃɑːt]	type of graph in the shape of a circle	Tortendiagramm

page 86

social media	[ˌsəʊʃl ˈmiːdiə]	online platform on which users can communicate	soziale Medien
tune	[tjuːn]	song	Lied, Song
to **warn**	[wɔːn]	*n* warning	warnen, (auf etw) hinweisen
interviewee	[ˌɪntəvjuːˈiː]	<> interviewer	*Person, die interviewt wird*

page 87

weird	[wɪəd]	<> normal	verrückt, schräg, gaga
contributor	[kənˈtrɪbjuːtə]	author of a magazine article	Autor/in *(eines Magazins)*

to make a living from sth	[ˌmeɪk ə ˈlɪvɪŋ frəm]	to earn money doing sth	seinen Lebensunterhalt mit etw verdienen
to broadcast	[ˈbrɔːdkɑːst]	*n* broadcasting	senden, verbreiten, ausstrahlen
subscriber	[səbˈskraɪbə]	sb who pays to receive a regular service	Abonnent/in
virtual	[ˈvɜːtʃuəl]	<> real	virtuell
to convert	[kənˈvɜːt]	to change	umwandeln
feeling	[ˈfiːlɪŋ]	opinion, view, impression	Gefühl, Ansicht, Meinung
circus skills *pl*	[ˈsɜːkəs skɪlz]	e.g. He learnt his circus skills from a famous clown.	Zirkuskünste
musician	[mjuːˈzɪʃn]	sb who makes music	Musiker/in
concert	[ˈkɒnsət]	where sb goes to listen to live music	Konzert
relaxed	[rɪˈlækst]	<> stressed	locker, entspannt
to request sth	[rɪˈkwest]	to ask for sth	um etw bitten, sich etw wünschen
to connect with sb	[kəˈnekt wɪð]	to come into contact with sb for the first time	mit jdm in Kontakt kommen
publicity	[pʌbˈlɪsəti]	public attention	öffentliche Aufmerksamkeit, Werbung
to release	[rɪˈliːs]	to bring out	veröffentlichen
lack of sth	[ˈlæk əv]	not enough of sth	Mangel an etw
identity theft	[aɪˈdentəti θeft]	to steal sb's details	Identitätsdiebstahl

page 88

to advertise	[ˈædvətaɪz]	*n* advertisement	werben, Werbung machen
developer	[dɪˈveləpə]	sb who creates sth	Entwickler/in
circus act	[ˈsɜːkəs ækt]	part of a circus show that demonstrates a skill	Zirkusnummer
in return	[ɪn rɪˈtɜːn]	when sb receives sth for sth they have given or done	als Gegenleistung
lucrative	[ˈluːkrətɪv]	when a lot of money can be made out of sth	lukrativ
intimate	[ˈɪntɪmət]	very personal	intim

page 89

to dislike	[dɪsˈlaɪk]	<> to like	nicht mögen
recently	[ˈriːsntli]	lately	neulich
to pretend to do sth	[prɪˈtend tə duː]	to give the impression that sth is being done	vorgeben, etw zu tun; so tun, als ob
especially	[ɪˈspeʃəli]	specifically	besonders, insbesondere
channel	[ˈtʃænl]	*phr* TV channel	Kanal
sense of fun	[ˌsens əf ˈfʌn]	sb's ability to be funny	Sinn für Humor

page 90

gazing	[ˈgeɪzɪŋ]	staring	(abwesendes) Starren
cell phone *AE*	[ˈsel fəʊn]	*BE:* mobile phone	Handy
at the same time	[ət ðə seɪm ˈtaɪm]	simultaneously	gleichzeitig
to cross	[krɒs]	to go across a street	überqueren
to step out in front of a car	[step ˌaʊt ɪn ˌfrʌnt əv ə ˈkɑː]	e.g. He didn't look, and stepped out in front of a car.	vor ein Auto laufen
to risk	[rɪsk]	*n* risk	riskieren
injury	[ˈɪndʒəri]	*v* to injure	Verletzung
council	[ˈkaʊnsl]	local government	Rat, Gremium
statistics *pl*	[stəˈtɪstɪks]	e.g. The statistics showed an increase in sales.	Statistiken
evidence	[ˈevɪdəns]	proof	Indizien
silly	[ˈsɪli]	stupid	albern
in a hurry	[ɪn ə ˈhʌri]	having to be quick	in Eile
to keep on doing sth	[ˈkiːp ɒn duːɪŋ]	to carry on doing sth	etw weiterhin tun
worrying	[ˈwʌrɪŋ]	discomforting	Besorgnis erregend, beunruhigend
hardly ever	[ˌhɑːdli ˈevə]	very rarely	kaum, so gut wie nie
to look up	[ˌlʊk ˈʌp]	<> to look down	aufsehen
pedestrian	[pɪˈdestriən]	sb who is on foot	Fußgänger/in
traffic	[ˈtræfɪk]	*phr* traffic jam	Verkehr
death	[deθ]	*v* to die	Todesfall
to decrease	[dɪˈkriːs]	<> to increase	abnehmen, sinken
to increase	[ɪnˈkriːs]	to go up	zunehmen, steigen
sharply	[ˈʃɑːpli]	suddenly	drastisch, stark, plötzlich
to rise	[raɪz]	<> decrease	ansteigen
usage	[ˈjuːsɪdʒ]	*v* to use	Benutzung
to surf the internet	[ˌsɜːf ði ˈɪntənet]	to look around on the internet	im Internet surfen
to text	[tekst]	to send a message on a mobile phone	SMS senden, simsen
vehicle	[ˈviːəkl]	automobile	Fahrzeug
to be related	[bi rɪˈleɪtɪd]	to be connected, to be linked	zusammenhängen
behaviour	[bɪˈheɪvjə]	*v* to behave	Verhalten
illegal	[ɪˈliːgl]	forbidden	verboten, illegal
police officer	[pəˈliːs ɒfɪsə]	policeman or policewoman	Polizeibeamte/r
traffic lights *pl*	[ˈtræfɪk laɪts]	lights regulating traffic at a cossroads	Ampel
ground	[graʊnd]	floor	Boden
possibility	[ˌpɒsəˈbɪləti]	chance	Möglichkeit
to keep sb safe	[ˌkiːp ˈseɪf]	to protect sb	jdn beschützen
warning	[ˈwɔːnɪŋ]	*v* to warn	Warnung, Warnhinweis
to walk towards sb	[ˈwɔːk təwɔːdz]	<> to walk away from sb	auf jdn zugehen
road crossing	[ˈrəʊd krɒsɪŋ]	crossroads	Straßenquerung

page 91

graph	[grɑːf]	diagram showing figures	Diagramm, Grafik
to **level off**	[ˌlevl ˈɒf]	to become even	sich abschwächen, sich einpendeln
pattern	[ˈpætn]	arrangement	Muster
placemat	[ˈpleɪsmæt]	a small mat	Tischset
sheet (of paper)	[ʃiːt]	piece of paper	Blatt (Papier)
step	[step]	*phr* step by step	Schritt
individual	[ˌɪndɪˈvɪdʒuəl]	single	einzeln, individuell
corner	[ˈkɔːnə]	e.g. There is a bird in the corner of the photo.	Ecke

page 92

insurance	[ɪnˈʃʊərəns]	financial protection against loss or damage	Versicherung
policy	[ˈpɒləsi]	way a company or institution does sth	Vorgehensweise, Linie, Politik
to **apply (to sb/sth)**	[əˈplaɪ]	e.g. Club rules apply to all members.	(für jdn/etw) gelten
employee	[ɪmˈplɔɪiː]	<> employer	Beschäftigte/r, Mitarbeiter/in
to **disturb**	[dɪˈstɜːb]	to interrupt	stören
to **turn sth off**	[ˌtɜːn ˈɒf]	<> to turn sth on	etw ausschalten
to **silence**	[ˈsaɪləns]	to make quiet	*(Handy)* stummschalten
to **log on**	[ˌlɒg ˈɒn]	<> to log out	sich einloggen
brief	[briːf]	short and to the point	knapp, kurz
official	[əˈfɪʃl]	<> inofficial	offiziell

page 93

to **bother sb**	[ˈbɒðə]	to annoy sb	jdn stören
corridor	[ˈkɒrɪdɔː]	hallway	Flur

page 94

to **blame sb/sth**	[bleɪm]	to say sb is guilty	jdm/etw die Schuld geben
study	[ˈstʌdi]	investigation, research	Untersuchung, Studie
news organization	[ˈnjuːz ɔːgənaɪzeɪʃn]	company reporting and selling news items	Nachrichtenagentur
to **fail to do sth**	[ˈfeɪl tə duː]	to not do something	versäumen, etw zu tun
to **separate sth from sth**	[ˈsepəreɪt]	<> to bring two things together	etw auseinanderhalten
fiction	[ˈfɪkʃn]	<> non-fiction	Erfindung, Fiktion
rumour	[ˈruːmə]	a story that has not been proven	Gerücht
rather than	[ˈrɑːðə ðən]	as opposed to	anstatt
to **act as sth**	[ˈækt əz]	to function as sth	als etw fungieren
accurate	[ˈækjərət]	precise	korrekt, präzise
frequently	[ˈfriːkwəntli]	often	oft, häufig
to **promote sth**	[prəˈməʊt]	to encourage sth, to support sth	etw begünstigen, etw fördern
misinformation	[ˌmɪsɪnfəˈmeɪʃn]	information that is not true	Falschinformation
attempt	[əˈtempt]	try	Versuch
to **drive sth**	[draɪv]	to move sth forward	etw antreiben
practice	[ˈpræktɪs]	e.g. It's common practice for interns to work for free.	Praktik
to **accelerate**	[əkˈseləreɪt]	to get faster	beschleunigen
damn	[dæm]	used to express frustration and anger	verdammt
to **apply sth (to sth)**	[əˈplaɪ]	to use sth for/on sth	etw (auf etw) anwenden
verification	[ˌverɪfɪˈkeɪʃn]	proof	Prüfung
claim	[kleɪm]	stating sth as a fact	Behauptung
to **rely on sth**	[rɪˈlaɪ ɒn]	to be dependent on sth	sich auf etw verlassen
extent	[ɪkˈstent]	amount, scale	Ausmaß
slayer	[ˈsleɪə]	sb who kills animals	Schlächter/in
angel	[ˈeɪndʒəl]	e.g. Sweetheart, you're an angel.	Engel
to **purport**	[pəˈpɔːt]	to claim	behaupten, zum Inhalt haben
Islamic	[ɪzˈlæmɪk]	linked with Islam	islamisch
to **spread**	[spred]	to disseminate, to distribute	(sich) verbreiten
tabloid journal	[ˈtæblɔɪd dʒɜːnl]	type of newspaper which aims to shock readers	Boulevardblatt
quality journalism outlets *pl*	[ˌkwɒləti ˈdʒɜːnəlɪzəm aʊtlets]	a news source which is serious	seriöse Medien
to **follow up**	[ˌfɒləʊ ˈʌp]	to keep investigating	nachfassen
explosive	[ɪkˈspləʊsɪv]	likely to shock or surprise	hochbrisant
fighter	[ˈfaɪtə]	sb who fights, like a soldier	Kämpfer/in
to **apprehend sb**	[ˌæprɪˈhend]	to arrest sb	jdn fassen, jdn festnehmen
border	[ˈbɔːdə]	e.g. There are no border controls between France and Germany.	Grenze
to **refute**	[rɪˈfjuːt]	to prove sth to be false	etw entkräften, etw widerlegen
yet	[jet]	however	dennoch
percent, per cent	[pəˈsent]	out of one hundred	Prozent
initial	[ɪˈnɪʃl]	first, original	ursprünglich, anfänglich
disturbing	[dɪˈstɜːbɪŋ]	upsetting	verstörend, bestürzend
to **found**	[faʊnd]	to start	gründen
particularly	[pəˈtɪkjələli]	especially	besonders
to **pass sth along/on**	[ˌpɑːs əˈlɒŋ/ˈɒn]	to share	etw weitergeben
fast-moving	[ˌfɑːst ˈmuːvɪŋ]	rapid, changing quickly	schnelllebig

nature	[ˈneɪtʃə]	e.g. It's not in his nature to be angry.	Wesen, Natur
to **tweet**	[twiːt]	to post a message on Twitter	twittern
sheer	[ʃɪə]	pure	rein, schier
repetition	[ˌrepəˈtɪʃn]	*v* to repeat	Wiederholung
entirely	[ɪnˈtaɪəli]	totally	völlig, gänzlich
over time	[ˌəuvə ˈtaɪm]	as time goes by	mit der Zeit
to **emerge**	[ɪˈmɜːdʒ]	to come out in the open	ans Licht kommen
correction	[kəˈrekʃn]	when a mistake is made right	Richtigstellung
to **tend to be sth**	[ˈtend tə biː]	to often be a certain way	dazu neigen, etw zu sein
widely distributed	[ˌwaɪdli dɪˈstrɪbjuːtɪd]	passed on to many people	weit verbreitet
to **be a believer in sth**	[bi ə bɪˈliːvər ɪn]	e.g. I'm a great believer in positive thinking.	an etw (fest) glauben, von etw (fest) überzeugt sein
value	[ˈvæljuː]	worth	Wert

page 95

instead of	[ɪnˈsted əv]	e.g. We took the bus instead of walking all the way.	anstatt
original material	[əˌrɪdʒənl məˈtɪəriəl]	material that an author writes based on his or her own ideas	eigene Beiträge
untrue	[ʌnˈtruː]	false	unwahr, unzutreffend
to **correct**	[kəˈrekt]	to make right	richtigstellen
unchecked	[ʌnˈtʃekt]	sth that has not been checked	ungeprüft
deliberately	[dɪˈlɪbərətli]	on purpose	absichtlich
concerned	[kənˈsɜːnd]	worried	besorgt, beunruhigt
although	[ɔːlˈðəu]	even though, though	obwohl

page 96

occasionally	[əˈkeɪʒənəli]	from time to time	gelegentlich, ab und zu
success	[səkˈses]	*v* to succeed	Erfolg

UNIT 9

page 97

currency	[ˈkʌrənsi]	the type of money that is used in a country	Währung
attraction	[əˈtrækʃn]	famous building or place that many people visit	Sehenswürdigkeit
cliff	[klɪf]	high rocks at the beach	Felsen, Klippe
castle	[ˈkɑːsl]	where kings and queens live	Burg, Schloss
railway	[ˈreɪlweɪ]	*phr* railway station	Eisenbahn
to make up	[ˈmeɪk ˌʌp]	to form, to put sth together from different things	bilden

page 98

bed and breakfast	[ˌbed ən ˈbrekfəst]	a place to stay (often a family home) that offers breakfast	Frühstückspension, Übernachtung mit Frühstück
camper van	[ˈkæmpə væn]	motor home	Wohnmobil
resort	[rɪˈzɔːt]	e.g. holiday resort	Ferienort
dormitory	[ˈdɔːmɪtri]	a large room (often in a hostel) where many people can sleep	Schlafsaal
unaccompanied	[ˌʌnəˈkʌmpənid]	without anyone else, alone	ohne Begleitung
campsite	[ˈkæmpsaɪt]	a place where sb goes camping	Campingplatz
unless	[ənˈles]	e.g. She can't go to the disco unless an adult is with her.	außer wenn, es sei denn
host	[həust]	<> guest	Gastgeber
to **rent**	[rent]	to pay money every month to live somewhere	mieten
flat *BE*	[flæt]	*AE:* apartment	Wohnung

page 99

guide	[gaɪd]	a book with information about a place for tourists	Reiseführer
traveller	[ˈtrævələ]	sb who goes on a trip or journey	Reisende/r
base	[beɪs]	starting point	Ausgangspunkt, Basis
major	[ˈmeɪdʒə]	large, important	groß, bedeutend
landscape	[ˈlændskeɪp]	scenery	Landschaft
association	[əˌsəusiˈeɪʃn]	organization	Verband, Vereinigung
booking	[ˈbukɪŋ]	reservation	Reservierung, Buchung
countryside	[ˈkʌntrisaɪd]	area outside of the city with large fields	Land, Landschaft
seaside	[ˈsiːsaɪd]	coast (beside the sea)	Küste
horrible	[ˈhɒrəbl]	awful	schrecklich
sadly	[ˈsædli]	unfortunately	leider
to **cause trouble**	[kɔːz ˈtrʌbl]	to cause problems	Ärger machen
sociable	[ˈsəuʃəbl]	friendly, likes people	gesellig, umgänglich
National Trust	[ˌnæʃnl ˈtrʌst]	an organization that aims to protect monuments and nature	*brit. Organisation für Denkmalpflege und Naturschutz*
to **plant**	[plɑːnt]	to put seeds in the ground	pflanzen
to **repair**	[rɪˈpeə]	to fix	reparieren
footpath	[ˈfutpɑːθ]	a path for people to walk on (often beside a road)	Weg, Pfad
to **participate in sth**	[pɑːˈtɪsɪpeɪt ɪn]	to take part in sth	an etw teilnehmen

fee	[fiː]	costs for a service	Gebühr
hospitality	[ˌhɒspɪˈtæləti]	treating guests in a friendly way	Bewirtung, Gastfreundschaft
rent	[rent]	e.g. The rent in London has risen a lot.	Miete
expense	[ɪkˈspens]	costs	Kosten, Ausgabe(n), Aufwendung(en)

page 100

to show sb around	[ˌʃəʊ əˈraʊnd]	to give sb a tour	jdn herumführen
adventure	[ədˈventʃə]	exciting experience or journey	Abenteuer
consequence	[ˈkɒnsɪkwəns]	result	Konsequenz

page 101

opposite	[ˈɒpəzɪt]	<> the same	gegenteilig, entgegengesetzt
inconvenient	[ˌɪnkənˈviːniənt]	unpractical	unpraktisch, unbequem
ugly	[ˈʌgli]	<> pretty	hässlich
uncomfortable	[ʌnˈkʌmftəbl]	<> comfortable	unbequem, unkomfortabl
unfriendly	[ʌnˈfrendli]	<> friendly	unfreundlich
review	[rɪˈvjuː]	a critical article or report (about food, hotels, etc.)	Rezension, Kritik
to rewrite	[ˌriːˈraɪt]	to write again in a different way	umformulieren, neu schreiben
opposite	[ˈɒpəzɪt]	word of the opposite meaning	Gegenwort
star	[stɑː]	e.g. We stayed in a 3-star hotel.	Stern
location	[ləʊˈkeɪʃn]	place, situation	Standort, Lage
bus route	[ˈbʌs ruːt]	bus line	Buslinie
surroundings *pl*	[səˈraʊndɪŋz]	the area around a place	Umgebung
tired	[ˈtaɪəd]	sleepy	müde

page 102

voicemail	[ˈvɔɪsmeɪl]	e.g. He left me a voicemail message yesterday.	Mailbox
to hop on/off	[ˌhɒp ˈɒn/ˈɒf]	to jump on/off	ein-/aussteigen
murder mystery	[ˌmɜːdə ˈmɪstri]	crime thriller	Krimi
amazing	[əˈmeɪzɪŋ]	fantastic	erstaunlich, super
puzzle	[ˈpʌzl]	a game with problems to be solved	Rätsel
to spare sth	[speə]	*phr* to have time to spare	etw übrig haben
architecture	[ˈɑːkɪtektʃə]	the design of the buildings	Architektur
entertaining	[ˌentəˈteɪnɪŋ]	enjoyable, amusing	unterhaltsam
scary	[ˈskeəri]	frightening	gruselig, unheimlich
steep	[stiːp]	e.g. Castles were often built on top of really steep hills.	steil
hill	[hɪl]	e.g. She ran down the hill.	Hügel, Berg
monarch	[ˈmɒnək]	ruler of a country, e.g. king or queen	Herrscher/in, Monarch/in
surrounded	[səˈraʊndɪd]	e.g. The village is surrounded by trees.	umgeben
view	[vjuː]	sight	Aussicht, Ausblick
history	[ˈhɪstri]	events that happened in the past	Geschichte
colourful	[ˈkʌləfl]	e.g. This picture is very colourful.	bunt, farbenfroh

page 103

sight	[saɪt]	place of interest that tourists visit	Sehenswürdigkeit
to let sb know	[ˌlet ˈnəʊ]	to inform sb	jdm Bescheid sagen
to explore	[ɪkˈsplɔː]	to investigate	erkunden
to pick up the phone	[ˌpɪk ˈʌp ðə fəʊn]	to answer a call	ans Telefon gehen
guided tour	[ˌgaɪdɪd ˈtʊə]	e.g. The guided tour in the History Museum is fantastic.	Führung
to pack	[pæk]	to put sth in a suitcase	packen
to catch the train	[ˌkætʃ ðə ˈtreɪn]	e.g. He caught the train just in time!	den Zug erwischen
wheel	[wiːl]	e.g. A car has four wheels.	Rad
soldier	[ˈsəʊldʒə]	sb who serves in an army	Soldat/in
image	[ˈɪmɪdʒ]	picture	Bild
tour guide	[ˈtʊə gaɪd]	sb who takes people on a trip or sightseeing	Reiseleiter/in, Fremdenführer/in
sophisticated	[səˈfɪstɪkeɪtɪd]	advanced	modern, technisch fortgeschritten
walkway	[ˈwɔːkweɪ]	bridge or path that people can walk along	Fußgängersteg
Victorian	[vɪkˈtɔːriən]	from the time of Queen Victoria	viktorianisch
engine	[ˈendʒɪn]	motor	Motor
column	[ˈkɒləm]	e.g. Nelson's Column on Trafalgar Square in London	Säule
step	[step]	e.g. To reach the top, we had to climb 400 steps.	Stufe
balcony	[ˈbælkəni]	e.g. I love sitting on my balcony in summer.	Balkon, Galerie
panoramic view	[pænəˌræmɪk ˈvjuː]	a wide view showing all directions	Panoramablick
parliament	[ˈpɑːləmənt]	e.g. the Houses of Parliament in London	Parlament
tower	[ˈtaʊə]	e.g. the Eiffel Tower	Turm
bell	[bel]	e.g. Big Ben must be the most famous bell in the world.	Glocke
deep	[diːp]	low	tief
iconic landmark	[aɪˌkɒnɪk ˈlændmɑːk]	an object or building that is famous in a particular place	Wahrzeichen
palace	[ˈpæləs]	where a king or queen lives	Palast, Schloss
politics	[ˈpɒlətɪks]	*n* politician	Politik
to blow sth up	[ˌbləʊ ˈʌp]	to destroy sth by explosion	etw in die Luft sprengen/jagen
century	[ˈsentʃʊri]	period of 100 years	Jahrhundert
gun powder	[ˈgʌn paʊdə]	explosive, used for guns, cannons and bombs	Schießpulver
plot	[plɒt]	e.g. the Gunpowder Plot	Verschwörung
to be unsuccessful	[bi ˌʌnsəkˈsesfl]	not to succeed	scheitern

resident	[ˈrezɪdənt]	inhabitant	Bewohner, Einwohner
House of Commons	[ˌhaʊs əv ˈkɒmənz]	UK parliament chamber consisting of elected members	Unterhaus *(des brit. Parlaments)*
House of Lords	[ˌhaʊs əv ˈlɔːdz]	UK parliament chamber consisting of unelected members	Oberhaus *(des brit. Parlaments)*
to **strike the hour**	[ˌstraɪk ði ˈaʊə]	e.g. At non, Big Ben struck the hour.	die Stunde schlagen
river cruise	[ˈrɪvə kruːz]	a trip on a boat along a river	Flussrundfahrt
fabulous	[ˈfæbjələs]	fantastic	fabelhaft, großartig
observation wheel	[ˌɒbzəˈveɪʃn wiːl]	e.g. the London Eye	Riesenrad
pod	[pɒd]	cabin on an observation wheel	Gondel
celebration	[ˌselɪˈbreɪʃn]	*v* to celebrate	Feier
to **lift**	[lɪft]	to raise	heben
incredible	[ɪnˈkredəbl]	unbelievable	unglaublich
queue	[kjuː]	line of people	Warteschlange
weather forecast	[ˈweðə fɔːkɑːst]	e.g. Today's weather forecast predicted rain.	Wettervorhersage
on board	[ɒn ˈbɔːd]	on a bus, ship, plane or other vehicle	an Bord
presenter	[prɪˈzentə]	TV host	Moderator/in
to **refer to sth**	[rɪˈfɜː tə]	*n* reference	sich auf etw beziehen
city break	[ˈsɪti breɪk]	short holiday in a city	(kurzer) Städteurlaub
to be honest, …	[tə bi ˈɒnɪst]	e.g. To be honest, I don't really want to go.	ehrlich gesagt …

page 104

trade fair	[ˈtreɪd feə]	exhibition	(Branchen-/Handels-)Messe
luggage	[ˈlʌgɪdʒ]	suitcases, bags, etc.	Gepäck
restriction	[rɪˈstrɪkʃn]	limit	Beschränkung
maximum	[ˈmæksɪməm]	<> minimum	Maximal-, Höchst-
to **present**	[prɪˈzent]	to show	vorzeigen
resealable	[riːˈsiːləbl]	e.g. This bottle is resealable.	wiederverschließbar
cream	[kriːm]	e.g. You can only take 100ml of hand cream on board a plane.	Creme
exempt	[ɪgˈzempt]	e.g. students are exempt from paying tax	befreit, ausgenommen
razor blade	[ˈreɪzə bleɪd]	e.g. You cannot take razor blades in your hand luggage.	Rasierklinge
tool	[tuːl]	e.g. This is not the right tool for the job.	Werkzeug
permitted	[pəˈmɪtɪd]	allowed	gestattet, erlaubt
inflammable	[ɪnˈflæməbl]	sth that easily catches fire	brennbar, entflammbar
aircraft	[ˈeəkrɑːft]	e.g. aeroplane, balloon	Flugzeug
bleach	[bliːtʃ]	e.g. Bleach cannot be taken on board a plane.	Bleichmittel
gas cylinder	[ˈgæs sɪlɪndə]	used to store gas under pressure	Gasflasche, Gaskartusche
battery	[ˈbætəri]	e.g. Insert the battery, please.	Akku, Batterie

page 105

boarding pass	[ˈbɔːdɪŋ pɑːs]	document you need to be allowed on a plane	Bordkarte
to **board**	[bɔːd]	to get onto (a plane)	an Bord gehen, einsteigen
aeroplane	[ˈeərəpleɪn]	e.g. Aeroplanes are faster than trains.	Flugzeug
passenger	[ˈpæsɪndʒə]	sb who travels in a car, on a train, bus, plane, boat, etc.	Passagier, Fluggast
seat	[siːt]	place where sb sits	Sitz, Platz
security check	[sɪˈkjʊərəti tʃek]	where passengers and their hand luggage are checked	Sicherheitskontrolle
security officer	[sɪˈkjʊərəti ɒfɪsə]	sb who works at security in an airport	Sicherheitsbeamte/r, -mitarbeiter/in
bin	[bɪn]	box, basket, etc. for rubbish	Mülltonne, Mülleimer
tray	[treɪ]	e.g. At security check, he put his keys and money in a tray.	Schale
glasses *pl*	[ˈglɑːsɪz]	e.g. She can't see without her glasses.	Brille
to **hand sb sth**	[hænd]	to pass sth to sb	jdm etw (über)geben
coin	[kɔɪn]	piece of currency	Münze
dish	[dɪʃ]	plate	Teller
belongings *pl*	[bɪˈlɒŋɪŋz]	what beings to sb	persönliche Sachen

page 106

radio advertisement	[ˈreɪdiəʊ ədvɜːtɪsmənt]	e.g. the radio advertisement was annoying	Werbespot (im Radio)
across	[əˈkrɒs]	all over	in ganz
What's the point?	[ˌwɒts ðə ˈpɔɪnt]	What's this all about?	Was soll das? Was hat das für einen Sinn?
to **switch off**	[ˌswɪtʃ ˈɒf]	to turn off	ausschalten, ausmachen
provided	[prəˈvaɪdɪd]	under the condition that	vorausgesetzt, dass
spending	[ˈspendɪŋ]	money spent	Ausgabe(n)
purchase	[ˈpɜːtʃəs]	act of buying, things bought	Kauf, Einkauf
in itself	[ɪn ɪtˈself]	e.g. In itself, this change was not so bad.	an sich
harmful	[ˈhɑːmfl]	dangerous	schädlich, nachteilig
to concentrate on sth	[ˈkɒnsntreɪt ɒn]	to focus on sth	sich auf etw konzentrieren
population	[ˌpɒpjuˈleɪʃn]	all of the people who live in a town or country	Bevölkerung
resources *pl*	[rɪˈsɔːsɪz]	materials	Rohstoffe, Ressourcen
distribution of wealth	[dɪstrɪˌbjuːʃn əv ˈwelθ]	how money or materials are spread across the population	Wohlstandsverteilung
to **put out the word**	[pʊt ˈaʊt ðə ˈwɜːd]	to spread a piece of information	die Nachricht verbreiten
convinced	[kənˈvɪnst]	*v* to convince	überzeugt
tough	[tʌf]	very difficult	hart

to **make a difference**	[ˌmeɪk ə ˈdɪfrəns]	to change sth	etw bewirken
lasting	[ˈlɑːstɪŋ]	with permanent effect	dauerhaft
impact	[ˈɪmpækt]	influence	Einfluss, Auswirkung(en)
to **consider sth**	[kənˈsɪdə]	to think about sth	Rücksicht auf etw nehmen
Count me in!	[ˌkaʊnt miː ˈin]	being enthusiastic about taking part in sth	Ich bin dabei!
to **intend to do sth**	[ɪnˈtend tə duː]	*n* intention	die Absicht haben, etw zu tun
degree	[dɪˈgriː]	e.g. It was freezing – minus five degrees.	Grad
freezing cold	[ˌfriːzɪŋ ˈkəʊld]	e.g. In Alaska, it was freezing cold even in April.	eiskalt
sleeping bag	[ˈsliːpɪŋbæg]	e.g. I forgot my sleeping bag when I went camping.	Schlafsack
to **be miserable**	[bi ˈmɪzrəbl]	to be very sad	sich elend fühlen
mattress	[ˈmætrəs]	e.g. My new mattress is too hard – I've now got back pain!	Matratze
fair enough	[ˌfeər ɪˈnʌf]	OK then	na gut

page 107

economic research	[iːkəˌnɒmɪk rɪˈsɜːtʃ]	e.g. Research shows that the poor have got poorer.	Wirtschaftsforschung
based in	[ˈbeɪst ɪn]	being located in	mit Sitz in, ansässig in
to **publish**	[ˈpʌblɪʃ]	to release	veröffentlichen, publizieren
entertainment	[ˌentəˈteɪnmənt]	*v* to entertain	Unterhaltung
electronics	[ˌɪlekˈtrɒnɪks]	e.g. the electronics company was doing well	Elektronik
to **find**	[faɪnd]	to show, to identify	feststellen
increasingly	[ɪnˈkriːsɪŋli]	more and more	zunehmend
informal	[ɪnˈfɔːml]	<> formal	zwanglos, informell
drama lesson	[ˈdrɑːmə lesn]	a class teaching people how to act	Schauspielunterricht
furthermore	[ˌfɜːðəˈmɔː]	moreover	außerdem, darüber hinaus
to **go out of fashion**	[gəʊ ˌaʊt əf ˈfæʃn]	to become unpopular	aus der Mode kommen
to **make sth happen**	[ˌmeɪk ˈhæpən]	to put sth into effect	etw verwirklichen, etw ermöglichen
organizing committee	[ˈɔːgənaɪzɪŋ kəmɪti]	group that organizes an event	Organisationskomitee
to **involve**	[ɪnˈvɒlv]	to contain sth, to consist of	beinhalten, mit sich bringen
to **be in charge of sth**	[bi ɪn ˈtʃɑːdʒ əv]	to be responsible for sth	für etw zuständig sein
cancellation	[ˌkænsəˈleɪʃn]	*v* to cancel	Absage
running order	[ˈrʌnɪŋ ɔːdə]	time schedule	Ablaufplan
rewarding	[rɪˈwɔːdɪŋ]	satisfying	erfüllend, befriedigend
pleasure	[ˈpleʒə]	enjoyment	Vergnügen
in good spirits	[ɪn ˌgʊd ˈspɪrɪts]	in a good mood	guter Dinge, gut gelaunt
common sense	[ˌkɒmən ˈsens]	good judgement	gesunder Menschenverstand
to **get badly burned**	[get ˌbædli ˈbɜːnd]	to have a bad sunburn	einen schweren Sonnenbrand bekommen
steward	[stjuːəd]	sb who takes care of audience members at a festival	Ordner/in
to **give directions**	[ˌgɪv dəˈrekʃnz]	to tell sb the way	den Weg erklären
to **reunite sb/sth with sb**	[ˌriːjuːˈnaɪt wɪð]	to bring sb/sth back together with sb	jdn/etw mit jdm wieder zusammenbringen
lost property	[lɒst prɒpəti]	belongings that have been lost	Fundsachen
owner	[ˈəʊnə]	sb who possesses sth	Besitzer/in
you name it	[ˌjuː ˈneɪm ɪt]	anything	alles Mögliche
runner at large	[ˌrʌnər ət ˈlɑːdʒ]	messenger dealing with all sorts of tasks at a festival	*etwa:* Laufbursche für besondere Aufgaben
performer	[pəˈfɔːmə]	anyone who performs on a stage, e.g. actor, musician, etc.	Künstler/in, Darsteller/in
stage	[steɪdʒ]	e.g. The stage is very large in this theatre.	Bühne
unexpected	[ˌʌnɪkˈspektɪd]	sudden	unvorhergesehen
event	[ɪˈvent]	sth that is happening	Ereignis
sensibly	[ˈsensəbli]	<> in a silly way	vernünftig
varied	[ˈveərid]	*n* variety	abwechslungsreich

page 108

to **have terrible luck**	[həv ˌterɪbl ˈlʌk]	to be very unlucky	furchtbares Pech haben
massive	[ˈmæsɪv]	huge	riesengroß
by oneself	[baɪ wʌnˈself]	alone, on one's own	allein
to **ride**	[raɪd]	*phr* to ride a motorbike	fahren
pub	[pʌb]	bar	Kneipe, Gasthaus
rental	[ˈrentl]	*n* rent	Miete, Miet-

UNIT 10

page 109

tradition	[trəˈdɪʃn]	*adj* traditional	Sitte, Tradition
carnival	[ˈkɑːnɪvl]	e.g. Carnival in Rio de Janeiro	Karneval
New Year's Eve	[ˌnjuː jɪəz ˈiːv]	31 December	Silvester
wedding	[ˈwedɪŋ]	act of getting married	Hochzeit
to **dress up**	[ˌdres ˈʌp]	to put on nice clothes	sich fein anziehen, sich schick machen
fireworks *pl*	[ˈfaɪəwɜːks]	e.g. The fireworks this year were very loud.	Feuerwerk

Chronological word list

page 110

to **enter** sth	['entə]	to take part in sth	*(Wettbewerb usw.:)* an etw teilnehmen
short story	[ˌʃɔːt 'stɔːri]	e.g. Ernest Hemingway was famous for his short stories.	Kurzgeschichte
prize	[praɪz]	e.g. I won a prize for my photograph.	Preis, Gewinn
to **attend**	[ə'tend]	to go to	*(Veranstaltung usw.)* besuchen
stadium	['steɪdiəm]	e.g. The football stadium was huge!	Stadion
in general	[ɪn 'dʒenrəl]	generally	im Allgemeinen

page 111

day out	[ˌdeɪ 'aʊt]	trip away for a day	freier Tag, Ausflug
mysterious(ly)	[mɪ'stɪəriəs]	*n* mystery	geheimnisvoll, rätselhaft
treat	[triːt]	e.g. Dad took me to the cinema as a treat.	Vergnügen, (kleines) Geschenk
patient(ly)	['peɪʃnt]	*n* patience	geduldig
polite	[pə'laɪt]	*n* politeness	höflich
disappointed	[ˌdɪsə'pɔɪntɪd]	*n* disappointment	enttäuscht
unfortunately	[ʌn'fɔːtʃənətli]	<> fortunately	leider, unglücklicherweise
to **disappoint** sb	[ˌdɪsə'pɔɪnt]	to let sb down	jdn enttäuschen
terrifying	['terɪfaɪɪŋ]	very scary	entsetzlich, furchteinflößend
crowd	[kraʊd]	a large number of people in one place	Menschenmenge
to **be scared of heights**	[bi ˌskeəd əv 'haɪts]	I won't climb this mountain – I'm scared of heights!	Höhenangst haben
to **stamp one's feet**	[ˌstæmp wʌnz 'fiːt]	e.g. Everybody stamped their feet at the stadium.	mit den Füßen trampeln
deafening	['defnɪŋ]	really loud	ohrenbetäubend
thunder	['θʌndə]	e.g. Did you hear the thunder last night?	Donner
to **rush**	[rʌʃ]	to go somewhere very quickly	eilen
bucket	['bʌkɪt]	e.g. a bucket of water	Eimer
foot	[fʊt]	e.g. He is six feet tall.	Fuß *(ca. 30,5 cm)*
opening ceremony	[ˌəʊpnɪŋ 'serəməni]	a small show at the beginning of an event	Eröffnungszeremonie
brass band	[ˌbrɑːs 'bænd]	a musical group with brass and percussion instruments	Blasorchester
national anthem	[ˌnæʃnəl 'ænθəm]	a song officially accepted as a country's song	Nationalhymne
opposing	[ə'pəʊzɪŋ]	competing	gegnerisch
speed	[spiːd]	how fast sth moves	Geschwindigkeit
inactivity	[ˌɪnæk'tɪvəti]	<> activity	Untätigkeit
burst	[bɜːst]	*phr* burst of action	Ausbruch, Explosion
violent	['vaɪələnt]	*n* violence	brutal, gewalttätig
to **knock** sb **down**	[ˌnɒk 'daʊn]	e.g. The players knocked each other down.	jdn niederschlagen, jdn umhauen
to **kick a ball**	[ˌkɪk ə 'bɔːl]	e.g. She kicked the ball hard.	einen Ball schießen
halfway though sth	[ˌhɑːfweɪ 'θruː]	midway through sth	mitten in etw, während etw
to **enjoy oneself**	[ɪn'dʒɔɪ wʌnself]	to have fun	sich gut amüsieren
a bunch of people	[ə ˌbʌntʃ əf 'piːpl]	a group of people	ein Haufen Leute, ein paar Leute
to **cheer**	[tʃɪə]	to shout encouragingly	jubeln, anfeuern
to **score**	[skɔː]	to win or get a point	einen Punkt machen, ein Tor erzielen
thrilling	['θrɪlɪŋ]	very exciting	aufregend, überwältigend

page 112

to **be about to do** sth	[bi ə'baʊt tə]	e.g. The game was about to start when it started to rain.	etw gleich tun; im Begriff sein, etw zu tun
autograph	['ɔːtəgrɑːf]	e.g. She waited to get the player's autograph.	Autogramm
perspective	[pə'spektɪv]	point of view	Perspektive, Sicht, Blickwinkel

page 113

fear of heights	[ˌfɪər əv 'haɪts]	scared of places that are high	Höhenangst
apparently	[ə'pærəntli]	supposedly	anscheinend
to **bang**	[bæŋ]	to stamp	schlagen, hauen, hämmern
frequent	['friːkwənt]	often	häufig
to **drag** sb **into** sth	[dræg]	e.g. I was dragged into the atmosphere of the game.	jdn in etw hineinziehen
score	[skɔː]	point in a game	Punkt
to **celebrate**	['selɪbreɪt]	*n* celebration	feiern

page 114

Thanksgiving	['θæŋksgɪvɪŋ]	day of giving thanks for the harvest	Erntedankfest
to **get** sth **ready**	[get 'redi]	to prepare sth	etw vorbereiten
public holiday	[ˌpʌblɪk 'hɒlədeɪ]	official day on which no-one has to go to work or school	gesetzlicher Feiertag
harvest	['hɑːvɪst]	time when agricultural crops are collected	Ernte
turkey	['tɜːki]	e.g. Turkey for Christmas dinner is a UK tradition.	Truthahn
corn	[kɔːn]	e.g. Corn was first grown in Mexico.	Mais
squash	[skwɒʃ]	e.g. Pumpkin is a type of squash.	Speisekürbis
pumpkin	['pʌmpkɪn]	vegetable often eaten on Thanksgiving	Kürbis
delicious	[dɪ'lɪʃəs]	really tasty	köstlich
immigrant	['ɪmɪgrənt]	*v* to immigrate	Einwanderer/-in
Native American	[ˌneɪtɪv ə'merɪkən]	original American people before the Europeans arrived	amerikanische/r Ureinwohner/in
to **cover** sth **up**	[ˌkʌvər 'ʌp]	to hide sth	etw übertünchen
settler	['setlə]	sb who comes to a new region to live there	Siedler/in
to **be the case**	[bi ðə 'keɪs]	e.g. Is he really dead? – I'm afraid that is the case.	der Fall sein
original(ly)	[ə'rɪdʒənl]	in the first place	ursprünglich

pie	[paɪ]	type of cake	Torte
variation	[ˌveəri'eɪʃn]	difference	Variante, Variation
to **import**	[ɪm'pɔːt]	to bring in	importieren
grown-up	['grəʊnʌp]	adult	erwachsen
roof	[ruːf]	top of a building	Dach
It depends.	[ɪt dɪ'pendz]	e.g. How long will the match be? – It depends.	Das kommt darauf an.
special deal	[ˌspeʃl 'diːl]	bargain offer	Sonderangebot

page 115

extract	['ekstrækt]	short text taken from a longer article or book	Auszug, Ausschnitt
daughter-in-law	['dɔːtər ɪn lɔː]	the wife of one's son or daughter	Schwiegertochter
to **hug**	[hʌg]	e.g. He hugged her tightly.	umarmen
to **bark**	[bɑːk]	the sound a dog makes	bellen
smell	[smel]	odour	Geruch
oven	['ʌvn]	a device used for cooking, roasting or baking	Ofen
to **cook**	[kʊk]	e.g. Cook the turkey for three hours.	garen, braten
ancient	['eɪnʃənt]	very old and no longer in existence	alt, uralt
indigenous	[ɪn'dɪdʒənəs]	native to	einheimisch, eingeboren
annual	['ænjuəl]	yearly	jährlich
people	['piːpl]	ethnic group	Volk
showcase	['ʃəʊkeɪs]	exhibition	Schau, Ausstellung
range	[reɪndʒ]	variety	Reihe, Auswahl, Vielfalt
performance	[pə'fɔːməns]	staging	Darbietung, Aufführung
structure	['strʌktʃə]	construction	Bauwerk, Konstruktion
marketplace	['mɑːkɪtpleɪs]	market square	Marktplatz
clinic	['klɪnɪk]	intense lesson or course	Workshop
food stall	['fuːd stɔːl]	where food is sold at a market	Essensstand
theme	[θiːm]	topic	Thema
to **matter**	['mætə]	to be important	wichtig sein, von Belang sein
to **draw attention to sth**	[ˌdrɔː ə'tenʃn tə]	to highlight sth	Aufmerksamkeit auf etw lenken
richness	['rɪtʃnəs]	variety	Reichtum, Vielfalt, Fülle
shore	[ʃɔː]	coast	Küste
honour	['ɒnə]	glory	Ehre
unity	['juːnəti]	togetherness	Einheit, Einigkeit
significance	[sɪg'nɪfɪkəns]	importance	Bedeutung
invitation	[ˌɪnvɪ'teɪʃn]	e.g. They sent out fifty invitations for their wedding.	Einladung

page 116

to **head off**	[ˌhed 'ɒf]	to leave	losfahren/-gehen
to **rest**	[rest]	e.g. After two hours' walking, I had to rest my feet.	ausruhen
straight	[streɪt]	direct	direkt
to **pick sb up**	[ˌpɪk 'ʌp]	to collect sb	jdn abholen
nearby	['nɪəbaɪ]	<> far	in der Nähe
to **drop sb off**	[ˌdrɒp 'ɒf]	e.g. Dad dropped me off at school.	jdn absetzen
entrance	['entrəns]	<> exit	Eingang
restroom *AE*	['restruːm]	toilet	Toilette
straight ahead	[ˌstreɪt ə'hed]	directly in front	geradeaus
to **turn right/left**	[ˌtɜːn 'raɪt/'left]	e.g. Turn right at the end of the hall.	rechts/links abbiegen
special exhibition	[ˌspeʃl eksɪ'bɪʃn]	e.g. We went to see the special exhibition last week.	Sonderausstellung
to **manage sth**	['mænɪdʒ]	to cope with sth	etw bewältigen, etw schaffen
to **be thirsty**	[bi 'θɜːsti]	to want sth to drink	Durst haben
to **wonder**	['wʌndə]	to question	sich fragen
ATM	[ˌeɪ tiː 'em]	machine where sb can take money from their account	Geldautomat
cloakroom	['kləʊkruːm]	place where people leave their coats or jackets	Garderobe

page 117

Your turn.	['jɔː tɜːn]	e.g. Peter said, "It's your turn."	Sie sind dran.
to **take charge of sth**	[teɪk 'tʃɑːdʒ əv]	to become leader of sth	die Leitung von etw übernehmen
to **have/get a turn**	[ˌhəv/ˌget ə 'tɜːn]	to have a go	drankommen
lobby	['lɒbi]	entrance hall	Empfangshalle, Eingangshalle

page 118

brightly lit	[ˌbraɪtli 'lɪt]	<> dimly lit	hell erleuchtet
shot	[ʃɒt]	photo	Foto, Aufnahme
gig	[gɪg]	concert	(Rock-, Pop-, Jazz-)Konzert
seriously irritating	[ˌsɪəriəsli 'ɪrɪteɪtɪŋ]	incredibly annoying	ganz schön lästig
wobbly	['wɒbli]	unsteady	wacklig, verwackelt
reputation	[ˌrepju'teɪʃn]	the general opinion people have about sb	Ruf
harmony	['hɑːməni]	singing together	mehrstimmiger Gesang
concern	[kən'sɜːn]	doubt, worry	Bedenken
venue	['venjuː]	place where an event takes place	Veranstaltungsort
to **lock**	[lɒk]	to close	verschließen, abschließen
magnetic pouch	[mægˌnetɪk 'paʊtʃ]	small bag that can be closed using a magnet	Magnettasche
magnetism	['mægnətɪzəm]	the power of metals to attract one another	Magnetismus

Chronological word list

device	[dɪˈvaɪs]	machine, gadget	Gerät
unusable	[ˌʌnˈjuːzəbl]	<> usable	unbrauchbar
to **unlock**	[ˌʌnˈlɒk]	to open	wieder aufschließen, entriegeln
hectare	[ˈhekteə]	10,000 metres squared	Hektar
full-time	[ˌfʊl ˈtaɪm]	<> part-time	Vollzeit-
machinery	[məˈʃiːnəri]	different machines	Maschinen, Geräte
crop	[krɒp]	plants grown on a large scale, especially cereals	Ackerpflanze
produce	[ˈprɒdjuːs]	farm products, including milk and vegetables	(landwirtschaftliche) Erzeugnisse, Lebensmittel
chain	[tʃeɪn]	e.g. Most people by their food from supermarket chains.	Kette
quantity	[ˈkwɒntəti]	amount	Menge
profit	[ˈprɒfɪt]	money earned from selling sth	Gewinn
chemicals *pl*	[ˈkemɪklz]	e.g. pesticide	Chemikalien
to **feed the soil**	[ˌfiːd ðə ˈsɔɪl]	to give the ground nutrients	den Boden mit Nährstoffen versorgen
to **control pests**	[kənˌtrəʊl ˈpests]	to kill harmful insects	Schädlinge bekämpfen
efficient	[ɪˈfɪʃnt]	effective	leistungsfähig, effizient
bare	[beə]	without anything on it	kahl
organic	[ɔːˈgænɪk]	produced without the use of chemicals	organisch, biologisch, Bio-
sustainable	[səˈsteɪnəbl]	*v* to sustain	nachhaltig
page 119			
reduction	[rɪˈdʌkʃn]	*v* to reduce	(Preis-)Nachlass
replacement	[rɪˈpleɪsmənt]	alternative	Ersatz
in addition	[ɪn əˈdɪʃn]	furthermore	außerdem
label	[ˈleɪbl]	manufacturer, tag	Marke, Etikett, Kennzeichnung
transaction	[trænˈzækʃn]	business deal	Geschäft, Transaktion
trader	[ˈtreɪdə]	sb whose business is buying and selling	Händler/in
criteria *pl*	[kraɪˈtɪəriə]	criterium *sing*	Kriterien
seal	[siːl]	the official symbol of an organization	Siegel
to **operate**	[ˈɒpəreɪt]	to work, to function	funktionieren, vorgehen
property	[ˈprɒpəti]	sth that sb owns	Eigentum
to **entrust sb/sth with sth**	[ɪnˈtrʌst wɪð]	e.g. My mum entrusted me with her wedding dress.	jdm/einer Sache etw anvertrauen
protection	[prəˈtekʃn]	*v* to protect	Schutz
worth	[wɜːθ]	*phr* to be worth it	wert
faulty	[ˈfɔːlti]	with defects	defekt
to **advertise sth**	[ˈædvətaɪz]	*n* advertisement	etw bewerben, für etw Werbung machen
retailer	[ˈriːteɪlə]	seller to individual customers	Einzelhändler/in
to **refund**	[rɪˈfʌnd]	to give money back for sth	rückerstatten
to **direct sb to sb**	[dəˈrekt tə]	to send sb to sb	jdn an jdn verweisen
manufacturer	[ˌmænjuˈfæktʃərə]	producer	Hersteller/in
additional	[əˈdɪʃənl]	extra	zusätzlich, Zusatz-
refund	[ˈriːfʌnd]	money received for returning a product	Rückerstattung
to **be entitled to sth**	[bi ɪnˈtaɪtld tə]	to have a claim to sth	etw verlangen können, Anspruch auf etw haben
to **insist**	[ɪnˈsɪst]	to not accept no for an answer	darauf bestehen
postage	[ˈpəʊstɪdʒ]	the money you pay to send sth by post	Porto, Versandkosten
guarantee	[ˌgærənˈtiː]	e.g. The TV set comes with a special 5-year guarantee.	Garantie
it doesn't matter	[ɪt dʌznt ˈmætə]	it is not important	es ist egal
mail order	[ˌmeɪl ˈɔːdə]	buying goods by mail delivery	Versand
Beware.	[bɪˈweə]	Careful.	Vorsicht!
individual	[ˌɪndɪˈvɪdʒuəl]	a single person	Person, Einzelperson
to **cover sth**	[ˈkʌvə]	to protect sth	etw absichern
to **bear in mind**	[ˌbeər ɪn ˈmaɪnd]	to not forget	daran denken, nicht vergessen
auction	[ˈɔːkʃn]	where things are sold to the person who offers the most money	Versteigerung, Auktion
to **protect**	[prəˈtekt]	*n* protection	schützen, beschützen
to **be confident**	[bi ˈkɒnfɪdənt]	*n* confidence	zuversichtlich sein, sich sicher sein
to **conform to sth**	[kənˈfɔːm tə]	*phr* to conform to rules	einer Sache entsprechen
standard	[ˈstændəd]	*phr* to meet the standards	Norm
genuine	[ˈdʒenjuɪn]	real	echt, wirklich
data *pl*	[ˈdeɪtə]	e.g. Let me enter your personal data into the database.	Daten
page 120			
to **queue**	[kjuː]	to stand in line	sich (in einer Warteschlange) anstellen
gate	[geɪt]	large door	Tor
to **sign sb**	[saɪn]	*phr* to sign a football player	jdn unter Vertrag nehmen
height	[haɪt]	how tall sb is	Höhe
object	[ˈɒbdʒɪkt]	item	Gegenstand, Objekt
airport	[ˈeəpɔːt]	e.g. Will the new Berlin airport ever be opened?	Flughafen
caption	[ˈkæpʃn]	explanation under a picture or illustration	Bildunterschrift
bear	[beə]	e.g. Grizzly bear	Bär
to **feed**	[fiːd]	to give food to	füttern

UNIT 11

page 121

pollution	[pə'lu:ʃn]	*v* to pollute	(Umwelt-)Verschmutzung
transportation	[ˌtrænspɔ:'teɪʃn]	e.g. Today, there are many types of transportation.	Transport, Verkehr
to **require**	[rɪ'kwaɪə]	to need	erfordern

page 122

paper cup	['peɪpə kʌp]	e.g. 3 million paper cups are thrown away every day in Germany.	Pappbecher
to **come up with sth**	[ˌkʌm 'ʌp wɪð]	to think of sth	sich etw ausdenken, sich etw einfallen lassen
disposable	[dɪ'spəʊzəbl]	designed to be thrown away	Einweg-, Wegwerf-
stage	[steɪdʒ]	step	Phase, Abschnitt, Schritt
to **transport**	[træn'spɔ:t]	*n* transportation	befördern, transportieren
industrial	[ɪn'dʌstriəl]	*phr* industrial process	industriell, Industrie-
process	['prəʊses]	a series of actions	Verfahren, Verarbeitung
log	[lɒg]	tree stem that has been cut	(gefällter) Baumstamm
to **turn sth into sth**	['tɜ:n ɪntə]	to make sth into sth	etw zu etw machen
chip	[tʃɪp]	small piece of wood that has been hacked off	Hackschnitzel
pulp	[pʌlp]	base product for making paper	Papierbrei, Zellstoff
pulp mill	['pʌlp mɪl]	where pulp is created	Zellstofffabrik
to **bleach**	[bli:tʃ]	to make white	bleichen
paper mill	['peɪpəmɪl]	where paper is produced	Papierfabrik
warehouse	['weəhaʊs]	where products are stored	Lager, Lagerhalle

page 123

to **stop off**	[ˌstɒp 'ɒf]	to take a break somewhere	Station machen, einkehren
wood	[wʊd]	e.g. This house is completely made of wood.	Holz
chipping plant	['tʃɪpɪŋ plɑ:nt]	factory where wood chips are made	Hackschnitzelanlage
steel disk	['sti:l dɪsk]	e.g. Sharp steel disks cut the wood into tiny pieces.	Stahlscheiben
tiny	['taɪni]	very small	klein, winzig
tonne	[tʌn]	1,000kg	Tonne
to **unload**	[ˌʌn'ləʊd]	<> to load	entladen, löschen
to **process**	['prəʊses]	*n* process	verarbeiten
dock	[dɒk]	area of port where goods are loaded onto ships	Kai, Dock
to **spray**	[spreɪ]	e.g. Graffiti artists spray their pictures on walls.	sprühen
metal screen	['metl skri:n]	e.g. Pulp is sprayed onto large metal screens.	Metallsieb
to **squeeze**	[skwi:z]	to put pressure on sth	drücken, quetschen
roller	['rəʊlə]	e.g. The paper is squeezed dry between rollers.	Walze
to **coat**	[kəʊt]	to put on an extra layer	beschichten
polyethylene	[ˌpɒli'eθəli:n]	a type of plastic	Polyäthylen
cardboard	['kɑ:dbɔ:d]	e.g. cardboard box	Pappe
shipping container	['ʃɪpɪŋ kənteɪnə]	large metal box in which goods are shipped	Schiffscontainer
on arrival	[ɒn ə'raɪvl]	the moment sb/sth arrives	bei Ankunft
to **load**	[ləʊd]	to fill up	laden, verladen
truck	[trʌk]	lorry	Lastwagen
van	[væn]	e.g. delivery van	Lieferwagen
rubbish bin	['rʌbɪʃ bɪn]	box, basket etc. for rubbish	Mülleimer, Abfalltonne
landfill	['lændfɪl]	place where rubbish is buried between layers of dirt	Mülldeponie
along with	[ə'lɒŋ wɪð]	together with	zusammen mit

page 124

ordinary	['ɔ:dnri]	normal	gewöhnlich, normal
to **pollute**	[pə'lu:t]	to make sth dirty	verschmutzen
raw material	[ˌrɔ: mə'tɪəriəl]	material before it is made into sth else	Rohstoff
mass	[mæs]	a large and uniform quantity of sth	Masse
flow chart	['fləʊ tʃɑ:t]	e.g. She had to made a flow chart for her homework.	Flussdiagramm
life cycle	['laɪf saɪkl]	sequence from birth to death	Lebenszyklus

page 125

to **break**	[breɪk]	to fall apart	zerbrechen, zerfallen
vending machine	['vendɪŋ məʃi:n]	a machine where drinks, snacks, etc. can be bought	(Getränke-)Automat
recyclable	[ˌri:'saɪkləbl]	able to be processed and used again	recyclebar
composite material	[ˌkɒmpəzɪt mə'tɪəriəl]	material made from two or more materials	Verbundmaterial
plastic liner	[ˌplæstɪk 'laɪnə]	plastic coating on the inside	Plastikauskleidung, Kunststoff-innenbeschichtung
to **favour sth**	['feɪvə]	to choose sth	sich für etw entscheiden
merit	['merɪt]	good feature	Vorzug
to **implement**	['ɪmplɪmənt]	to put in place, to carry out	in die Tat umsetzen, durchführen

page 126

repair	[rɪ'peə]	fixing sth	Reparatur
to **break**	[breɪk]	to stop working	kaputt gehen
to **fix**	[fɪks]	to repair	reparieren, flicken

meeting space	[ˈmiːtɪŋ speɪs]	place where people go to meet with one another	Begegnungsstätte
furniture	[ˈfɜːnɪtʃə]	e.g. chairs, tables, desks, etc.	Möbel
to **get involved in sth**	[ˌget ɪnˈvɒlvd ɪn]	*n* involvement	bei etw mitmachen
spare part	[ˌspeə ˈpɑːt]	replacement for old or broken parts	Ersatzteil
to **tidy (up)**	[ˈtaɪdi]	to clear up	aufräumen, saubermachen
to **bring sth along**	[ˌbrɪŋ əˈlɒŋ]	to take sth	etw mitbringen
to **upcycle**	[ʌpˈsaɪkl]	making old or useless products into sth new and better	veredeln, aufwerten
broken	[ˈbrəʊkən]	not working	kaputt
pallet	[ˈpælət]	e.g. Some people turn old pallets into furniture.	Palette
jewellery	[ˈdʒuːəlri]	e.g. My grandmother has very expensive jewellery.	Schmuck
tin can	[ˈtɪn kæn]	container to keep food fresh for a long time	Blechdose
backpack	[ˈbækpæk]	rucksack	Rucksack
to **have a taste of sth**	[həv ə ˈteɪst əv]	to try sth	etw probieren
restoration	[restəˈreɪʃn]	*v* to restore	Restaurierung
hopefully	[ˈhəʊpfli]	e.g. Jermaine is hopefully away next weekend	hoffentlich
delighted	[dɪˈlaɪtɪd]	very happy	begeistert, hocherfreut
satisfaction	[ˌsætɪsˈfækʃn]	when sb is happy with what they have or have achieved	Zufriedenheit, Genugtuung
to **catch on**	[ˌkætʃ ˈɒn]	to become popular	Schule machen, sich durchsetzen
to **reckon**	[ˈrekən]	to believe	meinen, glauben
marvellous	[ˈmɑːvələs]	fantastic	großartig
piece of furniture	[ˌpiːs əf ˈfɜːnɪtʃə]	e.g. sofa, wardrobe, table, etc.	Möbelstück
to **get rid of sth**	[get ˈrɪd əv]	to throw sth away	etw loswerden
slightly damaged	[ˌslaɪtli ˈdæmɪdʒd]	a little bit flawed	leicht beschädigt
professional	[prəˈfeʃənl]	*phr* on a professional basis	professionell
business idea	[ˈbɪznəs aɪdɪə]	e.g. Megan developed her own business idea.	Geschäftsidee

page 127

maintenance	[ˈmeɪntənəns]	*v* to maintain	Wartung, Instandhaltung
screwdriver	[ˈskruːdraɪvə]	tool used to put in / take out screws	Schraubenzieher, -dreher

page 128

eco-friendly	[ˈiːkəʊ frendli]	environmentally-friendly	umweltfreundlich
workplace	[ˈwɜːkpleɪs]	place where you work	Arbeitsplatz
to **print**	[prɪnt]	*n* printer	drucken
to **put sth up**	[ˌpʊt ˈʌp]	to hang sth up	etw aufhängen
to **remove sth from sth**	[rɪˈmuːv frəm]	to take sth out of sth	etw aus etw nehmen
keycard	[ˈkiːkɑːd]	card required to get into a building or hotel room	Schlüsselkarte
holder	[ˈhəʊldə]	e.g. keycard holder	Halter
air conditioning	[ˈeə kəndɪʃnɪŋ]	system to control air temperature in a building	Klimaanlage
to **activate**	[ˈæktɪveɪt]	to turn on	aktivieren, einschalten
power	[ˈpaʊə]	energy	Strom
toiletries *pl*	[ˈtɔɪlətriz]	hygiene products normally used in a bathroom	Hygieneartikel, Kosmetikartikel
conditioner	[kənˈdɪʃənə]	product used to improve the condition of hair	Haarspülung
moisturizer	[ˈmɔɪstʃəraɪzə]	product used to stop skin from becoming dry	Feuchtigkeitscreme
dispenser	[dɪˈspensə]	e.g. soap dispenser	Spender
container	[kənˈteɪnə]	used to hold a product	Behälter
brand	[brænd]	e.g. a brand name	Marke
in order to	[ɪn ˈɔːdə tə]	e.g. You'll have to do some sport in order to keep fit.	um … zu
towel	[ˈtaʊəl]	used to dry your body/hands/face after washing	Handtuch
to **require**	[rɪˈkwaɪə]	to want, to need	wünschen, benötigen
breakfast buffet	[ˈbrekfəst bʊfeɪ]	a self-service hotel breakfast	Frühstücksbüfett
unnecessary	[ʌnˈnesəsəri]	<> necessary	unnötig
packaging	[ˈpækɪdʒɪŋ]	wrapping	Verpackung
complaint	[kəmˈpleɪnt]	*v* to complain	Klage, Beschwerde, Reklamation
hygienic	[haɪˈdʒiːnɪk]	*n* hygiene	hygienisch
to **smell**	[smel]	*n* smell	riechen
heating	[ˈhiːtɪŋ]	*v* to heat	Heizung

page 129

bar of soap	[ˌbɑːr əf ˈsəʊp]	a block of soap	Stück Seife
basin	[ˈbeɪsn]	sink	Waschbecken
We'll manage.	[ˌwiːl ˈmænɪdʒ]	We'll be fine.	Wir kommen schon zurecht.

page 130

globalization	[ˌgləʊbəlaɪˈzeɪʃn]	e.g. What are your views on globalization?	Globalisierung
salutation	[ˌsæljuˈteɪʃn]	greeting in a letter	*(Brief:)* Anrede
close	[kləʊs]	end line in a letter	*(Brief:)* Schlussformel
to **pick**	[pɪk]	to choose	auswählen
to **entertain sb**	[ˌentəˈteɪn]	*n* entertainment	jdn unterhalten
to **harm**	[hɑːm]	*adj* harmful	schaden
technical advances *pl*	[ˌteknɪkl ədˈvɑːnsɪz]	progress in technology	technische Fortschritte
technician	[tekˈnɪʃn]	sb who makes sure machines are working	Techniker/in
happiness	[ˈhæpinəs]	*adj* happy	Zufriedenheit, Glück
partly	[ˈpɑːtli]	to a certain extent	teilweise, zum Teil

page 131

to **come true**	[ˌkʌm ˈtruː]	*phr* a dream has come true	sich verwirklichen, wahr werden
baggage carousel	[ˈbæɡɪdʒ kærəsel]	conveyor belt for luggage	Gepäckband
to **hurry**	[ˈhʌri]	to go quickly	eilen
football practice	[ˈfʊtbɔːl præktɪs]	e.g. Susan goes to football practice once a week.	Fußballtraining
elderly	[ˈeldəli]	older	ältere/r/s
to **act strangely**	[ˌækt ˈstreɪndʒli]	to not behave normally	sich seltsam verhalten
confused	[kənˈfjuːzd]	*n* confusion	verwirrt
frightened	[ˈfraɪtnd]	scared	verängstigt

page 132

to **last long**	[ˌlɑːst ˈlɒŋ]	<> to be short-lived	lang halten
government	[ˈɡʌvənmnt]	officials and ministers running a state or regian	Regierung, öffentliche Verwaltung
public transport	[ˌpʌblɪk ˈtrænspɔːt]	buses, trains, trams, etc.	öffentliche Verkehrsmittel
valuable	[ˈvæljuəbl]	worth a lot of money, very important	wertvoll
plastic bag	[ˌplæstɪk ˈbæɡ]	e.g. Plastic bags now cost 5p in the UK.	Plastiktüte
appliance	[əˈplaɪəns]	a machine that is used in the home	Haushaltsgerät
energy-efficient	[ˌenədʒi ɪˈfɪʃnt]	not using too much energy	energieeffizient
to **exploit**	[ɪkˈsplɔɪt]	*n* exploitation	*(Bodenschätze)* abbauen
to **install**	[ɪnˈstɔːl]	*n* installation	einbauen, installieren
waste	[weɪst]	rubbish	Verschwendung, Abfall
scientist	[ˈsaɪəntɪst]	*adj* scientific	(Natur-)Wissenschaftler/in
waste food	[ˈweɪst fuːd]	food that is not eaten and so thrown away	Lebensmittelabfälle
to **predict**	[prɪˈdɪkt]	*n* prediction	vorhersagen
to **prevent**	[prɪˈvent]	to stop happening	verhindern

UNIT 12

page 133

percentage	[pəˈsentɪdʒ]	parts out of one hundred	Anteil, Prozentsatz
official language	[əˌfɪʃl ˈlæŋɡwɪdʒ]	e.g. English is the official language of the UK.	Amtssprache
native speaker	[ˌneɪtɪv ˈspiːkə]	sb who has spoken a language since they were a baby	Muttersprachler/in
independence	[ˌɪndɪˈpendəns]	*adj* independent	Unabhängigkeit
Labor Day *AE*	[ˈleɪbə deɪ]	a public holiday in the United States	Tag der Arbeit
president	[ˈprezɪdənt]	the person with the highest political position (in the US)	Präsident/in
to **host**	[həʊst]	to accommodate, to have	beherbergen

page 134

open day	[ˈəʊpən deɪ]	day on which an organization allows the public to visit	Tag der offenen Tür
to **ask for directions**	[ˌɑːsk fə dəˈrekʃnz]	to ask the way	nach dem Weg fragen
lyrics *pl*	[ˈlɪrɪks]	text of a song	Liedtext
socializing	[ˈsəʊʃəlaɪzɪŋ]	to meet other people socially, e.g. at a party	Geselligkeit

page 135

to **profile**	[ˈprəʊfaɪl]	to describe sb in a short article	porträtieren
passion	[ˈpæʃn]	powerful emotion, enthusiasm	Leidenschaft
role-playing game	[ˈrəʊl pleɪɪŋ ɡeɪm]	game where the players pretend to be sb else	Rollenspiel
stereotype	[ˈsteriətaɪp]	cliché	Klischee
social misfit	[ˌsəʊʃl ˈmɪsfɪt]	sb who does not fit in, outsider	Außenseiter, Sonderling
fantasy world	[ˈfæntəsi wɜːld]	world that does not actually exist	Traumwelt, Phantasiewelt
unsociable	[ʌnˈsəʊʃəbl]	sb who avoids contact with others	kontaktarm, menschenscheu
strategy	[ˈstrætədʒi]	*adj* strategic	Strategie
to **collaborate**	[kəˈlæbəreɪt]	to work together	zusammenarbeiten
guild	[ɡɪld]	professional organization of a single trade	Zunft, Gilde
common	[ˈkɒmən]	shared	gemeinsam
multilingual	[ˌmʌltiˈlɪŋɡwəl]	able to speak more than one language	mehrsprachig
aptitude	[ˈæptɪtjuːd]	natural talent	Talent, Befähigung
to **keep up sth**	[ˌkiːp ˈʌp]	to carry on with sth	mit etw weitermachen
native language	[ˌneɪtɪv ˈlæŋɡwɪdʒ]	mother tongue	Muttersprache
unusual	[ʌnˈjuːʒuəl]	<> usual	ungewöhnlich
savings *pl*	[ˈseɪvɪŋz]	money that is saved rather than spent	Ersparnisse
casual job	[ˌkæʒuəl ˈdʒɒb]	temporary work	Gelegenheitsarbeit
building site	[ˈbɪldɪŋ saɪt]	place where building work takes place	Baustelle
realistic	[ˌriːəˈlɪstɪk]	likely to happen	realistisch
nomad	[ˈnəʊmæd]	sb who has no permanent home	Nomade/-in
exotic	[ɪɡˈzɒtɪk]	unusual and exciting	exotisch
fluent	[ˈfluːənt]	*adv* fluently	*(Sprache:)* fließend
foreign language	[ˌfɒrən ˈlæŋɡwɪdʒ]	a language you are not a native speaker of	Fremdsprache
preparation	[ˌprepəˈreɪʃn]	*v* to prepare	Vorbereitung
career prospects *pl*	[kəˈrɪə prɒspekts]	chances regarding work	Berufsaussichten

page 136

to **promise**	[ˈprɒmɪs]	*n* promise	versprechen

Chronological word list

page 137

to **be embarrassed by sth**	[bi ɪmˈbærəst baɪ]	*n* embarrassment	etw ist jdm peinlich
cute	[kjuːt]	sweet	süß, niedlich
higher education	[ˌhaɪə edʒuˈkeɪʃn]	university education	Hochschulbildung
to **invent**	[ɪnˈvent]	*n* invention	erfinden
quotation	[kwəʊˈteɪʃn]	*v* to quote	Zitat
provocative	[prəˈvɒkətɪv]	*v* to provoke	provokant, provozierend
career goal	[kəˈrɪə gəʊl]	aim regarding work	berufliches Ziel
testimony	[ˈtestɪməni]	statement	Aussage, Erfahrungsbericht
persuasive	[pəˈsweɪsɪv]	convincing	überzeugend, schlagkräftig
to **emphasize**	[ˈemfəsaɪz]	to highlight	betonen, herausstellen
to **catch sb's attention**	[ˌkætʃ əˈtenʃn]	to make sb aware of sb/sth	jds Aufmerksamkeit fesseln

page 138

photoshoot	[ˈfəʊtəʊʃuːt]	e.g. The photoshoot took three hours to complete.	Fotoaufnahmen, Shooting
to **shoot sb**	[ʃuːt]	e.g. The kidnappers were shot by the police.	jdn erschießen
bodybag	[ˈbɒdibæg]	large bag used to transport a dead body	Leichensack
dead	[ded]	<> alive	tot
victim	[ˈvɪktɪm]	sb who has suffered a crime	Opfer
messenger bag	[ˈmesɪndʒə bæg]	bag used to transport mail and messages	Kuriertasche
excellent	[ˈeksələnt]	very good	ausgezeichnet, hervorragend
to **get it wrong**	[ˌget ɪt ˈrɒŋ]	to be mistaken	etw falsch sagen
handy	[ˈhændi]	useful	praktisch, handlich
to **mail**	[meɪl]	to send via post	(per Post) senden, versenden
cross(ly)	[krɒs]	angry (angrily)	verärgert
finance	[ˈfaɪnæns]	e.g. My husband works in finance – he's a banker.	Finanzwesen
to **arrange**	[əˈreɪndʒ]	to make (an appointment)	*(Termin)* ausmachen
workout	[ˈwɜːkaʊt]	fitness training	Fitnesstraining, Trainingseinheit
sweaty	[ˈsweti]	e.g. After their workout, they were sweaty.	verschwitzt
misunderstanding	[ˌmɪsʌndəˈstændɪŋ]	failure to understand correctly	Missverständnis
to **embarrass oneself**	[ɪmˈbærəs wʌnself]	to make a fool of oneself	sich lächerlich machen
to **misunderstand**	[ˌmɪsʌndəˈstænd]	to not understand correctly	missverstehen, falsch verstehen

page 139

motoring	[ˈməʊtərɪŋ]	driving a car	Autofahren
hire company	[ˈhaɪə kʌmpəni]	company where you can hire cars	(Auto-)Vermietung
key fob	[ˈkiː fɒb]	object attached to key ring	Schlüsselanhänger
whereabouts	[ˌweərəˈbaʊts]	the place where a person or thing is	wo ungefähr?

page 140

automotive	[ˌɔːtəˈməʊtɪv]	e.g. automotive company	Automobil-, Auto-
motor show	[ˈməʊtə ʃəʊ]	exhibition of cars and other vehicles	Automobilmesse
to **exhibit**	[ɪgˈzɪbɪt]	*n* exhibition	ausstellen
exhibitor	[ɪgˈzɪbɪtə]	sb who owns something shown in an exhibition	Aussteller/in
floor plan	[ˈflɔː plæn]	drawing of a floor of a building	Grundriss, Übersichtsplan
exhibition	[ˌeksɪˈbɪʃn]	show, trade fair	Ausstellung, Messe
press	[pres]	the media and their journalists and reporters	Presse
brand new	[ˌbrænd ˈnjuː]	e.g. a brand new car	brandneu, nagelneu
car dealership	[ˈkɑː diːləʃɪp]	business that sells new or used cars	Autohaus, Autohändler/in
model	[ˈmɒdl]	e.g. I want to buy a new car, but don't know which model to choose.	Modell
concept car	[ˈkɒnsept kɑː]	car made to show new style or design	Konzeptauto
to **cater for all tastes**	[ˌkeɪtə fər ˌɔːl ˈteɪsts]	to offer something for everybody	für jeden Geschmack etw bieten
display	[dɪˈspleɪ]	presentation of sth	Ausstellung, (Messe-)Stand, Display

page 141

thrilling	[ˈθrɪlɪŋ]	very exciting	spannend, mitreißend
ride	[raɪd]	journey	Fahrt
alike	[əˈlaɪk]	similar	gleichermaßen, ebenso
response	[rɪˈspɒns]	answer, reaction	Reaktion, Antwort
brochure	[ˈbrəʊʃə]	small book with product information	Prospekt, Broschüre
Formula One	[ˌfɔːmjələ ˈwʌn]	e.g. She loves watching Formula One on TV.	Formel 1

page 142

pros and cons *pl*	[ˌprəʊz ənd ˈkɒnz]	advantages and disadvantages	Für und Wider, Argumente dafür und dagegen
spy	[spaɪ]	sb who secretly collects information about others	Spion/in
secret agent	[ˌsiːkrət ˈeɪdʒənt]	e.g. Hi, my name's James Bond. – What, like the famous secret agent?	Geheimagent/in
set in …	[ˈset ɪn]	takes place in …	das in … spielt
Cold War	[ˌkəʊld ˈwɔː]	e.g. The Cold War took place between the United States and Soviet Union.	Kalter Krieg
to **assist**	[əˈsɪst]	to help	helfen, unterstützen
enemy	[ˈenəmi]	<> friend	Feind/in, feindlich

to **succeed**	[sək'si:d]	*n* success	Erfolg haben, erfolgreich sein
original	[ə'rɪdʒənl]	new	originell
original thinking	[əˌrɪdʒənl 'θɪŋkɪŋ]	thinking like nobody else	Scharfsinn, Originalität
smart	[smɑ:t]	clever	intelligent, klug
level	['levl]	degree	Niveau
briefing	['bri:fɪŋ]	short talk during which a task is discussed	Einweisung, Lagebesprechung
flexibility	[ˌfleksə'bɪləti]	*adj* flexible	Flexibilität
unique	[ju'ni:k]	different to everything else	einzigartig
cycle path	['saɪkl pɑ:θ]	separate path for cyclists	Fahrradweg
canal	[kə'næl]	man-made river used to transport goods	Kanal
cuisine	[kwɪ'zi:n]	style of cooking in a particular country	(Länder-)Küche
adrenaline rush	[ə'drenlɪn rʌʃ]	e.g. Sport gives people an adrenaline rush.	Adrenalinrausch
suddenly	['sʌdnli]	<> gradually	plötzlich
to **twist**	[twɪst]	*phr* to twist and turn	sich winden
to **turn**	[tɜ:n]	to change direction	sich drehen
gentle	['dʒentl]	e.g. We slowed down and walked on at a gentle pace.	sanft
pace	[peɪs]	speed	Tempo
awesome	['ɔ:səm]	great	beeindruckend, toll
husky	['hʌski]	wolf-like dog	Schlittenhund
dog team	['dɒg ti:m]	a group of dogs which pull a sled	Hundegespann
hands-on	[ˌhændz 'ɒn]	practical	praktisch, lebensnah
to **sit back**	[ˌsɪt 'bæk]	*phr* sit back and relax	sich zurücklehnen
scenery	['si:nəri]	surroundings	Landschaft, Kulisse
working dog	[ˌwɜ:kɪŋ 'dɒg]	a dog suitable for useful work	Arbeitshund
taster session	['teɪstə seʃn]	trial	Schnupperkurs

page 143

to put sth into action	[ˌpʊt ɪntu 'ækʃn]	to implement	etw in die Tat umsetzen
to ban sb from doing sth	['bæn]	to not allow sb to do sth	jdm verbieten, etw zu tun
significant(ly)	[sɪg'nɪfɪkənt]	substantial(ly)	erheblich
brain	[breɪn]	e.g. Walking is good for the brain.	Gehirn
metabolic rate	[metəˌbɒlɪk 'reɪt]	how fast food is burnt in the body	Stoffwechsel
to **burn sth**	[bɜ:n]	*phr* to burn off calories	etw verbrennen
body fat	['bɒdi fæt]	the amount of fat in the body	Körperfett
balance	['bæləns]	*phr* to keep your balance	Gleichgewicht
compulsory	[kəm'pʌlsəri]	obligatory	obligatorisch
in particular	[ɪn pə'tɪkjələ]	especially	speziell
to **connect with sb**	[kə'nekt wɪð]	*n* connection	sich mit jdm (intensiv) austauschen
teammate	['ti:mmeɪt]	sb who plays on the same team	Mannschaftskamerad/in
school premises *pl*	['sku:l premɪsɪz]	land belonging to a school	Schulgelände
unhealthy	[ʌn'helθi]	<> healthy	ungesund
high-energy	[ˌhaɪ'enədʒi]	with lots of calories	energiereich
to **gain weight**	[geɪn 'weɪt]	<> to lose weight	zunehmen
sugar-rich	['ʃʊgə rɪtʃ]	with lots of sugar	stark zuckerhaltig
to **coat**	[kəʊt]	to cover	auskleiden, beschichten
to **attack**	[ə'tæk]	e.g. Sugar attacks your teeth.	angreifen
dietary fibre	[ˌdaɪətri 'faɪbə]	part of plant-based foods that cannot be digested	Ballaststoff
digestive system	[daɪˌdʒestɪv 'sɪstəm]	system of organs that get food in and out of the body	Verdauungssystem
mood	[mu:d]	feeling	Stimmung, Laune
low in sth	['ləʊ ɪn]	not having a lot of sth	arm an etw
saturated fat	[ˌsætʃəreɪtɪd 'fæt]	*phr* high/low in saturated fats	gesättigtes Fett
high in sth	['haɪ ɪn]	having a lot of sth	reich an etw
news story	['nju:z stɔ:ri]	news report	Bericht *(in den Medien)*
contradictory	[kɒntrə'dɪktəri]	meaning the opposite	widersprüchlich
to **tell sth from sth**	['tel frəm]	to recognize the difference between	etw von etw unterscheiden
abuse	[ə'bju:s]	e.g. alcohol abuse, drug abuse	Missbrauch

page 144

except for	[ɪk'sept fə]	apart from	außer

UNIT 13

page 145

art	[ɑ:t]	e.g. paintings, sculptures, etc.	Kunst
air pump	['eə pʌmp]	device for pushing air into or out of sth	Luftpumpe, Vakuumpumpe
intellectual	[ˌɪntə'lektʃuəl]	clever	intellektuell
artistic	[ɑ:'tɪstɪk]	good at drawing or painting	künstlerisch

page 146

graphic novel	[ˌgræfɪk 'nɒvl]	comic	Bildroman, Comicroman
vandalism	['vændəlɪzəm]	destroying public property	Vandalismus
to **be bored with sth**	[bi 'bɔ:d wɪð]	to find sth boring	etw langweilt jdn
Suit yourself.	[ˌsu:t jə'self]	As you like.	Wie du willst.

Chronological word list

paint	[peɪnt]	e.g. wall paint, oil paint	(Mal-)Farbe
police station	[pəˈliːs steɪʃn]	place where policemen work	Polizeiwache

page 147

criminal conviction	[ˌkrɪmɪnl kənˈvɪkʃn]	when sb is found guilty of a crime	strafrechtliche Verurteilung
to **deserve**	[dɪˈzɜːv]	e.g. He was a good colleague – he didn't deserve to be fired!	verdienen
offender	[əˈfendə]	sb who commited a crime	Straffällige/r, Straftäter/in
No way.	[ˌnəʊ ˈweɪ]	No chance.	Auf keinen Fall!
to **fuel sth**	[ˈfjuːəl]	to make sth worse	etw anheizen, etw befeuern
storm	[stɔːm]	negative reaction to sth	Sturm
to **cancel**	[ˈkænsl]	to end	beenden, abbrechen
to **cover sth up**	[ˌkʌvər ˈʌp]	to hide sth	*hier:* etw übermalen
mural	[ˈmjʊərəl]	a large painting on a wall	Wandmalerei

page 148

court	[kɔːt]	*phr* to go to court	Gericht
to **have a criminal record**	[həv ə ˌkrɪmɪnl ˈrekɔːd]	e.g. It's difficult to get a job if you have a criminal record.	vorbestraft sein
luckily	[ˈlʌkɪli]	thankfully	glücklicherweise
magistrate	[ˈmædʒɪstreɪt]	judge in a court that deals with less serious crimes	Richter/in
to **invite sb to do sth**	[ɪnˈvaɪt]	to give sb the opportunity to do sth	jdn auffordern, etw zu tun
vandal	[ˈvændl]	sb who damages public property	Vandale
to **vandalize**	[ˈvændəlaɪz]	to damage public property	verwüsten, mutwillig beschädigen
mess	[mes]	*phr* to clean up a mess	Schweinerei, Gesudel
to **blame sth on sb**	[bleɪm]	to say sb is guilty of sth	jdm für etw die Schuld geben
to **claim**	[kleɪm]	*n* claim	behaupten
local council	[ˌləʊkl ˈkaʊnsɪl]	government of an area, such as a city or town	Gemeinderat
to **paint**	[peɪnt]	e.g. Graffiti artists paint amazing murals on walls.	malen
to **brighten sth up**	[ˌbraɪtn ˈʌp]	to make sth lighter and more pleasant	etw aufhellen, etw aufheitern
proud	[praʊd]	e.g. He was proud of his work.	stolz
anonymous	[əˈnɒnɪməs]	having no special characteristics	anonym
concrete	[ˈkɒŋkriːt]	building material using cement	Beton
rubbish	[ˈrʌbɪʃ]	waste	Müll, Abfall
to **pass the time**	[pɑːs ðə ˈtaɪm]	to make time go more quickly	sich die Zeit vertreiben
excitement	[ɪkˈsaɪtmənt]	*adj* excited	Reiz, Spannung, Nervenkitzel
tag	[tæg]	a graffiti artist's mark	Marke, Kennzeichnung
surface	[ˈsɜːfɪs]	flat top part or outside of sth	Oberfläche, Fläche
post	[pəʊst]	sign on the street	Pfosten, Säule
childish	[ˈtʃaɪldɪʃ]	<> grown-up	kindisch
subway *BE*	[ˈsʌbweɪ]	!! subway *AE* = U-Bahn !!	Fußgängerunterführung
spray can	[ˈspreɪ kæn]	can of paint graffiti artists use	Sprühdose
to **find sb guilty of sth**	[ˌfaɪnd ˈgɪlti əv]	e.g. She was found guilty of a serious crime.	jdn einer Sache für schuldig befinden
to **break the law**	[ˌbreɪk ðə ˈlɔː]	e.g. You can go to prison for breaking the law.	gegen das Gesetz verstoßen
painting	[ˈpeɪntɪŋ]	e.g. painting on a wall	Gemälde

page 149

hate	[heɪt]	strong dislike	Hass
swastika	[ˈswɒstɪkə]	symbol of the Nazis	Hakenkreuz
harmless	[ˈhɑːmləs]	<> harmful	harmlos
cartoon	[kɑːˈtuːn]	comic	Karikatur, Zeichnung
heir	[eə]	sb who will inherit sth	Erbe
billiard ball	[ˈbɪljəd bɔːl]	e.g. Snooker is played with 22 coloured billiard balls.	Billardkugel
to **rid sth of sth**	[ˈrɪd əv]	to free sth of sth	etw von etw befreien
to **take to the streets**	[ˌteɪk tə ðe ˈstriːts]	to go out on the streets, often to demonstrate	auf die Straße gehen
to **be on the lookout for sth**	[bi ɒn ðe ˈlʊkaʊt fə]	to search for sth	auf der Suche nach etw sein
armed	[ɑːmd]	with a weapon	bewaffnet
to **run riot**	[ˌrʌn ˈraɪət]	to behave without control	ausschweifen
hateful	[ˈheɪtfl]	filled with anger	hasserfüllt
approach	[əˈprəʊtʃ]	way of doing sth	Herangehensweise, Ansatz
racist	[ˈreɪsɪst]	sb who hates others of a different race	rassistisch
to **assess**	[əˈses]	to judge, to evaluate	beurteilen, bewerten
effectiveness	[ɪˈfektɪvnəs]	*adj* effective	Effektivität
to **justify**	[ˈdʒʌstɪfaɪ]	to give reasons	begründen, rechtfertigen
controversial	[ˌkɒntrəˈvɜːʃl]	*n* controversy	umstritten
artist	[ˈɑːtɪst]	e.g. a painter or sculptor	Künstler/in
run down	[ˌrʌn ˈdaʊn]	in bad condition	heruntergekommen
to sum up	[tə ˌsʌm ˈʌp]	summarizing, in conclusion	zusammenfassend

page 150

snap	[snæp]	photo	Schnapschuss
technique	[tekˈniːk]	method	Technik, Methode
pose	[pəʊz]	*phr* to strike a pose	Haltung, Pose
flash	[flæʃ]	bright light on a camera	Blitz(licht)

angle	['æŋgl]	perspective	Winkel, Blickwinkel, Perspektive
to **edit**	['edɪt]	to change	bearbeiten
to **crop**	[krɒp]	to cut	beschneiden
to **rotate**	[rəʊ'teɪt]	to turn	drehen
spontaneous	[spɒn'teɪniəs]	natural and sudden without being planned	spontan
photographer	[fə'tɒgrəfə]	sb who takes photos professionally	Fotograf/in
guideline	['gaɪdlaɪn]	rule, recommendation	Richtlinie, Empfehlung
subject	['sʌbdʒɪkt]	main person or thing in a photo	Motiv, Gegenstand
cheeky	['tʃi:ki]	*phr* a cheeky smile	frech
portrait	['pɔ:treɪt]	likeness	Porträt
features *pl*	['fi:tʃəz]	characteristics	Gesichtszüge
ID card	[ˌaɪ 'di: kɑ:d]	form of identification	Personalausweis
effort	['efət]	*phr* to make an effort	Mühe, Anstrengung
shape	[ʃeɪp]	form	Form, Gestalt
contrast	['kɒntrɑ:st]	difference in lighting	Kontrast
shade	[ʃeɪd]	shadow	Schatten
to **light**	[laɪt]	to make bright with lights	beleuchten
tense	[tens]	<> relaxed	angespannt
unrelaxed	[ˌʌnrɪ'lækst]	uncomfortable	unentspannt

page 151

to **distract sb from sth**	[dɪ'strækt]	to move the attention away from sth	jdn von etw ablenken
overexposed	[ˌəʊvərɪk'spəʊzd]	too much light	überbelichtet
sunny	['sʌni]	with a lot of sun	sonnig

page 152

printing plant	['prɪntɪŋ plɑ:nt]	large factory where books and magazines are printed	Großdruckerei
hazard	['hæzəd]	danger	Gefahr
safety procedures *pl*	['seɪfti prəsi:dʒəz]	e.g. You have to follow safety procedures to avoid injury in the workplace.	Sicherheitsmaßnahmen, Sicherheitsbestimmungen
induction	[ɪn'dʌkʃn]	session organized to introduce sb to a new job	Einarbeitung
health and safety	[ˌhelθ ənd 'seɪfti]	measures against accidents	Arbeitsschutz, Arbeitssicherheit
safety sign	['seɪfti saɪn]	warning sign	Sicherzeitszeichen, Warnzeichen
ear protectors *pl*	[ɪə pr'tektəz]	e.g. Ear protectors must be worn in the factory at all times.	Gehörschutz
to **enter**	['entə]	to go inside	betreten
to **operate**	['ɒpəreɪt]	e.g. It's my job to operate printing machinery.	*(Geräte)* bedienen
safety glasses *pl*	['seɪfti glɑ:sɪz]	e.g. Wear safety glasses for eye protection!	Schutzbrille
forklift truck	[ˌfɔ:klɪft 'trʌk]	vehicle used to lift lots of pallets at once	Gabelstapler
to **catch fire**	[ˌkætʃ 'faɪə]	to start burning	Feuer fangen, in Brand geraten
to **beware of sth**	[bɪ'weər əv]	to be careful so that sth doesn't happen	sich vor etw in Acht nehmen
electric shock	[ɪˌlektrɪk 'ʃɒk]	e.g. The broken hairdryer gave him an electric shock.	Stromschlag
protective gloves *pl*	[prəˌtektɪv 'glʌvz]	gloves that stop sb's hands from being hurt, burnt, etc.	Schutzhandschuhe
to pull down	[ˌpʊl 'daʊn]	hold and move sth. down firmly	herunterziehen
guard	[gɑ:d]	safety cover	Schutzhaube
to **crush**	[krʌʃ]	to squash, to squeeze heavily	zerquetschen
protective clothing	[prəˌtektɪv 'kləʊðɪŋ]	clothes that stop sb from being hurt, burnt, etc.	Schutzkleidung

page 153

case study	['keɪs stʌdi]	example	Fallstudie
printing works	['prɪntɪŋ wɜ:ks]	factory in which things are printed	Druckerei
ink	[ɪŋk]	e.g. The printing press uses four different inks.	Druckfarbe
printing press	['prɪntɪŋ pres]	machine used for printing, especially books or newspapers	Druckmaschine
print run	['prɪnt rʌn]	number of copies that are printed at one time	Auflage
to **afford sth**	[ə'fɔ:d]	to be able to buy sth	sich etw leisten
cloth	[klɒθ]	piece of fabric for cleaning	Tuch
to **shut down**	[ˌʃʌt 'daʊn]	to turn off	abschalten
procedure	[prə'si:dʒə]	process, measure	Vorgang
to **get stuck**	[get 'stʌk]	to get caught	hängen bleiben, sich verfangen
to **pull**	[pʊl]	<> to push	ziehen
to **let go (of sth)**	[ˌlet 'gəʊ]	to release sth	(etw) loslassen
fortunately	['fɔ:tʃənətli]	<> unfortunately	glücklicherweise, zum Glück
wedding ring	['wedɪŋ rɪŋ]	ring worn as a symbol of marriage	Ehering
skin	[skɪn]	e.g. The doctors took skin from his foot.	Haut
representation	[ˌreprɪzen'teɪʃn]	*v* to represent	Vertretung
workplace safety	['wɜ:kpleɪs seɪfti]	e.g. The company is strict about workplace safety.	Sicherheit am Arbeitsplatz

page 154

comparison	[kəm'pærɪsn]	*v* to compare	Vergleich, *(Grammatik:)* Steigerung
to **take sth into account**	[ˌteɪk ɪntu ə'kaʊnt]	to consider sth	etw berücksichtigen
means of transport	[ˌmi:nz əf 'trænspɔ:t]	vehicle that can carry people or goods	Transportmittel
air travel	['eə trævl]	travelling in an aeroplane or helicopter	Flugreisen, Flugverkehr
road travel	['rəʊd trævl]	travelling with a car, bus, or motorbike	Straßenverkehr

rail travel	[ˈreɪl trævl]	travelling by train	Bahnverkehr
to **rush into it**	[ˈrʌʃ intʊ ɪt]	to do sth too fast and without thinking	es überstürzen
qualified	[ˈkwɒlɪfaɪd]	*n* qualification	mit Abschluss, ausgebildet
electrician	[ɪˌlekˈtrɪʃn]	sb who works with electrical equipment	Elektriker/in
running water	[ˌrʌnɪŋ ˈwɔːtə]	water that comes from a tap	fließendes Wasser

page 155

to **steal**	[stiːl]	to take sth without permission	stehlen
otherwise	[ˈʌðəwaɪz]	e.g. Open the door, otherwise I can't get in.	sonst

page 156

industrial estate	[ɪnˌdʌstriəl ɪˈsteɪt]	local area reserved for production facilites and large retail outlets	Gewerbegebiet
to **obey sth**	[əˈbeɪ]	to do what sth requires you to do	etw befolgen
to **ignore sth**	[ɪgˈnɔː]	to not pay attention to sth	etw ignorieren
warning	[ˈwɔːnɪŋ]	e.g. The judge gave him a warning.	Verwarnung
to **win the lottery**	[ˌwɪn ðə ˈlɒtəri]	e.g. If I win the lottery, I'll buy myself a house.	im Lotto gewinnen

UNIT 14

page 157

similarity	[ˌsɪməˈlærəti]	<> difference	Ähnlichkeit
to **be intolerant of sb**	[bi ɪnˈtɒlərənt əv]	<> to tolerate sb	intolerant gegenüber jdm sein
to **be suspicious of sb**	[bi səˈspɪʃəs əv]	*n* suspicion	jdm gegenüber misstrauisch sein
race	[reɪs]	*adj racist*	Rasse
disability	[ˌdɪsəˈbɪləti]	adj disabled	Behinderung
fear	[fɪə]	feeling sb has when they are scared	Angst
ambition	[æmˈbɪʃn]	aim, goal	Ziel, Wunschtraum, Ehrgeiz

page 158

robot	[ˈrəʊbɒt]	e.g. The robot could talk and walk.	Roboter
monkey	[ˈmʌŋki]	e.g. There are lots of monkeys in the zoo.	Affe
appearance	[əˈpɪərəns]	how sb or sth looks	Erscheinung(sbild)
deceptive	[dɪˈseptɪv]	*v* to deceive	trügerisch
chimpanzee	[ˌtʃɪmpænˈziː]	type of monkey	Schimpanse

page 159

to **slide**	[slaɪd]	to move along smoothly	gleiten
clay	[kleɪ]	raw material for pottery	Ton
to **relish**	[ˈrelɪʃ]	to enjoy	genießen
moisture	[ˈmɔɪstʃə]	*adj* moist	Feuchtigkeit
to **ooze**	[uːz]	to run slowly out of sth	hervorquellen
to **mat down**	[ˌmæt ˈdaʊn]	to make flat	*(Haare:)* plattstreichen
human	[ˈhjuːmən]	like a person	menschlich
potter's wheel	[ˌpɒtəz ˈwiːl]	turning wheel used for shaping clay	Töpferscheibe
prehensile	[prɪˈhensaɪl]	(hand or foot:) made for holding on to an object	zum Greifen geeignet
to **shape**	[ʃeɪp]	to form	formen
vase	[vɑːz]	a container used to hold flowers	Vase
to **pinch**	[pɪntʃ]	to press together, to squeeze	kneifen, zwicken, zusammendrücken
to **spin**	[spɪn]	to turn	drehen
pen	[pen]	closed area that animals are kept in	Pferch, Gehege
to **scream**	[skriːm]	to shout loudly	schreien
to **spin**	[spɪn]	to turn	sich herumdrehen
to **hurl**	[hɜːl]	to throw hard	schleudern
feces *AE*	[ˈfiːsiːz]	*BE:* faeces	Kot
to **spatter**	[ˈspætə]	e.g. The water spattered on the wall.	spritzen
to **slide down**	[ˌslaɪd ˈdaʊn]	to run down	herunterrutschen
courtyard	[ˈkɔːtjɑːd]	an area surrounded by buildings	Innenhof
beyond sth	[bɪˈjɒnd]	further than sth	jenseits von etw
to **swing**	[swɪŋ]	e.g. Monkeys swing from trees.	schwingen, schlenkern, schaukeln
to **ape**	[eɪp]	to imitate	nachäffen
crude(ly)	[kruːd]	rough(ly)	derb, grob
to **bare one's teeth**	[ˌbeə wʌnz ˈtiːθ]	to show one's teeth aggressively	die Zähne fletschen
grin	[grɪn]	smile	Grinsen
threat	[θret]	*v* to threaten	Drohung
stool	[stuːl]	small chair with no back	Hocker
to **cross**	[krɒs]	to go from one side to the other	durchqueren
stride	[straɪd]	a way of walking with big steps	(großer) Schritt
to **grin**	[grɪn]	*phr* to grin from ear to ear	grinsen
to **reverse**	[rɪˈvɜːs]	to go back	umkehren
to **flush**	[flʌʃ]	to turn red in the face	erröten
in heat	[ɪn ˈhiːt]	state of sexual excitement	läufig, rollig
to **grab**	[græb]	to take hold of sth roughly	anfassen, packen
naked	[ˈneɪkɪd]	not wearing anything	nackt

to rest sth against sth	[rest əˈgenst]	to lean sth on sth	etw an etw lehnen
skull	[skʌl]	e.g. The brain is inside the skull.	Schädel
to thunk against sth	[ˈθʌŋk əgenst]	to hit against sth	dumpf gegen etw schlagen
handler	[ˈhændlə]	person taking care of an animal	(Tier-)Betreuer/in
to make pottery	[ˌmeɪk ˈpɒtəri]	to produce cups, plates, and pots	töpfern
to lope	[ləʊp]	to move or run with big steps	springen, laufen
to kick	[kɪk]	to hit with one's foot	treten
movement	[ˈmuːvmənt]	*v* to move	Bewegung
vision	[ˈvɪʒn]	*phr* field of vision	Blickfeld
to snick open	[ˌsnɪk ˈəʊpən]	to open with a quiet screak	sich mit einem leisen Knarren öffnen
to spin to a halt	[ˌspɪn tʊ ə ˈhɒlt]	to suddenly stop	zum Stehen kommen
to crumple	[ˈkrʌmpl]	to destroy by squeezing together	zerknautschen
to poke sth through sth	[pəʊk]	to put sth through sth small	etw durch etw stecken
to sigh	[ɔɪːɔɪːɑɔˈə]	e.g. He sighed sadly.	seufzen
emphatic(ally)	[ɪmˈfætɪk]	with emphasis	nachdrücklich
to point at sth	[ˈpɔɪnt ət]	to use one's finger to show sth	auf etw zeigen, auf etw deuten
in submission	[ɪn sʌbˈmɪʃn]	*adj* submissive(ly)	unterwürfig
to bury sth in sth	[ˈberi]	to put sth in sth	etw in etw (ver)graben
to silence sth	[ˈsaɪləns]	*n* silence	etw zum Schweigen bringen
to scowl	[skaʊl]	to look angry	ein böses Gesicht machen
to yank	[jæŋk]	to pull forcefully	zerren, reißen
implant	[ˈɪmplɑːnt]	an object put in sb's body	Implantat

page 160

to kneel	[niːl]	to get down on one's knees	knieen
to sedate sb	[sɪˈdeɪt]	*n* sedative	jdn ruhigstellen, jdn sedieren
to reach out	[ˌriːtʃ ˈaʊt]	to stretch out one's hands	die Hand/Hände ausstrecken
to snap sth	[snæp]	to break sth in two	etw (entzwei)brechen
neck	[nek]	part of the body between the head and shoulders	Hals
lousy	[ˈlaʊzi]	nasty, terrible	lausig, beschissen
hellish	[ˈhelɪʃ]	terrible	höllisch
to be in limbo	[bi ɪn ˈlɪmbəʊ]	to be stuck without anything to do	in der Luft hängen, in der Schwebe sein
to raise one's eyebrows	[ˌreɪz wʌnz ˈaɪbraʊz]	e.g. He raised his eyebrows at the suggestion.	die Stirn runzeln
show	[ʃəʊ]	performance	Vorstellung
to mask	[mɑːsk]	to hide	verbergen, verdecken
manners *pl*	[ˈmænəz]	*phr* to learn good/bad manners	Manieren
upset	[ˌʌpˈset]	annoyed	verärgert, aufgebracht
to hoot	[huːt]	to shout excitedly	johlen
Serves her right.	[ˌsɜːvz hɜː ˈraɪt]	She deserved it.	Das geschieht ihr recht.
to discipline sb	[ˈdɪsəplɪn]	to tell sb off	jdn maßregeln, jdn disziplinieren
anger	[ˈæŋgə]	*adj* angry	Zorn, Ärger
display	[dɪˈspleɪ]	show	Zurschaustellung
lip	[lɪp]	e.g. He wiped his lips.	Lippe
to draw sth back	[ˌdrɔː ˈbæk]	to pull back	etw zurückziehen
grimace	[grɪˈmeɪs]	ugly expression	Grimasse
rage	[reɪdʒ]	anger	Wut
to threaten	[ˈθretn]	*n* threat	drohen
to blind	[blaɪnd]	to stop sb seeing clearly	blenden
to hold on	[ˌhəʊld ˈɒn]	to hang on to sth	durchhalten, sich festhalten
to lose it	[ˈluːz ɪt]	to become angry, to lose control	die Nerven verlieren, durchdrehen
rational	[ˈræʃnəl]	clear-thinking	vernünftig, rational
reach	[riːtʃ]	*phr* out of reach	Reichweite
panting	[ˈpæntɪŋ]	breathing heavily	keuchend
firm	[fɜːm]	strong	fest
smooth	[smuːð]	<> rough	geschmeidig, weich
nostril	[ˈnɒstrəl]	openings in nose to let air in and out	Nüster, Nasenloch
kernel	[ˈkɜːnl]	core	Kern
to subsume	[səbˈsjuːm]	to absorb	aufnehmen, vereinnahmen
to slow	[sləʊ]	<> to quicken	sich verlangsamen
to blink	[blɪŋk]	to close one's eyes for a fraction of a second	blinzeln
rim	[rɪm]	edge	Rand
moist	[mɔɪst]	*n* moisture	feucht
kiln	[kɪln]	large oven to bake pottery	Brennofen
to nod	[nɒd]	to move one's head up and down	nicken
to stare at sth	[ˈsteər ət]	to look at sth for a long time with your eyes open	etw anstarren
to snort at sth	[ˈsnɔːt ət]	to show disapproval with sth	etw verächtlich anschnauben
to sober	[ˈsəʊbə]	calm down in a serious manner	nüchtern werden, ernst werden
to crawl	[krɔːl]	to move on one's hands and knees	kriechen
spine	[spaɪn]	line of bones down the centre of the back	Rückgrat, Rücken
pile	[paɪl]	e.g. The books lay in a pile on the floor.	Haufen
to scoop sth up	[ˈskuːp ʌp]	to pick sth up	etw zusammenschaufeln

Chronological word list

page 161

to embarrass sb	[ɪm'bærəs]	*n* embarrassment	jdn in Verlegenheit bringen
to punish	['pʌnɪʃ]	*n* punishment	bestrafen
respectful	[rɪ'spektfl]	showing respect for sth	respektvoll
animal	['ænɪml]	like an animal	tierisch
to give evidence	[ˌgɪv 'evɪdəns]	to prove	(etw) belegen, (etw) nachweisen

page 162

flatshare	['flætʃeə]	to live with other people in a flat	Wohngemeinschaft
multicultural	[ˌmʌlti'kʌltʃərəl]	containing lots of different cultures within a society	multikulturell
after all	[ˌɑ:ftər 'ɔ:l]	e.g. I don't want to criticize her – she's my wife after all.	nun mal
mining	['maɪnɪŋ]	e.g. The Ruhrgebiet used to be a vast mining region.	Bergbau
Catholic	['kæθəlɪk]	linked to the Catholic Church	katholisch; Katholik/in
engineering	[ˌendʒɪ'nɪərɪŋ]	construction and design of machinery	Maschinenbau
flatmate	['flætmeɪt]	sb with whom sb lives with in a flat	Mitbewohner/in
strict	[strɪkt]	e.g. My parents are very strict – I have to be home by 9 o'clock.	streng
bacon	['beɪkən]	*phr* bacon and eggs	Speck
horrified	['hɒrɪfaɪd]	very shocked	entsetzt
pan	[pæn]	e.g. She burnt the pan cooking.	Topf, Pfanne
spicy	['spaɪsi]	with lots of spices	würzig, scharf
mint	[mɪnt]	e.g. mint sauce	Minze
pickled	['pɪkld]	preserved in vinegar	(sauer) eingelegt
dish	[dɪʃ]	meal	Gericht, Speise
preference	['prefrəns]	*v* to prefer	Vorliebe

page 163

cynical	['sɪnɪkl]	e.g. My brother's comments are always cynical, never friendly.	zynisch
figure	['fɪgə]	character	Figur
to reflect	[rɪ'flekt]	e.g. Her friendly face reflected her positive attitude.	widerspiegeln, wiedergeben

page 164

fundraiser	['fʌndreɪzə]	sb who collects money for a charity	Spendensammler/in
to shadow sb	['ʃædəʊ]	to follow sb around and learn from them	mit jdm *(zur Einarbeitung)* mitlaufen
phone duty	['fəʊn dju:ti]	e.g. Over 100 clients called while I was on phone duty!	Telefondienst
to be on a break	[bi ɒn ə 'breɪk]	e.g. The receptionist was on a 15-minute break.	Pause machen
to put sb through	[ˌpʊt 'θru:]	to pass sb to sb else on the phone	*(Telefon:)* jdn durchstellen
to catch sth	[kætʃ]	to understand sth	etw verstehen, etw mitbekommen
to hold the line	[ˌhəʊld ðə 'laɪn]	to stay on the phone	*(Telefon:)* am Apparat bleiben
to answer the phone	[ˌɑ:nsə ðə 'fəʊn]	e.g. John never answers the phone!	ans Telefon gehen
to leave a message	[ˌli:v ə 'mesɪdʒ]	e.g. She left a message for him.	eine Nachricht hinterlassen
to let sb know sth	[ˌlet 'nəʊ]	to inform sb about sth	jdm etw ausrichten
You're welcome.	[jɔ: 'welkəm]	e.g. Thank you for your help! – You're welcome!	Bitte (sehr). Gern geschehen.
Speaking.	['spi:kɪŋ]	That's me.	*(Telefon:)* Am Apparat.
to take a message	[ˌteɪk ə 'mesɪdʒ]	<> to leave a message	*(Telefon:)* jdm etw ausrichten
Don't mention it.	[dəʊnt 'menʃn ɪt]	No problem.	Nichts zu danken.

page 165

digit	['dɪdʒɪt]	figure, number from 0–9	Ziffer

page 166

to come to mind	[kʌm tə 'maɪnd]	to suddenly think of sth	jdm in den Sinn kommen
chest	[tʃest]	e.g. His chest hurt every time he coughed.	Brust
abdominal	[æb'dɒmɪnl]	e.g. She had strong abdominal muscles.	Bauch-
biceps	['baɪseps]	muscles in the upper arm	Bizeps
thigh	[θaɪ]	upper part of the leg	Oberschenkel
rippled	[rɪpld]	e.g. He was so fit, his abs were rippled!	gewellt, *(Muskeln:)* definiert
draining board	['dreɪnɪŋ bɔ:d]	*phr* to have a stomach like a draining board	*(Spüle:)* Abtropfbrett
to strive for sth	['straɪv fə]	to try hard to get sth	nach etw streben, etw anstreben
to soar	[sɔ:]	to increase greatly	in die Höhe schnellen
to make up	[ˌmeɪk 'ʌp]	e.g. Men make up two thirds of our gym members.	*(Anteil)* ausmachen
to account for sth	[ə'kaʊnt fə]	e.g. Women account for one third of our gym members.	*(Anteil)* ausmachen
disorder	[dɪs'ɔ:də]	e.g. eating disorder	Krankheitsbild, Störung
muscle dysmorphia	[ˌmʌsl dɪs'mɔ:fɪə]	mental disorder thinking one is not muscular enough	Muskeldysmorphie, Muskelsucht
anorexia	[ænə'reksiə]	eating disorder involving fear of faining weight	Magersucht
in reverse	[ɪn rɪ'vɜ:s]	the other way around	umgekehrt
whereas	[ˌweər'æz]	while	während
anorexic	[ˌænə'reksɪk]	*n* anorexia	Magersüchtge/r; magersüchtig
puny	['pju:ni]	small and weak	schwächlich, mickrig
muscular	['mʌskjələ]	e.g. Weight lifters are very muscular.	muskulös
obsession	[əb'seʃn]	*phr* to have an unhealthy obsession with sth	Besessenheit, Zwang
sufferer	['sʌfərə]	sb who is affected by an illness	Leidende/r, Patient/in
devastating	['devəsteɪtɪŋ]	*phr* to have a devastating impact on sth	verheerend
clerk	[klɑ:k]	sb who works in an office	Sachbearbeiter/in

to get in the way of sth	[ˌget ɪn ðə ˈweɪ əv]	e.g. The gym gets in the way of his relationships.	einer Sache im Weg stehen
to weigh	[weɪ]	e.g. Tom weighs 69 kilograms.	wiegen
stone	[stəʊn]	measurement of weight	*≈ 6,35 kg*
height	[haɪt]	how tall sb is	Körpergröße
throughout the day	[θruːˌaʊt ðə ˈdeɪ]	during the day	den ganzen Tag über
skinny	[ˈskɪni]	very thin	mager, dürr
to put on weight	[ˌpʊt ɒn ˈweɪt]	to get heavier	zunehmen
extreme	[ɪkˈstriːm]	*phr* to go from one extreme to the other	Extrem
personal best	[ˌpɜːsnl ˈbest]	sb's best performance of a task so far	persönliche Bestleistung
refrigerator	[rɪˈfrɪdʒəreɪtə]	*inf* fridge	Kühlschrank
stacked with sth	[ˈstækt wɪð]	completely full of sth	voll von etw, mit etw beladen
to urge sb to do sth	[ɜːdʒ]	to push sb to do sth	jdn dringend auffordern, etw zu tun
surgery	[ˈsɜːdʒəri]	operation	Operation
to spot	[spɒt]	to see, to detect	erkennen

page 167

to step away from sth	[ˌstep əˈweɪ frəm]	e.g. The policeman said, "Step away from the car."	von etw zurückgehen/-treten
constantly	[ˈkɒnstəntli]	continuously	andauernd
long-awaited	[ˌlɒŋ əˈweɪtɪd]	expected for a long time	lang erwartet, lang ersehnt
to cherish sth	[ˈtʃerɪʃ]	to love sth a lot	etw wertschätzen, etw lieben
to snap	[snæp]	to take a quick photo	einen Schnappschuss machen
to end up doing sth	[ˌend ˈʌp]	e.g. You could end up forgetting it all.	schließlich etw tun
in a flash	[ɪn ə ˈflæʃ]	in next to no time	im Nu
memory	[ˈmeməri]	images of past events in your mind	Erinnerung, Gedächtnis
to photograph	[ˈfəʊtəgrɑːf]	to take a photo	fotografieren
work of art	[ˌwɜːk əv ˈɑːt]	piece of art	Kunstwerk
historical	[hɪˈstɒrɪkl]	e.g. This little sculpture is an important historical artifact.	historisch
to recall sth	[rɪˈkɔːl]	to remember sth	sich an etw erinnern
to conduct sth	[kənˈdʌkt]	to carry sth out	etw durchführen
mindless(ly)	[ˈmaɪndləs]	without thinking	sinnfrei, hirnlos
previous	[ˈpriːviəs]	earlier	frühere/r/s
to suggest	[səˈdʒest]	e.g. Survey results suggest an improvement in public health.	nahelegen
to review sth	[rɪˈvjuː]	to look at sth again after a some time	etw nochmals betrachten
to access sth	[ˈækses]	to get to sth	auf etw zugreifen
to interact with sth	[ˌɪntərˈækt wɪð]	to think about and react to sth	sich mit etw auseinandersetzen

page 168

competitor	[kəmˈpetɪtə]	sb who takes part in a competition	Teilnehmer/in *(an einem Wettbewerb)*
vest	[vest]	t-shirt without sleeves that runners wear	Laufshirt
official	[əˈfɪʃl]	sb who is in charge of the rules of a competition	*(Sport:)* Kampfrichter/in
sex	[seks]	gender	Geschlecht
press kit	[ˈpres kɪt]	information material given to journalists	Pressemappe

UNIT 15

page 169

horizon	[həˈraɪzn]	*phr* on the horizon	Horizont
to look ahead	[ˌlʊk əˈhed]	to think about the future	nach vorne schauen
to represent	[ˌreprɪˈzent]	to show	darstellen, wiedergeben
aspiration	[ˌæspəˈreɪʃn]	ambition, aim	Ziel, Bestreben
to start a family	[ˌstɑːt ə ˈfæmli]	to decide to have children	eine Familie gründen

page 170

(registered) nurse	[nɜːs]	sb qualified to take care of the ill or injured	(examinierte/r) Krankenpfleger/-schwester
motor mechanic	[ˈməʊtə mɪkænɪk]	sb who repairs cars	Automechaniker/in
to convert	[kənˈvɜːt]	to change, to transform	umbauen
currently	[ˈkʌrəntli]	at the moment	zur Zeit, momentan
off piste	[ˌɒf ˈpiːst]	away from conventional paths	jenseits ausgetretener Pfade
ski instructor	[ˈskiː ɪnstrʌktə]	sb who teaches people how to ski	Skilehrer/in
bush	[bʊʃ]	Australian term for land outside main towns	Busch
to get pregnant	[ˌget ˈpregnənt]	*n* pregnancy	schwanger werden

page 171

globetrotting	[ˈgləʊbtrɒtɪŋ]	regular travel to different parts of the world	Weltenbummeln, Weltreise(n)
whenever	[wenˈevə]	e.g. I go running whenever I can.	immer wenn, wann immer
diverse	[daɪˈvɜːs]	varied	vielfältig
on the road	[ɒn ðə ˈrəʊd]	travelling	unterwegs
nursing	[ˈnɜːsɪŋ]	the job performed by nurses	Krankenpflege
to busk	[bʌsk]	to perform music on the street for money	Straßenmusik machen
to sing along	[ˌsɪŋ əˈlɒŋ]	to sing with others	mitsingen
impossible	[ɪmˈpɒsəbl]	<> possible	unmöglich
up close	[ˌʌp ˈkləʊs]	near sth	aus nächster Nähe

Chronological word list

to **rob** sb	[rɒb]	to steal sth from sb	jdn bestehlen
to **shake** with **fear**	[ʃeɪk wɪð ˈfɪə]	to be extremely scared	vor Angst zittern
inequality	[ˌɪnɪˈkwɒləti]	<> equality	Ungleichheit
crime	[kraɪm]	*phr* to commit a crime	Verbrechen, Kriminalität
eccentric	[ɪkˈsentrɪk]	unusual and slightly crazy	exzentrisch
wide open spaces *pl*	[waɪd ˌəʊpən ˈspeɪsɪz]	large areas not covered by housing, etc.	weites Land
harsh	[hɑːʃ]	*phr* harsh climate	rau
to **attract**	[əˈtrækt]	*n* attraction	anziehen, anlocken
to **head east**	[ˌhed ˈiːst]	to go east	gen Osten aufbrechen
flexible	[ˈfleksəbl]	happy to change	flexibel
to **set off**	[ˌset ˈɒf]	to start a journey	losfahren
apprenticeship	[əˈprentɪʃɪp]	traineeship	Lehre, Ausbildung
freedom	[ˈfriːdəm]	*adj* free	Freiheit
to **widen**	[ˈwaɪdn]	to extend	erweitern
to **settle into** sth	[ˈsetl ɪntə]	to become comfortable in/with sth	sich in etw einrichten
health care	[ˈhelθ keə]	*phr* health care system	Gesundheitswesen
health insurance	[ˈhelθ ɪnʃʊərəns]	type of insurance one needs to get medical care	Krankenversicherung
crocodile	[ˈkrɒkədaɪl]	a large reptile with long jaws	Krokodil
snake	[sneɪk]	a long thin reptile with no legs	Schlange
shark	[ʃɑːk]	a large fish with sharp teeth	Hai
mechanical failure	[mɪˌkænɪkl ˈfeɪljə]	when sth stops working	technisches Versagen, Motorschaden
to **break down**	[ˌbreɪk ˈdaʊn]	e.g. Our car broke down right on the motorway.	eine Panne haben
It's just as well that …	[ɪts ˌdʒʌst əz ˈwel ðət]	it's good that …	Da ist es gut, dass …

page 173

proxy	[ˈprɒksi]	representative	Stellvertreter/in, stellvertretend
broadcast	[ˈbrɔːdkɑːst]	a radio or television programme	Sendung, Übertragung, Ausstrahlung
Congratulations! *pl*	[kənˌgrætʃʊˈleɪʃnz]	*v* to congratulate	Herzlichen Glückwunsch!
wage	[weɪdʒ]	pay	Lohn
credit	[ˈkredɪt]	point you get instead of money	Guthabenpunkt
His heart missed a beat.	[hɪz ˌhɑːt mɪst ə ˈbiːt]	His heart skipped a beat.	Dies ließ ihm sein Herz höher schlagen.
universal	[ˌjuːnɪˈvɜːsl]	general	allgemein, universell
to **take up**	[ˌteɪk ˈʌp]	*phr* to take up a lot of space	*(Platz, Raum)* einnehmen
to **reply**	[rɪˈplaɪ]	to answer	antworten, entgegnen
trial period	[ˌtraɪəl ˈpɪəriəd]	*phr* to be on a trial period	Probezeit
permanent	[ˈpɜːmənənt]	<> temporary	dauerhaft, unbefristet
to **approach**	[əˈprəʊtʃ]	to get closer to	sich nähern
skyscraper	[ˈskaɪskreɪpə]	tall building	Wolkenkratzer
storey	[ˈstɔːri]	floor	Stockwerk
talkative	[ˈtɔːkətɪv]	chatty	gesprächig
chatty	[ˈtʃæti]	always happy to chat	geschwätzig
confusing	[kənˈfjuːzɪŋ]	*n* confusion	verwirrend

page 174

to **step out of** sth	[ˌstep ˈaʊt əv]	to get out of sth	aus etw steigen, aus etw treten
cheerful	[ˈtʃɪəfl]	<> sad	fröhlich
to **zoom off**	[ˌzuːm ˈɒf]	to leave quickly	wegsausen
identical	[aɪˈdentɪkl]	the same	identisch
robotic	[rəʊˈbɒtɪk]	*n* robot	Roboter-
to **lose sight of** sth	[ˌluːz ˈsaɪt əv]	to forget about sth	etw aus den Augen verlieren
to **adjust**	[əˈdʒʌst]	*adj* adjustable	einstellen, justieren
to **shine**	[ʃaɪn]	to glow	scheinen
breeze	[briːz]	light wind	Brise, (leichter) Wind
eager(ly)	[ˈiːgə]	wanting to do or have sth	eifrig, ungeduldig
unlike sth	[ˌʌnˈlaɪk]	different from sth	anders als etw
dome	[dəʊm]	a spherical roof of a building	Kuppel
home town	[ˌhəʊm ˈtaʊn]	the town sb is from or lives in	Heimatstadt
rooftop garden	[ˌruːftɒp ˈgɑːdn]	garden on the roof of a building	Dachgarten
to **pass** sb	[pɑːs]	to go past sb	jdn überholen, an jdm vorbeigehen
old-fashioned	[ˌəʊldˈfæʃənd]	<> modern	altmodisch
translator	[trænsˈleɪtə]	*v* to translate	Übersetzer/in
to **beat**	[biːt]	*n* heartbeat	schlagen, pochen
bench	[bentʃ]	e.g. We sat on a bench in the park.	Bank
contented(ly)	[kənˈtentɪd]	happy (happily)	zufrieden, wunschlos glücklich
paper plate	[ˈpeɪpə pleɪt]	plate made of cardboard	Pappteller
fork	[fɔːk]	*phr* knives and forks	Gabel
gardening tool	[ˈgɑːdnɪŋ tuːl]	tools for garden work	Gartengerät
gardener	[ˈgɑːdnə]	sb who works in a garden	Gärtner/in
grass	[grɑːs]	e.g. Lawn tennis is played on grass.	Gras
to **walk by**	[ˌwɔːk ˈbaɪ]	to pass by	vorbeilaufen, vorübergehen
thrill	[θrɪl]	feeling of excitement	Nervenkitzel, Kick
middle-aged	[ˌmɪdlˈeɪdʒd]	neither young nor old	mittleren Alters
authentic	[ɔːˈθentɪk]	real	echt, authentisch

page 175

prediction	[prɪˈdɪkʃn]	*v* to predict	Voraussage, Vorhersage
transport	[ˈtrænspɔːt]	*phr* means of transport	Verkehr
assignment	[əˈsaɪnmənt]	task	Aufgabe, Auftrag

page 176

contents	[ˈkɒntents]	e.g. On page three you find the table of contents.	Inhalt
to **turn to sb**	[ˈtɜːn tə]	to ask sb for advice	sich an jdn wenden
employment	[ɪmˈplɔɪmənt]	being employed	Beschäftigung, Anstellung
head of department	[ˌhed əv dɪˈpɑːtmənt]	sb who leads a part of a company	Abteilungsleiter/in
to **fit in**	[ˌfɪt ˈɪn]	to have a place in sth	hineinpassen
housekeeping issues *pl*	[ˈhaʊskiːpɪŋ ɪʃuːz]	anything to do with in-house procedures and regulations	Haushaltsfragen
security pass	[sɪˈkjʊərəti pɑːs]	e.g. I can't get into the lab – I forgot my security pass!	Firmenausweis
organization	[ˌɔːɡənaɪˈzeɪʃn]	business, firm	Unternehmen
to **recruit**	[rɪˈkruːt]	to employ	*(Personal)* einstellen
to **report to sb**	[rɪˈpɔːt tə]	to be under sb	jdm unterstehen
board of directors	[ˌbɔːd əv dəˈrektəz]	group of leaders of a company	Vorstand, Geschäftsführung
organizational chart	[ɔːɡənaɪˌzeɪʃənl ˈtʃɑːt]	chart showing the structure of a company	Organigramm
to **manufacture**	[ˌmænjuˈfæktʃə]	to produce	fertigen, herstellen
allocation	[ˌæləˈkeɪʃn]	*v* to allocate	Zuweisungs, Zuteilung
to **maintain**	[meɪnˈteɪn]	*n* maintenance	warten, instandhalten
to **upgrade**	[ˌʌpˈɡreɪd]	to install a newer version of sth	aktualisieren, auf den neuesten Stand bringen
finished product	[ˌfɪnɪʃt ˈprɒdʌkt]	end product	Endprodukt
to **supply**	[səˈplaɪ]	to deliver, to provide	liefern
to **store**	[stɔː]	to keep	lagern
Finance	[ˈfaɪnæns]	department in a company in charge of money	Finanzabteilung
Production (department)	[prəˈdʌkʃn]	department in a company in charge of making a product	Produktion(sabteilung)
Research & Development (R&D)	[rɪˌsɜːtʃ ən dɪˈveləpmənt]	department which makes products better or designs new ones	Forschung(s-) und Entwicklung(sabteilung)
distribution	[ˌdɪstrɪˈbjuːʃn]	*v* to distribute	Vertrieb, Auslieferung
Sales	[seɪlz]	*v* to sell	Verkauf(sabteilung)

page 177

day-to-day	[ˌdeɪ tə ˈdeɪ]	daily	laufend, tagtäglich
eventually	[ɪˈventʃuəli]	in the end	schließlich, am Ende
to **swap**	[swɒp]	to exchange	(die Seite) wechseln
to **settle in**	[ˈsetl ɪn]	to get used to a new place etc.	sich eingewöhnen
branch	[brɑːntʃ]	e.g. Where are all of the branches of the company based?	Niederlassung

page 178

industrial waste	[ɪnˈdʌstriəl weɪst]	waste produced by an industrial activity	Industriemüll
to **dump**	[dʌmp]	to dispose of waste illegally	*(Müll)* (wild) abkippen
risk	[rɪsk]	*adj* risky	Risiko
to **take a risk**	[ˌteɪk ə ˈrɪsk]	e.g. He took a huge risk investing in that company.	ein Risiko eingehen
wise	[waɪz]	clever	klug
risky	[ˈrɪski]	dangerous	gefährlich, riskant

page 179

phone-in	[ˈfəʊn ɪn]	TV or radio show which you can call on the phone to give your opinion	*Sendung mit Hörerbeteiligung per Telefon*
regarding	[rɪˈɡɑːdɪŋ]	with regards to	betreffend, bezüglich
A levels *pl BE*	[ˈeɪ levlz]	*AE* high school exams	Abitur
exhausted	[ɪɡˈzɔːstɪd]	*n* exhaustion	erschöpft
to **take time out**	[teɪk ˌtaɪm ˈaʊt]	e.g. I'm so stressed out, I have to take some time out.	sich freinehmen
to **make sense**	[meɪk ˈsens]	to be clear	vernünftig sein, einleuchten
walking holiday	[ˈwɔːkɪŋ hɒlədeɪ]	e.g. I went on a walking holiday in Cornwall last year.	Wanderurlaub
to **finalise**	[ˈfaɪnəlaɪz]	to add the last details to a plan or project	(endgültig) festlegen
to **confirm**	[kənˈfɜːm]	*n* confirmation	bestätigen
to **assume**	[əˈsjuːm]	to believe, to think	davon ausgehen, annehmen
senior management	[ˌsiːniə ˈmænɪdʒmənt]	people at the top of a company	Geschäftsleitung
to **separate**	[ˈsepəreɪt]	to divide	trennen, teilen
to **evaluate**	[ɪˈvæljueɪt]	to assess, to judge	beurteilen, bewerten
to **be free to do sth**	[bi ˈfriː tə duː]	to be allowed to do sth	etw (gern) tun dürfen
to **reimburse sb sth**	[ˌriːɪmˈbɜːs]	to pay sb back for sth	jdm etw erstatten
travel expenses *pl*	[ˈtrævl ɪkspensɪz]	costs of travel	Reisekosten

page 180

impression	[ɪmˈpreʃn]	*v* to impress	Eindruck

FURTHER READING

page 200

canned	[kænd]	Konserven-, in Dosen, konserviert
fresh(ly)	[freʃ]	frisch
recent	[ˈriːsnt]	aktuell
study	[ˈstʌdi]	Untersuchung, Studie
to **find out**	[ˌfaɪnd ˈaʊt]	herausfinden
case	[keɪs]	Fall
amount	[əˈmaʊnt]	Menge
minerals *pl*	[ˈmɪnərəlz]	Mineralien
can	[kæn]	(Konserven-)Dose
researcher	[rɪˈsɜːtʃə]	Forscher/in
to **test**	[test]	untersuchen, prüfen
dairy products *pl*	[ˈdeəri prɒdʌkts]	Milchprodukte
low in fat	[ˌləʊ ɪn ˈfæt]	fettarm
homemade	[ˌhəʊmˈmeɪd]	hausgemacht, selbstgemacht
stuff	[stʌf]	Sachen, Zeug
three times	[ˈθriː taɪmz]	dreimal
twice	[twaɪs]	zweimal
producer	[prəˈdjuːsə]	Produzent/in, Hersteller/in
bone	[bəʊn]	*(Fisch:)* Gräte
tuna fish	[ˈtjuːnə fɪʃ]	Thunfisch
salt water	[ˈsɔːlt wɔːtə]	Salzwasser
saturated fat	[ˌsætʃəreɪtɪd ˈfæt]	gesättigtes Fett
pea	[piː]	Erbse
third	[θɜːd]	Drittel
goodness	[ˈgʊdnəs]	wertvolle Inhaltsstoffe
to **prepare**	[prɪˈpeə]	*(Essen)* zubereiten
frozen	[ˈfrəʊzn]	Gefrier-, eingefroren

page 201

to **highlight**	[ˈhaɪlaɪt]	hervorheben
meaning	[ˈmiːnɪŋ]	Bedeutung
to **look sth up**	[ˌlʊk ˈʌp]	etw *(in einem Wörterbuch)* nachschlagen
nutritious	[njuˈtrɪʃəs]	nahrhaft, nährstoffreich
research	[rɪˈsɜːtʃ]	Forschung, Untersuchung(en)
to **feel bad about sth**	[ˌfiːl ˈbæd əbaʊt]	wegen etw ein schlechtes Gewissen haben
scientist	[ˈsaɪəntɪst]	(Natur-)Wissenschaftler/in
to **study sth**	[ˈstʌdi]	etw erforschen
report	[rɪˈpɔːt]	Bericht
sea fish	[ˈsiː fɪʃ]	Meeresfisch
however	[haʊˈevə]	dagegen, allerdings, jedoch

page 202

grade	[greɪd]	Note
recent	[ˈriːsnt]	aktuell
survey	[ˈsɜːveɪ]	Umfrage
likely	[ˈlaɪkli]	wahrscheinlich
to **study sth**	[ˈstʌdi]	etw untersuchen, etw erforschen
data *pl*	[ˈdeɪtə]	Daten
urban	[ˈɜːbən]	städtisch, Stadt-
suburban	[səˈbɜːbən]	Vorstadt-, am Stadtrand
rural	[ˈrʊərəl]	ländlich
acting society	[ˈæktɪŋ səsaɪəti]	Schauspiel-AG
connection	[kəˈnekʃn]	Verbindung
to **perform**	[pəˈfɔːm]	*(in einer Prüfung usw.)* abschneiden
successful	[səkˈsesfl]	erfolgreich
day-to-day	[ˌdeɪ tə ˈdeɪ]	laufend, tagtäglich
self-esteem	[ˌself ɪˈstiːm]	Selbstwertgefühl
determination	[dɪˌtɜːmɪˈneɪʃn]	Entschlossenheit
to **succeed**	[səkˈsiːd]	Erfolg haben, erfolgreich sein
to **enter higher education**	[entə ˌhaɪər edʒuˈkeɪʃn]	ein Studium beginnen
peers *pl*	[pɪəz]	Gleichaltrige, Schulkameraden
feeling	[ˈfiːlɪŋ]	Gefühl, Ansicht
to **encourage**	[ɪnˈkʌrɪdʒ]	ermutigen, fördern
focused	[ˈfəʊkəst]	zielstrebig
ability	[əˈbɪləti]	Fähigkeit
to **deal with sth**	[ˈdiːl wɪð]	mit etw umgehen
headline	[ˈhedlaɪn]	Überschrift

page 203

report	[rɪˈpɔːt]	Bericht
competitive sport	[kəmˈpetətɪv spɔːt]	Wettkampfsport
will-power	[ˈwɪl paʊə]	Willenskraft
mark	[mɑːk]	Note
score	[skɔː]	Punktzahl, Ergebnis
competence	[ˈkɒmpɪtəns]	Kompetenz
football pitch	[ˈfʊtbɔːl pɪtʃ]	Fußballfeld, Fußballplatz
serious	[ˈsɪəriəs]	ernst, ernsthaft
background	[ˈbækgraʊnd]	Hintergrund
to **invite sb to do sth**	[ɪnˈvaɪt]	jdn auffordern, etw zu tun
to **join**	[dʒɔɪn]	sich dazugesellen
member	[ˈmembə]	Mitglied
opposing team	[əˌpəʊzɪŋ ˈtiːm]	gegnerische Mannschaft
in the sunshine	[ɪn ðə ˈsʌnʃaɪn]	in der Sonne
goal post	[ˈgəʊl pəʊst]	Torpfosten
net	[net]	Netz

page 204

to **study sth**	[ˈstʌdi]	sich mit etw (eingehend) beschäftigen
real-life	[ˌrɪəl ˈlaɪf]	aus dem wirklichen Leben
to **pick**	[pɪk]	auswählen
to **warm with pride**	[ˌwɔː wɪð ˈpraɪd]	von Stolz erfüllt werden
to **run**	[rʌn]	*(Betrieb)* führen, betreiben
admirable	[ˈædmrəbl]	bewundernswert
to **put**	[pʊt]	formulieren
to **swing the competition in sb's favour**	[ˌswɪŋ ðə kɒmpəˌtɪʃn ɪn sʌmbədiz ˈfeɪvə]	das Pendel zu jds Gunsten umschlagen lassen
power	[ˈpaʊə]	Kraft, Energie
infectious enthusiasm	[ɪnˌfekʃəs ɪnˈθjuːziæzəm]	ansteckende Begeisterung
to **matter**	[ˈmætə]	wichtig sein, von Belang sein
ego	[ˈiːgəʊ]	Ego
aside	[əˈsaɪd]	beiseite, abgesehen von
to **be thrilled**	[bi ˈθrɪld]	sich wahnsinnig freuen
kindness	[ˈkaɪndnəs]	Liebenswürdigkeit
grand	[grænd]	großartig
to **encounter sth**	[ɪnˈkaʊntə]	auf etw treffen
assignment	[əˈsaɪnmənt]	Aufgabe, Auftrag

page 205

especially	[ɪˈspeʃəli]	besonders, insbesondere
feeling	[ˈfiːlɪŋ]	Ansicht, Meinung
subject	[ˈsʌbdʒɪkt]	Gegenstand, Thema
Yours sincerely	[ˌjɔːz sɪnˈsɪəli]	Mit freundlichen Grüßen

page 206

to **name sb sth**	[neɪm]	jdn zu etw ernennen
ceremony	[ˈserəməni]	Feier, Zeremonie
to **take up**	[ˌteɪk ˈʌp]	*(Posten)* antreten
bright	[braɪt]	*(Zukunft:)* aussichtsreich
purpose	[ˈpɜːpəs]	Ziel, Zweck
originally	[əˈrɪdʒənəli]	ursprünglich
to **shoot**	[ʃuːt]	schießen
valley	[ˈvæli]	Tal
to **speak out against sb**	[ˌspiːk ˈaʊt əgenst]	sich (öffentlich) gegen jdn aussprechen, jdn kritisieren
secretary-general	[ˌsekrətri ˈdʒenrəl]	Generalsekretär/in
statement	[ˈsteɪtmənt]	(öffentliche) Erklärung
just	[dʒʌst]	gerecht
committed	[kəˈmɪtɪd]	engagiert
generous	[ˈdʒenərəs]	großzügig
to **invent**	[ɪnˈvent]	erfinden
explosive	[ɪkˈspləʊsɪv]	Sprengstoff
movement	[ˈmuːvmənt]	Bewegung
to **found**	[faʊnd]	gründen

second world war	[ˌsekənd ˌwɜːld ˈwɔː]	Zweiter Weltkrieg

page 207

equality	[ɪˈkwɒləti]	Gleichberechtigung
fear	[fɪə]	Angst
ruler	[ˈruːlə]	Herrscher/in
to **take action**	[ˌteɪk ˈækʃn]	etwas unternehmen
political	[pəˈlɪtɪkl]	politisch
for good	[fə ˈgʊd]	*hier:* zum Allgemeinwohl
to **move forward**	[ˌmuːv ˈfɔːwəd]	vorankommen
leader	[ˈliːdə]	Führer/in
bomb	[bɒm]	Bombe
bullet	[ˈbʊlɪt]	(Gewehr-)Kugel
to **succeed**	[səkˈsiːd]	Erfolg haben, erfolgreich sein
to **attempt**	[əˈtempt]	versuchen

page 208

prosthetic arm	[prɒsˌθetɪk ˈɑːm]	Armprothese
inventor	[ɪnˈventə]	Erfinder/in
lower arm	[ˌləʊər ˈɑːm]	Unterarm
barely	[ˈbeəli]	kaum
decade	[ˈdekeɪd]	Jahrzehnt
bionic	[baɪˈɒnɪk]	bionisch
limbs *pl*	[lɪmz]	Gliedmaßen, Extremitäten
to **experiment**	[ɪkˈsperɪmənt]	experimentieren
to **feature sth**	[ˈfiːtʃə]	etw (*Merkmal usw.*) aufweisen
pattern	[ˈpætn]	Muster
the key	[ðə ˈkiː]	das Entscheidende
to **bully**	[ˈbʊli]	schikanieren, mobben
to **assemble**	[əˈsembl]	montieren, zusammenbauen
solar-powered air-conditioning	[səʊləˌpaʊəd ˈeə kəndɪʃnɪŋ]	Solar-Klimaanlage
narrow temperature range	[ˌnærəʊ ˈtemprətʃə reɪndʒ]	schmaler Temperaturbereich
along with sb	[əˈlɒŋ wɪð]	zusammen mit jdm
to **charge sb for sth**	[ˈtʃɑːdʒ fə]	von jdm Geld für etw verlangen
to **unwrap sth**	[ʌnˈræp]	etw auspacken
to **manage**	[ˈmænɪdʒ]	zurechtkommen
to **volunteer**	[ˌvɒlənˈtɪə]	sich bereit erklären
to **fall in love with sb/sth**	[ˌfɔːl ɪn ˈlʌv wɪð]	sich in jdn/etw verlieben

page 209

artificial	[ˌɑːtɪˈfɪʃl]	künstlich
to **pick on sb**	[ˈpɪk ɒn]	jdn drangsalieren
donation	[dəʊˈneɪʃn]	Spende
to **line sth with sth**	[laɪn]	etw mit etw auskleiden, etw mit etw tapezieren
for free	[fə ˈfriː]	umsonst, kostenlos
self-confident	[ˌself ˈkɒnfɪdənt]	selbstbewusst

page 210

counselling service	[ˌkaʊnsəlɪŋ ˈsɜːvɪs]	Beratung, Beratungsdienst
sadness	[ˈsædnəs]	Traurigkeit
anxiety	[æŋˈzaɪəti]	Angst
to **own**	[əʊn]	besitzen
to **take one's mind off sth**	[ˌteɪk wʌnz ˈmaɪnd ɒf]	jdn von etw ablenken
to **buy into sth**	[!baɪ ɪntə]	an etw glauben
persona	[pəˈsəʊnə]	Ich, Selbst
high	[haɪ]	Hochstimmung, Rausch
worthless	[ˈwɜːθləs]	wertlos
to **cheer sb up**	[ˌtʃɪər ˈʌp]	jdn aufmuntern
to **beg sb to do sth**	[beg]	jdn anflehen, etw zu tun
debt	[det]	Schulden
to **get into debt**	[ˌget ɪntə ˈdet]	sich verschulden
threat	[θret]	Gefahr, Bedrohung
to **go to court**	[ˌgəʊ tə ˈkɔːt]	vor Gericht gehen, prozessieren
to **manage**	[ˈmænɪdʒ]	es schaffen
to **acknowledge**	[əkˈnɒlɪdʒ]	anerkennen
recovery	[rɪˈkʌvəri]	Genesung
to **advise**	[ədˈvaɪz]	raten, Rat erteilen
to **pound**	[paʊnd]	hämmern, stampfen
fraction	[ˈfrækʃn]	Bruchteil
odd	[ɒd]	gelegentlich
weak	[wiːk]	schwach
spending	[ˈspendɪŋ]	Ausgaben
sth is firmly under control	[ɪz ˌfɜːmli ʌndə kənˈtrəʊl]	jd hat etw fest im Griff

page 211

loan	[ləʊn]	Darlehen, Kredit
to **feel bad about sth**	[ˌfiːl ˈbæd əbaʊt]	wegen etw ein schlechtes Gewissen haben
stressed out	[ˌstrest ˈaʊt]	gestresst
to **swap sth for sth**	[swɒp]	etw gegen etw eintauschen
membership card	[ˈmembəʃɪp kɑːd]	Mietgliedskarte
to **get rid of sth**	[get ˈrɪd əv]	etw loswerden
short-term	[ˌʃɔːtˈtɜːm]	kurzfristig
to **apply for sth**	[əˈplaɪ fə]	etw beantragen

page 212

recent	[ˈriːsnt]	aktuell
disagreement	[ˌdɪsəˈgriːmənt]	Meinungsverschiedenheit
romance	[rəʊˈmæns]	Liebesaffäre, Romanze
pay rise	[ˈpeɪ raɪz]	Lohnerhöhung
sick day	[sɪk ˈdeɪ]	Krankentag
minor	[ˈmaɪnə]	kleinere/r/s, unbedeutend
overtime	[ˈəʊvətaɪm]	Überstunden
chief executive	[ˌtʃiːf ɪgˈzekjətɪv]	Geschäftsführer/in
to **commission sth**	[kəˈmɪʃn]	etw in Auftrag geben
ups and downs *pl*	[ˌʌps ən ˈdaʊnz]	Höhen und Tiefen
revealing	[rɪˈviːlɪŋ]	aufschlussreich
to **ensure**	[ɪnˈʃʊə]	dafür sorgen
to **seek**	[siːk]	suchen
surroundings *pl*	[səˈraʊndɪŋz]	Umgebung, Umfeld
fellow colleague	[ˌfeləʊ ˈkɒliːg]	Kollege/-in
job satisfaction	[ˈdʒɒb sætɪsfækʃn]	Zufriedenheit im Beruf
to **suit sb**	[suːt]	zu jdm passen
to **enter**	[ˈentə]	betreten
to **aim for sth**	[ˈeɪm fə]	etw anstreben
promotion	[prəˈməʊʃn]	Beförderung

page 213

dictionary entry	[ˈdɪkʃənri entri]	Stichwort, Wörterbucheintrag
beside	[bɪˈsaɪd]	neben
to **be in charge of sb**	[bi ɪn ˈtʃɑːdʒ əv]	jdm vorgesetzt sein
rank	[ræŋk]	Stellung, Rang
outline	[ˈaʊtlaɪn]	Übersicht, Stichpunkte
findings *pl*	[ˈfaɪndɪŋz]	Ergebnisse
to **occur**	[əˈkɜː]	vorkommen
further training	[ˌfɜːðəˈtreɪnɪŋ]	Fortbildung
to **indicate**	[ˈɪndɪkeɪt]	angeben, zu verstehen geben
to **be the case**	[bi ðə ˈkeɪs]	der Fall sein
nowadays	[ˈnaʊədeɪz]	heute, heutzutage

page 214

to **publish**	[ˈpʌblɪʃ]	veröffentlichen, publizieren
to **reflect**	[rɪˈflekt]	widerspiegeln
readership	[ˈriːdəʃɪp]	Leser, Leserschaft
news agency	[ˈnjuːz eɪdʒənsi]	Nachrichtenagentur
press release	[ˈpres rɪliːs]	Presseerklärung
press conference	[ˈpres kɒnfərəns]	Pressekonferenz
trusted contact	[ˌtrʌstɪd ˈkɒntækt]	vertrauenswürdige Kontaktperson
confidential	[ˌkɒnfɪˈdenʃl]	vertraulich, geheim
potential	[pəˈtenʃl]	potentiell
to **select**	[sɪˈlekt]	auswählen
news agenda	[ˈnjuːz ədʒendə]	Schwerpunkte der Berichterstattung

Chronological word list

ethos	[ˈiːθɒs]	Gesinnung, Ethos
owner	[ˈəʊnə]	Inhaber/in, Besitzer/in
editor	[ˈedɪtə]	Herausgeber/in
senior	[ˈsiːniə]	leitende/r
to **make the headlines**	[ˌmeɪk ðə ˈhedlaɪnz]	Schlagzeilen machen
breaking news	[ˌbreɪkɪŋ ˈnjuːz]	Eilmeldung(en)
attack	[əˈtæk]	Angriff
competitive	[kəmˈpetətɪv]	umkämpft
to **affect sb**	[əˈfekt]	jdn betreffen
casualties *pl*	[ˈkæʒuəltiz]	Opfer, Tote und Verletzte
hoax bomb alert	[ˌhəʊks ˈbɒm əlɜːt]	vorgetäuschter Bombenalarm
continuity	[ˌkɒntɪnˈjuːəti]	Dauer, Kontinuität
ongoing	[ˈɒngəʊɪŋ]	laufend, fortdauernd
event	[ɪˈvent]	Ereignis
simplicity	[sɪmˈplɪsəti]	Einfachheit
lottery win	[ˈlɒtəri wɪn]	Lottogewinn
long-term court case	[lɒŋ ˌtɜːm ˈkɔːt keɪs]	Gerichtsverfahren, das sich lange hinzieht
tabloid	[ˈtæblɔɪd]	Boulevardblatt
broadsheet	[ˈbrɔːdʃiːt]	(seriöse) Tageszeitung

page 215

predictability	[prəˌdɪktəˈbɪləti]	Vorhersehbarkeit
eventful	[ɪˈventfl]	ereignisreich
to **cover sth**	[ˈkʌvə]	über etw berichten
to **pass off**	[ˌpɑːs ˈɒf]	*(Ereignis)* verlaufen
unexpectedness	[ˌʌnɪkˈspektɪdnəs]	Unvermutetheit
negativity	[negəˈtɪvəti]	Negativität
heroic	[həˈrəʊɪk]	heldenhaft
member of the general public	[ˌmembər əv ðə ˌdʒenrəl ˈpʌblɪk]	(einfache/r) Bürger/in
angle	[ˈæŋgl]	(journalistischer) Ansatz
meaningfulness	[ˈmiːnɪŋflnəs]	Wichtigkeit, Aussagekraft
availability	[əˌveɪləˈbɪləti]	Verfügbarkeit
partly	[ˈpɑːtli]	zum Teil, teilweise
decline	[dɪˈklaɪn]	Rückgang
to **make an impact on sth**	[ˌmeɪk ən ˈɪmpækt ɒn]	sich auf etw auswirken
to **evaluate**	[ɪˈvæljueɪt]	beurteilen, bewerten
score	[skɔː]	Punktzahl
to **turn sth into sth**	[ˈtɜːn ɪntə]	etw zu etw machen, etw zu etw umwandeln
abandoned	[əˈbændnd]	verlassen, stillgelegt
to **predict**	[prɪˈdɪkt]	vorhersagen
to **hit sth**	[hɪt]	auf etw treffen
civilian	[səˈvɪliən]	Zivilist/in
drone	[drəʊn]	Drohne
to **disappear**	[ˌdɪsəˈpɪə]	verschwinden

page 216

to **merge**	[mɜːdʒ]	zusammenfügen
exit	[ˈeksɪt]	Abgang, Austritt
referendum	[ˌrefəˈrendəm]	Volksentscheid
vote	[vəʊt]	Abstimmung
voting age	[ˈvəʊtɪŋ eɪdʒ]	Wahlalter
turnout	[ˈtɜːnaʊt]	Wahlbeteiligung
to **negotiate**	[nɪˈgəʊʃieɪt]	verhandeln
process	[ˈprəʊses]	Verfahren
negotiation	[nɪˌgəʊʃiˈeɪʃn]	Verhandlung
terms *pl*	[tɜːmz]	Bedingungen
treaty	[ˈtriːti]	Vertrag, Abkommen
decision-making	[dɪˈsɪʒn meɪkɪŋ]	Entscheidungsfindung
to **charge**	[tʃɑːdʒ]	*(Geld)* verlangen
membership fees *pl*	[ˈmembəʃɪp fiːz]	Mitgliedsbeiträge
shared	[ʃeəd]	gemeinsam
supporter	[səˈpɔːtə]	Befürworter/in
principle	[ˈprɪnsəpl]	Grundsatz, Prinzip
membership	[ˈmembəʃɪp]	Mitgliedschaft
free movement	[ˌfriː ˈmuːvmənt]	Freizügigkeit
to **campaign for sth**	[kæmˈpeɪn fə]	für etw eintreten, für etw kämpfen
to **argue**	[ˈɑːgjuː]	argumentieren
flow	[fləʊ]	Strom, Zustrom
to **fuel**	[ˈfjuːəl]	antreiben, anheizen
economic growth	[iːkəˌnɒmɪk ˈgrəʊθ]	Wirtschaftswachstum
public services *pl*	[ˌpʌblɪk ˈsɜːvɪsɪz]	öffentliche Dienstleistungen
status	[ˈsteɪtəs]	Ansehen
to **be in favour of sth**	[bi ɪn ˈfeɪvər əv]	etw befürworten, für etw sein

page 217

breakdown	[ˈbreɪkdaʊn]	Verteilung, Aufschlüsselung
campaigner	[kæmˈpeɪnə]	Wahlkämpfer/in, Aktivist/in
proportion	[prəˈpɔːʃn]	Anteil
deal	[diːl]	Abmachung
incorrect	[ɪnkəˈrekt]	falsch, unzutreffend

page 218

bonfire	[ˈbɒnfaɪə]	Freudenfeuer
formerly	[ˈfɔːməli]	ehemals
fireworks *pl*	[ˈfaɪəwɜːks]	Feuerwerk
straw dummy	[ˌstrɔː ˈdʌmi]	Strohpuppe
contemporary	[kənˈtemprəri]	zeitgenössisch, heutig
figure	[ˈfɪgə]	Figur
to **drive away evil spirits**	[draɪv əˈweɪ ˌiːvɪl ˈspɪrɪts]	böse Geister vertreiben
sacrifice	[ˈsækrɪfaɪs]	Opfer, Opferung
effigy	[ˈefɪdʒi]	Bildnis
passer-by	[ˈpɑːsə baɪ]	Passant/in
explosive	[ɪkˈspləʊsɪv]	Sprengstoff
plotter	[ˈplɒtə]	Verschwörer/in
barrel	[ˈbærəl]	Fass
soaked	[səʊkt]	getränkt
tar	[tɑː]	Teer
to **set sth alight**	[ˌset əˈlaɪt]	etw anzünden
distinctly	[dɪˈstɪŋktli]	ausgesprochen
local flavour	[ˌləʊkl ˈfleɪvə]	Lokalkolorit, lokaler Bezug
to **stretch back for generations**	[stretʃ ˌbæk fə dʒenəˈreɪʃnz]	sich um Generationen zurückerstrecken
flaming	[ˈfleɪmɪŋ]	lodernd
procession	[prəˈseʃn]	Umzug, Prozession
costumed	[ˈkɒstjuːmd]	kostümiert, in Kostümen
to **mark**	[mɑːk]	*(Gedenktag usw.)* begehen
bang	[bæŋ]	Knall
to **attract**	[əˈtrækt]	anziehen, anlocken
to **explode sth**	[ɪkˈspləʊd]	etw zünden, etw in die Luft jagen
to **fail**	[feɪl]	scheitern
to **execute**	[ˈeksɪkjuːt]	hinrichten
anonymous	[əˈnɒnɪməs]	anonym
dystopian (novel)	[dɪsˈtəʊpiən]	*(Roman usw.:)* Schreckens-vision
in recent years	[ɪn ˈriːsnt jɪəz]	in den letzten Jahren
supporter	[səˈpɔːtə]	Anhänger/in, Vertreter/in
Capitalist	[ˈkæpɪtəlɪst]	kapitalistisch
to **take to the streets**	[ˌteɪk tə ðə ˈstriːts]	auf die Straße gehen
oppression	[əˈpreʃn]	Unterdrückung

page 219

brave	[breɪv]	mutig
firework display	[ˈfaɪəwɜːk dɪspleɪ]	Feuerwerk
from … onwards	[ˈfrəm ɒnwədz]	seit …
to **represent**	[ˌreprɪˈzent]	darstellen, wiedergeben

page 220

campaigner	[kæmˈpeɪnə]	Aktivist/in
industrial estate	[ɪnˌdʌstriəl ɪˈsteɪt]	Gewerbegebiet
desperate	[ˈdespərət]	verzweifelt
to **struggle to do sth**	[ˈstrʌgl tə duː]	Mühe haben, etw zu tun
sb is diagnosed with sth	[ɪz ˈdaɪəgnəʊzd wɪð]	bei jdm wird etw *(Krankheit)* festgestellt
chronic pain condition	[ˌkrɒnɪk ˈpeɪn kəndɪʃn]	chronische Schmerz-erkrankung

care	[keə]	Betreuung
overnight	[ˌəʊvəˈnaɪt]	über Nacht
to be reduced to nothing	[bi rɪˌdjuːst tə ˈnʌθɪŋ]	zunichte gemacht werden
founder	[ˈfaʊndə]	Gründer/in
surplus produce	[ˌsɜːpləs ˈprɒdjuːs]	überschüssige Lebensmittel
to obtain	[əbˈteɪn]	erhalten, bekommen
central storage	[ˌsentrəl ˈstɔːrɪdʒ]	Zentrallager
otherwise	[ˈʌðəwaɪz]	sonst
to expand	[ɪkˈspænd]	ausweiten
investigation	[ɪnˌvestɪˈgeɪʃn]	Untersuchung, Recherche
edible	[ˈedəbl]	essbar

page 221

to manage	[ˈmænɪdʒ]	zurechtkommen
effort	[ˈefət]	Mühe(n), Anstrengung(en)
to outline	[ˈaʊtlaɪn]	skizzieren, umreißen

page 222

to switch to sth	[ˈswɪtʃ tə]	auf etw umsteigen
motion technology	[ˈməʊʃn teknɒlədʒi]	Bewegungstechnik
engineering	[ˌendʒɪˈnɪərɪŋ]	Maschinenbau
senior staffer	[ˌsiːniə ˈstɑːfə]	leitende/r Angestellte/r
to be considered sth	[bi kənˈsɪdəd]	als etw gelten, als etw angesehen werden
corporate	[ˈkɔːpərət]	Unternehmens-
to adopt sth	[əˈdɒpt]	etw übernehmen
exclusively	[ɪkˈskluːsɪvli]	ausschließlich
cultural shift	[ˌkʌltʃərəl ˈʃɪft]	Kulturwandel
in their primary years	[ɪn ðeə ˌpraɪmri ˈjɪəz]	im Grundschulalter
we have a revolt on our hands	[wiː həv ə rɪˈvəʊlt ɒn aʊə hændz]	eine Revolte kommt auf uns zu
primarily	[praɪˈmerəli]	hauptsächlich, vorrangig
executive	[ɪgˈzekjətɪv]	Manager/in
even so	[ˈiːvn səʊ]	aber dennoch
entire	[ɪnˈtaɪə]	ganze/r/s, vollständig
compassion	[kəmˈpæʃn]	Mitgefühl
peers *pl*	[pɪəz]	Kollegen
alike	[əˈlaɪk]	ebenso, gleichermaßen
fully	[ˈfʊli]	vollständig, völlig
awkwardness	[ˈɔːkwədnəs]	Verlegenheit
plant tour	[ˈplɑːnt tʊə]	Betriebsbesichtigung
to cross a wall	[ˌkrɒs ə ˈwɔːl]	eine Mauer überqueren

page 223

perceived	[pəˈsiːvd]	(individuell) empfunden
language barrier	[ˈlæŋgwɪdʒ bæriə]	Sprachbarriere
input	[ˈɪnpʊt]	Beitrag
to lose face	[ˌluːz ˈfeɪs]	das Gesicht verlieren
accidentally	[ˌæksɪˈdentəli]	aus Versehen
to be conscious of sth	[bi ˈkɒnʃəs əv]	sich einer Sache bewusst sein
requirement	[rɪˈkwaɪəmənt]	Bestimmung, Anforderung
to affect sb	[əˈfekt]	jdn betreffen

page 224

portfolio	[pɔːtˈfəʊliəʊ]	Mappe
rather	[ˈrɑːðə]	eher, vielmehr
Here's another go at the same thing.	[hɪəz ənʌðə ˌgəʊ ət ðə ˌseɪm ˈθɪŋ]	Ich versuch's nochmal.
to pass sth on	[ˌpɑːs ˈɒn]	etw weitersagen
graphic art	[ˌgræfɪk ˈɑːt]	Malerei und Grafik
nothing whatsoever	[ˌnʌθɪŋ wɒtsəʊˈevə]	überhaupt nichts
to carry out a function	[kæri ˌaʊt ə ˈfʌŋkʃn]	eine Funktion wahrnehmen
to detach	[dɪˈtætʃ]	ablösen
to tip	[tɪp]	kippen
galaxy	[ˈgæləksi]	*hier:* Unmenge
to redefine	[ˌriːdɪˈfaɪn]	neu definieren
in relation to sth	[ɪn rɪˈleɪʃn tə]	in Bezug auf etw
fountain	[ˈfaʊntən]	Brunnen
to sign sth sth	[saɪn]	etw mit etw signieren
to reject	[rɪˈdʒekt]	ablehnen
to select	[sɪˈlekt]	auswählen
to set aside	[set əˈsaɪd]	*(Zeit)* reservieren
to carry out	[ˌkæri ˈaʊt]	*(Tätigkeit)* ausführen
obviously	[ˈɒbviəsli]	vordergründig
to transform	[trænsˈfɔːm]	verwandeln
painted mark	[ˌpeɪntɪd ˈmɑːk]	Mal, Zeichnung
timeless	[ˈtaɪmləs]	zeitlos
to head out	[ˌhed ˈaʊt]	losziehen
demanding	[dɪˈmɑːndɪŋ]	anspruchsvoll
sequence of execution	[ˌsiːkwəns əv ˌeksɪˈkjuːʃn]	Ausführungsreihenfolge
to work sth out	[ˌwɜːk ˈaʊt]	etw erarbeiten
in detail	[ɪn ˈdiːteɪl]	genau, detailliert
in advance	[ɪn ədˈvɑːns]	im Voraus
enterprise	[ˈentəpraɪz]	Unternehmen, Unterfangen

page 225

to consider sth sth	[kənˈsɪdəz]	etw für etw halten
similarity	[ˌsɪməˈlærəti]	Ähnlichkeit

page 226

in sign of sth	[ɪn ˈsaɪn əv]	im Zeichen von etw
policy shift	[ˈpɒləsi ʃɪft]	Politikwandel
to pick sb up	[ˌpɪk ˈʌp]	jdn festnehmen
ahead of	[əˈhed əv]	vor, im Vorfeld von
imminent	[ˈɪmɪnənt]	bevorstehend
to set	[set]	festsetzen, festlegen
rushed	[rʌʃt]	übereilt
removal	[rɪˈmuːvl]	Ausweisung
stark example	[ˌstɑːk ɪgˈzɑːmpl]	krasses Beispiel
push	[pʊʃ]	Vorstoß
previously	[ˈpriːviəsli]	zuvor, bislang
substantially	[səbˈstænʃəli]	wesentlich, erheblich
to sustain	[səˈsteɪn]	halten, aufrechterhalten
considerable	[kənˈsɪdərəbl]	beträchtlich, erheblich
anecdotal evidence	[ænɪkˌdəʊtl ˈevɪdəns]	vereinzelte Anhaltspunkte
Immigration and Customs Enforcement	[ɪmɪˌgreɪʃnz ən ˈkʌstəmz ɪnfɔːsmnt]	*US-Behörde für Einwanderung und Zoll*
agent	[ˈeɪdʒənt]	Beamte/r
without a (criminal) record	[wɪðˈaʊt ə ˈrekɔːd]	nicht vorbestraft
to be regarded as sth	[bi rɪˈgɑːdɪd əz]	als etw gelten
of low priority	[əv ˌləʊ praɪˈɒrəti]	unwichtig, unbedeutend
to inflict harm	[ɪnˌflɪkt ˈhɑːm]	Schaden zufügen
to fall into a category	[ˌfɔːl ɪntu ə ˈkætəgəri]	zu einer Kategorie gehören
to indicate	[ˈɪndɪkeɪt]	zu verstehen geben
to grant permission	[ˌgrɑːnt pəˈmɪʃn]	Erlaubnis erteilen
to present sb with a choice	[prɪˌzent wɪð ə ˈtʃɔɪs]	jdn vor die Wahl stellen
to abandon sb	[əˈbændən]	jdn verlassen
potentially	[pəˈtenʃəli]	potentiell
to detain sb	[dɪˈteɪn]	jdn inhaftieren
spokesman	[ˈspəʊksmən]	Sprecher
to review	[rɪˈvjuː]	prüfen
case	[keɪs]	Fall
court	[kɔːt]	Gericht
legal basis	[ˌliːgl ˈbeɪsɪz]	Rechtsgrundlage
to pose sth with sb	[pəʊz]	jdn vor etw stellen
to order sb removed	[ˌɔːdə rɪˈmuːvd]	jds Ausweisung anordnen
to relocate	[riːləʊˈkeɪt]	umziehen, übersiedeln
to struggle with sth	[ˈstʌgl wɪð]	mit etw ringen
scarcely anything	[ˌskeəsli ˈeniθɪŋ]	kaum etwas
to lament	[ləˈment]	klagen

Alphabetical word list

Dieses Wörterverzeichnis enthält alle Wörter aus **Work with English 5th Edition** in alphabetischer Reihenfolge. Nicht aufgeführt sind internationale Wörter wie *hotel, email* usw. Wörter, die in den Audio- und Videotexten vorkommen, sind mit einem T bzw. einem V, und Wörter, die in den *Differentiation files* vorkommen, mit einem F hinter der Seitenzahl gekennzeichnet.

A

to **abandon sb** 226 jdn verlassen, jdn im Stich lassen
abandoned 215 verlassen, stillgelegt
abdominal 166 Bauch-
able, to **be ~ to do sth** 50 in der Lage sein, etw zu tun
ability 58, 202 Fähigkeit, Möglichkeit
about, to **be ~ to do sth** 112 etw gleich tun; im Begriff sein, etw zu tun
abroad 75 im/ins Ausland
abuse 143 Missbrauch
to **accelerate** 94 beschleunigen
to **accept** 28 akzeptieren, annehmen
access 51 Zugang, Zugriff
to **access sth** 167 auf etw zugreifen
accessory 72 Accessoire
accident 56 Unfall
accidentally 223 aus Versehen
accommodation 67 Unterkunft
account 28 Konto; to **take sth into ~** 154 etw berücksichtigen
to **account for sth** 166 *(Anteil)* ausmachen
accurate 94 korrekt, präzise
to **achieve sth** 45 etw erreichen
to **acknowledge** 210 anerkennen
across 106T in ganz
to **act: ~ as sth** 94 als etw fungieren; **~ sth out** 23 etw (mit verteilten Rollen) spielen; **~ out** 83 spielen, aufführen; **~ strangely** 131 sich seltsam verhalten
act, circus ~ 88 Zirkusnummer
acting society 202 Schauspiel-AG
action, to **call for ~** 51 zu Maßnahmen aufrufen, Maßnahmen fordern; to **put sth into ~** 143 etw in die Tat umsetzen; to **take ~** 207 Maßnahmen ergreifen, etwas unternehmen
to **activate** 128 aktivieren, einschalten
active(ly) 50T aktiv
activity 26 Tätigkeit, Beschäftigung, Aktivität
actor 50T Schauspieler
actress 37 Schauspielerin
to **adapt to sth** 67 sich an etw anpassen, sich an etw gewöhnen
to **add** 6 hinzufügen
addict 70T Süchtige/r
addicted, to **be ~ to sth** 56 nach etw süchtig sein, von etw abhängig sein
addition, in ~ 119 außerdem
additional 119 zusätzlich, Zusatz-
to **adjust** 174 einstellen, justieren
admirable 204 bewundernswert
to **admire** 50T bewundern
to **admit** 70T zugeben, eingestehen
to **adopt** 37 adoptieren; **~ sth** 222 etw übernehmen
adoption 37 Adoption; to **give sb up for ~** 37 jdn zur Adoption freigeben
adoptive family 37 Adoptivfamilie
to **adore sb/sth** 37 jdn/etw über alles lieben
adrenaline rush 142 Adrenalinrausch
adult 32 Erwachsene/r
advance, in ~ 224 im Voraus; **technical ~s** *pl* 130 technische Fortschritte, technische Entwicklungen
advantage 43 Vorteil
adventure 100 Abenteuer
advert 79 Anzeige
to **advertise** 88 werben, Werbung machen; **~ sth** 119 etw bewerben, für etw Werbung machen
advertisement 32 Anzeige, Werbung; **job ~** 76 Stellenanzeige; **radio ~** 106 Werbespot (im Radio)
advice 57 Rat, Ratschlag; to **give sb ~** 63 jdn beraten
to **advise** 210 raten, Rat erteilen; **~ sb** 63 jdn beraten
aeroplane 105 Flugzeug
affairs *pl* 52T Geschäfte, geschäftliche Angelegenheiten
to **affect sb/sth** 40T jdn/etw beeinflussen, sich auf jdn/etw auswirken; 214 jdn/etw betreffen
to **afford sth** 153 sich etw leisten
afraid, to **be ~ of sb/sth** 12 vor jdm/etw Angst haben, sich vor jdm/etw fürchten
after all 162T nun mal
age, for ~s 40T eine Ewigkeit
aged: ~ … 32 im Alter von … Jahren; **middle-~** 174 mittleren Alters
agency 37 Agentur; **news ~** 214 Nachrichtenagentur
agenda, news ~ 214 Schwerpunkte der Berichterstattung
agent 226 Beamte/r; **call centre ~** 7 Telefonagent/in, Callcenteragent/in; **secret ~** 142 Geheimagent/in
to **agree** 31 zustimmen, einverstanden sein
agreement 50T Abkommen, Vereinbarung; 64 Übereinkunft, Übereinstimmung
agricultural 77 landwirtschaftlich
agriculture 17 Landwirtschaft
ahead of 226 vor, im Vorfeld von
aid, first ~ 33 Erste Hilfe; **first-~ kit** 58 Erste-Hilfe-Kasten, Verbandskasten; **~ group** 50T Hilfsorganisation
aim 64 Ziel
to **aim for sth** 212 etw anstreben
air conditioning 128 Klimaanlage; **solar-powered ~** 208 Solar-Klimaanlage
aircraft 104 Flugzeug
airport 120 Flughafen
air pump 145 Luftpumpe, Vakuumpumpe
air travel 154 Flugreisen, Flugverkehr
alert, hoax bomb ~ 214 vorgetäuschter Bombenalarm
A levels *pl BE* 179T Abitur
alight, to **set sth ~** 218 etw anzünden
alike 141, 222 gleichermaßen, ebenso
all, at ~ 36 überhaupt; **most of ~** 42 vor allem
allergy 20 Allergie
allocation 176 Zuweisungs, Zuteilung
allowed, to **be ~ to do sth** 21V etw tun dürfen
along 33 entlang
along with 123, 208 zusammen mit
to **alter** 43F *(Kleidung)* ändern
although 95 obwohl
to **amass sth** 167 etw anhäufen
amazing 102 erstaunlich, super
ambassador 50 Botschafter/in
ambition 157 Ziel, Wunschtraum, Ehrgeiz
ambitious 49 ehrgeizig
ambulance 56 Rettungswagen
among 51 unter, bei
amount 57, 200 Menge
anaemia 20 Blutarmut, Anämie
ancient 115 alt, uralt
anecdotal evidence 226 vereinzelte Anhaltspunkte
angel 94 Engel
anger 43T Wut; 160 Zorn, Ärger
angle 150 Winkel, Blickwinkel, Perspektive; 215 (journalistischer) Ansatz
animal 161 tierisch
to **animate** 51V antreiben, mit Leben erfüllen
to **announce** 44 verkünden
announcement 52 Ankündigung, Mitteilung
annual 115V jährlich
anonymous 148, 218 anonym
anorexia 166 Magersucht
anorexic 166 Magersüchtge/r; magersüchtig
to **answer the phone** 164T ans Telefon gehen
anthem, national ~ 111 Nationalhymne
antibiotics *pl* 17 Antibiotika
anxiety 210 Angst
apart from 69F abgesehen von, außer
to **ape** 159 nachäffen
apparently 113 anscheinend
to **appear** 19 vorkommen, auftauchen; **~ on TV** 50T im Fernsehen auftreten
appearance 158 Erscheinung(sbild)
appliance 132 Haushaltsgerät
applicant 82 Bewerber/in
application 52 Bewerbung
to **apply: ~ for sth** 42 sich um etw bewerben; 211 etw beantragen; **~ to sb/sth** 92 (für jdn/etw) gelten; **~ sth (to sth)** 94 etw (auf etw) anwenden
to **appoint sb sth** 45 jdn zu etw ernennen
appointment 59 Termin
to **apprehend sb** 94 jdn fassen, jdn festnehmen
apprenticeship 171 Lehre, Ausbildung
approach 149V Herangehensweise, Ansatz
to **approach** 173 sich nähern
appropriate 46 passend
to **approve of sth** 78 etw gutheißen, etw billigen
aptitude 135 Talent, Befähigung
architecture 102 Architektur
area 33 Bereich, Zone; 34 Gegend, Gebiet
to **argue** 216 argumentieren
argument, to **have an ~** 40 sich streiten

arm, lower ~ 208 Unterarm; **prosthetic ~** 208 Armprothese
armed 149V bewaffnet
to **arrange** 138T *(Termin)* ausmachen
arrangements *pl* 74 Vorbereitungen
arrival, on ~ 123 bei Ankunft
to **arrive** 9 eintreffen, ankommen
art 145 Kunst; **work of ~** 167 Kunstwerk; **graphic ~** 224 Malerei und Grafik; **~ college** 43F Kunstakademie, Kunsthochschule
artery 21V Ader, Arterie
article 19 Artikel
artificial 209 künstlich
artist 149F Künstler/in
artistic 145 künstlerisch
as 57 während; **~ long as** 20T solange
aside 204 beiseite, abgesehen von
aspect 28 Gesichtspunkt, Aspekt, Seite
aspiration 169 Ziel, Bestreben
to **assemble** 208 montieren, zusammenbauen
to **assess** 149V beurteilen, bewerten
assignment 175, 204 Aufgabe, Auftrag
to **assist** 142 helfen, unterstützen
assistance 60 Hilfe, Unterstützung; to **call for ~** 60 um Hilfe ersuchen
assistant, shop ~ 72 Verkäufer/in
association 99 Verband, Vereinigung
to **assume** 179T davon ausgehen, annehmen
at all 36 überhaupt
athlete 26 Sportler/in
ATM 116T Geldautomat
atmosphere 28 Atmosphäre
attack 214 Angriff; **heart ~** 57 Herzinfarkt
to **attack** 143 angreifen
attempt 94 Versuch
to **attempt** 207 versuchen
to **attend sth** 83 an etw teilnehmen; 110 etw *(Veranstaltung usw.)* besuchen
attendant, flight ~ 7 Flugbegleiter/in
attention 31 Aufmerksamkeit; to **catch sb's ~** 137 jds Aufmerksamkeit fesseln; to **draw ~ to sth** 115V Aufmerksamkeit auf etw lenken; to **pay ~** 224 aufpassen; to **pay ~ to sth** 31 auf etw achten
attitude 42 Einstellung, Haltung
to **attract** 171, 218 anziehen, anlocken
attraction 97 Sehenswürdigkeit
attractive 34 ansprechend, attraktiv
attractiveness 24 Attraktivität
auction 119 Versteigerung, Auktion
audience 44 Publikum
authentic 174 echt, authentisch
autograph 112 Autogramm
automatic(ally) 60 automatisch
automotive 140 Automobil-, Auto-
availability 215 Verfügbarkeit
average 17 Durchschnitt(s-), durchschnittlich
to **avoid** 82 vermeiden, meiden
awaited, long-~ 167 lang erwartet, lang ersehnt
to **award** 45 *(Preis)* verleihen
aware, to **be ~ of sth** 52T etw kennen, sich einer Sache bewusst sein; to **make sb ~ of sth** 50T jdm etw bewusst machen, jdn auf etw hinweisen
awesome 142 beeindruckend, toll
awkwardness 222 Verlegenheit

B

background 21V Herkunft; 54, 203 Hintergrund, Vorgeschichte
backpack 126 Rucksack
backpacker 80T Rucksackreisende/r
backpacking 80 Rucksackreisen
bacon 162T Speck
bad, to **feel ~ about sth** 201 wegen etw ein schlechtes Gewissen haben
bag, plastic ~ 132 Plastiktüte
baggage carousel 131 Gepäckband
baking soda 67 Natron
balance 143 Gleichgewicht
balanced 21V ausgewogen
balcony 103V Balkon, Galerie
ban (on sth) 56 Verbot (von etw)
to **ban sb from doing sth** 143 jdm verbieten, etw zu tun
bang 218 Knall
to **bang** 113 schlagen, hauen, hämmern
bar: chocolate ~ 17 Schokoriegel; **~ of soap** 129 Stück Seife; **~ chart** 85 Säulendiagramm
bare 118 kahl
to **bare one's teeth** 159 die Zähne fletschen
barely 208 kaum
to **bark** 115 bellen
barrel 218 Fass
barrier, language ~ 223 Sprachbarriere
base 99 Ausgangspunkt, Basis
based: ~ in 107 mit Sitz in, ansässig in; **~ on** 18 auf Grundlage von
basic 52T einfach, grundlegend, elementar
basically 30T im Prinzip, grundsätzlich
basics *pl* 43T Grundlagen
basin 129 Waschbecken
basis, legal ~ 226 Rechtsgrundlage
bathrobe 62 Bademantel
battery 104 Akku, Batterie
battle 21V Kampf, Schlacht
bear 120 Bär
to **bear in mind** 119 daran denken, nicht vergessen
to **beat** 174 schlagen, pochen
beat, His heart missed a ~. 173 Dies ließ ihm sein Herz höher schlagen.
beauty 43T Schönheit
to **become (sth)** 10 (etw / zu etw) werden
bed and breakfast 98 Frühstückspension, Übernachtung mit Frühstück
beer 13 Bier
to **beg** 47 betteln; **~ sb to do sth** 210 jdn anflehen, etw zu tun
to **behave** 45 sich verhalten, sich benehmen
behaviour 90T Verhalten
being, human ~ 224 Mensch, menschliches Wesen
belief 78 Überzeugung, Glaube
believer, to **be a ~ in sth** 94 an etw (fest) glauben, von etw (fest) überzeugt sein
bell 103V Glocke
belongings *pl* 105T persönliche Sachen
bench 174 Bank
benefit 19 Nutzen, Vorteil
besides 45 außer; 69V außerdem; 213 neben
best, personal ~ 166 persönliche Bestleistung
to **bet** 30T wetten
to **beware: ~ of sth** 152 sich vor etw in Acht nehmen; **B~** 119 Vorsicht!

beyond sth 159 jenseits von etw
biceps 166 Bizeps
bill 23 Rechnung
billiard ball 149V Billardkugel
billion 17 Milliarde
bin 105T Mülltonne, Mülleimer; **rubbish ~** 123 Mülleimer, Abfalltonne
bionic 208 bionisch
birth mother 36 leibliche Mutter
blade, razor ~ 104 Rasierklinge
to **blame sb/sth on sb** 94 jdm/etw für etw die Schuld geben
bleach 104 Bleichmittel
to **bleach** 122 bleichen
blended family 35 Patchworkfamilie
blind 60 Blinde/r, blind
to **blind** 160 blenden
to **blink** 160 blinzeln
blood, red ~ cells *pl* 20 rote Blutkörperchen; **~ pressure** 21V Blutdruck
to **blow sth up** 103V etw in die Luft sprengen/jagen
board 8 (Wand-)Tafel; **on ~** 103V an Bord; **draining ~** 166 *(Spüle:)* Abtropfbrett; **notice ~** 64 Schwarzes Brett; **~ of directors** 176T Vorstand, Geschäftsführung
to **board** 105 an Bord gehen, einsteigen
boarding pass 105 Bordkarte
body contact 52T Körperkontakt
body fat 143 Körperfett
body language 52T Körpersprache
bodybag 138T Leichensack
bomb, hoax ~ alert 214 vorgetäuschter Bombenalarm
bone 200 *(Fisch:)* Gräte
bonfire 218 Freudenfeuer
booking 99 Reservierung, Buchung
to **boost consumption** 69V den Konsum ankurbeln
border 94 Grenze
bored, to **be ~ with sth** 146 etw langweilt jdn
to **bother sb** 93T jdn stören
bowl 10 Schale, Schüssel, Napf
bracket 11 Klammer
brain 143 Gehirn
to **brainstorm** 8 Ideen sammeln
branch 84 Zweig; 177 Niederlassung
brand 128 Marke; **~ new** 140 brandneu, nagelneu
brass band 111 Blasorchester
brave 219 mutig
break, to **be on a ~** 164 Pause machen; to **take a ~** 62 eine Pause machen; **city ~** 103V (kurzer) Städteurlaub; **lunch ~** 57 Mittagspause
to **break** 125 zerbrechen, zerfallen; 126 kaputt gehen; **~ down** 70T kaputtgehen; 171 eine Panne haben; **~ the law** 148 gegen das Gesetz verstoßen
breakdown 217 Verteilung, Aufschlüsselung
breakfast buffet 128 Frühstücksbüfett
breaking news 214 Eilmeldung(en)
breeze 174 Brise, (leichter) Wind
bridesmaid 81 Brautjungfer
brief 92 knapp, kurz
briefing 142 Einweisung, Lagebesprechung
bright 52T *(Farbe:)* kräftig, bunt; 206 *(Zukunft:)* aussichtsreich, vielversprechend
to **brighten sth up** 148 etw aufhellen, etw aufheitern

brightly lit 118 hell erleuchtet
to **bring: ~ sb up** 35 jdn großziehen, jdn aufziehen; **~ sth along** 126 etw mitbringen
broadcast 173 Sendung, Übertragung, Ausstrahlung
to **broadcast** 87 senden, verbreiten, ausstrahlen
broadsheet 214 (seriöse) Tageszeitung
brochure 141 Prospekt, Broschüre
broken 126 kaputt
bubble, speech ~ 11 Sprechblase
bucket 111 Eimer
budget 42 Budget, Etat, Haushalt
building site 135 Baustelle
bullet 207 (Gewehr-)Kugel
to **bully** 208 schikanieren, mobben
a bunch of people 111 ein Haufen Leute, ein paar Leute
to **burn** 143 verbrennen
burned, to **get badly ~** 107T einen schweren Sonnenbrand bekommen
burst 111 Ausbruch, Explosion
to **bury sth in sth** 159 etw in etw (ver) graben
bus route 101 Buslinie
bush 170 Busch
business idea 126 Geschäftsidee
to **busk** 171 Straßenmusik machen
to **buy into sth** 210 an etw glauben
buyer 69V Käufer/in
by oneself 108 allein

C

caffeinated 56 koffeinhaltig
caffeine 56 Koffein
call, to **take a ~** 60T einen Anruf entgegennehmen; **voice ~** 85 Sprachanruf
call centre agent 7 Telefonagent/in, Callcenteragent/in
to **camp** 47 kampieren
campaign 56 Kampagne, Aktion
to **campaign for sth** 216 für etw eintreten, für etw kämpfen
campaigner 217 Wahlkämpfer/in, Aktivist/in
camper van 98 Wohnmobil
campsite 98 Campingplatz
can 200 (Konserven-)Dose; **spray ~** 148 Sprühdose; **tin ~** 126 Blechdose
canal 142 Kanal
to **cancel** 147 beenden, abbrechen
cancellation 107T Absage
canned 200 Konserven-, in Dosen, konserviert
canteen 24 Kantine
capital 10 Hauptstadt
caption 120 Bildunterschrift
car: concept ~ 140 Konzeptauto; **~ crash** 41 Autounfall; **~ dealership** 140 Autohaus, Autohändler/in
caravan 67 Wohnwagen
cardboard 123 Pappe
care 220 Betreuung; **health ~** 171 Gesundheitswesen, Krankenversorgung
to **care about sth** 67 sich um etw kümmern, jdm ist an etw gelegen
career 32 Karriere, Laufbahn; **~ goal** 137F berufliches Ziel; **~ prospects** *pl* 135 Berufsaussichten

careful, to **be ~ with sth** 13 bei etw aufpassen, vorsichtig bei/mit etw sein
carnival 109 Karneval
carousel, baggage ~ 131 Gepäckband
to **carry out** 224 *(Tätigkeit)* ausführen; **~ a function** 224 eine Funktion wahrnehmen
cartoon 149V Karikatur, Zeichnung
case 200 Fall; **in ~** 58 falls; für den Fall, dass; to **be the ~** 114T der Fall sein; **long-term court ~** 214 Gerichtsverfahren, das sich lange hinzieht; **test-~** 21V Probelauf; **~ study** 153 Fallstudie
cash desk 73 Kasse
castle 97 Burg, Schloss
casual job 135 Gelegenheitsarbeit
casualties *pl* 214 Opfer, Tote und Verletzte
catalogue 70T Katalog
to **catch: ~ sth** 164T etw verstehen, etw mitbekommen; **~ on** 126T Schule machen, sich durchsetzen; **~ sb's attention** 137 jds Aufmerksamkeit fesseln; **~ fire** 152 Feuer fangen, in Brand geraten; **~ the train** 103T den Zug erwischen
category 24 Rubrik, Kategorie; to **fall into a ~** 226 zu einer Kategorie gehören
to **cater for all tastes** 140 für jeden Geschmack etw bieten
cathedral 14 Dom, Kathedrale
Catholic 162T katholisch; Katholik/in
cause 50 (gute) Sache, Anliegen
to **cause** 20 verursachen; **~ trouble** 99 Ärger machen
to **celebrate** 113 feiern
celebration 103V Feier
celebrity 51 Prominente/r, Promi
cell phone *AE* 90 Handy
central storage 220 Zentrallager
century 103V Jahrhundert
cereal 22 Müsli, Getreideflocken
ceremony 206 Feier, Zeremonie; **opening ~** 111 Eröffnungszeremonie
certain 10 bestimmte/r/s, gewisse/r/s
chain 118 Kette
challenge 30 Herausforderung, (schwierige) Aufgabe
to **challenge sth** 67 etw infrage stellen
chance: ~es are 51 aller Wahrscheinlichkeit nach
change 72 Wechselgeld
to **change: ~ (into sth)** 33 sich umziehen, sich etw anziehen; **~ one's mind** 68 seine Meinung ändern
changing room 73 Umkleidekabine
changing tent 33 Umkleidezelt
channel 89 Kanal
character 44 (Roman-/Film-)Figur, Charakter
characteristic 32 Merkmal, Eigenschaft
charge, free of ~ 43T gebührenfrei, kostenlos; to **be in ~ of sth** 107T für etw zuständig sein; to **be in ~ of sb** 213 jdm vorgesetzt sein; to **take ~ of sth** 117 die Leitung von etw übernehmen
to **charge** 61 aufladen; 216 *(Geld)* verlangen; **~ sb for sth** 208 von jdm Geld für etw verlangen
charity 45 Wohltätigkeitsorganisation(en), wohltätige Zwecke; **~ shop** 43F Second-Hand-Laden *(für wohltätige Zwecke)*

chart 14 Tabelle; **bar ~** 85 Säulendiagramm; **flow ~** 124 Flussdiagramm; **organizational ~** 176 Organigramm; **pie ~** 85 Tortendiagramm
chatty 173 geschwätzig
to **cheat on sb with sb** 40T jdn mit jdm betrügen
cheating 40 Fremdgehen
cheeky 150T frech
to **cheer** 111 jubeln, anfeuern; **~ sb up** 210 jdn aufmuntern
cheerful 174 fröhlich
to **cherish sth** 167 etw wertschätzen, etw lieben
cheesecake 22 Käsekuchen
chef 62 (Chef-)Koch/Köchin
chemicals *pl* 118 Chemikalien
chest 166 Brust
chicken 13 Huhn, Hühnchen
chief executive 212 Geschäftsführer/in
child, only ~ 37 Einzelkind
childhood 39 Kindheit
childish 148 kindisch
to **chill** 64 chillen, relaxen
chimpanzee 158 Schimpanse
chip 122 Hackschnitzel
chipping plant 123 Hackschnitzelanlage
chocolate bar 17 Schokoriegel
choice 13 Wahl; to **present sb with a ~** 226 jdn vor die Wahl stellen
cholesterol 21V Cholesterin
chronic pain condition 220 chronische Schmerzerkrankung
church 9 Kirche
cinema 9 Kino
circus: ~ act 88 Zirkusnummer; **~ skills** *pl* 87 Zirkuskünste
to **cite** 94 zitieren
city break 103V (kurzer) Städteurlaub
civilian 215 Zivilist/in
claim 94 Behauptung
to **claim** 148 behaupten
clay 159 Ton
clerk 166 Sachbearbeiter/in
client 62 Kunde/-in
cliff 97 Felsen, Klippe
climate 50T Klima
climate change 50T Klimawandel
clinic 115V Workshop
cloakroom 116 Garderobe
close 130 *(Brief:)* Schlussformel; **up ~** 171 aus nächster Nähe; to **grow ~er** 37 sich näherkommen, die Beziehung intensivieren
cloth 153 Tuch
clothing 72 Kleidung, Bekleidung, Kleider; **protective ~** 152 Schutzkleidung
cloudy 81 bewölkt
to **clutch sth** 29F etw umklammern, etw festhalten
coach 30T Trainer/in
to **coat** 123 beschichten; 143 auskleiden
coin 105T Münze
Cold War 142 Kalter Krieg
to **collaborate** 135 zusammenarbeiten
to **collapse** 56 zusammenbrechen
colleague 22 Kollege/-in
colourful 102 bunt, farbenfroh
column 6 *(Text:)* Spalte; 103V Säule
coma 56 Koma
to **combat sth** 64 etw bekämpfen
combination offer 62 Kombi-Angebot

Alphabetical word list

ego 204 Ego
elderly 131 ältere/r/s
electric shock 152 Stromschlag
electrician 154 Elektriker/in
electricity 67 Strom, Elektrizität
electronics 107T Elektronik
to **embarrass: ~ oneself** 138 sich lächerlich machen; **~ sb** 161 jdn in Verlegenheit bringen
embarrassed, to **be ~ by sth** 137 etw ist jdm peinlich
embassy 50T Botschaft
to **emerge** 94 ans Licht kommen
to **emphasize** 137 betonen, herausstellen
emphatic(ally) 159 nachdrücklich
employee 92 Beschäftigte/r, Mitarbeiter/in
employer 33 Arbeitgeber/in
employment 176T Beschäftigung, Anstellung
to **encounter sth** 204 auf etw treffen
to **encourage** 50, 202 ermutigen, fördern
end, towards the ~ 80T gegen Ende
to **end up doing sth** 167 schließlich etw tun
endless(ly) 51V unendlich
enemy 142 Feind/in, feindlich
energetic 27 voller Energie, tatkräftig
energy 42 Energie
energy-efficient 132 energieeffizient
enforcement, Immigration and Customs E~ 226 *US-Behörde für Einwanderung und Zoll*
engine 103V Motor
engineer 7 Ingenieur/in, Techniker/in
engineering 162T, 222 Maschinenbau
engineering Maschinenbau
to **enjoy: ~ oneself** 111 sich gut amüsieren; **E~ your meal!** 23 Guten Appetit!
to **ensure** 212 dafür sorgen
to **enter** 152, 212 betreten; **~ sth** 110 *(Wettbewerb usw.:)* an etw teilnehmen; **~ higher education** 202 ein Studium beginnen
enterprise 224 Unternehmen, Unterfangen
to **entertain sb** 130 jdn unterhalten
entertaining 102 unterhaltsam
entertainment 107T Unterhaltung
enthusiasm, infectious ~ 204 ansteckende Begeisterung
enthusiastic 42 begeisterungsfähig
entire 222 ganze/r/s, vollständig
entirely 94 völlig, gänzlich
entitled, to **be ~ to sth** 119 etw verlangen können, Anspruch auf etw haben
entrance 116 Eingang
to **entrust sb/sth with sth** 119 jdm/einer Sache etw anvertrauen
entry 27 Eintrag; 62 Eintritt; **dictionary ~** 213 Stichwort, Wörterbucheintrag; **~ fee** 33 Anmeldegebühr
environment 17 Umwelt
environmental 50T Umwelt-
equal(ly) 45 gleich
equality 207 Gleichheit, Gleichberechtigung
equipment 30 Ausrüstung, Geräte; **piece of ~** 70T Gerät
equivalent 60 Entsprechung, Äquivalent
errand, to **run ~s** 69V Besorgungen machen
especially 205 besonders, insbesondere
especially 89 besonders, insbesondere
essential 42 wesentlich, unerlässlich
estate, industrial ~ 156, 220 Gewerbegebiet
esteem, self-~ 202 Selbstachtung, Selbstwertgefühl
ethos 214 Gesinnung, Ethos
to **evaluate** 179T, 215 beurteilen, bewerten
eve, New Year's E~ 109 Silvester
even: ~ so 222 aber dennoch; **~ though** 45 obwohl
event 32 Veranstaltung; 107T, 214 Ereignis
eventful 215 ereignisreich
eventually 177T schließlich, am Ende
ever, hardly ~ 90T kaum, so gut wie nie
evidence 90T Indizien; to **give ~** 161 (etw) belegen, (etw) nachweisen; **anecdotal ~** 226 vereinzelte Anhaltspunkte
evil 51 böse; to **drive away ~ spirits** 218 böse Geister vertreiben
to **examine** 58 untersuchen
example, to **set an ~** 50 ein Beispiel geben; **stark ~** 226 krasses Beispiel
excellent 138T ausgezeichnet, hervorragend
except for 144 außer
exception (to sth) 10 Ausnahme (von etw)
exchange 67 Austausch; **~ student** 34 Austauschschüler/in
to **exchange** 43 austauschen; 72 umtauschen
excited 37 aufgeregt, begeistert, gespannt
excitement 148 Reiz, Spannung, Nervenkitzel
exciting 52 aufregend, spannend
exclusively 222 ausschließlich
to **execute** 218 hinrichten
execution, sequence of ~ 224 Ausführungsreihenfolge
executive 222 Manager/in; **chief ~** 212 Geschäftsführer/in
exempt, to **be ~ from sth** 104 von etw ausgenommen sein
exhausted 179T erschöpft
exhibit 167 Ausstellungsstück
to **exhibit** 140 ausstellen
exhibition 140 Ausstellung, Messe; **special ~** 116T Sonderausstellung
exhibitor 140 Aussteller/in
exit 216 Abgang, Austritt
exotic 135 exotisch
to **expand** 220 ausweiten
expense 99 Kosten, Ausgabe(n), Aufwendung(en); **travel ~es** *pl* 179T Reisekosten
experience 33 Erlebnis(se), Erfahrung(en); **work ~** 72 Praktikum
to **experiment** 208 experimentieren
expert 18 Fachmann/-frau, Experte/-in
to **explode sth** 218 etw zünden, etw in die Luft jagen
to **exploit** 67 ausbeuten; 132 *(Bodenschätze)* abbauen
to **explore** 103T erkunden
explosive 94 hochbrisant; 206 Sprengstoff
to **express** 58 ausdrücken
extended 35 erweitert
extent 94 Ausmaß
extract 115 Auszug, Ausschnitt
extracurricular 64 außerhalb des Stundenplans, außerschulisch
extreme 166 Extrem
eyebrow to **raise one's ~s** 160 die Stirn runzeln
eye contact 82 Blickkontakt
eyesight, poor ~ 60T Sehschwäche

F

fabulous 103V fabelhaft, großartig
face, to **lose ~** 223 das Gesicht verlieren
facilities *pl* 9 Einrichtung(en), Ausstattung
factor 74 Faktor
to **fail** 78 *(Prüfung)* nicht bestehen, durchfallen; 218 scheitern; **~ to do sth** 94 versäumen, etw zu tun
failure, mechanical ~ 171 technisches Versagen, Motorschaden
fair: ~ enough 106T na gut; **~ game** 94 Freiwild; **trade ~** 104 (Branchen-/Handels-)Messe
to **fall: ~ behind** 47 zurückbleiben, zurückfallen; **~ in love with sb/sth** 70T sich in jdn/etw verlieben; **~ into a category** 226 zu einer Kategorie gehören
famine 17 Hungersnot
familiar, to **be ~ with sth** 35 mit etw vertraut sein, etw kennen
family, adoptive ~ 37 Adoptivfamilie; **blended ~** 35 Patchworkfamilie; **nuclear ~** 35 Kernfamilie, Kleinfamilie; **single-parent ~** 35 Einelternfamilie; to **start a ~** 169 eine Familie gründen
fantasy 7 Phantasie-; **~ world** 135 Traumwelt, Phantasiewelt
fashion 37 Mode; to **go out of ~** 107T aus der Mode kommen
fast-moving 94 schnelllebig
to **fasten one's seat belt** 80T sich anschnallen
fat, body ~ 143 Körperfett; **saturated ~** 143, 200 gesättigtes Fett; **low in ~** 200 fettarm
fatty streaks *pl* 21V Schaumzellen, Verkalkungen
faulty 119 defekt
favour, to **be in ~ of sth** 216 etw befürworten, für etw sein; to **swing the competition in sb's ~** 204 das Pendel zu jds Gunsten umschlagen lassen
to **favour sth** 125 sich für etw entscheiden
fear 157, 207 Angst; **~ of heights** 113 Höhenangst; to **shake with ~** 171 vor Angst zittern
to **feature sth** 208 etw *(Merkmal usw.)* aufweisen
features *pl* 150T Gesichtszüge
feces *AE* 159 Kot
federal 76 Bundes-
fee 99 Gebühr; **entry ~** 33 Anmeldegebühr; **membership ~s** *pl* 216 Mitgliedsbeiträge
to **feed** 16 ernähren; 120 füttern; **~ bad about sth** 201 wegen etw ein schlechtes Gewissen haben; **~ the soil** 118 den Boden mit Nährstoffen versorgen
feedback 61 Rückmeldung, Reaktion(en)
feeling 87, 202 Gefühl, Ansicht, Meinung
fellow: ~ colleague 212 Kollege/-in; **~ student** 56 Mitschüler/in
fibre 17 Ballaststoffe; **dietary ~** 143 Ballaststoff
fiction 94 Erfindung, Fiktion
fighter 94 Kämpfer/in
figure 163, 218 Figur
to **figure sth out** 67 etw herausfinden
figures *pl* 85 Zahlen
to **fill** 6 füllen; **~ in** 14 eintragen, ausfüllen

final 20T letzte/r/s
to **finalise** 179T (endgültig) festlegen
finance 138T Finanzwesen; **F~** 176 Finanzabteilung
to **find** 107T feststellen; **~ out** 200 herausfinden; **~ sb guilty of sth** 148 jdn einer Sache für schuldig befinden
findings *pl* 85, 213 Ergebnisse
finish 33 Ziel
finished product 176 Endprodukt
firefighter 45 Feuerwehrmann/-frau
fireworks *pl* 109, 218 Feuerwerk; **~ display** 219 Feuerwerk
firm 160 fest; **sth is ~ly under control** 210 jd hat etw fest im Griff
first aid 33 Erste Hilfe; **~ kit** 58 Erste-Hilfe-Kasten, Verbandskasten
to **fit** 73 passen; **~ sth** 16 zu etw passen; **~ in** 176T hineinpassen; **~ into sth** 76 sich in etw einfügen
to **fix** 126 reparieren, flicken
flaming 218 lodernd
flash 150 Blitz(licht); **in a ~** 167 im Nu
flat *BE* 98 Wohnung
flatmate 162T Mitbewohner/in
flatshare 162 Wohngemeinschaft
flavour 22 Geschmacksrichtung, Aroma; **local ~** 218 Lokalkolorit, lokaler Bezug
flexibility 142 Flexibilität
flexible 171 flexibel
flight 53 Flug; **~ attendant** 7 Flugbegleiter/in
floor, shop ~ 72 Verkaufsfläche; **~ plan** 140 Grundriss, Übersichtsplan
flour 17 Mehl
flow 216 Strom, Zustrom; **~ chart** 124 Flussdiagramm
fluent 135 *(Sprache:)* fließend
to **flush** 159 erröten
flyer 34 Handzettel, Broschüre
fob, key ~ 139 Schlüsselanhänger
focus 36 Schwerpunkt, Hauptaugenmerk
to **focus on sth** 18 sich auf etw konzentrieren
focused 202 zielstrebig
to **follow up** 94 nachfassen
follow-up 56 Nachfassen
food: waste ~ 132 Lebensmittelabfälle; **~ hall** 72 Lebensmittelabteilung; **~ stall** 115V Essensstand
fool 70 Narr
foot 111 Fuß *(ca. 30,5 cm)*; to **stamp one's feet** 111 mit den Füßen trampeln
football: ~ pitch 203 Fußballfeld, Fußballplatz; **~ practice** 131 Fußballtraining
footpath 99 Weg, Pfad
forecast, weather ~ 103V Wettervorhersage
foreign 80 ausländisch, fremd; **~ language** 135 Fremdsprache
forest 66 Wald
fork 174 Gabel
forklift truck 152 Gabelstapler
to **form** 78 bilden
formerly 218 ehemals
Formula One 141 Formel 1
fortunately 153 glücklicherweise, zum Glück
to **forward sth** 60T etw weiterleiten
forward, to **move ~** 207 vorankommen
to **found** 94, 206 gründen
foundation 45 Stiftung
founder 220 Gründer/in
fountain 224 Brunnen
fraction 210 Bruchteil
to **frame** 43F *(Bildmotiv)* gestalten, Bildausschnitt wählen
to **freak out** 37 ausrasten, durchdrehen
free, to **be ~** 63 Zeit haben; to **be ~ to do sth** 47 etw (gern) tun dürfen; **for ~** 209 umsonst, kostenlos; **~ movement** 216 Freizügigkeit; **~ of charge** 43T gebührenfrei, kostenlos
freedom 171 Freiheit
freezing cold 106T eiskalt
frequent 113 häufig
frequently 94 oft, häufig; **~ asked questions (FAQs)** 33 häufig gestellte Fragen
fresh(ly) 62, 200 frisch
fridge 12 Kühlschrank
friend, to **make ~s** 26 Freunde finden/gewinnen
friendship 37 Freundschaft
frightened 131 verängstigt
front, in ~ of 8 vor
frozen 200 Gefrier-, eingefroren
to **fuel** 216 antreiben, anheizen; **~ sth** 147 etw anheizen, etw befeuern
to **fulfil** 80T erfüllen
full-time 118 Vollzeit-
fully 222 vollständig, völlig
fun, just for ~ 61 nur zum Spaß; **sense of ~** 89 Sinn für Humor
function, to **carry out a ~** 224 eine Funktion wahrnehmen
fundraiser 164 Spendensammler/in
funds *pl*, to **raise ~** 37 Spenden sammeln
furniture 126 Möbel; **piece of ~** 126 Möbelstück
further 82 weiter, weitergehend; **~ education** 52 Weiterbildung; **~ training** 213 Fortbildung
furthermore 107T außerdem, darüber hinaus

G

to **gain** 17 *(Gewicht)* zunehmen; 67 erwerben, erlangen; **~ weight** 143 zunehmen
galaxy 224 *hier:* Unmenge
game, fair ~ 94 Freiwild
gap 29 Lücke
gapped 22 mit Lücken
gardener 174 Gärtner/in
gardening tool 174 Gartengerät
gas cylinder 104 Gasflasche, Gaskartusche
gate 120 Tor
gazing 90 (abwesendes) Starren
gear 33 (Sport-)Kleidung
general, in ~ 110 im Allgemeinen; **member of the ~ public** 215 (einfache/r) Bürger/in
generation 35 Generation; to **stretch back for ~s** 218 sich um Generationen zurückerstrecken
generous 206 großzügig
gentle 142 sanft
gentleman 52T Herr
genuine 119 echt, wirklich
to **get: ~ sth across** 57 etw vermitteln; **~ by with sth** 70T mit etw auskommen; **~ on well with sb** 79 gut mit jdm auskommen; **~ in the way of sth** 166 einer Sache im Weg stehen, einer Sache in die Quere kommen; **~ it wrong** 138T etw falsch machen, etw falsch verstehen
gig 118 (Rock-, Pop-, Jazz-)Konzert
the gist 51V das Wesentliche, die Hauptpunkte
to **give: ~ up** 27 aufgeben; **~ sb up for adoption** 37 jdn zur Adoption freigeben
glad, to **be ~** 40T sich freuen, froh sein
glasses *pl* 105T Brille; **safety ~** 152 Schutzbrille
global 16 global, weltumspannend
globalization 130 Globalisierung
globetrotting 171 Weltenbummeln, Weltreise(n)
glove 43T Handschuh; **protective ~es** *pl* 152 Schutzhandschuhe
to **go: ~ off with sb** 47 mit jdm ein Verhältnis anfangen; **Off we ~.** 80T Los geht's! **~ on** 47 *(Dinge:)* laufen, gehen; 52T weitermachen, fortfahren; **out with sb** 40T mit jdm ausgehen; **~ for walks** 69V spazieren gehen; to **let ~ (of sth)** 153 (etw) loslassen
go, Here's another ~ at the same thing. 224 Ich versuch's nochmal.
goal 47 Ziel; **career ~** 137F berufliches Ziel; **~ post** 203 Torpfosten
good, for ~ 207 *hier:* zum Allgemeinwohl
goods *pl*, **consumer ~** 67 Konsumgüter
goodness 200 wertvolle Inhaltsstoffe
government 132 Regierung, öffentliche Verwaltung
to **grab** 159 anfassen, packen
grade 78, 202 Note
gram 17 Gramm
grand 204 großartig
grandparents *pl* 29F Großeltern
to **grant** 79 gewähren; **~ permission** 226 Erlaubnis erteilen
graph 91 Diagramm, Grafik
graphic: ~ art 224 Malerei und Grafik; **~ novel** 146 Bildroman, Comicroman
grass 174 Gras
grateful, to **be ~ to sb** 47 jdm dankbar sein
greenhouse gas 17 Treibhausgas
greens *pl* 21V Grünzeug, Gemüse
to **greet** 52 begrüßen
greeting 82 Begrüßung
grimace 160 Grimasse
grin 159 Grinsen
to **grin** 159 grinsen
ground 90T Boden
to **grow** 17 wachsen, zunehmen; 67 *(Pflanzen)* anbauen; **~ up** 37 aufwachsen; **~ to do sth** 21V (allmählich) dahin kommen, etw zu tun; **~ closer** 37 sich näherkommen, die Beziehung intensivieren
grown-up 114T erwachsen
growth, economic ~ 216 Wirtschaftswachstum
guarantee 119 Garantie
guard 152 Schutzhaube
guest 7 Gast
guide 99 Reiseführer; **tour ~** 103V Reiseleiter/in, Fremdenführer/in
guided tour 103T Führung
guideline 150T Richtlinie, Empfehlung
guild 135 Zunft, Gilde

guilty, to **find sb ~ of sth** 148 jdn einer Sache für schuldig befinden
gun powder 103V Schießpulver
guy 31 Typ, Kerl
gym 27 Fitness-Studio

H

habit 20 Gewohnheit
halfway though sth 111 mitten in etw, während etw
halt, to **spin to a ~** 159 zum Stehen kommen
hand, to **shake ~s** 52T die Hand geben, die Hände schütteln; **second-~** 67 gebraucht, aus zweiter Hand; **we have a revolt on our ~s** 222 eine Revolte kommt auf uns zu
to **hand: ~ sth in** 50T etw abgeben; **~ sth out** 44 etw verteilen; **~ sb sth** 105T jdm etw (über)geben; **~ in one's notice** 67 die Kündigung einreichen, kündigen
to **handle sth** 58 etw anfassen
handler 159 (Tier-)Betreuer/in
handout 54 Arbeitsblatt, Handzettel
hands-on 142 praktisch, lebensnah
handy 138T praktisch, handlich
to **happen** 20 geschehen, passieren
happiness 130 Zufriedenheit, Glück
happy, to **be ~ to do sth** 68 etw gern tun
hardly ever 90T kaum, so gut wie nie
harm, to **inflict ~** 226 Schaden zufügen
to **harm** 47 schaden
harmful 106T schädlich, nachteilig
harmless 149V harmlos
harmony 118 mehrstimmiger Gesang
harsh 171 rau
harvest 114 Ernte
hate 149V Hass
hateful 149V hasserfüllt
hazard 152 Gefahr
to **head: ~ off** 116T losfahren/-gehen; **~ out** 224 losziehen; **~ east** 171 gen Osten aufbrechen
head of department 176T Abteilungsleiter/in
heading 32 Überschrift; **sub-~** 18 Zwischenüberschrift
headline 56, 202 Überschrift; to **make the ~s** 214 Schlagzeilen machen
health 17 Gesundheit; **~ and safety** 152 Arbeitsschutz, Arbeitssicherheit; **~ care** 171 Gesundheitswesen, Krankenversorgung; **~ insurance** 171 Krankenversicherung
healthy 17 gesund
heart: ~ attack 57 Herzinfarkt; **~ disease** 21V Herzerkrankung; **His ~ missed a beat.** 173 Dies ließ ihm sein Herz höher schlagen.
heat, in ~ 159 läufig, rollig
heating 128T Heizung
hectare 118 Hektar
height 120 Höhe; 166 Körpergröße
heights *pl*, to **be scared of ~** 111 nicht schwindelfrei sein, Höhenangst haben; **fear of ~** 113 Höhenangst
heir 149V Erbe
hellish 160 höllisch
helmet 58 Helm
helper 60 Helfer/in
herbs *pl* 67 Kräuter
hero 9 Held
heroic 215 heldenhaft
hidden 56 verborgen, versteckt
high 210 Hochstimmung, Rausch; **~ in sth** 143 reich an etw
high-energy 143 energiereich
higher education 137 Hochschulbildung; to **enter ~** 202 ein Studium beginnen
highlight 32T Höhepunkt
to **highlight** 50 hervorheben
hill 102 Hügel, Berg
hire company 139 (Auto-)Vermietung
historical 167 historisch
history 102 Geschichte
to **hit sth** 215 auf etw treffen
hoax bomb alert 214 vorgetäuschter Bombenalarm
to **hold: ~ on** 160 durchhalten, sich festhalten; **~ sth up** 29F etw hochhalten; **~ the line** 164T *(Telefon:)* am Apparat bleiben
holder 128 Halter
holiday, public ~ 114 gesetzlicher Feiertag; **walking ~** 179T Wanderurlaub; **~ resort** 14 Urlaubsort, Ferienort
home: ~ town 174 Heimatstadt; **~ visit** 58 Hausbesuch
homemade 200 hausgemacht, selbstgemacht
homework 13 Hausaufgaben
honest 82 ehrlich, aufrichtig; **to be ~** 103 ehrlich gesagt …
honour 115V Ehre
to **hoot** 160 johlen
to **hop on/off** 102 ein-/aussteigen
hopefully 126T hoffentlich
horizon 169 Horizont
hormone 17 Hormon
horrible 99 schrecklich
horrified 162T entsetzt
hospitality 99 Bewirtung, Gastfreundschaft
host 98 Gastgeber
to **host** 50T moderieren; 133 beherbergen
hour, to **strike the ~** 103V die Stunde schlagen
house: H~ of Commons 103V Unterhaus *(des brit. Parlaments)*; **H~ of Lords** 103V Oberhaus *(des brit. Parlaments)*
household items *pl* 72 Haushaltsartikel
housekeeping issues *pl* 176T Haushaltsfragen
housework 47 Hausarbeit(en)
however 29, 201 allerdings, doch, jedoch, dagegen
to **hug** 115 umarmen
human 20T Mensch; 159 menschlich
humour 42 Humor
to **hurl** 159 schleudern
to **hurry** 131 eilen; **~ up** 12 sich beeilen
hurry, in a ~ 90T in Eile
hurt 40T verletzt
to **hurt** 40 wehtun, schmerzen, verletzen
husky 142 Schlittenhund
hygienic 128T hygienisch

I

ice cream 22 Eis, Eiskrem
iced tea 8 Eistee
iconic landmark 103V Wahrzeichen
ID card 150T Personalausweis
identical 174 identisch
identical twins *pl* 37 eineiige Zwillinge
to **identify** 15 identifizieren
identity theft 87 Identitätsdiebstahl
idiom 69 Redensart
to **ignore sth** 156 etw ignorieren
illegal 90T verboten, illegal
illness 55 Krankheit
to **illustrate** 24 illustrieren
image 103V Bild
to **imagine sth** 33 sich etw vorstellen
immediately 33 sofort
immigrant 114T Einwanderer/-in
immigration, I~s and Customs Enforcement 226 *US-Behörde für Einwanderung und Zoll*
imminent 226 bevorstehend
impact 106T Einfluss, Auswirkung(en); to **make an ~ on sth** 215 sich auf etw auswirken
implant 159 Implantat
to **implement** 125 in die Tat umsetzen, durchführen
to **import** 114T importieren
importance 26 Bedeutung, Wichtigkeit
impossible 171 unmöglich
to **impress** 50T beeindrucken
impressed 47 beeindruckt
impression 180 Eindruck
to **improve** 24 verbessern
in: ~ itself 106T an sich
inactivity 111 Untätigkeit
income 77 Einkommen
inconvenient 101 unpraktisch, unbequem
incorrect 217 falsch, unzutreffend
to **increase** 90T zunehmen, steigen; **~ sth** 29 etw steigern, etw erhöhen
increasingly 107T zunehmend
incredible 103V unglaublich
indeed 37 tatsächlich, in der Tat
independence 133 Unabhängigkeit
independent 60T unabhängig
to **indicate** 213 angeben, zu verstehen geben
indigenous 115V einheimisch, eingeboren
individual 91 einzeln, individuell; 119 Person, Einzelperson
indoor pool 62 Hallenbad
induction 152 Einarbeitung
industrial 122 industriell, Industrie-; **~ estate** 156, 220 Gewerbegebiet; **~ waste** 178 Industriemüll
inequality 171 Ungleichheit
infectious enthusiasm 204 ansteckende Begeisterung
inflammable 104 brennbar, entflammbar
to **inflict harm** 226 Schaden zufügen
influence 50 Einfluss
to **influence** 50 beeinflussen
to **inform** 16 informieren
informal 107T zwanglos, informell
initial 94 ursprünglich, anfänglich
injury 90T Verletzung
ink 153 Druckfarbe
input 223 Beitrag
insect 17 Insekt
to **insist** 119 darauf bestehen
to **inspire** 50 anregen, inspirieren
to **install** 132 einbauen, installieren
instead 31 stattdessen; **~ of** 60 anstelle von etw; 95 anstatt
instruction 60T Anleitung, Anweisung
instructor, ski ~ 170 Skilehrer/in

J

K

L

lottery, to **win the ~** 156 im Lotto gewinnen; **~ win** 214 Lottogewinn
lousy 160 lausig, beschissen
love, to **fall in ~ with sb/sth** 208 sich in jdn/etw verlieben
low: ~ in sth 143 arm an etw; **~ in fat** 200 fettarm; **of ~ priority** 226 unwichtig, unbedeutend
low-carb 21 kohlenhydratarm
low-cut top 52T tief ausgeschnittenes Oberteil
to **lower** 21V senken
lower arm 208 Unterarm
luck, to **have terrible ~** 108 furchtbares Pech haben
luckily 148 glücklicherweise
lucrative 88 lukrativ
luggage 104 Gepäck
lunch break 57 Mittagspause
luxury 62 Luxus
lyrics *pl* 134 Liedtext

M

machinery 118 Maschinen, Geräte
made up, to **be ~ of sth** 35 aus etw bestehen
magistrate 148 Richter/in
magnetic pouch 118 Magnettasche
magnetism 118 Magnetismus
magnitude 51V Größe
to **mail** 138T (per Post) senden, versenden
mail order 119 Versand
to **maintain** 176 warten, instandhalten
maintenance 127 Wartung, Instandhaltung
major 99 groß, bedeutend
to **make: ~ sb do sth** 11 jdn dazu bringen, etw zu tun; **~ up** 97 *(Anteil)* ausmachen; **~ sense** 179T vernünftig sein, einleuchten; **~ sure** 58 dafür sorgen, sicherstellen; **~ sth happen** 20 dafür sorgen, dass etw geschieht; 107T etw verwirklichen, etw ermöglichen; to **be made up of sth** 35 aus etw bestehen
to **manage** 208 zurechtkommen; 210 es schaffen; **~ sth** 32 etw verwalten, etw organisieren, etw managen; 63 etw bewältigen; 116T etw bewältigen, etw schaffen; **We'll ~.** 129 Wir kommen schon zurecht.
management, senior ~ 179T Geschäftsleitung
manager 43 Leiter/in
manners *pl* 160 Manieren
to **manufacture** 176 fertigen, herstellen
manufacturer 119 Hersteller/in
map 34 Landkarte, Karte
mark 203 Note; **painted ~** 224 Mal, Zeichnung
to **mark** 218 *(Gedenktag usw.)* begehen
marketplace 115V Marktplatz
married: ~ to sb 38 mit jdm verheiratet; to **get ~** 81 heiraten
marvellous 126T großartig
to **mask** 160 verbergen, verdecken
mass 124 Masse
massive 108 riesengroß
to **mat down** 159 *(Haare:)* plattstreichen
match 30 Spiel, Partie
to **match** 6 zuordnen; 38 zusammenpassen
material, composite ~ 125 Verbundmaterial; **original ~** 95 eigene Beiträge; **raw ~** 124 Rohstoff
maths 11 Mathe
matter 43T Sache, Angelegenheit; **no ~** 26 egal, ganz gleich
to **matter** 115V, 204 wichtig sein, von Belang sein; **it doesn't ~** 119 es ist egal
mattress 106T Matratze
maximum 104 Maximal-, Höchst-
meal, Enjoy your ~! 23 Guten Appetit!
to **mean** 6 bedeuten; 51V meinen
meaning 36, 201 Bedeutung
meaningfulness 215 Wichtigkeit, Aussagekraft
means of transport 154 Transportmittel
mechanic, motor ~ 170 Automechaniker/in
mechanical failure 171 technisches Versagen, Motorschaden
media *pl* 41 Medien; **social ~** 86 soziale Medien
to **mediate** 51V vermitteln, übersetzen
medical 60 medizinisch
medicine 21V Medikament(e); 61 Medizin
meeting space 126 Begegnungsstätte
to **melt** 17 schmelzen
member 35, 203 Mitglied; **~ of the general public** 215 (einfache/r) Bürger/in
membership 216 Mitgliedschaft; **~ card** 211 Mietgliedskarte; **~ fees** *pl* 216 Mitgliedsbeiträge
memory 167 Erinnerung, Gedächtnis
menswear 72 Herrenbekleidung
mental 27 geistig, mental
to **mention** 36 erwähnen, nennen; **Don't ~ it.** 164 Nichts zu danken.
mentor 42 Mentor/in
menu 21V Speisekarte, Speiseplan
to **merge** 216 zusammenfügen
merit 125 Vorzug
mess 148 Schweinerei, Gesudel
message, to **leave a ~** 164T eine Nachricht hinterlassen; to **take a ~** 164 *(Telefon:)* jdm etw ausrichten; **text ~** 85 SMS
messenger 45 Botschafter/in; **~ bag** 138T Kuriertasche
metabolic rate 143 Stoffwechsel
metal screen 123 Metallsieb
middle 62 Mitte
middle-aged 174 mittleren Alters
mill, paper ~ 122 Papierfabrik; **pulp ~** 122 Zellstofffabrik
to **mind** 39 etw dagegen haben; **Never ~.** 40T Das macht nichts.
mind, to **bear in ~** 119 daran denken, nicht vergessen; to **change one's ~** 68 seine Meinung ändern; to **come to ~** 166 jdm einfallen, jdm in den Sinn kommen; to **take one's ~ off sth** 210 jdn von etw ablenken
mind-blowing 51V irre, überwältigend
mindless(ly) 167 sinnfrei, hirnlos
mineral 17 Mineral
minerals *pl* 200 Mineralien
minimum 80 Mindest-
mining 162T Bergbau
minor 212 kleinere/r/s, unbedeutend
minority 21V Minderheit
mint 162T Minze
mirror 74 Spiegel
miserable, to **be ~** 106T sich elend fühlen
misfit, social ~ 135 Außenseiter, Sonderling
misinformation 94 Falschinformation
missing 32 fehlend; to **be ~** 32 fehlen
mistake 51 Fehler
to **misunderstand** 138 missverstehen, falsch verstehen
misunderstanding 138 Missverständnis
to **mix** 17 mischen, vermischen, anrühren
mixture 17 Mischung
mobile (phone) *BE* 8 Handy
model 140 Modell; **role ~** 42 Vorbild
moist 160 feucht
moisture 159 Feuchtigkeit
moisturizer 128 Feuchtigkeitscreme
monarch 102 Herrscher/in, Monarch/in
moneyless 67 ohne Geld
monkey 158 Affe
monument 14 Denkmal
mood 143 Stimmung, Laune
mosque 43F Moschee
most, to **make the ~ of sth** 47 das Beste aus etw machen, etw ausnutzen
most of all 42 vor allem
mostly 31 hauptsächlich, meistens
mother tongue 79 Muttersprache
motion technology 222 Bewegungstechnik
motivated 27 motiviert
motor: ~ mechanic 170 Automechaniker/in; **~ show** 140 Automobilmesse
motoring 139 Autofahren
mountain 14 Berg
to **move: ~ forward** 207 vorankommen; **~ in** 47 einziehen; **~ on (to sth)** 52T (mit etw) weitermachen; **~ up** 30T aufsteigen
movement 159, 206 Bewegung; **free ~** 216 Freizügigkeit
multicultural 162 multikulturell
multilingual 135 mehrsprachig
mural 147 Wandmalerei
murder mystery 102 Krimi
muscle 13 Muskel; **~ dysmorphia** 166 Muskeldysmorphie, Muskelsucht
muscular 166 muskulös
mushroom 67 Pilz
musician 87 Musiker/in
a must 52 ein Muss
mysterious(ly) 111 geheimnisvoll, rätselhaft
mystery, murder ~ 102 Krimi

N

naked 159 nackt
to **name: ~ sb sth** 206 jdn zu etw ernennen; **you ~ it** 107T alles Mögliche
narrow temperature range 208 schmaler Temperaturbereich
nasty 50T gemein, böse
nation 21V Land, Nation; **United N~s** *pl* 17 Vereinte Nationen
national: ~ anthem 111 Nationalhymne; **N~ Trust** 99 *brit. Organisation für Denkmalpflege und Naturschutz*
nationality 14 Staatsangehörigkeit, Nationalität
native: N~ American 114T amerikanische/r Ureinwohner/in; **~ language** 135 Muttersprache; **~ speaker** 133 Muttersprachler/in
natural 17 natürlich
nature 94 Wesen, Natur
nearby 116T in der Nähe
neck 160 Hals
need, to **satisfy one's ~s** 65 jds Bedürfnisse befriedigen; to **be in ~ of sth** 69V etw brauchen, etw benötigen

negative 8 verneinend, negativ
negativity 215 Negativität
to **negotiate** 216 verhandeln
negotiation 216 Verhandlung
neighbour 48 Nachbar/in
net 203 Netz
never 20 nie
New Year's Eve 109 Silvester
news: ~ **agency** 214 Nachrichtenagentur; ~ **agenda** 214 Schwerpunkte der Berichterstattung; ~ **organization** 94 Nachrichtenagentur; ~ **story** 143 Bericht *(in den Medien)*; ~ **value** 214 Nachrichtenwert
next to 6 neben
Nobel Peace Prize 45 Friedensnobelpreis
to **nod** 160 nicken
nomad 135 Nomade/-in
noon 33 Mittag
normally 31 normalerweise
nostril 160 Nüster, Nasenloch
nothing whatsoever 224 überhaupt nichts
notice 24 Ankündigung, Mitteilung, Aushang; to **hand in one's** ~ 67 die Kündigung einreichen, kündigen; ~ **board** 64 Schwarzes Brett
to **notice** 25 bemerken, feststellen
nourishing 24 nahrhaft
novel, dystopian ~ 218 *(Roman usw.:)* Schreckensvision; **graphic** ~ 146 Bildroman, Comicroman
nowadays 213 heute, heutzutage
nuclear family 35 Kernfamilie, Kleinfamilie
(registered) nurse 170 (examinierte/r) Krankenpfleger/-schwester
nursing 171 Krankenpflege
nutrient 17 Nährstoff
nutrition 21V Nahrung, Ernährung
nutritionist 17 Ernährungswissenschaftler/in
nutritious 201 nahrhaft, nährstoffreich

O

obesity 21V Fettleibigkeit
to **obey sth** 156 etw befolgen
object 120 Gegenstand, Objekt
obligation 58 Verpflichtung
observation wheel 103V Riesenrad
obsession 166 Besessenheit, Zwang
obstacle 30T Hindernis
to **obtain** 220 erhalten, bekommen
obvious 78 klar (erkennbar), offensichtlich
obviously 32T, 224 natürlich, offensichtlich
occasionally 96 gelegentlich, ab und zu
to **occur** 213 vorkommen
odd 210 gelegentlich
off: O~ we go. 80T Los geht's!; ~ **piste** 170 jenseits ausgetretener Pfade; to **be** ~ **to a promising start** 21V vielversprechend angelaufen sein
offender 147 Straffällige/r, Straftäter/in
offer 62 Angebot; **on** ~ 62 im Angebot, angeboten; **combination** ~ 62 Kombi-Angebot; **special** ~ 62 Sonderangebot
to **offer** 64 bieten, anbieten
officer, police ~ 90T Polizeibeamte/r
official 168 *(Sport:)* Kampfrichter/in; 92 offiziell; ~ **language** 133 Amtssprache
old-fashioned 174 altmodisch
once 14 einmal; **at** ~ 57 auf einmal
oneself, by ~ 108 allein
ongoing 214 laufend, fortdauernd
only child 37 Einzelkind
onwards, from ... ~ 219 seit ...
to **ooze** 159 hervorquellen
open day 134 Tag der offenen Tür
opening ceremony 111 Eröffnungszeremonie
opening times *pl* 42 Öffnungszeiten
to **operate** 119 funktionieren, vorgehen; 152 *(Geräte)* bedienen
opinion, in my ~ 20T meiner Meinung nach
opportunity 34 Möglichkeit, Gelegenheit
opposing 111 gegnerisch; ~ **team** 203 gegnerische Mannschaft
opposite 16 gegenüber; 101 gegenteilig, entgegengesetzt; 101 Gegenteil
oppression 218 Unterdrückung
optimistic 42 optimistisch
option 43T Möglichkeit, Alternative
order 20 Reihenfolge; to **get sth in** ~ 26 etw auf die Reihe kriegen; **in** ~ **to** 128 um ... zu; **mail** ~ 119 Versand; **running** ~ 107T Ablaufplan
to **order** 15 bestellen; ~ **sb removed** 226 jds Ausweisung anordnen
ordinary 52 gewöhnlich, normal
organic 118 organisch, biologisch, Bio-
organization 176T Unternehmen; **news** ~ 94 Nachrichtenagentur
organizational chart 176 Organigramm
organizing committee 107T Organisationskomitee
original 142 originell; ~ **material** 95 eigene Beiträge; ~ **thinking** 142 Scharfsinn, Originalität
original(ly) 114T, 206 ursprünglich
otherwise 155, 220 sonst
out, time ~ 62 Auszeit
outline 213 Übersicht, Stichpunkte
to **outline** 221 skizzieren, umreißen
oven 115 Ofen
overall 24 Gesamt-, insgesamt
to **overcome sth** 46 etw überwinden
overdose 56 Überdosis
overexposed 151 überbelichtet
overnight 220 über Nacht
overtime 212 Überstunden
to **own** 71, 210 besitzen
owner 107T, 214 Inhaber/in, Besitzer/in

P

pace 142 Tempo
to **pack** 103T packen
package 17 Packung
packaging 128 Verpackung
paddle boarding, stand up ~ 43F Stehpaddeln
pain, chronic ~ **condition** 220 chronische Schmerzerkrankung
to **paint** 148 malen
paint 146 (Mal-)Farbe
painted mark 224 Mal, Zeichnung
painting 148 Gemälde
palace 103V Palast, Schloss
pallet 126 Palette
pan 162T Topf, Pfanne
panel, solar ~ 67 Solarzelle, Solarmodul
panoramic view 103V Panoramablick
panting 160 keuchend
paper: ~ **cup** 122 Pappbecher; ~ **mill** 122 Papierfabrik; ~ **plate** 174 Pappteller
paragraph 18 *(Text:) Absatz*
paramedic 56 Rettungssanitäter/in
parent, single ~ 35 Alleinerziehende/r; **single-**~ **family** 35 Einelternfamilie; **set of** ~**s** 37 Elternpaar
parking space 10 Parkplatz
parkour 30T Parkour
parliament 103V Parlament
part, to **take** ~ **in sth** 16 an etw teilnehmen; **spare** ~ 126 Ersatzteil
to **part** 70 auseinandergehen, (sich) trennen
participant 32 Teilnehmer/in
to **participate in sth** 99 an etw teilnehmen
particular 20 spezielle/r/s, bestimmt; **in** ~ 143 speziell; **sth in** ~ 72 etw Spezielles
particularly 94 besonders
partly 130, 215 teilweise, zum Teil
pass, security ~ 176T Firmenausweis
to **pass** 78 *(Prüfung)* bestehen; ~ **sb** 174 jdn überholen, an jdm vorbeigehen; ~ **off** 215 *(Ereignis, Veranstaltung:)* verlaufen; ~ **sth along/on** 94 etw weitergeben; ~ **sth on** 224 etw weitersagen; ~ **the time** 148 sich die Zeit vertreiben
passenger 105 Passagier, Fluggast
passer-by 218 Passant/in
passion 135 Leidenschaft
passionate(ly) 50T leidenschaftlich
passport 84 Pass, Reisepass
path, cycle ~ 142 Fahrradweg
patience 42 Geduld
patient(ly) 111 geduldig
pattern 91F, 208 Muster
pay 80T Lohn, Bezahlung; ~ **rise** 212 Lohnerhöhung
to **pay attention to sth** 31 auf etw achten
pea 200 Erbse
peace 45 Frieden; **Nobel P~ Prize** 45 Friedensnobelpreis
pedagogical staff 77 Lehrpersonal
pedestrian 90T Fußgänger/in
peers *pl* 202 Gleichaltrige, Schulkameraden; 222 Kollegen
pen 8 Stift; 159 Pferch, Gehege
pencil 8 Bleistift
people 115V Volk
perceived 223 (individuell) empfunden
percent, per cent 94 Prozent
percentage 133 Anteil, Prozentsatz
to **perform** 44 aufführen, spielen; 202 *(in einer Prüfung usw.)* abschneiden
performance 115V Darbietung, Aufführung
performer 107T Künstler/in, Darsteller/in
period 49 Zeitabschnitt, Zeit; **trial** ~ 173 Probezeit
permanent 173 dauerhaft, unbefristet
permission 58 Erlaubnis; to **grant** ~ 226 Erlaubnis erteilen
permit, work ~ 80 Arbeitserlaubnis
permitted 104 gestattet, erlaubt
person, in ~ 38 persönlich
persona 210 Ich, Selbst
personal 7 persönlich, privat; ~ **best** 166 persönliche Bestleistung
personality 52 Persönlichkeit
perspective 112 Perspektive, Sicht, Blickwinkel
pest, to **control** ~**s** 118 Schädlinge bekämpfen
to **persuade** 20 überzeugen, überreden
persuasive 137F überzeugend, schlagkräftig

phase 43 Phase
phone, to answer the ~ 164T ans Telefon gehen; to **pick up the ~** 103T ans Telefon gehen; **cell ~** *AE* 90 Handy; **mobile** *BE* 8 Handy; **~ duty** 164 Telefondienst
phone-in 179 *Sendung mit Hörerbeteiligung per Telefon*
photocopy 14 Fotokopie
to **photograph** 167 fotografieren
photographer 150T Fotograf/in
photography 43F Fotografie
photoshoot 138T Fotoaufnahmen, Shooting
piano 9 Klavier
to **pick** 130; 204 auswählen; **~ on sb** 209 jdn drangsalieren; **~ sb up** 116T jdn abholen; 226 jdn festnehmen; **~ sth up** 21V etw nehmen, etw holen; **~ up the phone** 103T ans Telefon gehen
pickled 162T (sauer) eingelegt
pie 114T Torte; **~ chart** 85 Tortendiagramm
pile 160 Haufen
to **pin** 24 (mit einer Nadel) anheften
to **pinch** 159 kneifen, zwicken, zusammendrücken
piste, off ~ 170 jenseits ausgetretener Pfade
pitch, football ~ 203 Fußballfeld, Fußballplatz
placemat 91 Tischset
plain 22 einfach, Natur
to **plant** 99 pflanzen
plant, chipping ~ 123 Hackschnitzelanlage; **printing ~** 152 Großdruckerei; **~ tour** 222 Betriebsbesichtigung
plastic: ~ bag 132 Plastiktüte; **~ liner** 125 Plastikauskleidung, Kunststoffinnenbeschichtung
plate, paper ~ 174 Pappteller
pleasure 107T Vergnügen
plot 103V Verschwörung
plotter 218 Verschwörer/in
pocket money 13 Taschengeld
pod 103V Gondel
point, at one ~ 69 an einer Stelle; **there's no ~ in doing sth** 70T es hat keinen Sinn, etw zu tun; **What's the ~?** 106T Was soll das? Was hat das für einen Sinn?
to **point: ~ sth at sth** 60T etw auf etw richten; **~ at sth** 159 auf etw zeigen, auf etw deuten; **~ out sth** 52 auf etw hinweisen
to **poke sth through sth** 159 etw durch etw stecken
police: ~ officer 90T Polizeibeamte/r; **~ station** 146 Polizeiwache
policy 92 Vorgehensweise, Linie, Politik; **~ shift** 226 Politikwandel
polite 52 höflich
political 207 politisch
politics 103V Politik
to **pollute** 124 verschmutzen
pollution 121 (Umwelt-)Verschmutzung
polyethylene 123 Polyäthylen
to **ponder sth** 69 über etw nachdenken
pool table 64 Billardtisch
popular 29 beliebt
population 106T Bevölkerung
pork 20T Schweinefleisch
port 37 Hafen
portfolio 224 Mappe
portrait 150T Porträt
to **portray** 44 darstellen, zeigen, porträtieren
pose 150 Haltung, Pose
to **pose sth with sb** 226 jdn vor etw stellen
position 76 Stelle, Stellung, Position
positive 8 bejahend, positiv
possibility 90T Möglichkeit
post 148 Pfosten, Säule; **goal ~** 203 Torpfosten
postage 119 Porto, Versandkosten
potential 214 potentiell
potentially 226 potentiell
potter's wheel 159 Töpferscheibe
pottery, to make ~ 159 töpfern
pouch, magnetic ~ 118 Magnettasche
pound 43T Pfund
to **pound** 210 hämmern, stampfen
poverty 51V Armut
powder, gun ~ 103V Schießpulver
powdered milk 17 Milchpulver
power 128 Strom; 204 Kraft, Energie; **will-~** 203 Willenskraft
practice 94 Praktik; to **put sth into ~** 69F etw in die Praxis umsetzen; **football ~** 131 Fußballtraining
to **practise** 6 üben
precise 34 genau, präzise
to **predict** 132, 215 vorhersagen
predictability 215 Vorhersehbarkeit
prediction 175 Voraussage, Vorhersage
preference 162 Vorliebe
pregnant, to get ~ 170 schwanger werden
prehensile 159 zum Greifen geeignet
premises *pl*, **school ~** 143 Schulgelände
preparation 135 Vorbereitung
to **prepare** 16 (sich) vorbereiten; 62, 200 *(Essen)* zubereiten
prepared, to be ~ to do sth 52T bereit sein, etw zu tun
prescription 58 (ärztliches) Rezept
present 12 Geschenk
to **present** 24 vorstellen, präsentieren; 104 vorzeigen; **~ sb with a choice** 226 jdn vor die Wahl stellen
presentation 31 Präsentation
presenter 103V Moderator/in
president 133 Präsident/in
press 41 Presse; **printing ~** 153 Druckmaschine; **~ conference** 214 Pressekonferenz; **~ kit** 168 Pressemappe; **~ release** 214 Presseerklärung
to **press** 60 drücken
pressure 28 Druck; **blood ~** 21V Blutdruck
to **pretend to do sth** 89 vorgeben, etw zu tun; so tun, als ob
to **prevent** 132 verhindern
previous 167 frühere/r/s
previously 226 zuvor, bislang
price 24 Preis
pride, to warm with ~ 204 von Stolz erfüllt werden
primarily 222 hauptsächlich, vorrangig
primary: ~ school *BE* 21V Grundschule; **in their ~ years** 222 im Grundschulalter
princess 41 Prinzessin
principal 21V Schuldirektor/in
principle 216 Grundsatz, Prinzip
print 19 gedruckt, Druck-; **~ run** 153 Auflage
to **print** 128 drucken
printer 71 Drucker; **3D ~** 208 3D-Drucker
printing: ~ plant 152 Großdruckerei; **~ press** 153 Druckmaschine; **~ works** 153 Druckerei
priority, of low ~ 226 unwichtig, unbedeutend
prize 110 Preis, Gewinn; **Nobel Peace P~** 45 Friedensnobelpreis
procedure 153 Vorgang; **safety ~es** *pl* 152 Sicherheitsmaßnahmen, Sicherheitsbestimmungen
process 122, 216 Verfahren, Verarbeitung
to **process** 123 verarbeiten
procession 218 Umzug, Prozession
produce 118 (landwirtschaftliche) Erzeugnisse, Lebensmittel; **surplus ~** 220 überschüssige Lebensmittel
to **produce** 17 produzieren
producer 200 Produzent/in, Hersteller/in, Erzeuger/in
product 20T Produkt, Erzeugnis; **finished ~** 176 Endprodukt
Production (department) 176 Produktion(sabteilung)
profession 33 Beruf
professional 75 beruflich; 126 professionell
to **profile** 135 porträtieren
profit 118 Gewinn
programmer 40 Programmierer/in
progress 27 Fortschritt(e), Entwicklung, Vorankommen
to **promise** 136 versprechen
promising start, to be off to a ~ 21V vielversprechend angelaufen sein
to **promote sth** 94 etw begünstigen, etw fördern
promotion 212 Beförderung
prompt 33 Stichwort
to **pronounce** 6 aussprechen
proper(ly) 58 richtig, ordentlich
property 119 Eigentum; **lost ~** 107T Fundsachen
proportion 217 Anteil
pros and cons *pl* 142 Für und Wider, Argumente dafür und dagegen
prospects *pl*, **career ~** 135 Berufsaussichten
prosthetic arm 208 Armprothese
to **protect** 119 schützen, beschützen
protection 119 Schutz
protective: ~ clothing 152 Schutzkleidung; **~ gloves** *pl* 152 Schutzhandschuhe
protectors *pl*, **ear ~** 152 Gehörschutz
protein 17 Eiweiß, Protein(e)
proud 148 stolz
to **prove** 37 beweisen, nachweisen
proverb 69 Sprichwort
to **provide** 26 liefen, bieten; 43F zur Verfügung stellen
provided 106T vorausgesetzt, dass
provocative 137F provokant, provozierend
proxy 173 Stellvertreter/in, stellvertretend
pub 108 Kneipe, Gasthaus
public: member of the general ~ 215 (einfache/r) Bürger/in; **~ holiday** 114 gesetzlicher Feiertag; **~ school** *AE* 21V staatliche Schule; **~ services** *pl* 216 öffentliche Dienstleistungen; **~ transport** 132 öffentliche Verkehrsmittel
to **publish** 107, 214 veröffentlichen, publizieren
publicity 87 öffentliche Aufmerksamkeit, Werbung

to **pull** 153 ziehen; to ~ **sth down** 152 etw absenken
pulp 122 Papierbrei, Zellstoff; ~ **mill** 122 Zellstofffabrik
pumpkin 114 Kürbis
to **punish** 161 bestrafen
puny 166 schwächlich, mickrig
purchase 106T Kauf, Einkauf
to **purport** 94 behaupten, zum Inhalt haben
purpose 206 Ziel, Zweck
push 226 Vorstoß
to **put** 204 formulieren; ~ **sth aside** 72 etw zurücklegen; ~ **sth up** 128 etw aufhängen; ~ **sb at risk** 57 jdn gefährden; ~ **on weight** 166 zunehmen; ~ **out the word** 106T die Nachricht verbreiten; ~ **sb through** 164T *(Telefon:)* jdn durchstellen; ~ **sth into action** 143 etw in die Tat umsetzen; ~ **sth into practice** 69F etw in die Praxis umsetzen
puzzle 102 Rätsel

Q

qualification 80T Abschluss, Ausbildung
qualified 154 mit Abschluss, ausgebildet
to **qualify** 80 (sich) qualifizieren
quality 42 Eigenschaft
quality journalism outlets *pl* 94 seriöse Medien
quantity 118 Menge
questionnaire 85 Fragebogen
queue 103V Warteschlange
to **queue** 120 sich (in einer Warteschlange) anstellen
quotation 137 Zitat

R

race 33 Rennen; 157 Rasse
racist 149V rassistisch
radio advertisement 106 Werbespot (im Radio)
rage 160 Wut
rail travel 154 Bahnverkehr
railway 97 Eisenbahn
to **raise:** ~ **funds** 37 Spenden sammeln; ~ **one's eyebrows** 160 die Stirn runzeln
ramp 43T Rampe
range 115V Reihe, Auswahl, Vielfalt; **narrow temperature** ~ 208 schmaler Temperaturbereich
rank 213 Stellung, Rang
to **rank** 24 einstufen, (nach Rang) ordnen
ranking list 43 Rangliste
rarely 31 selten, kaum
rate 21V Quote; **metabolic** ~ 143 Stoffwechsel
rather 224 eher, vielmehr; ~ **than** 94 anstatt
rational 160 vernünftig, rational
raw material 124 Rohstoff
razor blade 104 Rasierklinge
reach 160 Reichweite
to **reach** 64 erreichen; ~ **for sth** 17 nach etw greifen; ~ **out** 160 die Hand/Hände ausstrecken
to **react to sth** 67 auf etw reagieren
readership 214 Leser, Leserschaft
ready, to **get** ~ 28 sich fertigmachen, sich zurechtmachen; to **get sth** ~ 114 etw vorbereiten
real-life 204 real, aus dem wirklichen Leben
realistic 135 realistisch
to **realize: sb ~es sth** 47 jdm wird/ist etw klar, jdm wird/ist etw bewusst
reason 13 Grund, Begründung; to **give ~s** 15 begründen
to **recall sth** 167 sich an etw erinnern
receipt 73 Quittung, Beleg, Kassenbon
to **receive** 37 erhalten, bekommen
recent 200 aktuell; **in ~ years** 218 in den letzten Jahren
recently 89 neulich
receptionist 7 Empfangsmitarbeiter/in, Rezeptionist/in
to **reckon** 126T meinen, glauben
to **recommend** 22 empfehlen
record 28 Aufzeichnung(en), Protokoll; to **have a criminal** ~ 148 vorbestraft sein; **without a (criminal)** ~ 226 nicht vorbestraft
to **record** 27 aufzeichnen, protokollieren; ~ **sth** 66 etw aufnehmen
recording 66 Aufzeichnung, Aufnahme
to **recover** 57 sich erholen
recovery 210 Genesung
to **recruit** 176T *(Personal)* einstellen
recruiter 76 einstellendes Unternehmen, Personalvermittler/in
recyclable 125 recyclebar
red blood cells *pl* 20 rote Blutkörperchen
to **redefine** 224 neu definieren
reduced to nothing, to **be** ~ 220 zunichte gemacht werden
reduction 119 (Preis-)Nachlass
to **refer to sth** 103V sich auf etw beziehen
referee 79 Referenz
referendum 216 Volksentscheid
to **reflect** 163 widerspiegeln, wiedergeben; 214 widerspiegeln; ~ **on sth** 51 über etw nachdenken
refreshment point 33 Verpflegungspunkt
refrigerator 166 Kühlschrank
refugee 79 Flüchtling
refund 119 Rückerstattung
to **refund** 119 rückerstatten
to **refuse to do sth** 38 sich weigern, etw zu tun
to **refute** 94 etw entkräften, etw widerlegen
regarded, to **be ~ as sth** 226 als etw gelten
regarding 179 betreffend, bezüglich
to **register** 33 sich anmelden; 61 anmelden, eintragen
registration 33 Anmeldung
regularly 85 regelmäßig
regulations *pl*, **safety** ~ 7 Sicherheitsvorschriften, -vorkehrungen
to **reimburse sb sth** 179T jdm etw erstatten
to **reject** 224 ablehnen
related, to **be** ~ 90T zusammenhängen
relation, in ~ to sth 224 in Bezug auf etw
relationship 35 Beziehung
relaxation 62 Entspannung, Erholung
relaxed 87 locker, entspannt
release 37 Mitteilung, Veröffentlichung; **press** ~ 214 Presseerklärung
to **release** 87 veröffentlichen
relevant 33 relevant, wichtig (für etw)
relief, earthquake ~ 50T Erdbebenhilfe
religious 77 religiös
religious leader 43F Religionsführer/in
to **relish** 159 genießen
to **relocate** 226 umziehen, übersiedeln
to **rely on sth** 94 sich auf etw verlassen
remote control 29F Fernbedienung
removal 226 Ausweisung
to **remove** 21V entfernen; ~ **sth from sth** 128 etw aus etw nehmen; to **order sb ~ed** 226 jds Ausweisung anordnen
rent 99 Miete
to **rent** 98 mieten
rental 108 Miete, Miet-
repair 126 Reparatur
to **repair** 99 reparieren
repetition 94 Wiederholung
to **replace** 58 ersetzen, austauschen
replacement 119 Ersatz
to **reply** 173 antworten, entgegnen
report 56 Reportage, Bericht
to **report** 41 berichten, Bericht erstatten; ~ **sb/sth** 61 jdn/etw melden; ~ **to sb** 176T jdm unterstehen; ~ **back to sb** 8 jdm berichten, jdm Bericht erstatten
to **represent** 50 vertreten, repräsentieren; 169 darstellen, wiedergeben
to **request sth** 87 um etw bitten, sich etw wünschen
to **require** 121 erfordern; 128 wünschen, benötigen
representation 153 Vertretung
representative 83 Vertreter/in, Repräsentant/in
reputation 118 Ruf
requirement 223 Bestimmung, Anforderung
resealable 104 wiederverschließbar
research 34 Recherche, Nachforschungen; 201 Forschung, Untersuchung(en); **economic** ~ 107 Wirtschaftsforschung;
to **research sth** 34 etw recherchieren, Nachforschungen über etw anstellen
researcher 60, 200 Forscher/in
resident 103V Bewohner, Einwohner
resit, to **do ~s** 47 Prüfungen wiederholen
resort 98 Ferienort; **holiday** ~ 14 Urlaubsort, Ferienort
resources *pl* 106T Rohstoffe, Ressourcen
respect 52 Respekt
to **respect** 21 respektieren
respectful 161 respektvoll
to **respond** 82 antworten; ~ **to sth** 21V auf etw reagieren
response 141 Reaktion, Antwort
responsibility 46 Verantwortung, Verantwortlichkeit
rest 62 Erholung, Ruhe
to **rest** 116T (sich) ausruhen; ~ **sth against sth** 159 etw an etw lehnen
restoration 126T Restaurierung
restriction 104 Beschränkung
restroom *AE* 116T Toilette
result 17 Ergebnis, Resultat
retail 72 Einzelhandel
retailer 119 Einzelhändler/in
return, in ~ 88 als Gegenleistung
to **return sth** 73 etw zurückgeben
to **reunite sb/sth with sb** 107T jdn/etw mit jdm wieder zusammenbringen
revealing 212 aufschlussreich
reverse, in ~ 166 umgekehrt
to **reverse** 159 umkehren
review 101 Rezension, Kritik

S

sheer 94 rein, schier
sheet (of paper) 91 Blatt (Papier)
shelf, shelves 9 Regal, Regale
shift, cultural ~ 222 Kulturwandel; **policy ~** 226 Politikwandel
to **shine** 174 scheinen
shipping container 123 Schiffscontainer
shock, electric ~ 152 Stromschlag
shocked 51V schockiert
to **shoot** 206 schießen; **~ sb** 138T jdn erschießen
shop assistant 72 Verkäufer/in
shop floor 72 Verkaufsfläche
shopkeeper 43F Ladenbesitzer/in
shopping 58 Einkäufe; to **go ~** 58 einkaufen gehen
shore 115V Küste
short, to **be ~ on sth** 6 zu wenig von etw haben; **~ story** 110 Kurzgeschichte; **~-term** 211 kurzfristig
shot 118 Foto, Aufnahme
shoulder 40T Schulter
show 13 (TV-, Radio-)Sendung; 160 Vorstellung
to **show sb around** 100 jdn herumführen
showcase 115V Schau, Ausstellung
shower, to **have a ~** 33 duschen
to **shut down** 153 abschalten
sick, to **be ~ of sth** 66 etw satt haben; **~ day** 212 Krankentag
to **sigh** 159 seufzen
sight 103 Sehenswürdigkeit; to **lose ~ of sth** 174 etw aus den Augen verlieren
sign 81 Anzeichen; **in ~ of sth** 226 im Zeichen von etw; **safety ~** 152 Sicherzeitszeichen, Warnzeichen; **street ~** 60T Straßenschild
to **sign: ~ sb** 120 jdn unter Vertrag nehmen; **~ sth sth** 224 etw mit etw signieren; **~ off** 61 sich abmelden, *(Telefonat)* beenden
signature 39 Unterschrift
significance 115V Bedeutung
significant(ly) 143 erheblich
to **silence** 92 *(Handy)* stummschalten; **~ sth** 159 etw zum Schweigen bringen
silly 90T albern
similar 50, 200 ähnlich
similarity 157, 225 Ähnlichkeit
simplicity 214 Einfachheit
simply 67 einfach, schlichtweg, nur
since 47 seit
sincerely, Yours ~ 79, 205 Mit freundlichen Grüßen
to **sing along** 171 mitsingen
single parent 35 Alleinerziehende/r; **~ family** 35 Einelternfamilie
to **sit: ~ back** 142 sich zurücklehnen; **~ by** 94 tatenlos zusehen
site, building ~ 135 Baustelle
size 72 Größe
sketch 72 Skizze
ski instructor 170 Skilehrer/in
skill 16 Fähigkeit, Fertigkeit, Kompetenz
skillful 30T geschickt
to **skim** 66 *(Text)* überfliegen
skin 153 Haut
skinny 166 mager, dürr
skull 159 Schädel
skyscraper 173 Wolkenkratzer
slayer 94 Schlächter/in
to **sleep** 9 schlafen
sleeping bag 106T Schlafsack
slice 18 (Kuchen-)Stück
to **slide** 159 gleiten; **~ down** 159 herunterrutschen
slightly damaged 126 leicht beschädigt
to **slip** 58 ausrutschen
to **slow** 160 sich verlangsamen; **~ down** 6 langsamer sprechen
smallholder 67 Kleinbauer/-bäuerin
smallholding 67 Kleinbauernhof
smart(ly) 52T *(Kleidung:)* schick; 142 intelligent, klug
smell 115 Geruch
to **smell** 128T riechen
smooth(ly) 52T reibungslos, glatt; 160 geschmeidig, weich
snake 171 Schlange
snap 150 Schnapsschuss
to **snap** 167 einen Schnappschuss machen; **~ sth** 160 etw (entzwei)brechen
to **snick open** 159 sich mit einem leisen Knarren öffnen
to **snort at sth** 160 etw verächtlich anschnauben
soaked 218 getränkt
soap 67 Seife; **bar of ~** 129 Stück Seife
soapwort 67 Seifenkraut
to **soar** 166 in die Höhe schnellen
to **sober** 160 nüchtern werden, ernst werden
sociable 99 gesellig, umgänglich
social: ~ media 27 soziale Medien; **~ misfit** 135 Außenseiter, Sonderling; **~ worker** 47 Sozialarbeiter/in
socializing 134 Geselligkeit
society 49 Gesellschaft
soda, baking ~ 67 Natron
soil, to **feed the ~** 118 den Boden mit Nährstoffen versorgen
solar panel 67 Solarzelle, Solarmodul
solar-powered air-conditioning 208 Solar-Klimaanlage
soldier 103V Soldat/in
solution 60T Lösung
solvable 51V lösbar
to **solve** 51V lösen
sophisticated 103V modern, technisch fortgeschritten
to **sort** 48 einordnen, einsortieren; **~ out sth** 29 etw klären, etw regeln
sound 10 Laut, Klang
to **sound** 37 klingen
source 17 Quelle
soya 20T Soja
space: parking ~ 10 Parkplatz; **~ of time** 57 Zeitspanne; **meeting ~** 126 Begegnungsstätte; **wide open ~s** *pl* 171 weites Land
to **spare sth** 102 etw übrig haben
spare part 126 Ersatzteil
to **spatter** 159 spritzen
to **speak: ~ up** 6 lauter sprechen; **~ out against sb** 206 sich (öffentlich) gegen jdn aussprechen, jdn kritisieren; **Speaking.** 164 *(Telefon:)* Am Apparat.
special: ~ deal 114T Sonderangebot; **~ exhibition** 116T Sonderausstellung; **~ offer** 62 Sonderangebot
speech 43 Vortrag, Rede; **~ bubble** 11 Sprechblase
speed 111 Geschwindigkeit
to **spend** 13 *(Zeit:)* verbringen; 67 *(Geld)* ausgeben
spending 106T, 210 Ausgabe(n)
spicy 162T würzig, scharf
to **spin** 159 drehen; 159 sich herumdrehen; **~ to a halt** 159 zum Stehen kommen
spine 160 Rückgrat, Rücken
spirit, in good ~s 107T guter Dinge, gut gelaunt; **team ~** 30T Mannschaftsgeist; to **drive away evil ~s** 218 böse Geister vertreiben
to **split up** 31 sich trennen
spoken language 12 gesprochene Sprache
spokesman 226 Sprecher
spontaneous 150 spontan
sport, to **do ~** 25 Sport treiben
sportswear 72 Sportbekleidung
to **spot** 166 erkennen
to **spray** 123 sprühen
spray can 148 Sprühdose
spread 17 (Brot-)Aufstrich
to **spread** 94 (sich) verbreiten
spy 142 Spion/in
squash 114 Speisekürbis
to **squeeze** 123 drücken, quetschen
stable 41 stabil
stacked with sth 166 voll von etw, mit etw beladen
stadium 110 Stadion
staff 77 Personal; **pedagogical ~** 77 Lehrpersonal
staffer, senior ~ 222 leitende/r Angestellte/r
stage 107T Bühne; 122 Phase, Abschnitt, Schritt; **early ~** 21V Frühstadium
stairs *pl* 58 Treppe
stall, food ~ 115V Essensstand
to **stamp one's feet** 111 mit den Füßen trampeln
stand up paddle boarding 43F Stehpaddeln
standard 119 Norm
star 101 Stern
to **stare at sth** 160 etw anstarren
stark example 226 krasses Beispiel
to **start: ~ off** 6 anfangen; **~ a family** 169 eine Familie gründen
started, to **get ~** 6 loslegen, anfangen
starter 22 Vorspeise
state 14 Staat
statement 6 Aussage, Aussagesatz; 206 (öffentliche) Erklärung
statistics *pl* 90T Statistiken
status 216 Ansehen
stay 80T Aufenthalt
to **steal** 155 stehlen
steel disk 123 Stahlscheiben
steep 102 steil
step 91 Schritt; 103V Stufe
to **step: ~ away from sth** 167 von etw zurückgehen/-treten; **~ out in front of a car** 90 vor ein Auto laufen; **~ out of sth** 174 aus etw steigen, aus etw treten
stereotype 135 Klischee
steward 107T Ordner/in
to **stick to sth** 82 sich an etw halten
stir-fried 22 pfannengerührt
stone 166 ≈ *6,35 kg*
stone 62 Stein
stool 159 Hocker
to **stop off** 123 Station machen, einkehren
storage, central ~ 220 Zentrallager

store 70T Laden, Geschäft; **department ~** 72 Kaufhaus
to **store** 176 lagern
storey 173 Stockwerk
storm 147 Sturm
story, news ~ 143 Bericht *(in den Medien)*
stove, wood-burning ~ 67 Holzofen
straight 116T direkt; **~ ahead** 116T geradeaus
strangely, to **act ~** 131 sich seltsam verhalten
strategy 135 Strategie
straw dummy 218 Strohpuppe
streak, fatty ~s *pl* 21V Schaumzellen, Verkalkungen
street, to **take to the ~s** 149V, 218 auf die Straße gehen; **~ sign** 60T Straßenschild
strength 30 Stärke, Kraft
stressed 63 gestresst
stressed out 211 gestresst
stressful 64 anstrengend, stressig
to **stretch back for generations** 218 sich um Generationen zurückerstrecken
strict 162T streng
stride 159 (großer) Schritt
to **strike the hour** 103V die Stunde schlagen
to **strive for sth** 166 nach etw streben, etw anstreben
structure 115V Bauwerk, Konstruktion
structure 54 Aufbau
to **structure** 54 strukturieren
struggle 77 Kampf
to **struggle: ~ to do sth** 220 Mühe haben, etw zu tun; **~ with sth** 226 mit etw ringen
stuck, to **get ~** 153 hängen bleiben, sich verfangen
student 9 Schüler/in, Student/in
study 94, 200 Untersuchung, Studie
to **study** 37 studieren; **~ sth** 24 sich etw genau ansehen/durchlesen; 201 etw untersuchen, etw erforschen; 204 sich mit etw (eingehend) beschäftigen
stuff 70T, 200 Sachen, Zeug
style 72 Stil, Art
sub-heading 18 Zwischenüberschrift
sub-Saharan 17 südlich der Sahara
subject 150T Motiv, Gegenstand; 205 Thema
submission, in ~ 159 unterwürfig
subscriber 87 Abonnent/in
substantially 226 wesentlich, erheblich
substitute 58 Ersatz, Ersetzung
to **subsume** 160 aufnehmen, vereinnahmen
suburban 202 Vorstadt-, am Stadtrand
subway *BE* 148 Fußgängerunterführung
to **succeed** 142, 202 Erfolg haben, erfolgreich sein
success 96 Erfolg
successful 50, 202 erfolgreich
suddenly 142 plötzlich
to **suffer** 41 leiden; **~ from sth** 17 an etw *(Krankheit usw.)* leiden
sufferer 166 Leidende/r, Patient/in
sugar-rich 143 stark zuckerhaltig
to **suggest** 167 nahelegen
suggestion 29 Vorschlag
to **suit: ~ sb** 212 zu jdm passen; **~ sth** 69F zu etw passen; **Suit yourself.** 146 Wie du willst.
suitable 22 geeignet
to **sum up: to ~** 149F zusammenfassend
sunny 151 sonnig
sunshine, in the ~ 203 in der Sonne
supervisor 72 Vorgesetzte/r
to **supply** 176 liefern; **~ sth** 77 etw zur Verfügung stellen
to **support** 56 unterstützen; **~ sb** 41 jdm helfen, jdn unterstützen
supporter 216 Befürworter/in; 218 Anhänger/in, Vertreter/in
supportive 21V unterstützend
to **suppose** 78 annehmen, glauben
supposed, to **be ~ to do sth** 47 etw (eigentlich) tun sollen
sure, to **make ~** 58 dafür sorgen, sicherstellen
to **surf the internet** 90T im Internet surfen
surface 148 Oberfläche, Fläche
surgery 166 Operation
to **surround** 51V umgeben
surplus produce 220 überschüssige Lebensmittel
surprised 37 überrascht, erstaunt
surprisingly 21V erstaunlicherweise
surrounded 102 umgeben
surroundings *pl* 101 Umgebung; 212 Umfeld
survey 85, 202 Umfrage
to **survive** 20 überleben
to **suspect** 37 vermuten
suspicious, to **be ~ of sb** 157 jdm gegenüber misstrauisch sein
to **sustain** 226 halten, aufrechterhalten
sustainable 118 nachhaltig
to **swap** 65 tauschen; 177T (die Seite) wechseln; **~ sth for sth** 211 etw gegen etw eintauschen
swastika 149V Hakenkreuz
sweaty 138T verschwitzt
to **swing** 159 schwingen, schlenkern, schaukeln; **~ the competition in sb's favour** 204 das Pendel zu jds Gunsten umschlagen lassen
to **switch: ~ off** 106T ausschalten, ausmachen; **~ to sth** 222 auf etw umsteigen
system 57 Organismus

T

tabloid journal 94, 214 Boulevardblatt
tactic 21V Taktik
tag 148 Marke, Kennzeichnung; **~ line** 28 Bildunterschrift, Slogan
to **take: ~ up** 173 *(Platz, Raum)* einnehmen; 206 *(Posten)* antreten; **~ sth round** 58 etw vorbeibringen; **~ to the streets** 149V, 218 auf die Straße gehen
talented 50 talentiert
talk 47 Vortrag
talkative 173 gesprächig
tar 218 Teer
target group 24 Zielgruppe
task 16 Aufgabe
taste 20T Geschmack; to **have a ~ of sth** 126T etw probieren; to **cater for all ~s** 140 für jeden Geschmack etw bieten
to **taste (of sth)** 15 (nach etw) schmecken
taster session 142 Schnupperkurs
tasty 23 schmackhaft, lecker
team leader 32 Teamleiter/in
team spirit 30T Mannschaftsgeist
teammate 143 Mannschaftskamerad/in
technical advances *pl* 130 technische Fortschritte
technician 130 Techniker/in
technique 150 Technik, Methode
technological 60 technologisch, technisch
technology 18 Technologie, Technik
to **tell sth from sth** 143 etw von etw unterscheiden
temple 43F Tempel
temporary 80T befristet
temperature, narrow ~ range 208 schmaler Temperaturbereich
to **tend to be sth** 94 dazu neigen, etw zu sein
tense 150 angespannt
tent 33 Zelt; **changing ~** 33 Umkleidezelt
term, short-~ 211 kurzfristig
terms *pl* 216 Bedingungen
terrible 41 furchtbar; to **have ~ luck** 108 furchtbares Pech haben
terrifying 111 entsetzlich, furchteinflößend
to **test** 200 untersuchen, prüfen
test-case 21V Probelauf
testimony 137F Aussage, Erfahrungsbericht
to **text** 90T SMS senden, simsen
text (message) 85 SMS
Thanksgiving 114 Erntedankfest
theft, identity ~ 87 Identitätsdiebstahl
theme 115V Thema
thigh 166 Oberschenkel
thinking, original ~ 142 Scharfsinn, Originalität
third 200 Drittel
thirsty, to **be ~** 116T Durst haben
though, even ~ 45 obwohl
thought 31 Gedanke
thousand 37 tausend, Tausend
thread 41 Thema, Forumsthread
threat 159 Drohung; 210 Gefahr, Bedrohung
to **threaten** 160 drohen
thrill 174 Nervenkitzel, Kick
thrilled, to **be ~** 204 sich wahnsinnig freuen
thrilling 111 aufregend, überwältigend; 141 spannend, mitreißend
throne 51 Thron
throughout … 76 in ganz …
throughout the day 166 den ganzen Tag über
to **throw: ~ sth away** 47 etw wegwerfen; **~ sb out** 47 jdn hinauswerfen
thunder 111 Donner
to **thunk against sth** 159 dumpf gegen etw schlagen
to **tidy (up)** 126 aufräumen, saubermachen
tie 84 Bindung, Beziehung
time, at the same ~ 90 gleichzeitig; **full-~** 118 Vollzeit-; **on ~** 82 pünktlich; **over ~** 94 mit der Zeit; to **take ~ off/out** 80 sich freinehmen; to **take the ~ to do sth** 39 sich die Zeit nehmen, etw zu tun; **three ~s** 200 dreimal; **~ out** 62 Auszeit; **waste of ~** 71 Zeitverschwendung; **space of ~** 57 Zeitspanne; **opening ~s** *pl* 42 Öffnungszeiten
timeless 224 zeitlos
timetable 13 Fahrplan
tin can 126 Blechdose
tiny 123 klein, winzig
to **tip** 224 kippen
tired 101 müde

toiletries *pl* 128 Hygieneartikel, Kosmetikartikel
a ton of 70T jede Menge
tongue, mother ~ 79 Muttersprache
tonne 123 Tonne
tool 104 Werkzeug; **gardening** ~ 174 Gartengerät
tooth, teeth 10 Zahn, Zähne
toothpaste 67 Zahncreme
total 57 Gesamt-, Gesamtmenge/-betrag
to **touch** 52T berühren
touch, to **keep in** ~ 38 in Verbindung bleiben
tough 106T hart
tour, guided ~ 103T Führung; **plant** ~ 222 Werksführung, Betriebsbesichtigung; ~ **guide** 103V Reiseleiter/in, Fremdenführer/in
towards the end 80T gegen Ende
towel 128 Handtuch
tower 103V Turm
town council 52T Stadtrat, Stadtverwaltung
toxic 58 giftig
track, to **get back on** ~ 46 wieder in die Spur kommen
to **track sth** 37 etw nachverfolgen, etw nachzeichnen
traction, to **get** ~ 94 an Boden gewinnen
trade fair 104 (Branchen-/Handels-)Messe
trader 119 Händler/in
tradition 109 Sitte, Tradition
traditionally 30T üblicherweise, traditionell
traffic 90T Verkehr
traffic lights *pl* 90T Ampel
tragic 56 tragisch
to **train:** ~ **sb** 77 jdn schulen; ~ **for sth** 53 eine Ausbildung zu etw machen
trainer 52 Dozent/in, Ausbilder/in
training, further ~ 213 Fortbildung; **vocational** ~ 52 Berufsausbildung; ~ **session** 52 Schulungseinheit
transaction 119 Geschäft, Transaktion
to **transform** 224 verwandeln
to **translate** 11 übersetzen
translation 16 Übersetzung
translator 174 Übersetzer/in
transport 175 Verkehr; **means of** ~ 154 Transportmittel; **public** ~ 132 öffentliche Verkehrsmittel
to **transport** 122 befördern, transportieren
transportation 121 Transport, Verkehr
travel, rail ~ 154 Bahnverkehr; **road** ~ 154 Straßenverkehr; ~ **expenses** *pl* 179T Reisekosten
traveller 99 Reisende/r
tray 105T Schale
treadmill 31 Laufband
treat 111 Vergnügen, (kleines) Geschenk
to **treat** 45 behandeln
treatment 55 Behandlung; **course of** ~ 59 Therapie, Behandlung
treaty 216 Vertrag, Abkommen
trial period 173 Probezeit
trip 26 Reise
trolley 8 Wagen
trouble 47 Ärger, Schwierigkeiten, Probleme; to **cause** ~ 99 Ärger machen
truck 123 Lastwagen; **forklift** ~ 152 Gabelstapler
true, to **come** ~ 131 sich verwirklichen, wahr werden
trust, National T~ 99 *brit. Organisation für Denkmalpflege und Naturschutz*
to **trust** 66 (darauf) vertrauen
trusted contact 214 vertrauenswürdige Kontaktperson
to **try** 6 versuchen; ~ **sth on** 72 etw anprobieren
tuna fish 200 Thunfisch
tune 86 Lied, Song
turkey 114 Truthahn
turn, to **have/get a** ~ 117 drankommen; to **take** ~**s to do sth** 6 etw abwechselnd tun; **Your** ~. 117 Sie sind dran.
to **turn** 142 sich drehen; ~ **sth off** 92 etw ausschalten; ~ **out** 47 *(Dinge:)* sich ergeben; 67 sich herausstellen; ~ **out to be sb/sth** 51 sich als jd/etw herausstellen; ~ **sth into sth** 122, 215 etw zu etw machen, etw zu etw umwandeln; ~ **to sb** 176T sich an jdn wenden; ~ **up** 28 kommen, auftauchen; ~ **right/left** 116T rechts/links abbiegen; ~ **one's life around** 46 das eigene Leben umkrempeln
turnout 216 Wahlbeteiligung
TV show 13 Fernsehsendung
to **tweet** 94 twittern
twice 27,200 zweimal
twin 36 Zwilling; ~ **town** 52 Partnerstadt; **identical** ~**s** *pl* 37 eineiige Zwillinge
to **twist** 142 sich winden

U

ugly 101 hässlich
unaccompanied 98 ohne Begleitung
unchecked 95 ungeprüft
uncomfortable 101 unbequem, unkomfortabl
uncountable 12 unzählbar
to **undergird** 51V untermauern
underprivileged 45 benachteiligt, unterprivilegiert
to **understand** 6 verstehen
unexpected 107T unvorhergesehen
unexpectedness 215 Unvermutetheit
unfortunately 111 leider, unglücklicherweise
unfriendly 101 unfreundlich
unhealthy 143 ungesund
unique 142 einzigartig
United Nations *pl* 17 Vereinte Nationen
unity 115V Einheit, Einigkeit
universal 173 allgemein, universell
unless 98 außer wenn, es sei denn
unlike sth 174 anders als etw
unlikely 70T unwahrscheinlich
to **unload** 123 entladen, löschen
to **unlock** 118 wieder aufschließen, entriegeln
unnecessary 128 unnötig
unrelaxed 150 unentspannt
unsociable 135 kontaktarm, menschenscheu
unsuccessful, to **be** ~ 103V scheitern
unsure 66 unsicher
untrue 95 unwahr, unzutreffend
unusable 118 unbrauchbar
unusual 135 ungewöhnlich
unverified 94 unbestätigt, ungeprüft
to **unwrap sth** 208 etw auspacken
up, to **be** ~ **to sth** 69F einer Sache gewachsen sein; **What's** ~40T Was ist los?; ~ **close** 171 aus nächster Nähe; ~**s and downs** *pl* 67, 212 Höhen und Tiefen
to **upcycle** 126 veredeln, aufwerten
to **update** 33 aktualisieren, auf den neuesten Stand bringen
to **upgrade** 176 aktualisieren, auf den neuesten Stand bringen
to **upload** 66 hochladen
upset 160 verärgert, aufgebracht
urban 202 städtisch, Stadt-
to **urge sb to do sth** 166 jdn dringend auffordern, etw zu tun
usage 90T Benutzung
used, to **get** ~ **to sth** 68 sich an etw gewöhnen
user 60T Nutzer/in, Benutzer/in
usually 12 normalerweise, gewöhnlich

V

valley 206 Tal
valuable 132 wertvoll
value 94 Wert; **news** ~ 214 Nachrichtenwert, Neuigkeitswert
van 123 Lieferwagen; **camper** ~ 98 Wohnmobil
vandal 148 Vandale
vandalism 146 Vandalismus
to **vandalize** 148 verwüsten, mutwillig beschädigen
variation 114T Variante, Variation
varied 107 abwechslungsreich
variety 20 Vielfalt, Abwechslung; 22 Auswahl; 66 Vielzahl
various 22 verschiedene/r/s
vase 159 Vase
vegan 20 Veganer/in; vegan
vegetarian 20 Vegetarier/in; vegetarisch
vegetarianism 21V vegetarische Lebensweise
vehicle 90T Fahrzeug
vending machine 125 (Getränke-)Automat
venue 118 Veranstaltungsort
verification 94 Prüfung
vest 168 Laufshirt
via 33 mittels, über
victim 138T Opfer
Victorian 103V viktorianisch
view 42 Ansicht, Meinung; 102 Aussicht, Ausblick; **panoramic** ~ 103V Panoramablick
viewer 44 Zuschauer/in
violence 43T Gewalt
violent 111 brutal, gewalttätig
viral, to **go** ~ 94 sich rasant (im Internet) verbreiten
virtual 87 virtuell
visa 80 Visum
vision 159 Blickfeld
visitor 52 Besucher/in
vocational training 52 Berufsausbildung
voice call 85 Sprachanruf
voicemail 102 Mailbox
voluntary service 76 Freiwilligendienst
volunteer 32 (freiwilliger/ehrenamtlicher) Helfer/in
to **volunteer** 32 ehrenamtlich arbeiten, (freiwillig) helfen; 208 sich bereit erklären
vote 43F, 216 Wahl, Abstimmung, Stimmen
to **vote (on sb/sth)** 34 abstimmen, (jdn/etw) wählen
voting age 216 Wahlalter
vowel 9 Vokal

W

wage 173 Lohn
waiter 7 Kellner
to **wake up** 47 aufwachen
to **walk:** ~ **by** 174 vorbeilaufen, vorübergehen; ~ **towards sb** 90T auf jdn zugehen
walk, to **go for** ~**s** 69V spazieren gehen
walking holiday 179T Wanderurlaub
walkway 103V Fußgängersteg
wall, to **cross a** ~ 222 eine Mauer überqueren
wallet 12 Brieftasche, (Herren-)Portemonnaie
war, Cold W~ 142 Kalter Krieg; **second world** ~ 206 Zweiter Weltkrieg
warehouse 122 Lager, Lagerhalle
to **warm with pride** 204 von Stolz erfüllt werden
to **warn** 86 warnen, (auf etw) hinweisen
warning 90T Warnung, Warnhinweis; 156 Verwarnung
way, No ~. 147 Auf keinen Fall!; to **get in the** ~ **of sth** 166 einer Sache im Weg stehen, einer Sache in die Quere kommen
waste 132 Verschwendung, Abfall; ~ **of time** 71 Zeitverschwendung; **industrial** ~ 178 Industriemüll; ~ **food** 132 Lebensmittelabfälle
to **waste** 70 verschwenden, vergeuden
weak 210 schwach
weakness 51 Schwäche
wealth, distribution of ~ 106T Wohlstandsverteilung
wear, ladies' ~ 72 Damenbekleidung
weather forecast 103V Wettervorhersage
wedding 109 Hochzeit; ~ **ring** 153 Ehering
weekday 13 Wochentag, Werktag
to **weigh** 166 wiegen
weight 27 Gewicht; to **gain** ~ 143 zunehmen; to **lose** ~ 27 abnehmen; to **put on** ~ 166 zunehmen
weird 87 verrückt, schräg, gaga
welcome, You're ~. 164T Bitte (sehr). Gern geschehen.
well, It's just as ~ **that ...** 171 Da ist es gut, dass ...; ~ **known** 50T bekannt
wet 58 feucht, nass
whatsoever, nothing ~ 224 überhaupt nichts
wheel 103V Rad; **observation** ~ 103V Riesenrad; **potter's** ~ 159 Töpferscheibe
wheelchair 32 Rollstuhl
whenever 171 immer wenn, wann immer
whereabouts 139 wo ungefähr?
whereas 166 während
while 37 Weile
to **whip sth out** 167 etw zücken
wide open spaces *pl* 171 weites Land
widely distributed 94 weit verbreitet
to **widen** 171 erweitern
wife 35 Ehefrau
wild 41 wild
will-power 203 Willenskraft
willing 43 bereit, willens
to **win** 30T gewinnen
win, lottery ~ 214 Lottogewinn
winner 26 Gewinner/in, Sieger/in
wise 178 klug
wish 39 Wunsch; **Best** ~**es** 39 *(Brief:)* Mit besten Grüßen
within 60T innerhalb von, binnen
without, to **do** ~ **sth** 21V ohne etw auskommen
wobbly 118 wacklig, verwackelt
to **wonder** 116T sich fragen
wood 123 Holz
wood-burning stove 67 Holzofen
wooden house 67 Holzhaus
word, to **put out the** ~ 106T die Nachricht verbreiten
work: ~ **of art** 167 Kunstwerk; ~ **experience** 72 Praktikum; ~ **permit** 80 Arbeitserlaubnis
to **work:** ~ **out** 66 gut ausgehen; ~ **sth out** 80, 224 etw ausarbeiten, etw erarbeiten; 84 etw herausfinden, etw ausrechnen
worker, social ~ 47 Sozialarbeiter/in
working dog 142 Arbeitshund
workout 138T Fitnesstraining, Trainingseinheit
workplace 128 Arbeitsplatz; ~ **safety** 153 Sicherheit am Arbeitsplatz
works, printing ~ 153 Druckerei
workshop 52 Werkstatt
worried 13 besorgt, beunruhigt
to **worry about sb/sth** 57 sich um jdn/etw Sorgen machen
worrying 90T Besorgnis erregend, beunruhigend
worth 119 wert
worthless 210 wertlos
to **write up sth** 24 etw formulieren, etw ausarbeiten
wrong, to **get it** ~ 138T etw falsch sagen

Y

to **yank** 159 zerren, reißen
year, in recent ~**s** 218 in den letzten Jahren
yet 94 dennoch; **not ...** ~ 47 noch nicht
youngster 42 Jugendliche/r
youth: ~ **centre** 42 Jugendzentrum; ~ **worker** 42 Jugendarbeiter/in, Erzieher/in

Z

to **zoom off** 174 wegsausen

Irregular verbs

be	was/were	been	*sein*
beat	beat	beaten	*schlagen, besiegen*
become	became	become	*werden*
begin	began	begun	*anfangen, beginnen*
break	broke	broken	*brechen*
bring	brought	brought	*bringen*
build	built	built	*bauen*
burn	burnt/burned	burnt/burned	*(ver)brennen*
buy	bought	bought	*kaufen*
catch	caught	caught	*fangen*
choose	chose	chosen	*(aus)wählen*
come	came	come	*kommen*
cut	cut	cut	*schneiden*
do	did	done	*tun, machen*
draw	drew	drawn	*zeichnen*
dream	dreamt/dreamed	dreamt/dreamed	*träumen*
drink	drank	drunk	*trinken*
drive	drove	driven	*(Auto) fahren*
eat	ate	eaten	*essen*
fall	fell	fallen	*fallen*
feed	fed	fed	*füttern, ernähren*
feel	felt	felt	*(sich) fühlen, empfinden*
fight	fought	fought	*kämpfen*
find	found	found	*finden*
fit	fit/fitted	fitted	*passen, sitzen; anbringen*
fly	flew	flown	*fliegen*
forget	forgot	forgotten	*vergessen*
get	got	got (AE gotten)	*bekommen*
give	gave	given	*geben, schenken*
go	went	gone	*gehen, fahren*
grow	grew	grown	*wachsen*
hang	hung	hung	*hängen*
have	had	had	*haben*
hear	heard	heard	*hören*
hide	hid	hidden	*(sich) verstecken*
hit	hit	hit	*schlagen*
hold	held	held	*halten, festhalten*
keep	kept	kept	*behalten*
know	knew	known	*kennen, wissen*
lay	laid	laid	*legen*
learn	learnt/learned	learnt/learned	*lernen*
leave	left	left	*abfahren, verlassen, weggehen*
let	let	let	*lassen*
lie	lay	lain	*liegen*
light	lit	lit	*anzünden, beleuchten, anmachen*

lose	**lost**	**lost**	*verlieren*
make	**made**	**made**	*machen*
mean	**meant**	**meant**	*meinen, bedeuten*
meet	**met**	**met**	*treffen, kennen lernen*
pay	**paid**	**paid**	*bezahlen*
put	**put**	**put**	*setzen, stellen, legen*
quit	**quit/quitted**	**quit/quitted**	*verlassen, aufhören*
read	**read**	**read**	*lesen*
ride	**rode**	**ridden**	*reiten, fahren*
rise	**rose**	**risen**	*(an)steigen*
run	**ran**	**run**	*laufen, rennen*
say	**said**	**said**	*sagen*
see	**saw**	**seen**	*sehen*
sell	**sold**	**sold**	*verkaufen*
send	**sent**	**sent**	*senden, schicken*
set	**set**	**set**	*setzen, stellen*
show	**showed**	**shown**	*zeigen*
shut	**shut**	**shut**	*schließen*
sing	**sang**	**sung**	*singen*
sit	**sat**	**sat**	*sitzen*
sleep	**slept**	**slept**	*schlafen*
smell	**smelt/smelled**	**smelt/smelled**	*riechen*
speak	**spoke**	**spoken**	*sprechen*
spell	**spelt/spelled**	**spelt/spelled**	*buchstabieren*
spend	**spent**	**spent**	*ausgeben, verbringen*
stand	**stood**	**stood**	*stehen*
steal	**stole**	**stolen**	*stehlen*
swim	**swam**	**swum**	*schwimmen*
take	**took**	**taken**	*nehmen*
teach	**taught**	**taught**	*unterrichten, beibringen*
tell	**told**	**told**	*sagen, erzählen*
think	**thought**	**thought**	*denken*
throw	**threw**	**thrown**	*werfen*
understand	**understood**	**understood**	*verstehen*
wake	**woke**	**woken**	*aufwachen, aufwecken*
wear	**wore**	**worn**	*tragen*
win	**won**	**won**	*gewinnen*
write	**wrote**	**written**	*schreiben*

Quellenverzeichnis

S. 7.1: Fotolia/ Rido; **S. 7.2:** Fotolia/ michaeljung; **S. 7.3:** Fotolia/ Milissenta; **S. 7.4:** Fotolia/ Kalim; **S. 9:** Shutterstock/ Redshinestudi; **S. 14.1:** Fotolia/ olenatur; **S. 14.2:** Shutterstock/ Jaro68; **S. 14.3:** Shutterstock/ Baturina Yuliya; **S. 14.4:** Shutterstock/ Fotografie-Kuhlmann; **S. 15.1:** Fotolia/ uwimages; **S. 15.2:** Fotolia/ al62; **S. 15.3:** Shutterstock/ Anastasia_Panait; **S. 15.4:** Fotolia/ alotofpeople; **S. 15.5:** Fotolia/ travelphotos; **S. 15.6:** Fotolia/ Jenifoto; **S. 17.1:** Nutriset, www.nutriset.fr/ Bertrand Guillemot; **S. 17.2:** Fotolia/ inguaribile; **S. 19:** Shutterstock/ Great Divide Photography; **S. 20.1:** Fotolia/ ponomarencko; **S. 20.2:** Fotolia/ sumnersgraphicsinc; **S. 22.1:** Shutterstock/ El Nariz; **S. 22.2:** Shutterstock/ Elina Li; **S. 23:** ddp images/ Monkey Business Image; **S. 25.1:** Fotolia/ Izf; **S. 25.2:** Shutterstock/ ostill; **S. 25.3:** Shutterstock/ Sergey Nivens; **S. 25.4:** Shutterstock/ Dusan Petkovic; **S. 25.5:** Bildagentur Schapowalow/ Maurizio Rellini; **S. 25.6:** Shutterstock/ pio3; **S. 25.7:** Shutterstock/ iko; **S. 25.8:** Shutterstock/ Eugene Onischenko; **S. 26:** Fotolia/ Gstudio Group; **S. 27.1:** Fotolia/ the_lightwriter; **S. 27.2:** ImageSource/ Onoky; **S. 28:** Shutterstock/ Ross Petukhov; **S. 29.1:** Shutterstock/ ShutteCreat; **S. 29.2:** Shutterstock/ wavebreakmedia; **S. 31:** Shutterstock/ Thisislove; **S. 32:** Imago stock&people/ Rolf Kremming; **S. 33:** Fotolia/ okalinichenko; **S. 34:** Shutterstock/ matimix; **S. 35.1:** Shutterstock/ Fotoluminate LLC; **S. 35.2:** Glow Images/ **©JGI**/ Daniel Grill/ Blend Images LLC; **S. 35.3:** Fotolia/ ricardoferrando; **S. 35.4:** Shutterstock/ India Picture; **S. 35.5:** Fotolia/ Fotolia365; **S. 35.6:** F1online/ Rainer Berg/ Westend61/ F1online; **S. 36:** Fotolia/ yupachingping; **S. 37:** ddp images/ Capital Pictures; **S. 38:** Shutterstock/ create jobs 51; **S. 41:** ddp images/ Intertopics/ Empics/ Phil Noble; **S. 43.1–43.4:** Shutterstock; **S. 44:** Fotolia/ fergregory; **S. 45.1:** Imago stock&people/ Pacific Press Agency; **S. 45.2:** ddp images/ Sven Simon; **S. 45.3:** Bridgeman Images/ AGIP; **S. 45.4:** Fotolia/ gwimages; **S. 45.5:** Fotolia/ Sunny studio; **S. 45.6:** Shutterstock strizh; **S. 45.7:** Shutterstock/ Catalin Petolea; **S. 46:** Shutterstock/ kenary820; **S. 47.1:** Shutterstock/ Fresnel; **S. 47.2:** Shutterstock/ WAYHOME studio; **S. 50:** dpa Picture Alliance/ Jürgen Wacker; **S. 51:** Shutterstock/ Thinglass; **S. 52.1:** Fotolia/ Ilyes Laszlo; **S. 52.2:** YourPhotoToday/ Tetra_Images/ PaulBurns; **S. 55.1:** Fotolia/ Сергей Чирков; **S. 55.2:** Fotolia/ Max Tactic; **S. 55.3:** Shutterstock/ AWesleyFloyd; **S. 55.4:** Fotolia/ kinako; **S. 55.5:** F1online/ Julian winslow/ ableimages; **S. 55.6:** Shutterstock/ Monkey Business Images; **S. 55.7:** ddp images/ OLEKSANDR NIKOLAIENKO; **S. 55.8:** Fotolia/ WavebreakMediaMicro; **S. 57.1:** Shutterstock/ Brendan Howard; **S. 57.2:** Fotolia/ Cigdem; **S. 58:** Shutterstock/ Africa Studio; **S. 60:** Fotolia/ SFIO CRACHO; **S. 62.1:** Fotolia/ marrakeshh; **S. 62.2:** Shutterstock/ Christian Jung; **S. 63:** Fotolia/ starblue; **S. 65.1:** Fotolia/ Monkey Business; **S. 65.2:** Mauritius Images/ Alamy/ Gruffydd Thomas; **S. 65.3:** Fotolia/ Kzenon; **S. 65.4:** Fotolia/ beeboys; **S. 65.5:** Fotolia/ wavebreakmediaMicro; **S. 65.6:** Fotolia/ daviles; **S. 65.7:** Shutterstock/ YIUCHEUNG; **S. 65.8:** Shutterstock/ Rishiken; **S. 67.1:** Shutterstock/ moomsabuy; **S. 67.2:** Fotolia/ eugenesergeev; **S. 70.1:** Shutterstock/ vilax; **S. 70.2:** Shutterstock/ namtipStudio; **S. 70.3:** Shutterstock/ Nejron Photo; **S. 72.1:** Shutterstock/ Dasha Petrenko; **S. 72.2:** Shutterstock/ A and N Photography; **S. 72.3:** Shutterstock/ sabarwal; **S. 72.4:** Shutterstock/ Iakov Filimonov; **S. 72.5:** Shutterstock/ Dragon Images; **S. 72.6:** Shutterstock/ mimagephotography; **S. 72.7:** Fotolia/ Alex Ischenko; **S. 72.8:** Shutterstock/ Sergey Ryzhov; **S. 75.1:** Shutterstock/ ded pixto; **S. 75.2:** Shutterstock/ quinky; **S. 75.3:** Shutterstock/ wavebreakmedia; **S. 75.4:** Shutterstock/ Nestor Rizhniak; **S. 75.5:** Shutterstock/ Photodiem; **S. 75.6:** Shutterstock/ michaeljung; **S. 75.7:** Fotolia/ JackF; **S. 75.8:** Shutterstock/ Ikonoklast Fotografie; **S. 77.1:** Shutterstock/ szefei; **S. 77.2:** Shutterstock/ vepar5; **S. 77.3:** Shutterstock/ Sokolenko; **S. 80.1:** Shutterstock/ Franco Volpato; **S. 80.2:** Shutterstock/ Khongtham; **S. 80.3:** Shutterstock/ Sam Jonah; **S. 81.1:** ddp images/ ddp images; **S. 81.2:** Fotolia/ Luap Vision; **S. 83.1:** Shutterstock/ wavebreakmedia; **S. 83.2:** Fotolia/ Antonioguillem; **S. 83.3:** Shutterstock/ Dipak Shelare; **S. 85.1:** Fotolia/ canbedone; **S. 85.** Statistiken: www.teensafe.com; **S. 85.2:** Fotolia/ Milos; **S. 85.3:** Fotolia/ Olaf Speier; **S. 85.4:** laif/ Keystone Schweiz; **S. 85.5:** Shutterstock/ YAKOBCHUK VIACHESLAV; **S. 85.6:** Fotolia/ Dragon Images; **S. 86.1+3:** Fotolia/ alessandradesole; **S. 86.2+4:** Shutterstock/ Eugenio Marongiu; **S. 86.5:** Fotolia/ Mat Hayward; **S. 86.6:** Fotolia/ kues1; **S. 86.7:** Fotolia/ kues1; **S. 86.8:** Fotolia/ yellowpaul; **S. 86.9:** Fotolia/ mashimara; **S. 86.10:** Shutterstock/ Vasya Kobelev; **S. 87.1:** Shutterstock/ carlos castilla; **S. 87.2:** Fotolia/ Alex White; **S. 89:** Shutterstock/ Aa Amie; **S. 90:** akg-images/ Rainer Hackenberg; **S. 97.1:** Shutterstock/ skvoor; **S. 97.2:** Shutterstock/ Filip Bjorkman; **S. 97.3:** Shutterstock/ Kositlimsiri; **S. 97.4:** Mark Giles McKeown, Portadown, Co. Armagh, Northern Ireland; **S. 97.5:** Fotolia/ Aliaksandr Kazlou; **S. 97.6:** Fotolia/ chrisdorney; **S. 97.7:** Fotolia/ Photocreo Bednarek; **S. 97.8:** Shutterstock/ Ruth Black; **S. 97.9:** ddp images/ robertharding/ Michael; **S. 97.10:** Shutterstock/ Lukas Hejtman; **S. 98.1:** Shutterstock/ satit sewtiw; **S. 98.2:** Shutterstock/ Dmitry Naumov; **S. 98.3:** Shutterstock/ Dragon Images; **S. 98.4:** Shutterstock/ shutter_o; **S. 98.5:** Shutterstock/ Aleksey Stemmer; **S. 99:** Fotolia/ donfiore; **S. 100.1:** Shutterstock/ Syda Productions; **S. 100.2:** Shutterstock/ Phovoir; **S. 101.1:** Shutterstock/ Lekcha; **S. 101.2:** Shutterstock/ Uber Images; **S. 101.3:** Fotolia/ Kybele; **S. 101.4:** Fotolia/ imageegami; **S. 101.5:** Shutterstock/ Billion Photos; **S. 101.6:** Shutterstock/ Rawpixel.com; **S. 102.1:** Shutterstock/ David Ionut; **S. 102.2:** Shutterstock/ Evannovostro; **S. 102.3:** Shutterstock/ Mariusz S.Jurgielewicz; **S. 102.4:** Shutterstock/ Daxiao Productions; **S. 102.5:** Mauritius Images/ Paul Gabot; **S. 102.6:** Fotolia/ sonya kamoz; **S. 104.1:** Shutterstock/ Ovocim; **S. 104.1a:** Shutterstock/ DenisFilm; **S. 104.2:** Shutterstock/ Sergey85; **S. 104.3:** Shutterstock/ OlegSam; **S. 104.4:** Shutterstock/ Kostenko Maxim; **S. 104.5:** Shutterstock/ qwasder1987; **S. 104.6:** Shutterstock/ Tish1; **S. 104.7:** Shutterstock/ LanKS; **S. 104.8:** Shutterstock/ Maxx-Studio; **S. 104.9:** Shutterstock/ Tarzhanova; **S. 104.10:** Shutterstock/ SANNIK; **S. 105.2:** Fotolia/ Adrian Hillman; **S. 106:** Fotolia/ allouphoto; **S. 109.1:** Shutterstock/ Zurijeta; **S. 109.2:** ddp images/ Jürgen Wiesler; **S. 109.3:** Shutterstock/ Dmitry Sheremeta; **S. 109.4:** Reuters/ Eddie Keogh; **S. 109.5:** Shutterstock/ S.Borisov; **S. 109.6:** Shutterstock/ Monkey Business Images; **S. 109.7:** Shutterstock/ Noppasin; **S. 109.8:** Shutterstock/ wavebreakmedia; **S. 110.1:** Fotolia/ Tomasz Zajda; **S. 110.2:** action press/ DUOMO; **S. 110.3:** laif/ Sandro Di Carlo Darsa; **S. 111:** Fotolia/ BillionPhotos.com; **S. 112:** Shutterstock/ Africa Studio; **S. 113:** Shutterstock/ Jacob Lund; **S. 114.1:** Shutterstock/ Shutterstock; **S. 114.2:** Shutterstock/ OLGA KARPOVA; **S. 114.3:** Fotolia/ evgenyb; **S. 115.1:** Shutterstock/ Shutterstock; **S. 115.2:** Shutterstock/ OLGA KARPOVA; **S. 115.3:** Shutterstock/ d13; **S. 116.1:** Fotolia/ gornostaj; **S. 121.1:** Shutterstock/ kwest; **S. 121.2:** Shutterstock/ Toa55; **S. 121.3:** Shutterstock/ Romolo Tavani; **S. 121.4:** Shutterstock/ ssguy; **S. 121.5:** Shutterstock/ Travel mania; **S. 121.6:** Shutterstock/ William Potter; **S. 121.7:** Shutterstock/ huyangshu; **S. 123:** Fotolia/ efetova; **S. 125:** Shutterstock/ Andriy Lipkan; **S. 126.1:** Fotolia/ dashadima; **S. 128.1:** Fotolia/ Scanrail; **S. 128.2:**

Fotolia/ tanawatbig; **S. 128.3:** Imago stock&people GmbH/ blickwinkel; **S. 128.4:** Shutterstocl/ Stockforlife; **S. 131.1:** Fotolia/ Johan Larson; **S. 131.2:** Shutterstock/ Iryna Inshyna; **S. 133.1–4:** Shutterstock/ Filip Bjorkman; **S. 134.1:** Shutterstock/ F8 studio; **S. 134.2:** Shutterstock/ Syda Productions; **S. 134.3:** Shutterstock/ Phovoir; **S. 134.4:** Shutterstock/ michaeljung; **S. 135:** Fotolia/ Melpomene; **S. 138.1:** Shutterstock/ amixstudio; **S. 138.2:** Shutterstock/ N Azlin Sha; **S. 138.3:** Shutterstock/ kurhan; **S. 138.4:** Shutterstock/ Georgejmclittle; **S. 138.5:** Shutterstock/ one photo; **S. 138.6:** Shutterstock/ Syda Productions; **S. 140.1:** Fotolia/ pincasso; **S. 145.1:** Imago stock&people/ ZUMA Press; **S. 145.2:** Fotolia/ nirutft; **S. 145.3:** A1pix - Yourphoto today/ Panther Media/ AndreyPopov; **S. 145.4:** Mauritius Images/ Alamy/ Nadine Mitchell; **S. 145.5:** Mauritius Images/ United Archives; **S. 145.6:** Imago sportfotodienst GmbH/ Jan Huebner; **S. 145.7:** Your Photo Today/ PM/ studiostoks; **S. 151:** A1pix -YourPhotoToday/ PM; **S. 152.1:** Fotolia/ bartsadowski; **S. 152.2,5,6:** Shutterstock/ Barry Barnes; **S. 152.3,7:** Fotolia/ alona_s; **S. 152.4:** Fotolia/ nazar12; **S. 152.8:** Fotolia/ teracreonte; **S. 152.9:** Fotolia/ Barry Barnes; **S. 153.1:** Fotolia/ Kybele; **S. 153.2:** Shutterstock/ zefart; **S. 153.3:** Fotolia/ zefart; **S. 157.1:** Fotolia/ marino; **S. 157.2:** Shutterstock/ anna karwowska; **S. 157.3:** Fotolia/ Rafael Ben-Ari; **S. 157.4:** Fotolia/ Joshua Resnick; **S. 157.5:** Fotolia/ Robert Kneschke; **S. 157.6:** Fotolia/ stokkete; **S. 157.7:** Fotolia/ ink drop; **S. 157.8:** Fotolia/ Belish; **S. 161.1:** Shutterstock/ bezikus; **S. 161.2:** Shutterstock/ Piotr Wawrzyniuk; **S. 161.3:** Shutterstock/ Nadezda Murmakova; **S. 162:** Fotolia/ mihail39; **S. 163:** cartoonstock/ Mark Lynch; **S. 164:** Fotolia/ Gajus; **S. 169.1:** Shutterstock/ Peshkova; **S. 169.2:** Shutterstock/ Syda Productions; **S. 169.3:** Fotolia/ Hemant; **S. 169.4:** Fotolia/ BillionPhotos.com; **S. 169.5:** Shutterstock/ 1000 Words; **S. 169.6:** Fotolia/ lenets_tan; **S. 169.7:** Fotolia/ pressmaster; **S. 169.8:** Shutterstock/ Ditty_about_summer; **S. 169.9:** Shutterstock/ Roman Samborskyi; **S. 170.1:** Fotolia/ hanack; **S. 170.2:** Fotolia/ Candy (Debora) Dzenk; **S. 170.3:** Shutterstock/ Josu Ozkaritz; **S. 173:** Fotolia/ Algol; **S. 175.1:** Shutterstock/ Nejron Photo; **S. 175.2:** Shutterstock/ puhhha; **S. 176:** Shutterstock/ g-stockstudio; **S. 178:** ddp images; **S. 192.1:** Shutterstock/ gbreezy; **S. 192.2:** Shutterstock/ cobalt88; **S. 192.3:** Fotolia/ aleksangel; **S. 192.4:** Fotolia/ denisgorelkin; **S. 192.5:** Fotolia/ phuadiesta; **S. 193.1:** Fotolia/ Dmitry Naumov; **S. 193.2:** Shutterstock/ Dmitryp-k; **S. 193.3:** Fotolia/ Monkey Business; **S. 193.4:** Fotolia dmitrimaruta; **S. 193.5:** Fotolia/ Nikolai Sorokin; **S. 194:** AFPTV/ T. Urtizvérá, C.Notteghem; **S. 195:** AFPTV/ A. Buthier, N.Larson; **S. 196:** AFPTV/ B. Logan/ Wei Lan/ E.Malykhina; **S. 197:** Capitelrose/ Nico Bell; **S. 198:** AFPTV/ Glenda Kwek; **S. 199:** AFPTV/ Oceane Laze/ Legacy BLN; **S. 200.1:** Fotolia/ markobe; **S. 200.2:** Fotolia/ viperagp; **S. 200.3:** Shutterstock/ Arturs Budkevics; **S. 202:** Shutterstock/ monkey business; **S. 204:** Fotolia/ bonezboyz; **S. 214:** dpa Picture-Alliance/ Daniel Kalker; **S. 217:** Fotolia/ grandeduc; **S. 219.1:** ddp images; **S. 219.2:** Fotolia/ Adam Siese; **S. 219.3:** ddp images; **S. 221:** Imago stock&people GmbH/ viennaslide; **S. 224:** Succession Marcel Duchamp/ ADAGP, Paris and DACS, London 2017/ Photo: Tate; **S. 225.1:** Fotolia/ Mirko; **S. 225.2:** Mauritius Images/ Alamy/ Sergio Bondioni; **S. 225.3:** Fotolia/ meepoohyaphoto; **S. 225.4:** Fotolia/ Rafael Ben-Ari

The World

Greenland
Canada
United States of America
Mexico
San Francisco
Las Vegas
Montreal
New York
Mexico City
Bahamas
Cuba
Jamaica
Haiti
Dominican Rep.
Puerto Rico
Guatemala
El Salvador
Honduras
Nicaragua
Costa Rica
Panama
Venezuela
Columbia
Ecuador
Guyana
Surinam
Fr. Guyana
Peru
Brasil
Bolivia
Paraguay
Chile
Uruguay
Argentina
Buenos Aires
Rio de Janeiro
Pacific
Ocean
Atlantic
Ocean
Iceland
Norway
Sweden
Finland
United Kingdom
Leeds
London
Ireland
Germany
Paris
France
Portugal
Spain
Italy
Greece
Ukraine
Moscow
Russia
Kazakhstan
Mongolia
Georgia
Turkey
Uzbekistan
Turkmenistan
Kyrgystan
Tajikistan
China
Beijing
North Korea
South Korea
Japan
Tokyo
Yokohama
Shanghai
Taiwan
Hong Kong
Pacific
Ocean
Tunisia
Morocco
Algeria
Libya
Egypt
Western Sahara
Mauretania
Mali
Niger
Chad
Sudan
Eritrea
Yemen
Senegal
Burkina Faso
Guinea
Sierra Leone
Liberia
Côte d'Ivoire
Ghana
Nigeria
Cameroon
Central African Rep.
South Sudan
Ethiopia
Somalia
Gabun
Congo
Dem. Rep. of Congo
Uganda
Kenya
Tanzania
Angola
Zambia
Malawi
Zim-babwe
Mo-zam-bique
Madagascar
Namibia
Bots-wana
South Africa
Swaziland
Lesotho
Iraq
Iran
Kuwait
Saudi Arabia
UAE
Dubai
Oman
Afghanistan
Pakistan
Nepal
India
Mumbai
Bangla-desh
Myan-mar
Laos
Thai-land
Vietnam
Cam-bodia
Sri Lanka
Kuala Lumpur
Malaysia
Philippines
Indonesia
Jakarta
Papua New Guinea
Indian
Ocean
Australia
Sydney
New Zealand